BEYOND LANGUAGE:
Social and Cultural
Factors in Schooling
Language Minority Students

Developed by

BILINGUAL EDUCATION OFFICE
California State Department of Education
Sacramento, California

Published and Disseminated by

EVALUATION, DISSEMINATION AND ASSESSMENT CENTER
California State University, Los Angeles
Los Angeles, California

ISBN: 0-89755-024-2

This publication was funded in part with funds from the Office of Bilingual Educa-
tion and Minority Languages Affairs. The opinions expressed herein by the
various authors do not, however, necessarily reflect the position or policy of the
United States Department of Education or of the California State Department of
Education, and no official endorsement by the United States Department of
Education or the California State Department of Education should be inferred.

Developed by
BILINGUAL EDUCATION OFFICE
California State Department of Education
Sacramento, California

Published and Disseminated by
EVALUATION, DISSEMINATION AND ASSESSMENT CENTER
California State University, Los Angeles
5300 Paseo Rancho Castilla, #2105
Box 2-019
Los Angeles, California 90032

Printed in USA 1986
Second Printing 1986
Third Printing 1987
Fourth Printing 1990
Fifth Printing 1995

PREFACE

Wide open and unguarded stand our gates,
And through them presses a wild motley throng--
Men from the Volga and the Tartar steppes,
Featureless figures of the Hoang-Ho
Malayan, Scythian, Teuton, Kelt, and Slav...
These bringing with them unknown gods and rites,
Those, tiger passions, here to stretch their claws...
Accents of menace alien to our air,
Voices that once the Tower of Babel knew!

> -- Thomas Bailey Aldrich,
> from *Unguarded Gates and*
> *Other Poems*, 1895

Although written in the late 1800's, remnants of Aldrich's anxieties are evident in America's responses to immigrants today. Reactions toward immigrant minority groups alternate between ambivalence and antagonism, respect and paranoia, hospitality and rejection. While priding themselves on being democratic and inclusive, Americans remain troubled about just how much cultural and linguistic pluralism can be tolerated without the nation's identity and solidarity being undermined.

Nowhere is this dilemma more pronounced than within the United States educational system. Lay persons and trained educators alike debate the efficacy of schooling language minority students in their mother tongue, of teaching students about their native culture, of helping students to regard all cultures as equally viable systems of behavior, or of teaching students to cope with racially motivated antagonism. Educators have yet to develop a coherent set of approaches for dealing with the cultural and linguistic diversity represented by increasing numbers of immigrant minority students.

This book is about the educational challenges posed by American ideals of equality, diversity, and inclusion. Under pressures created by rapid immigration, tight budgets, and political conflict, schooling for minority students has often resulted in inequality, uniformity, and exclusion. The chapters that follow were written to help educators improve their understanding of minority students within the American social context. The authors offer perspectives and suggestions for helping educators and minority students interact in ways which will result in the students' experiencing their fullest academic potential while still realizing their freedom to enjoy and share with others their cultural and linguistic heritage.

The book's title, **Beyond Language,** reflects the authors' analyses of factors in addition to language which might suggest why some minority students tend to achieve below expectations, with implications for how educational programs can be improved. The factors which are addressed are implied in the subtitle: **Social and Cultural Factors in Schooling Language Minority Students.** To better understand minority schooling, educators must examine the relationship between social factors (e.g., socioeconomic status, attitudes toward minority groups, immigration patterns, etc.) and cultural factors (e.g., self-identity, child-rearing practices, language-use patterns, etc.). Although the title indicates that language minority students (i.e., those students with a non-English language background) are the focus of the volume, the authors emphasize the need to look beyond the students to the broader social and educational contexts to understand outcomes and formulate changes.

This book should be reviewed as a companion piece to two widely used publications on language minority education: **Schooling and Language Minority Students: A Theoretical Framework** and **Studies on Immersion Education: A Collection for United States Educators.** These volumes address first and second language issues in the education of minority and majority students. **Beyond Language** deals not only with language, but also with other social and cultural factors which affect educational outcomes of language minority students.

A central point of each of the following chapters is that influences flow in both directions between education and sociocultural factors. That is, educational success and failure should be understood as a product of the interaction among such factors as the student's cultural background, the educational setting, and wider social forces. For example, educational success depends in part on how students have learned to solve problems, use language, form relationships, work with peers, and regard themselves. On the other hand, educational experiences affect students' attitudes toward themselves, their teachers, and the value of schooling itself. These reactions, in turn, affect how the students (and eventually their children) respond to future educational experiences. The authors emphasize the significance of understanding not only variations in the equity of educational offerings, but also the different ways that individuals and groups respond to the same educational setting. Such an "interactionist" view considers the group's response to discrimination to be as significant as the nature of the discrimination itself.

The volume is divided into seven parts, each of which deals with a related aspect of sociocultural influences on education. The following is a brief summary with a selected excerpt from each of the chapters.

The introductory chapter provides an overview of a theory for how the many sociocultural factors influence language minority education. It is written by Carlos Cortés who uses his many years of experience in ethnic studies to place the volume in an historical as well as theoretical context.

> *...rather than a melting pot, a more cogent metaphor for the United States is that of a mosaic, but a constantly-shifting mosaic in which the multi-hued pieces do not always fit together perfectly, as if an ongoing historical earthquake has been challenging the society to attempt to resolve the unresolvable.*

> -- Carlos E. Cortés

Before dealing with specific minority groups later in the volume, the next chapter looks at historical explanations for why some groups do better in school than others. Stanley Sue and Amado Padilla discuss this history and provide a summary of the major value conflicts which have characterized the debate of minority-majority group relations in the United States.

> *Our belief is that many educational programs and practices reflect conflicts in which the clashes of values and the fruitlessness of single solutions have not been clearly recognized. Moreover, in trying to resolve issues, one side has been dominant, often to the detriment of ethnic minority groups.*

> -- Stanley Sue
> Amado Padilla

The next chapter analyzes sociocultural factors in detail: e.g., group attitudes toward education, self-identity, historical experiences, cultural values, job ceiling, etc. John Ogbu and María Matute-Bianchi present a typology of minority groups which is based on systematic differences in minority groups' experiences in the United States and their response to educational and occupational opportunities.

> *Basically, we think that the problem of persistent disproportionate school failure among some minorities has been too narrowly conceptualized in terms of discontinuities between the cultural and language backgrounds of the children on the one hand and the demands of the school milieu on the other.*
>
> -- John U. Ogbu
> María Matute-Bianchi

A discussion of language minority group education necessarily involves the issue of language, especially its relationship to culture and other sociocultural factors. Shirley Brice Heath's chapter places language as an integral part of the entire volume and helps to ensure that considerations of mother tongue and second language education are included in language minority educational reform.

> *Each group's ways are limited in terms of the full range of possibilities. Knowing the ways of other groups offers the possibility of expanding the abilities of all groups to create and learn new information and to adjust and adapt to new circumstances.*
>
> -- Shirley Brice Heath

A detailed illustration of how language development (e.g., reading and writing) can be improved, based on a positive link between the home and school, is provided in the chapter by Stephen Díaz, Luis Moll, and Hugh Mehan. The authors suggest an ethnographic method as a way for educators to observe more accurately the interplay between home and school settings, and between teachers and students in the school context.

> *The ethnographer working in a foreign land is attempting to make the strange familiar in order to understand it, while*

*the ethnographer in local scenes must reverse the process
and make the familiar strange in order to understand it.*

-- Stephen Díaz
Luis C. Moll
Hugh Mehan

In addition to language, educational programs should promote
positive psychological and social outcomes. Spencer Kagan
describes cooperative learning in detail--its rationale, methodology,
and research support--as an educational innovation for improving
students' acquisition of both academic and humanistic skills.

*If we are to have a population which is rational and adap-
tive, we must provide all types of learning experiences--
cooperative, competitive, and individualistic--so that our
students will develop the ability to adapt rationally to the full
range of human situations.*

-- Spencer Kagan

The concluding chapter of the book is designed to facilitate
educators' understanding and use of the hypotheses and approaches
proposed in the earlier chapters. Mary McGroarty discusses implications with several audiences in mind: parents, teachers, aides,
resource teachers, teacher-trainers, and administrators.

*(Adopting goals related to both academic achievement
and social orientation) could make the difference between
''more of the same''--a school experience sharply bounded,
as in the past, by linguistic and cultural barriers for certain
students--and ''more of the best''--a school experience that
offers all students a variety of ways to improve the mastery
of skills and concepts and learn to work with each other as
they do.*

-- Mary McGroarty

Becoming aware of one's own attitudes and behavior is part of the foundation upon which to build an understanding of and respect for others. The result of encounters among individuals, groups, societies, and nations is, after all, the product of many sets of forces in dynamic interaction. Improving such encounters depends on a sense of interdependence and a dedication to mutual adaptation. Suspicion, fear, antagonism, and ignorance of the type expressed by Aldrich above only perpetuate mutual distrust and insecurity, prolonging the discovery of solutions which benefit everyone involved. This book offers a way for people of minority and majority backgrounds to see one another in dynamic interaction. It provides language and concepts which people can use in order to discuss minority schooling issues more deeply and accurately. With an enlightened perspective and a set of alternative solutions for reform, educators lack only the will to help minority and majority students to reach their highest levels of academic and personal achievement.

Daniel D. Holt
Project Team Leader
Bilingual Education Office
California State Department
of Education

ACKNOWLEDGMENTS

Preparation of this volume began in 1981. Many dedicated individuals generously responded to our requests for assistance. We are most indebted to staff of the Bilingual Education Office, California State Department of Education for their expert guidance in designing the project and editing the individual chapters. Those staff with most significant responsibilities were Daniel Holt, project team leader, David Dolson, Norman Gold, Dennis Parker, and Fred Tempes. We are also grateful to Guillermo Lopez, Maria Ortiz, Leo Lopez, and Sarah Gomez for their administrative support during development of the volume.

As the project progressed, many educators were consulted and provided useful insights and words of encouragement: Edna Bonacich, University of California, Riverside; Thomas Carter, California State University, Sacramento; Edward DeAvila, Linguametrics; Eduardo Hernandez-Chavez, Instituto de Lengua y Cultura; Wallace Lambert, McGill University; Jane Mercer, University of California, Riverside; and Robert Politzer and George Spindler, Stanford University.

The following educators made valuable suggestions to drafts of the chapters from the viewpoint of practitioners and teacher-trainers: Tim Allen, San Diego City Schools; Margarita Calderon, University of California, Santa Barbara; Shelly Spiegel-Coleman, Los Angeles County Office of Education; Lily Ogden, Glendale Unified School District; Marta Martini, Orange County Office of Education; and Rocio Moss, San Diego Bilingual Education Service Center.

The authors deserve special recognition for their patience and perseverance during the preparation of the volume. They did more than simply write and submit chapters for publication. They met on numerous occasions in order to fuse their outlines and drafts into an integrated and coordinated whole. They reviewed each other's drafts and suggested revisions. Most importantly, they responded to their critics with a spirit of respect and cooperation.

Finally, special appreciation is due to staff at the EDAC, School of Education, California State University, Los Angeles whose attention to detail and overall conscientiousness were indispensable to the publication of the volume, especially that of Sherry Yang, Project Director.

Charles F. Leyba, Director
Evaluation, Dissemination and
    Assessment Center
California State University, Los Angeles

BIOGRAPHICAL SKETCHES

CARLOS E. CORTÉS (Ph.D., History, University of New Mexico, 1969) is Professor of History and Chair of the Department of History at the University of California, Riverside. Among his many publications are **Three Perspectives on Ethnicity, Gaucho Politics in Brazil,** and **A Filmic Approach to the Study of Historical Dilemmas,** as well as a three book series, **The Mexican American, The Chicano Heritage,** and **Hispanics in the United States.** He is the recipient of two book awards, his university's 1976 Distinguished Teaching Award, and the California Council for the Humanities' 1980 Distinguished California Humanist Award. He has lectured widely throughout the United States, Latin America, and Europe, has written film and television documentaries, and has appeared as guest host on the PBS national television series, "Why in the World?"

* * *

STANLEY SUE (Ph.D., Psychology, University of California, Los Angeles, 1971) is Professor of Psychology at UCLA. He was formerly a faculty member at the University of Washington and Director of Clinical-Community Psychology Training at the National Asian American Psychology Training Center, an APA approved internship program. His research focuses upon Asian American mental health and personality as well as service delivery systems for ethnic minority groups. He is particularly interested in bicultural adaptation.

* * *

AMADO M. PADILLA (Ph.D., Experimental Psychology, University of New Mexico, 1969) is Professor of Psychology at the University of California at Los Angeles. His research interests include acculturation, bilingualism, and psychological factors related to the well being of Hispanics. He is Director of the Spanish Speaking Mental Health Research Center at UCLA and the recently created Center for Language, Education and Research funded by the National Institute of Education. The author of approximately 100 publications including **Acculturation: Theory, Models, and Some New Findings** (Westview, 1980); he is also the founding editor of the **Hispanic Journal of Behavioral Sciences.**

JOHN U. OGBU (Ph.D., Anthropology, University of California, Berkeley, 1971) is Professor of Anthropology at the University of California, Berkeley. His research interests include minority-group academic achievement in comparative perspective, the influence of societal forces (economic, political, and social stratification systems) on schooling, social identity and schooling, schooling and youth transition to labor force and adulthood, and cross-cultural human development. He received the Margaret Mead Award in 1979 for his book, **The Next Generation: An Ethnography of Education in an Urban Neighborhood,** which was based on his research on minority education (primarily Blacks and Chicanos) in Stockton, California. He has published many works on education and culture, but is best known for his two books on minority education: **The Next Generation** (1974) and **Minority Education and Caste: The American System in Cross-Cultural Perspective** (1978).

*   *   *

MARÍA EUGENIA MATUTE-BIANCHI (Ph.D., in Education, Stanford University, 1979), is an Assistant Professor of Education at the University of California at Santa Cruz. She is an educational ethnographer with research interest in the education of ethnic linguistic minorities. Currently, she is engaged in an ethnography of schooling comparing variability in patterns of school performance among Chicano, Mexicano, and Japanese American youth.

*   *   *

SHIRLEY BRICE HEATH (Ph.D., Anthropology, Columbia University, 1970), Professor in the School of Education of Stanford University, is an anthropologist, linguist, and social historian. She has done ethnographic fieldwork in the southeastern United States, Guatemala, and Mexico; historical research on language policies in Mexico and the United States; and collaborative research with teachers of language minority children. A decade of such collaboration is reported in her best-known book, **Ways with Words: Language, Life and Work in Communities and Classrooms.** She has served as a member of the Board of Advisers of the National Center for Bilingualism Research and has taught writing and American literature at the Bread Loaf School of English since 1982. She was named a MacArthur Prize Fellow in 1984.

STEPHEN DÍAZ (Ed.D., Human Development, Harvard University, 1983) is co-director of the Community Educational Resource and Research Center and a researcher at the Laboratory of Comparative Human Cognition at the University of California at San Diego. He has conducted research in bilingual education, reading and cognitive development. His current research interests also include computer-mediated instruction of low-achieving minority students at all levels of the educational system.

*   *   *

LUIS C. MOLL (Ph.D., Educational Psychology, University of California, Los Angeles, 1978) is Lecturer in the Department of Communication and Assistant Research Psychologist in the Laboratory of Comparative Human Cognition at the University of California, San Diego. His research interests include child development and education, sociolinguistics, and literacy. His recent research explores the use of microcomputers in school and community settings to promote international communications, bilingualism, and literacy skills. Along with Alonzo Anderson and Stephen Díaz, he is co-founder of the Community Educational Resource and Research Center, a community-based research organization addressing issues of education, culture, and psychology in Latino and Black neighborhoods.

*   *   *

HUGH MEHAN (Ph.D., Sociology, University of California, Santa Barbara, 1971) is Professor of Sociology and Coordinator of Teacher Education at the University of California, San Diego. Approaching the role of schooling in society from an interactionist and sociolinguistic perspective, he has examined the construction of classroom lessons, educational tests and students' educational careers within the context of bilingual and special education. A member of the Social Science Research Council from 1976-1979, he is author of **The Reality of Ethnomethodology** (with Houston Wood), **Learning Lessons** and **Handicapping the Handicapped** (with Alma J. Hertweck and J. Lee Meihls) and numerous articles in sociological, linguistic, and educational journals. ·

SPENCER KAGAN (Ph.D., Psychology, University of California, Los Angeles, 1972) is Professor of Psychology and Cooperating Faculty, School of Education at the University of California, Riverside. His research documents the development of cooperative and competitive motives and behaviors among children of various cultures; most recently his work has focused on the academic and social impact of cooperative and competitive classroom structures on children with cooperative vs. competitive social motives, and training teachers in cooperative learning methods. A founding member and member of the board of directors of the International Association for the Study of Cooperation in Education, he was recently elected to Chair the California regional association of that organization.

*   *   *

MARY McGROARTY (Ph.D., Education, Stanford University, 1982) is an assistant professor in the TESL (Teaching English as a Second Language)/Applied Linguistics Programs and member of the research staff of the Center for Language Education and Research (CLEAR), the research center on bilingualism at the University of California, Los Angeles. She has worked in several language education programs and trained teachers in the U.S. and abroad. Research interests include theoretical and pedagogical aspects of bilingualism, with recent studies examining issues in language assessment, the nature of second language skills, cultural influences on language learning and teaching, and learner strategies.

CONTENTS

Page

BEYOND LANGUAGE:
Social and Cultural Factors in Schooling Language Minority Students

THE EDUCATION OF LANGUAGE MINORITY STUDENTS: A CONTEXTUAL INTERACTION MODEL

Carlos E. Cortés

University of California, Riverside

"I will not speak Spanish at school," wrote the young Mexican-American boy. The words increasingly covered the chalkboard, as he repeated and repeated the teacher-imposed penance. The punishment: to write that sentence 50 times after school. The crime: having been caught speaking Spanish with his Latino classmates during recess. Such was the process known as "Spanish Detention," once a hallowed type of traditional retribution aimed at imposing conformity on Hispanic students.

Fortunately, the protests of the 1960s, combined with a rising, more culturally-sensitive consciousness among educators, have reduced the occurrence of such draconian measures involving language minority students. Moreover, the reality of continuing--in some cases, growing--ethnic diversity in the classroom has increased the attention devoted to sociocultural issues in education. These issues have become an important part of educational policy debates, educational research, and efforts at educational reform, particularly during the past two decades.

This volume reflects a general concern with the relationship of sociocultural factors-- including language--to the process of education, especially of language minority students. In particular, the volume focuses on the relationship between sociocultural context, including the various facets of societal and ethnic cultures, and student educational outcomes. The book addresses two basic questions concerning educational achievement. First, why do members of some minority groups *tend* to have higher educational achievement than members of other minority groups? Second, why do members of some minority groups *tend* to have lower educational achievement than mainstream American students?

During the past decade, scholarship oriented toward improving the educational achievement of language minority students has shifted from a narrow focus on language alone as a causal factor to the examination of language in combination with other factors. To address the relationship of language to learning, the California State Department of Education's Bilingual Education Office (BEO) [formerly the Office of Bilingual-Bicultural Education (OBBE)] developed two publications, *Schooling and Language Minority Students: A Theoretical Framework* (1981) and *Studies on Immersion Education: A Collection for United States Educators* (1984). However, over the years, the BEO staff became convinced that the education of language minority students, including the learning of effective English, could only be understood within the larger sociocultural context of schools themselves and the society within which they functioned. Therefore, they determined the need for a thorough and cohesive scholarly examination of the social and cultural context of minority experience and its influence on the education of these language minority students.

With the impetus of these initial findings, a project was developed by the BEO staff, culminating in the publishing of this volume by the Evaluation, Dissemination and Assessment Center at California State University, Los Angeles. On the basis of a preliminary review of the literature, as well as current educational policies and practices, they identified a number of salient issues, including the following:

1. the powerful and dynamic relationship between sociocultural factors, including language, and schooling;

2. the fact that many current efforts and recommendations for educational reform do not address this relationship;

3. the dramatic demographic changes in the national and California population, particularly the recent and projected increases in the percentages of various language minority groups, raising even greater concern about the weaknesses of those general approaches to educational reform;

4. the educational underachievement of some language minority groups, in contrast to the superior achievement of other such groups; and

5. the need to more thoroughly examine the relationship between sociocultural factors and the schooling of language minority students, in terms of their effect on educational attainment, in order to recommend future educational reforms to deal with differential achievement outcomes.

This project involved scholars in a variety of disciplines-- anthropology, education, history, linguistics, psychology, and sociology-- from Stanford University and five University of California campuses. The resulting collection of analyses examines sociocultural factors that influence education, with the goal of bridging the gap between research and practice by drawing upon scholarship to suggest needed educational reforms. This volume builds upon the BEO's two previous volumes by examining language in relation to other sociocultural factors. Moreover, by combining sociocultural analysis with educational application, the volume provides educators with both a substantive basis for considering the educational significance of sociocultural issues and practical suggestions for responding more effectively and positively to the language, culture, heritage, and experiences of linguistically and ethnically diverse students, thereby improving their educational attainment.

Because of the scope and variety of the issues addressed by the authors, this volume can and should be of value to persons involved in various aspects of the school educational process. Teachers can derive insights into the learning process of students with whom they currently work and with whom they are likely to work in the nation's and state's increasingly multi-ethnic future. Administrators can gain a better understanding of sociocultural issues that should be considered in their daily decisions and long-range planning. Curriculum developers, resource people, and even textbook writers can find ideas that will assist them in better shaping their products for students of different sociocultural backgrounds and for multi-ethnic classrooms.

Teacher trainers and schools of education can extract ideas for strengthening their programs in order to better prepare teachers for the challenges of the demographically-changing future. Members of school boards can inform themselves more effectively of the dimensions of the sociocultural issues on which they should base their policymaking. Moreover, parents who desire to learn about the nature of their changing communities and the educational implications of such changes can find this a good source for general background. Overall, the volume provides insights that suggest directions for effective educational reform.

THE HISTORICAL CONTEXT OF ETHNIC DIVERSITY

An understanding of the historical context of ethnic diversity within education demands a consideration of two levels of that context. Obviously, such an understanding must include an examination of the historical development of the relationship between educational institutions and students of diverse ethnic backgrounds. However, it also requires a consideration of the larger society that surrounds and incorporates those educational institutions, particularly the general reactions of that society, or smaller geographical entities within that society, to the presence of ethnic diversity.

From the inception of the United States as a nation, ethnic diversity has been recognized and responded to. The Founding Fathers responded to this reality with such actions as defining Black people in the United States Constitution as "three fifths of all other Persons" and deciding not to establish an official national language (the First Amendment guarantees freedom of speech, but does not restrict that freedom to any particular language). Since then, much of United States history has revolved around the struggle to address the significance of ethnic diversity.

Many Native American (American Indian) nations were defeated militarily and sometimes relocated to remove them as obstacles to expansion, while some 450 treaties between the United States government and Native American nations gave the latter land, special privileges, and special protections as true "internal nations." The Civil War was fought to a considerable extent over the issue of slavery, yet the war did not resolve other societal issues involving Blacks, such as prejudice, economic inequities, political representation, segregation, and other forms of discrimination. Asian immigrants were alternately welcomed and barred, both formally through the 1882 Chinese Exclusion Act and informally, as through the 1906 Gentleman's Agreement with Japan.

Mexicans and Puerto Ricans became part of the United States through conquest and annexation: Mexicans via the 1845 United States annexation of Texas, the 1846-1848 United States-Mexican War, and the 1848 Treaty of Guadalupe Hidalgo; and Puerto Ricans through the 1898 Cuban-Spanish-American War and Treaty of Paris. However, citizenship for both annexed Latinos and Latino immigrants did not resolve such burning issues as land rights, language differences, cultural diversity, and societal discrimination. Even European immigrants became a source of societal dissension, with issues ranging from nativism to immigration restriction, which was applied most vigorously and inequitably to those from Eastern Europe (Higham, 1963). In short, rather than a melting pot, a more cogent metaphor for the United States is that of a mosaic, a constantly-shifting mosaic in which the multihued pieces do not always fit together perfectly, as if an on-going historical earthquake has been challenging the society to attempt to resolve the unresolvable.

Inevitably, schools as a major element of society have been in the forefront of institutions that have had to react to the reality of this changing societal diversity. Historically, a variety of issues have drawn the attention of schools and those people and institutions concerned with the relationship of schools to ethnic diversity. The maintenance or eradication of school segregation along racial lines (race as defined by specific governmental entities) has traditionally received the most school and public attention. A related issue has been unequal educational opportunity, a question of more recent vintage. Historically, such unequal educational opportunities have resulted from factors ranging from institutional restrictions on minority opportunities to the fact that segregated education has meant anything but equality, despite the "separate but equal" rhetoric of the 1896 *Plessy* v. *Ferguson* decision.

The role of schools *vis-à-vis* immigrants has been debated, with educators taking positions ranging from the use of schools to help immigrants maintain their ancestral cultures to the use of schools to Americanize, often without concern about negative side-effects for culturally different students. The questions of whether and how schools should become involved in directly working to improve interracial and interethnic relations surfaced with the intergroup education reform movement of the 1950s (Cook and Cook, 1954) and resurfaced in the 1960s and 1970s with the ethnic studies, multi-ethnic education, and multicultural education movements.

Language, too, has been an educational issue. In the late nineteenth and early twentieth centuries, bilingual education flourished in certain communities, particularly in the Midwest with bilingual programs using various European languages. However, World War I caused a crisis of perception in the United States, as many Americans became astounded with the revelation of the persistence of German language usage, not only in churches, private organizations, and the press, but also in schools (Higham, 1963). In the nearly-crazed reaction to these revelations, the use of languages other than English was virtually extinguished within public schools, except for foreign language classes at the high school level. Not until the 1960s did bilingual education return to the classroom, and supporters of this educational approach have had to contend constantly with public misunderstanding and distrust. Also, not until the 1974 *Lau* v. *Nichols* decision did the courts rule that the failure of schools to provide students with an education in a language they could understand (as well as the failure to teach them English) violated the Civil Rights Act of 1964.

Over the years, ethnicity-related issues have changed in prominence and importance. The school-by-school division of students on racial and linguistic grounds long dominated public debates over the impact of diversity in education. The past 30 years, in particular, have brought the slow, hard-won victory of legal desegregation, a process often marked both by fierce demands for change and equally fierce, sometimes violent, counter-attacks to preserve the status quo. Total victory--meaning total integration--has yet to be won.

However, with progress in this focal area has also come a growing awareness that simple school and even classroom mixing of diverse students has not laid ethnicity to rest as an educational issue. The civil rights movements of the 1960s and early 1970s dramatized many inequities within United States society. Schools, long a source of both hope and frustration for ethnic minorities, became a special focus of attention and reform efforts. In the past three decades, increased attention has been paid to such issues as inequitable testing, the controversy over placement and tracking, relations between schools and ethnic communities, the appropriateness of teaching styles, multicultural education, and the special questions of the education of linguistically-diverse students.

In short, there has been an on-going relationship between ethnicity and education. However, until recently this fact was often ignored by the general public and dealt with intermittently and often superficially by educators. Events of the past three decades have literally forced educators and the public to address more critically the implications of ethnicity for education. Two factors stand out. First, has been the widespread surfacing of minority protests against traditional policies and practices. Second, have been the extraordinary changes in the composition of United States society as well as the projections for future changes. This second factor deserves a moment of contemplation in underlining the significance of this volume.

A comparison of the 1970 and 1980 censuses dramatizes the nature of these changes. While any census in any nation contains a margin of error, while the United States Bureau of the Census has admitted that it has undercounted specific groups at various points in United States history, and while comparisons of censuses are distorted somewhat by changing census questions and categories, a comparison of these two censuses does provide an overall sense of the changes in our nation, even if statistical rigor is lacking.

According to the censuses, between 1970 and 1980, the United States population rose by 11.6 percent. However, the four major American minority groups grew at a far faster rate. The Black population rose by 17.8 percent, Hispanics by 61 percent, Native Americans by 71 percent, and Asian-Americans by 233 percent! Put another way, if you remove Blacks, Hispanics, Native Americans, and Asian-Americans from the the total population figure, the remaining Americans (essentially Anglos, white Americans other than those of Hispanic ancestry) grew by only 7 to 8 percent. Although these "remaining Americans" grew more in absolute numbers than did the four ethnic minority groups, the dynamics of population change indicate that the United States is becoming an increasingly multiracial, multi-ethnic society, not an ethnically more homogenous one. The major contributing factors are continuing sizable immigration from Asia and Latin America and the fact that the average age of ethnic minorities is about five years less than the national average. The latter translates into a larger percentage being in or entering the most active child-bearing years.

The California population-shifts paint an even more dramatic picture. According to economist, Stephen Levy (see Figure 1), between 1980 and the year 2000, California's Hispanic population is likely to increase by 109 percent (to 9.5 million), the Asian-American population by 90 percent (to 3 million), and the Black population by 34 percent (to 2.4 million), while the non-Hispanic white population should increase by less than 13 percent (to 17.8 million). Levy projects the state to be more than 45 percent ethnic minority by the year 2000 (Center for the Continuing Study of the California Economy). Other projections call for the state to be more than 50 percent ethnic minority, including Native Americans, by the same year (Willis, 1985).

Figure 1
The Increasing Ethnic Diversity of California's
Population 1980 to 2000

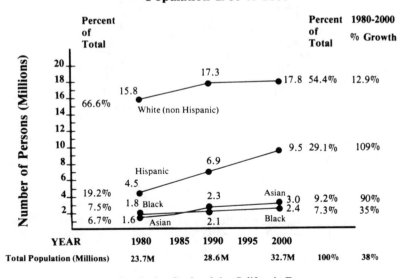

Source: Center for the Continuing Study of the California Economy.

Among school-age Californians (ages 5-17), the advent of the minority majority will come even sooner, with minorities projected to become 52 percent of this age group by the year 2000. Minorities grew from 27 percent of all public school enrollment in 1970 to 42 percent in 1980 (see Figure 2). In 1985, minorities comprised 47 percent of the 4.15 million students, including more than one-half million limited English proficient students. (California State Department of Education, 1985a, 1985b).

Figure 2

Growth of the Minority Component of California's School Age Population, 1970 to 2000

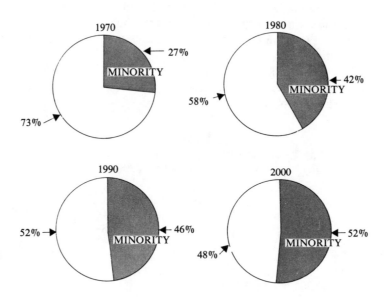

Source: Prepared by California State Department of Education projection from historical data and Center for the Continuing Study of California Economy.

Already many school districts, particularly in large urban areas, have student bodies that are more than one-half ethnic minorities. Los Angeles Unified School District, the largest in the state, now has more than 50 percent of its kindergarten through second grades composed of just one ethnic group, Hispanics. Clearly, the nation and the nation's student bodies are developing a more diverse linguistic, cultural, and racial hue.

These changes have had a dramatic impact on the nature and emphasis of the relationship between ethnicity and schools discussed earlier. Changes in the focus of the debate over desegregation exemplify this altered perspective. Historically, the major issue was the eradication or maintenance of segregation at the district level. Until the 1930s, school segregation along racial lines functioned throughout most of the nation. Such segregation survived from both de jure (laws or school attendance district gerrymandering) and de facto causes (residential segregation). However, in the 1930s, the National Association for the Advancement of Colored People began to force school segregation into the public consciousness. The 1946 *Mendez* v. *Westminster* decision, which outlawed the assigning of California Mexican-American students to segregated schools or classrooms on the basis of surname or heritage, and the 1954 *Brown* v. *Board of Education of Topeka* decision, which ruled that segregated schools were inherently unequal, marked the beginning of the end of legal segregation and gave an impetus for school desegregation.

The primary goal of reformers was the physical mixing of different colored bodies, with so-called solutions including busing, the redrawing of school attendance boundaries, the establishment of magnet schools, and even the creation of metropolitan school assignment patterns that crossed traditional district lines. However, increasingly the focus of the debate has shifted from desegregation (the mixing of bodies) to integration (the development of more effective understanding, cooperation, and personal relations within the educational system among persons of different backgrounds). Even the concept of integration has been broadened from merely students to include faculties, staffs, district administrations, and even curricula, through such processes as multicultural education.

The issues of desegregation and integration are far from being resolved. In fact, in some places resegregation has been occurring through such forces as changes in residency patterns (usually referred to as "white flight," but also involving some middle-class minority families), as well as the decision of some minority families to put their children in private schools. As a result, many large urban school districts are becoming increasingly, often predominantly, composed of both minority and poor children.

In recent years, the focus of ethnic educational reform has shifted more and more to the issue of student achievement. With the publication of the first Coleman report, *Equality of Educational Opportunity* (Coleman *et al.*, 1966), the report's titular topic became a national issue. The continuation of the academic underachievement of some ethnic minority groups has become a growing concern for educators and public alike. Some reformers of the past had hoped and even predicted that desegregation would inevitably bring increased minority educational achievement, but such dreams have been dashed. Desegregation often does not go beyond the physical mixing of students of different racial and ethnic backgrounds, with little effort made to increase the possibilities that the racially-mixed students will enjoy educational equity and have positive inter-group experiences (Hochschild, 1984). It has become starkly clear that more precise and thoughtful educational measures must be taken to reduce group differences in achievement and thereby move toward greater educational equity.

Recent statistics speak eloquently to this issue by demonstrating the sharp ethnic differences in educational attainment. Take, for example, the attrition of Hispanic students in California (see Figure 3). In the two years between Fall 1979 and Fall 1981, Hispanic students who were enrolled in ninth grade in Fall of 1979 had lost more than 14 percent of their class. The 1979 Hispanic class of tenth graders had lost almost 29 percent by Fall 1981, and the graduating class of June 1981 had 31 percent fewer Hispanics than it did in Fall of 1980 (California State Department of Education, 1982). More recent data indicates that more than 36 percent of Hispanics in ninth grade in 1981 failed to enroll in twelfth grade in 1984 (California State Department of Education, 1985b).

A national report documented comparable problems throughout the country: About 45 percent of Hispanic students who enter high school never finish, 40 percent of these departures occurring before the tenth grade. By comparison, about 17 percent of Anglo students drop out prior to completing high school (National Commission on Secondary Education for Hispanics, 1984). (Greater detail concerning ethnic inequities in educational achievement and attainment can be found in the chapter by Sue and Padilla in this volume.)

In attempting to grapple with this continuing problem, one of the significant areas of discussion has been the response of teachers and administrators to the growing diversity in their classrooms. Critical questions have arisen. How do educators perceive ethnic minority students,

Figure 3

**Attrition of Hispanic Students from California Public High Schools
(1979 to 1981)**

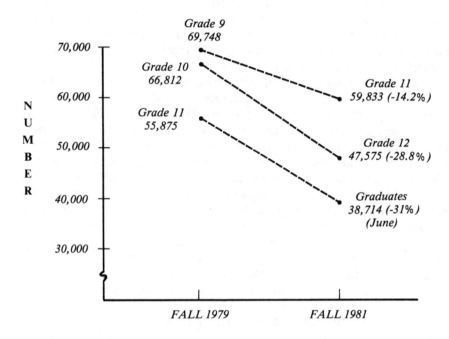

Source: California State Department of Education, 1980, 1982.

particularly those educators whose teacher education did not involve
specific training in working with minority students and whose previous
teaching experience has mainly involved work with non-minority
students? How much knowledge and knowledge-based understanding
do educators have about ethnic minorities? How does their knowledge
or lack of knowledge about ethnic minorities affect their attitudes and
behavior toward such students? Most important, in what respects have
they modified their teaching or administrative practices to increase the
educational achievement of their minority students?

SCHOLARSHIP ON MINORITY EDUCATION

It was almost inevitable that the rise in public concern with issues concerning relations between ethnicity and schools would ultimately be reflected in a rise in scholarly attention to that topic. As a result, the last two decades have seen a major expansion in scholarship on facets of this general theme. Such scholarship has provided new insights, but it has also revealed the enormous knowledge gaps that still exist and some of the critical directions that future scholarship should take.

There are many ways to group ethnicity-and-schools scholarship. For purposes of this volume, I will look at this scholarship in terms of three, necessarily overlapping, categories: (1) works that analyze the historical development of various relationships between ethnicity and schools or that document the current situation within education, although the lengthy delays that often exist between research, writing, and publication often transform such "contemporary" analyses into historical slices of life; (2) studies that identify those factors that influence the education of minority students and that need to be addressed in the process of attempting to improve that education; and (3) scholarly literature that provides recommendations for the modification of educational policies and practices. However, it must be recognized that many studies touch upon all three categories. (For example, Weinberg, 1977, provides historical analysis, needs assessment, and recommendations for action.)

Historical-Contemporary Analytical Scholarship

Numerous themes have emerged, with the following merely serving as examples. The struggle over desegregation continues to absorb scholars, particularly those with a bent toward reconstructing and analyzing the history of this process (Coleman *et al.*, 1966; Wollenberg, 1976; Weinberg, 1977). The educational experience of ethnic minority students has drawn the attention of other scholars, particularly educational anthropologists, who have documented these experiences through firsthand observation and interviews as well as by school records (Parsons, 1965; Rist, 1978; Kleinfeld, 1979; Philips, 1983). The development and modification of educational conditions affecting students have been examined, sometimes from a perspective of hope (things have improved or are improving), sometimes from one of despair (severe structural restraints in the educational system and society render educational change in favor of minorities relatively meaningless or virtually impossible) (Carnoy, 1974).

Factors that Influence the Education of Minority Students

In general, three types of factors have been identified:

1. Overall societal dynamics that influence education through such means as setting the societal agenda for school priorities, contributing to minority self-concept and teacher perceptions of minority students (such as through the mass media), and restraining or galvanizing educational reform (Kirp, 1982; Appleton, 1983).

2. School forces that influence minority education, such as teacher expectations and behavior, counseling practices, school structure, curriculum, and testing (Kane, 1970; Jencks *et al.*, 1972; "Perspectives on Inequality," 1973; Samuda, 1975; Longstreet, 1978). This second category of scholarship also includes those research studies that attempt to analyze and differentiate schools in which minority and poor students tend to achieve from those in which they tend to do poorly (Brookover *et al.*, 1979; Purkey and Smith, 1983; Cuban, 1984).

3. Educationally-relevant sociocultural factors within minority communities or identified as part of ethnic minority students such as language, culture, socio-economic situation, and personal and group experiences both within and outside of the educational system (Dinnerstein *et al.*, 1979; Clark, 1983; Grossman, 1984).

Prescriptions for Reform

Curricular and textbook reform aimed at making education more relevant to minority students by emphasizing their histories and cultures and at creating better intergroup understanding has been advocated by scholars dealing with the issues of multicultural, multi-ethnic, and bilingual education (Banks, 1981a, 1981b). Others have addressed various modifications of teacher behavior, ranging from raising their expectations for minority students to adopting culturally-sensitive teaching styles (Ramírez and Castañeda, 1974; García, 1982). Some have moved beyond the classroom into such areas as reform of testing, placement, counseling, and other school practices (Atkinson *et al.*, 1979). Finally, there is a growing, increasingly sophisticated body of scholarly literature on language aspects of instruction, addressing such topics as bilingual education and English-as-a-second-language (ESL) education (California State Department of Education, 1981; Fishman and Keller, 1982).

CONTEXTUAL INTERACTION MODEL

Yet, while this research has contributed to our understanding of the complex and changing relationships between ethnicity and education, no consensus has emerged concerning this volume's two basic questions. First, why do members of some minority group *tend* to have higher educational achievement than members of other minority groups? Second, why do members of some minority groups *tend* to have lower educational achievement than mainstream American students?

Over the years, analysts have posited a number of explanations for group achievements and underachievements. However, these explanations generally fall short of being convincing, for a number of reasons. These reasons are worth examining in order to establish the basis on which this book's new model has been developed.

First, some analyses have relied too heavily on single-cause explanations. Group educational differentials have been attributed, at various times, to language difference, to socio-economic status, to racism and other forms of prejudice, to cultural conflict, to discriminatory instruments (such as I.Q. tests), or to the cultural insensitivity of educators. Yet as surely as one of these has been posited as *the*, or at least *the principal*, cause of group achievement differentials, then other situations are discovered in which these factors exist, and yet group achievement differentials do not occur.

Second, a tendency that both distorts on its own and contributes to the misguided dependence on single-cause explanations is the confusion of correlation and cause. Sometimes correlations are found, as between language and educational achievement, between socio-economic status and educational achievement, or between race and educational achievement. Yet, without evidence-based demonstrations that these correlations actually reflect causation--for example, that language difference or socio-economic status or race have actually *caused* lower educational achievement--such correlations are no stronger than arguing that a cock's crowing "causes" the sun to rise, simply because the two phenomena are strongly correlated.

Third, and most important for this book, there has been a tendency to decontextualize explanations. That is, explanations about the relationships between sociocultural factors and educational achievement often posit causation without consideration of the context in which these factors operate. For example, while there may be causative connections between such sociocultural factors as language, race, ethnicity, socio-economic status, learning style, group history, and low educational achievement, there are also situations in which limited English proficient students, students of different racial and ethnic backgrounds, and students from poor families succeed dramatically in school. Why do students of similar linguistic, racial, ethnic, and socio-economic backgrounds vary so widely in their academic achievement? More specifically, under what conditions do students with similar sociocultural characteristics succeed educationally and under what conditions do they perform poorly in school? In other words, within what contexts-- educational and societal--do students of similar backgrounds succeed and within what contexts do they do less well?

The question of the educational influence of context stretches beyond our national borders. For example, why do Koreans tend to succeed in United States schools and society, but not in Japan? Why do native Maoris do worse in New Zealand schools than do those immigrant Polynesians who have language and culture similar to the Maoris? Why do West Indian students do better in United States schools than they do in the United Kingdom (Ogbu and Matute-Bianchi, this volume)? An analysis of group culture alone does not provide the answers to these questions. It is also necessary to evaluate the societal and school contexts in which those cultures operate.

This book moves beyond the three fallacious analytical tendencies that have been noted and posits a Contextual Interaction Model for evaluating the educational process, in general, and the educational experiences of language minority students, in particular. This model integrates two previous conceptual formulations: my historical concept of the Societal Curriculum (Cortés, 1981) and the Interaction Model for Language Minority Students developed by the Bilingual Education Office. The latter model, presented in the publication, *Basic Principles for the Education of Language-Minority Students: An Overview* (California State Department of Education, 1983), was adapted from James Cummins' article, "Linguistic Interdependence and the Educational Development of Bilingual Children" (Cummins, 1979).

The Contextual Interaction Model illustrates the way in which non-school societal factors affect three aspects of the school's context and process, which are labeled educational input factors, instructional elements, and student qualities (see Figure 4). Among these societal factors are:

1. family (including home culture and language use);

2. community (both the general community and subcommunities, such as ethnic communities);

3. non-school institutions (such as religious institutions, voluntary associations, and government agencies);

4. the mass media (including television, motion pictures, radio, newspapers, and magazines);

5. heritage, culture, and ethnicity (including individual backgrounds, ethnic group experiences and life styles, and varying societal elements from the local to the national level);

6. attitudes (ranging from national to local);

7. perceptions (including not only how individuals and groups perceive themselves and others, but also how they interpret how others perceive them);

8. socio-economic status (family and surrounding community); and

9. educational level (self, family, and peers).

Figure 4

School and Society

Contextual Interaction Model

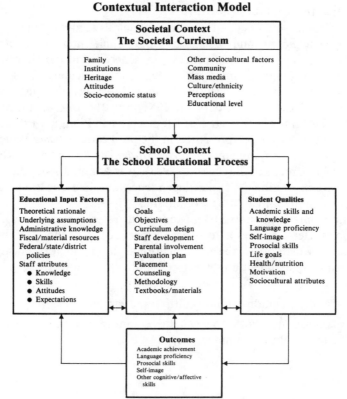

These and other factors create the societal context in which educational institutions function. Moreover, operating through the societal curriculum (the massive, on-going educational and socializing process carried on by society at large, as contrasted with the educational and socializing process conducted within schools), these societal factors directly affect the school's context and process. In particular, they influence at least three areas of school education:

1. *Educational input factors,* such as educators themselves (including the knowledge, skills, expectations, and attitudes of teachers, administrators, counselors, school board members, and other educational personnel), fiscal resources, governmental policies, and the educational theories and assumptions that undergird and inform the school educational process.

2. *Student qualities,* such as their proficiency in one or more languages, academic skills and knowledge, self-image, prosocial skills, educational motivation, and goals for the future.

3. *Instructional elements,* including curriculum, subject emphases, textbooks and other educational materials, pedagogical strategies, teaching styles, counseling, student placement, evaluation plan, staff development, and parent involvement.

In addition, these three components of the educational process affect one another. Both the general educational input factors and student qualities (including perceived qualities) influence the selection and implementation of instructional elements. Furthermore, these instructional elements affect students, with this impact sometimes observed and evaluated as cognitive and affective outcomes, although many of these outcomes are neither perceived nor assessed by schools. In turn, these student outcomes should be evaluated for purposes of modifying educational input factors and instructional elements.

Finally, the model illustrates the dynamism of these interactions over time. As days, weeks, months, years, and decades pass, the content of the model changes, continuously and sometimes dramatically. Society changes over time. The educational context and process--general educational factors, instructional treatments, students, and student outcomes--change over time. The ways in which society interacts with and influences schools--both via society in general and via specific societal elements, including ethnic groups--change over time. Finally, as the future adult citizens of our society, students who emerge from the schooling process ultimately influence, modify, and reinforce schools, the societal context, and the content of the societal curriculum. In other words, the Contextual Interaction Model is dynamic, interactive, and historically changing (see Figure 5).

Figure 5

Contextual Interaction Over Time

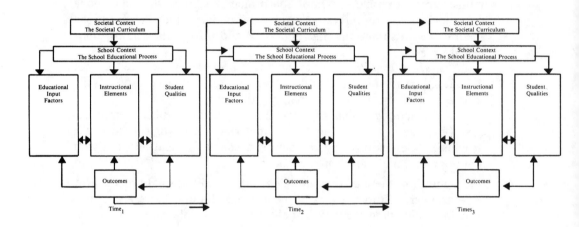

As conceptualized in this model, the school and societal educational processes are themselves extremely complex and interact in complex ways. For example, take one aspect of the societal curriculum, the visual media (motion pictures and television). Scholars and societal analysts have long recognized the impact of motion pictures on American society. Film historian, Lewis Jacobs (1939) noted:

> *The content of American motion pictures since their inception has been, in fact, not only an important historical source but a stimulant and educator to American life itself. Besides offering a social occasion and an emotional experience, they supplied audiences with information and ideas. (p. 3)*

The rise of television, through both its own programming and its recycling of theatrical feature films, has extended the impact of the visual media. In 1977, social psychologist, George Comstock reported that there had been more than 2,300 research papers on television and human behavior. He stated:

> *Several writers have argued that television is a powerful rein-forcer of the* status quo. *The ostensible mechanisms are the effects of its portrayals on public expectations and percep-tions. Television portrayals and particularly violent drama are said to assign roles of authority, power, success, failure, dependence, and vulnerability in a manner that matches the real-life social hierarchy, thereby strengthening that hierarchy by increasing its acknowledgement among the public and by failing to provide positive images for members of social categories occupying a subservient position. Content analyses of television drama support the contention that por-trayals reflect normative status. (pp. 20-21)*

Among those influenced by film and television are persons involved in the educational process, including teachers, administrators, counselors, curriculum developers, textbook writers, school board members, and students. It affects their perceptions of themselves and their perceptions and expectations of others, thereby influencing curricular content and pedagogical decisions. To the extent that media teaching conforms to or conflicts with school teaching, it reinforces or challenges school instruction.

Moreover, both school learning (student outcomes) and societal learning will affect the future societal context. Students of today become the societal decision makers and context providers of the future. In turn, that future societal curriculum will influence education in the future.

This example illustrates the complex and dynamic nature of the historical interaction between schools and society, as well as the multiplicity of factors that influence students, including their school achievement. Moreover, it demonstrates the need to examine both societal and school context in analyzing student achievement and in sug-gesting educational change to increase that achievement. In short, the Contextual Interaction Model provides a means of visualizing the total educational process for purposes of analysis.

While the Contextual Interaction Model applies to the school educa-tion of all students, it can be used to examine the education of specific groups of students, such as language minority students (see Figure 6). For example, the societal context influences the students' proficiency in

English (L$_2$) and their primary language (L$_1$), their motivation to strengthen their primary language and acquire proficiency in other languages, their perceptions and expectations of teachers and schools, and their self-image (including educational motivation, life goals, and hopes for the future). It influences educators, such as their knowledge, perceptions, and expectations of language minority students, their multiple language facility, and their beliefs and underlying assumptions about education, including language learning. Therefore, it influences the instructional elements adopted by these educators in addressing language minority students, including approaches to language use and instruction, the treatment and coordination of other subject areas, their interaction with students, and the use (or non-use) of student or community sociocultural factors in developing instruction. The result will be educational outcomes, including English language learning, the further development of the students' home languages, cognitive achievement in other subject areas, improvement in prosocial skills, and such elements of the students' affective domain as self-image, perceptions of others, and orientation toward society.

Figure 6
The Education of
Language Minority Students
A Contextual Interaction Model

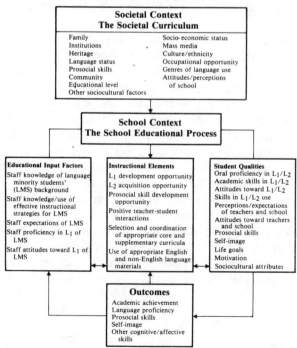

Societal Context
The Societal Curriculum

Family	Socio-economic status
Institutions	Mass media
Heritage	Culture/ethnicity
Language status	Occupational opportunity
Prosocial skills	Genres of language use
Community	Attitudes/perceptions
Educational level	of school
Other sociocultural factors	

School Context
The School Educational Process

Educational Input Factors
Staff knowledge of language minority students' (LMS) background
Staff knowledge/use of effective instructional strategies for LMS
Staff expectations of LMS
Staff proficiency in L$_1$ of LMS
Staff attitudes toward L$_1$ of LMS

Instructional Elements
L$_1$ development opportunity
L$_2$ acquisition opportunity
Prosocial skill development opportunity
Positive teacher-student interactions
Selection and coordination of appropriate core and supplementary curricula
Use of appropriate English and non-English language materials

Student Qualities
Oral proficiency in L$_1$/L$_2$
Academic skills in L$_1$/L$_2$
Attitudes toward L$_1$/L$_2$
Skills in L$_1$/L$_2$ use
Perceptions/expectations of teachers and school
Attitudes toward teachers and school
Prosocial skills
Self-image
Life goals
Motivation
Sociocultural attributes

Outcomes
Academic achievement
Language proficiency
Prosocial skills
Self-image
Other cognitive/affective skills

The examination of a wide variety of societal and school factors, including their interaction both at one point in time and dynamically over time, provides the essence of the Contextual Interaction Model. This model rejects single-cause explanations and instead seeks to incorporate a multiplicity of factors that may influence educational achievement. It rejects static correlations and instead substitutes the consideration of observable dynamic interactions over time in an attempt to assess causation. It rejects the examination of societal and school factors outside of a specific context and instead examines the dynamic operation of these multiple factors with specific contexts. Finally, it provides a basis for the comparison of contexts in order to identify different ways in which sociocultural factors interact with the influence educational experience, including educational achievement.

Moreover, a careful examination of the contextualized relationship between sociocultural factors and educational achievement can lead to the identification of other school dilemmas. Analysts may determine that certain verifiable realities exist within an educational situation, but that the actors in that situation may perceive things quite differently and, most important, act and react on the basis of those assumptions. For example, within the Contextual Interaction Model, the *fact* that a teacher is not prejudiced against a linguistic minority group may be less important than the perception by students or parents that the teacher is prejudiced, with the resulting effect on the educational actions of those students or parents. Likewise, ''objective'' analysis may determine that certain curricular content exists within the educational system or within society itself, but within the Contextual Interaction Model the meaning and importance that individuals or groups assign to that content becomes additionally significant. The objective ''fact'' that educational opportunity exists is important, but also important is whether or not a student *believes* that opportunity exists within a specific school situation or that school education enhances future opportunities within society.

In other words, the Contextual Interaction Model incorporates both objective and subjective elements. It integrates a consideration not only of the existence of sociocultural factors, but also of the way in which these factors operate and the perception of their operation by the actors, primarily educators and students. Finally, it provides a framework for viewing the dynamic interaction of multiple factors over time.

A MULTIDISCIPLINARY APPROACH

The Contextual Interaction Model facilitates the integration of the diverse analyses in this volume. The book focuses on how societal and school sociocultural factors have influenced, do influence, and will continue to influence the education of ethnic minority students. It looks at ways in which these factors have affected that education historically. It addresses the contemporary educational situation. It analyzes selected educational responses to minority students and provides suggestions for making the educational process more equitable and effective for minority students. Moreover, it does so by drawing on perspectives from a variety of academic disciplines.

The chapter by psychologists Stanley Sue and Amado Padilla provides a general introduction to the theme of the relationship between ethnicity and educational achievement, with an emphasis on school and societal assumptions and value conflicts. They begin with an overview of the rapid growth of the ethnic minority population of the United States and the differential academic outcomes of various groups, with particular emphasis on California. Following this, they turn to two major types of interpretive problems that plague scholars and educators in addressing ethnic issues: (1) four basic perspectives that have been used explicitly or implicitly when attempting to explain the status and educational achievements of ethnic minority groups (including the weaknesses and educational implications of these models); and (2) five paradoxes, reflecting basic value conflicts, that make it difficult to arrive at compromise solutions for educational and societal problems concerning ethnic minority groups.

Sue and Padilla conclude by suggesting five approaches that may be of use in working *toward* resolutions of these values conflicts. In particular, they suggest that the traditional convergent thinking approach to searching for compromises among value conflicts may be less effective than alternative, less solution-oriented approaches, such as divergent thinking, mediation, alternation, co-existence, and moving to higher levels of abstraction. However, Sue and Padilla do not go so far as to claim that these approaches will solve all minority-related educational problems or totally resolve what may be basically unresolvable conflicts.

The chapter by anthropologists John Ogbu and Maria Matute-Bianchi focuses on the question: Why do some language minorities experience disproportionate school failure, while others do well despite language and cultural differences from the national mainstream? The answer, they say, is not language or cultural discontinuities between various language minorities and the schools, at least as these discontinuities have traditionally been described. To explain these differences in achievement, Ogbu and Matute-Bianchi propose a conceptual framework that includes the following components: (1) that different language minority groups experience differential success in schools, not only within the United States, but also in other nations; (2) that schools are linked to larger sociocultural and historical forces, particularly through the conscious and sometimes unconscious efforts of schools to prepare students to contribute to their nation's economic system; and (3) that this link affects groups' perceptions of schools and of the ways one gets ahead in United States society. In particular, they argue that, greatly through the influence of sociocultural and historical circumstances, each minority group develops its own "status mobility system," which they label a "folk theory of getting ahead." Some groups' folk theories enhance their ability to achieve in schools, while the folk theories of other groups limit their school achievement capacity.

Following an analysis of these three factors, the authors suggest that minority groups fall into three categories: autonomous minorities (who do not exist in the United States); immigrant minorities (who tend to succeed educationally); and caste-like minorities (who tend to underachieve educationally and socio-economically). Caste-like minority groups, they argue, develop what the authors call "oppositional cultural frames of reference" and culturally inverted survival strategies. These lead to alternative routes to success (as defined by the group) and may even lead group members to resist schooling, particularly if they view it to be of no tangible benefit and possibly even culturally destructive. As examples, the authors provide brief histories, including educational experiences, of Chinese-Americans (whom they classify as an immigrant group that has been educationally successful) and Mexican-Americans (whom they classify as a caste-like minority group that comparatively has been educationally unsuccessful). Finally, they present their conceptual framework that sociocultural forces--including a group's perception of the linkage between school success and adult employment and earnings--will influence academic efforts, which, in turn, influence academic achievement.

The chapter by anthropologist Shirley Brice Heath addresses the issue of the sociocultural environments of language learning for minority children and their relationship to traditional school expectations of what children bring to the classroom in terms of language learning. The author sees all language learning as cultural learning; in learning language, young people also learn language use in its cultural context, as well as role relationships associated with this language use. In some cases, this cultural learning may not include some of the types of language use expected by schools; it may also include certain language uses that schools fail to draw upon. Heath looks at the various primary social groups (family and community) and secondary social groups (such as institutions, including schools) that influence language learning. She also analyzes three types of ethnic families--Chinese-Americans, Mexican-Americans, and Indo-Chinese-Americans--in terms of three factors: parental assumptions about their teaching role, non-school opportunities for children to use oral and written language in a variety of ways, and links between primary and secondary social groups in terms of language learning. She concludes that the language use environments in some ethnic homes and communities tend to better prepare young people for English language learning in school because they engage in forms of language that are expected, required, and rewarded in school. Furthermore, schools penalize some language minority children through the inappropriate use of a single developmental model of language learning normed on mainstream students.

Based on her analysis, Heath concludes that parents should use their strongest language (even if it is not English) in order to provide their children with maximum opportunities to use language in diverse settings and for diverse purposes in order to develop language facility in its broadest and richest sense. According to Heath, those students who have the most diverse, well-developed, and extensive patterns of language use (even in a language other than English) will be best prepared to learn a rich and powerful English in schools. Moreover, schools should emphasize constant, multiple uses of language and, wherever possible, should incorporate sociocultural knowledge of their students' backgrounds to help make teaching more appropriate to the students' needs and strengths.

The chapter by educational ethnographers, Stephen Díaz, Luis Moll, and Hugh Mehan suggests an interactionist approach to education. Starting from the universalist assumption that children in all cultures have about the same capacity for early language acquisition and cognitive development, the authors present what they believe to be the major explanations for cultural differentials in the school performance of students from different ethnic backgrounds. They divide these explanations into two basic categories: context-free interpretations (biological determinism and cultural determinism) and context-specific interpretations (that the demonstration of language ability and intelligence are influenced by, sometimes determined by, the interactional context, that is, the actions of the participants).

Following this introduction, Díaz et al. focus on two school situations, one in bilingual reading instruction and one in second-language writing instruction. They describe their ethnographic observations and analyses of adult-child interactions both at the school and in the home, as well as their pedagogical interventions in the two situations, including an assessment of results. Finally, they compare their experiments with two other school studies that combine ethnography and intervention. On the basis of their own experiments and an evaluation of these other studies, the authors conclude that the sociocultural organization of schooling--not language alone--is the major obstacle to the educational achievement of language minority students. Furthermore, they assert that school achievement can be fostered if schools identify their students' special social, linguistic, and academic strengths, build from these, and draw upon community data to create learning opportunities.

The chapter by psychologist, Spencer Kagan, confronts what he sees as three interrelated failures of United States schools: their failure to retain and educate sociocultural minority students; their failure to successfully integrate desegregated classrooms and foster positive student race relations; and their failure to socialize students with prosocial and cooperative values and behaviors. Moreover, he provides a general analysis of the roots and expressions of these problems, including schools' overemphasis on competitive learning. He believes that this emphasis on school competition has had particularly harmful effects on the school achievement of many minority students (as well as students of low income and rural backgrounds) who come from homes and communities with a more cooperative orientation.

Kagan believes that schools should set goals that go beyond the development of academic skills to also include the improvement of interethnic relations, prosocial values, and cooperative behavior. Kagan posits what he considers to be a potentially powerful strategy for addressing all three issues: the increased adoption of pedagogical strategies that incorporate cooperative learning. He argues that an increased use of cooperative learning would help all students, with special benefits for minority students, who have demonstrated special responsiveness to such learning strategies. The major portion of this article deals with cooperative learning, including discussions of its basic characteristics, various classroom and teacher training models, the academic and social gains that have been achieved through the use of this approach, and the factors in cooperative learning that contribute to such gains.

The concluding chapter, by applied linguist, Mary McGroarty, synthesizes the interactional relationships among culture, context, and education. It also addresses the implications of the earlier chapters for educational practice. In particular, she discusses the implications of the book for four groups who are involved in the educational process--

parents, teachers, resource teachers and teacher trainers, and administrators--and offers suggestions for each group.

McGroarty's recommendations range widely. She calls for greater parental emphasis on developing their children's language skills and on involving children in both cooperative and competitive activities. She urges increased teacher efforts to develop better understanding of their own and their students' cultures and interactional styles in order to apply this understanding to the educational process. She suggests modifications in teacher training and staff development to incorporate more emphasis on the educational significance of sociocultural factors and to draw upon a knowledge of interactional experiences, alternative pedagogical strategies, and the impact of different contexts. She cites the need for stronger administrator emphasis on improving school climate and communications and on building educational communities of commitment involving teachers, students, and parents. Taken as a whole, this article can serve as a basic plan of action for the practical application of the insights provided by the previous chapters.

CONCLUSION

Overall, this volume poses a challenge to current educational thinking and practices. Yet, three limitations need to be recognized in reading the following chapters: (1) some sociocultural issues and other questions related to the education of language minority students are not discussed; (2) the articles raise numerous issues and questions that can only be answered through additional research; and (3) the authors' alternative interpretations and recommendations reflect various theoretical positions, philosophical perspectives, and disciplinary approaches.

First, the book concentrates on the various relationships between the sociocultural context, the schooling process, and the educational outcomes of language minority students. Therefore, of space-imposed necessity, it cannot address a number of other critical, related issues. For example, the book does not look at such continuing significant minority issues as desegregation, the relatively small percentage of minority educators (contrasted with the demographics of the general population), textbook treatment of minorities, the integration of minority content and perspectives into the mainstream curriculum, and the role of minority communities in affecting the educational process through such means as political activity, community organizations, and participation on school boards. Nor does it look at a number of general educational issues that have vital implications for minority education, such as school financing,

the problems of implementing educational change, the changing significance of education for careers, the organizational culture of schools, and
the cross-cutting influences of such factors as race, class, gender, and
regional background of language minorities. Also, it does not devote
considerable attention to the value or process of maintaining and
developing minority languages as an academic skill both for the inherent
value of facility in a second language and for the career opportunities
increased by functional bilingualism. (See the Cummins' article in
Schooling and Language Minority Students: A Theoretical Framework,
EDAC, California State University, Los Angeles.)

Second, more research needs to be done on some of the issues suggested by these papers. How unyielding to compromise are the value
conflicts identified by Sue and Padilla and how effective are their suggested alternative approaches? How valid are the minority categoriza-
tions and descriptions of various folk theories of success presented by
Ogbu and Matute-Bianchi, and what steps can be taken to improve
minority student attitudes toward education? How can families,
schools, and other institutions increase the opportunities for language
minority youth to engage in language development, as suggested by
Heath? What other types of strategies can be developed to link home
and community culture with learning, and what are the various long-
range educational benefits or limitations to the approaches recommended by Díaz *et al.*? What are some of the additional applications of
cooperative learning, besides the ones suggested by Kagan, and what are
the limitations to its use, including its varying applicability to different
subject areas? How effective would McGroarty's recommendations be if
adopted and implemented consistently over a long period of time?

Third, these chapters provide alternative responses to a number of
questions, such as the following: What are the primary causes of
language minority student academic successes and failures? What
should be the main focus of efforts to bring about change in minority
educational achievement: the groups themselves, schools, institutions of
teacher education, or society at large? In what respects do language and
culture create obstacles for minority educational attainment; and in what
respects do they provide opportunities for minority students, schools,
and society as a whole? In what respects and how can basic sociocultural
and value conflicts be resolved, particularly when these reflect deeply
held, historically ingrained societal and ethnic values? Can sufficient
changes be made in the schooling process in order to provide students
from all backgrounds an equal chance to succeed educationally?

Despite some disagreement on these questions, a remarkable amount
of concurrence emerges from these authors of varying disciplines,

theoretical perspectives, and interpretive points of view. They concur that minority students have had an unconscionably low level of educational attainment. They concur that sociocultural factors have contributed to that inequitable situation due to unfortunate incongruences between the cultures and social experiences of some language minority groups and historical and current educational policies and practices. They concur about the importance of culture and language as major factors in both educational and societal success. They concur that major changes are necessary, with most concluding that schools both have an obligation to provide quality educational equity and have an opportunity to bring about effective educational reform.

Finally, all six papers contribute to a better understanding of the educational process as viewed through a dynamic Contextual Interaction Model. Obgu and Matute-Bianchi describe a societal context in which folk cultures of success develop within ethnic groups, influencing their behavior and achievement within different educational contexts. Sue and Padilla identify certain basic value conflicts that defy compromise and impede ethnic minority achievement within the context of schools, but suggest some non-traditional approaches for altering the school context to facilitate positive interaction and improve minority education. Heath recommends the modification of the educational context, both by abandoning an erroneous, misleading single model of language development and by building more from sociocultural knowledge of the students, including their unique home-developed language use repertoires.

Díaz, Moll, and Mehan also suggest school contextual reform to achieve educationally more effective teacher-student interactions, based on teacher ethnography and analysis, so that schools can better build from students' special strengths. Kagan calls for an increased use of cooperative learning strategies as a major change in the school context, not only to increase minority achievement but also to improve interethnic relations and strengthen all students' prosocial attitudes and behaviors. McGroarty sketches a broad plan of action to provide avenues of educational reform within the model.

The publication of this volume comes at a critical time in the history of our nation and the development of our educational system. Given current demographic trends, projections for the future, and our increasing knowledge of the significance of minorities both for society and for education, a serious rethinking of our school policies and practices should be an on-going part of the educational process. This rich volume provides a major contribution to this process, and for that reason should be read and seriously contemplated by educators.*

REFERENCES

Appleton, Nicholas. *Cultural Pluralism in Education: Theoretical Foundations.* New York: Longman, 1983.

Atkinson, Donald R., Morten, George, and Sue, Derald Wings (Eds.). *Counseling American Minorities: A Cross-Cultural Perspective.* Dubuque, Iowa: William C. Brown, 1979.

Banks, James A. (Ed.). *Education in the 80s: Multiethnic Education.* Washington, D.C.: National Education Association, 1981a.

_____. *Multiethnic Education: Theory and Practice.* Boston: Allyn and Bacon, 1981b.

_____, and Lynch, James (Eds.). *Multicultural Education in Western Societies.* London: Holt, Rinehart and Winston, 1986.

Brookover, Wilbur, Beady, Charles, Flood, Patricia, Schweitzer, John, and Wisenbaker, Joe. *School Social Systems and Student Achievement: Schools Can Make a Difference.* New York: Praeger, 1979.

California State Department of Education. *Basic Principles for the Education of Language-Minority Students: An Overview.* Sacramento: California State Department of Education, 1983.

_____. *Language Census Report.* Sacramento: California State Department of Education, Spring, 1985a.

_____. *Racial or Ethnic Distribution of Staff and Students in California Public Schools, 1979-80.* Sacramento: California State Department of Education, 1980.

_____. *Racial or Ethnic Distribution of Staff and Students in California Public Schools, 1981-82.* Sacramento: California State Department of Education, 1982.

_____. *Racial or Ethnic Distribution of Staff and Students in California Public Schools, 1984-85.* Sacramento: California State Department of Education, 1985b.

_____. *Schooling and Language Minority Students: A Theoretical Framework.* Los Angeles: Evaluation, Dissemination and Assessment Center, California State University, Los Angeles, 1981.

_____. *Studies on Immersion Education: A Collection for United States Educators.* Sacramento, California: California State Department of Education, 1984.

Carnoy, Martin. *Education as Cultural Imperialism.* New York: David McKay, 1974.

Center for the Continuing Study of the California Economy. *Projections of Ethnic Population for California, 1980-2000.* Palo Alto, California: Center for the Continuing Study of the California Economy.

Clark, Reginald M. *Family Life and School Achievement: Why Poor Black Children Succeed or Fail.* Chicago: University of Chicago Press, 1983.

*I would like to thank Daniel Holt and Dennis Parker for their insightful comments on earlier drafts of this chapter, and James Banks both for his critique of this chapter and for allowing me to read a chapter of his forthcoming book, *Multicultural Education in Western Societies,* which he co-authored with James Lynch.

Coleman, James S. *et al. Equality of Educational Opportunity.* Washington D.C.: U.S. Government Printing Office, 1966.

Comstock, George. *The Impact of Television on American Institutions and the American Public.* Honolulu: East-West Communication Institute, East-West Center, 1977.

Cook Lloyd, and Cook, Elaine. *Intergroup Education.* New York: McGraw-Hill, 1954.

Cortés, Carlos E. The societal curriculum: Implications for multiethnic education. In James A. Banks (Ed.), *Education in the 80s: Multiethnic Education.* Washington, D.C.: National Education Association, 1981.

Cuban, Larry. Transforming the frog into a prince: Effective schools research, policy, and practice at the district level. *Harvard Educational Review,* 1984, *54*(2), 129-151.

Cummins, James. Linguistic interdependence and the educational development of bilingual children. *Review of Educational Research,* 1979, *49*(2), 222-251.

————. The role of primary language development in promoting educational success for language minority students. In *Schooling and Language Minority Students: A Theoretical Framework.* Los Angeles, California: Evaluation, Dissemination and Assessment Center, California State University, Los Angeles, 1981.

Díaz, Stephen, Moll, Luis C., and Mehan, Hugh. Sociocultural resources in instruction: A context-specific approach. In *Beyond Language: Social and Cultural Factors in Schooling Language Minority Students.* Los Angeles, California: Evaluation, Dissemination and Assessement Center, California State University, Los Angeles, 1986.

Dinnerstein, Leonard, Nichols, Roger L., and Reimers, David M. *Natives and Strangers: Ethnic Groups and the Building of America.* New York: Oxford University Press, 1979.

Fishman, Joshua A., and Keller, Gary D. (Eds.). *Bilingual Education for Hispanic Students in the United States.* New York: Teachers College Press, 1982.

García, Ricardo L. *Teaching in a Pluralistic Society: Concepts, Models, Strategies.* New York: Harper & Row, 1982.

Grossman, Herbert. *Educating Hispanic Students: Cultural Implications for Instruction, Classroom Management, Counseling, and Assessment.* Springfield, Illinois: Charles C. Thomas, 1984.

Heath, Shirley Brice. Sociocultural contexts of language development. In *Beyond Language: Social and Cultural Factors in Schooling Language Minority Students.* Los Angeles, California: Evaluation, Dissemination and Assessment Center, California State University, Los Angeles, 1986.

Highman, John. *Strangers in the Land: Patterns of American Nativism, 1860-1925.* New Brunswick, New Jersey: Rutgers University Press, 1963.

Hochschild, Jennifer L. *The New American Dilemma: Liberal Democracy and School Desegregation.* New Haven: Yale University Press, 1984.

Jacobs, Lewis. *The Rise of the American Film: A Critical History.* New York: Harcourt, Brace and Company, 1939.

Jencks, Christopher, Smith, Marshall, Acland, Henry, Bane, Mary Jo, Cohen, David, Gintis, Herbert, Heyns, Barbara, and Michelson, Stephan. *Inequality: A Reassessment of the Effect of Family and Schooling in America.* New York: Basic Books, 1972.

Kagan, Spencer. Cooperative learning and sociocultural factors in schooling. In *Beyond Language: Social and Cultural Factors in Schooling Language Minority Students.* Los Angeles, California: Evaluation, Dissemination and Assessment Center, California State University, Los Angeles, 1986.

Kane, Michael B. *Minorities in Textbooks: A Study of Their Treatment in Social Studies Texts.* Chicago: Quadrangle Books, 1970.

Kirp, David L. *Just Schools: The Idea of Racial Equality in American Education.* Berkeley: University of California Press, 1982.

Kleinfeld, Judith S. *Eskimo School on the Andreafsky: A Study of Effective Bicultural Education.* New York: Praeger, 1979.

Longstreet, Wilma S. *Aspects of Ethnicity: Understanding Differences in Pluralistic Classrooms.* New York: Teachers College Press, 1978.

McGroarty, Mary. Educators' responses to sociocultural diversity: Implications for practice. In *Beyond Language: Social and Cultural Factors in Schooling Language Minority Students.* Los Angeles, California: Evaluation, Dissemination and Assessment Center, California State University, Los Angeles, 1986.

National Commission on Secondary Education for Hispanics. *Make Something Happen: Hispanics and Urban High School Reform.* Washington, D.C.: Hispanic Policy Development Project, 1984.

Ogbu, John U., and Matute-Bianchi, Maria Eugina. Understanding sociocultural factors: Knowledge, identity, and school adjustment. In *Beyond Language: Social and Cultural Factors in Schooling Language Minority Students.* Los Angeles, California: Evaluation, Dissemination and Assessment Center, California State University, Los Angeles, 1986.

Parsons, Theodore William, Jr. Ethnic Cleavage in a California School. Unpublished doctoral dissertation, Stanford University, 1965.

Perspectives on inequality. *Harvard Educational Review,* Reprint Series No. 8, 1973.

Philips, Susan Urmston. *The Invisible Culture: Communication in Classroom and Community on the Warm Springs Indian Reservation.* New York: Longman, 1983.

Purkey, Stewart C., and Smith, Marshall S. Effective schools--a review. *Elementary School Journal,* 1983, *83*(4), 427-452.

Ramírez, Manuel III, and Castañeda, Alfredo. *Cultural Democracy, Bicognitive Development, and Education.* New York: Academic Press, 1974.

Rist, Ray C. *The Invisible Children: School Integration in American Society.* Cambridge: Harvard University Press, 1978.

Samuda, Ronald J. *Psychological Testing of American Minorities: Issues and Consequences.* New York: Dodd, Mead & Co., 1975.

Sue, Stanley, and Padilla, Amado. Ethnic minority issues in the United States: Challenges for the educational system. In *Beyond Language: Social and Cultural Factors in Schooling Language Minority Students.* Los Angeles, California: Evaluation, Dissemination and Assessment Center, California State University, Los Angeles, 1986.

Weinberg, Meyer. *A Chance to Learn: A History of Race and Education in the United States.* Cambridge, England: Cambridge University Press, 1977.

Willis, Doug. California 2005: Racially diverse. *Riverside Press-Enterprise,* February 10, 1985, pp. B1-B4.

Wollenberg, Charles. *All Deliberate Speed: Segregation and Exclusion in California Schools, 1855-1975.* Berkeley, California: University of California Press, 1976.

ETHNIC MINORITY ISSUES IN THE UNITED STATES: CHALLENGES FOR THE EDUCATIONAL SYSTEM

Stanley Sue

University of California, Los Angeles

Amado Padilla

University of California, Los Angeles

For decades, public school systems have been confronted with a major problem: How can the education and achievement of ethnic minority students, particularly those with limited-English proficiency, be enhanced? In addressing this question, much attention has been placed upon English language acquisition (e.g., bilingual or English-as-a-second-language programs for immigrants or for those ethnic minorities with limited-English skills). There is no question that English proficiency is essential to education success, occupational achievement, and socio-economic mobility, but these occur in a sociocultural context. Understanding this context can help to explain educational attainments of ethnic minority students and to provide alternatives that can lead to improved educational outcomes for these students.

The contributors to this book examine sociocultural factors that influence educational achievements. These factors include the background and culture of particular ethnic groups, including their values and attitudes; educational practices in the United States; race and ethnic relations; socialization strategies; ethnic identity, etc. The contributors generally conceptualize how sociocultural factors affect academic performance and educational experiences. They also indicate the significance of sociocultural considerations in the formulation of programs and policies to facilitate the educational outcomes of ethnic minority students. Thus, implications are drawn for parents, teachers, administrators, and social scientists.

This chapter provides a brief overview of the educational achievements of various ethnic minority groups. The achievement levels should be cause for great concern, since on different indices of outcomes, ethnic minorities are not faring well. The problem is further complicated by population projections and by the need to prepare students to meet new demands as adults in American society. Our central thesis is that underlying educational practices and policies are two fundamental sociocultural variables: (1) *assumptions* about the achievement levels and potential of ethnic minorities, and (2) *value conflicts* that occur in the planning of educational policies. We will argue that assumptions influence how problems are defined and what kinds of solutions are sought. Furthermore, in an attempt to initiate reforms in the educational system, several value conflicts emerge. How these conflicts are resolved has direct relevance for educational policies.

Reactions to this and the other chapters will undoubtedly be varied. Some readers will strongly disagree with various analyses that are made. Indeed, one can also find differences of opinion among the contributors. Other readers will find the contributions insightful and refreshing. From our experience, issues involving ethnicity and education invariably provoke strong emotions, perhaps reflecting the magnitude of the problems confronting our multi-ethnic society. Our hope is to stimulate examination of issues and to demonstrate the importance of sociocultural factors and education.

Several points should be kept in mind while reading this and other chapters. First, culture, race, ethnicity, minority group, and limited-English proficiency are terms that appear throughout this book. The terms are sometimes loosely and interchangeably used. In general, we are focusing upon issues common to Native Americans (including Eskimos and Aleuts), Asian Americans (including Pacific Islanders), Blacks, and Hispanics. These four major populations are included in our references to ethnicity, minority groups, and culture. Obviously, there are many other populations that can be considered ethnic or cultural groups. Our primary interest, however, is in the four groups (although little direct discussion is made of Native Americans).

Consensus is lacking over the definition of race. Some anthropologists divide human beings into three races: Asians, Blacks, and Caucasians. Others use many more categories. In this chapter, terms such as race, race relations, and racism appear because research in the field of intergroup relations is pertinent to our discussion of sociocultural factors. Most of this research has involved black-white relations so that we draw implications from this work and apply them to our discussions of ethnicity.

Another distinction we would like to make from the very outset is the term "limited-English proficiency" (LEP). Many members of the four ethnic groups have limited-English proficiency. This is particularly true of Asian Americans and Hispanics, many of whom are immigrants. Therefore, when we speak of LEP students, we are referring to members of ethnic minority groups who are not fully proficient in English and who have a language other than English in the home.

Second, the various ethnic groups differ considerably from one another in educational attainments, cultural background, experiences, etc. Heterogeneity can also be seen within a particular ethnic group. The contributors to this volume may formulate hypotheses that apply to all groups, or they may also compare and contrast different ethnic groups. Their purpose is to illustrate general principles rather than to deny between-group variability or specific within-group differences. Similarly, the contributors do not necessarily endorse generalizations about groups applied to specific individuals or those of individual case studies applied to groups.

Third, an examination of sociocultural variables in explaining differential schooling outcomes and in directing school-based programs suggests that the educational system alone cannot achieve the necessary reforms. This is strongly argued in Heath's chapter (this volume), which points to the necessity of having various institutions contribute to language learning. The home and community environments must provide opportunities to develop "genres of language use" or occasions in which speakers questions, evaluate, support, deny, and contribute to the talk of others. Families, communities, and the institutional structures of society must be actively involved. An analysis of sociocultural factors in education serves only as a point of departure.

DIFFERENTIAL ACADEMIC OUTCOMES

The fact that many ethnic minority students are not successful in school is no secret. Parents complain that their children are receiving poor grades. Many students feel alienated and unmotivated. Teachers often find it difficult to communicate with LEP students and to stimulate ethnic minority pupils. Concerns over the educational outcomes of various ethnic groups are reflected in various indices of achievement shown in Figure 1. In terms of persons in California over 24 years of age in 1980, 77 percent of whites, 69 percent of Blacks, 66 percent of Native Americans, and 44 percent of Hispanics graduated from high school. Only Asians showed a rate similar to whites (i.e., 76 percent). Even more striking are the data on persons who have completed a bachelor's degree. Here, whites have a rate twice that of Blacks and Native Americans, and three and one-half times that of Hispanics; the proportion of college graduates among Asians, on the other hand, exceeds that of whites.

Figure 1

Educational Attainment by Race and Spanish Origin
of Persons Aged 25 and Over, 1980
—California—

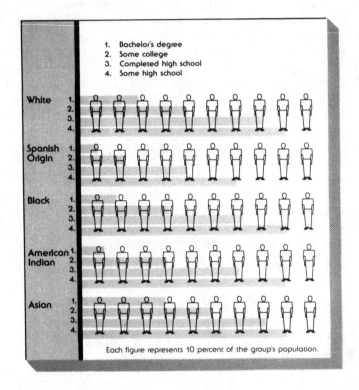

Source: Kaufman, N. S. and G. Dolman, Jr. *Minorities in Higher Education: The Changing Southwest, California.* Boulder, Colorado: Western Interstate Commission
for Higher Education, 1984, p. 13.

Other measures of achievement also reveal discrepancies in the performances of whites versus ethnic minorities. Figure 2 shows the scores of
various groups on the 1984 National Scholastic Aptitude Test (SAT).
Whites outperform all the ethnic groups in average overall scores on the
test. On the verbal subtest, whites exceed the different ethnic groups, including Asians, by 50 to 110 ponts in average scores. With the exception
of Asians, all ethnic groups were lower than whites on the mean score for
the mathematics subtest.

Figure 2

National Mean SAT Scores by Ethnic Group, 1984

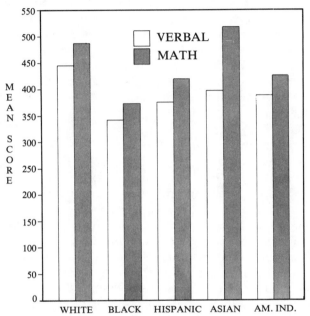

Source: College Entrance Examination Board. *Profile, College-Bound Seniors, 1984.*
New York: College Entrance Examination Board, 1984.

These indicators of differential academic achievement outcomes result in a series of questions. For example, why do some ethnic minorities lag behind whites? How can we explain why ethnic groups themselves differ in performance? What can be done to close the gap in educational outcomes between minority and majority group students? These questions are more fully addressed in this and other chapters. It should be noted that even in the case of Asian Americans, who perform well on measures such as college graduation and SAT mathematics subtest scores, a rather mixed picture emerges. Although they have succeeded in higher education, they paradoxically have more than four times the proportion of persons failing to have any education whatsoever, compared to whites. In addition, they appear to be underrepresented at levels of middle and upper management compared to the level of educational attainment of those who successfully graduate from universities (United States Department of Commerce, 1983).

FUTURE TRENDS

While the current educational status of ethnic minority groups is of great concern, the issue takes on special significance in view of projections of future population changes and educational needs. Population projections are hazardous since assumptions must be made about birth and mortality rates, and immigration and emigration.   However, substantial evidence suggests that ethnic minority groups will show significant increases over the next two decades. Between 1980 and 2000, the rate of increase of ethnic minority groups will exceed that of whites. Blacks will increase by 34 percent, Hispanics and Asians by 97 percent, while whites will increase by only 16 percent. These projections mean that whereas whites constituted 67 percent of the state's population in 1980, their portion of the total state population will decrease to 55 percent by the year 2000. Importantly, much of the population shift is attributed to immigration from Latin America and Southeast Asia.

A direct impact of the demographic changes in the composition of the state population will be felt by the school system. In California, there are more than four million students in grades K-12. Of these, approximately 44 percent were ethnic minority students in 1981. By 1990, they will comprise about 48 percent of the student population. About 500,000 of the students are classified as LEP pupils, a figure expected to grow at an annual rate of 6-10 percent, even though LEP students are reclassified (from LEP to full English proficiency) annually at a rate of 10-13 percent.

These statistics and projections portend a number of challenges for the educational system in particular and our multi-ethnic society in general. With the projected population changes, there will be an even more urgent need to address the educational problems of ethnic minority students, especially since education is viewed as a means to socialize and prepare individuals for productive and meaningful roles in society. This constitutes the challenge confronting education today and for the foreseeable future.

VALUE OF EDUCATION

In our society, education is highly valued for its own sake. It is also a way to increase socio-economic mobility and to prepare students for meeting the demands of society. Although there is controversy over the exact relationship between educational attainments and income/occupational levels (i.e., whether education is a cause, consequence, or simply a correlate of socio-economic status), the connection between education and income is well-documented (United States Commission on Civil Rights, 1978; Jencks *et al.,* 1979). Ethnic minority groups not only attain lower levels of education (except for Asians), but also show poorer outcomes than whites on other measures. For example, in California, during 1979, 5.5 percent of white families had incomes below poverty levels (United States Department of Commerce, 1983). The percentages were much higher for Native Americans (14.4 percent), Asians (9.7 percent), Blacks (20.6 percent), and Hispanics (16.8 percent). A study by the United States Commission on Civil Rights (1978) revealed that with the exception of certain Asian groups, ethnic minorities were also less likely to hold high prestige occupations. Even among college graduates, all ethnic groups, including Asians, averaged less income than did whites. The Commission also found that Asians were frequently "overqualified" for their occupations so that whites with less education held the same jobs as Asians. Thus, while educational attainment is directly related to income and occupational prestige, ethnic minorities who have comparable levels of education to whites may earn less income, for one reason or another.

Today, more than ever before, education has taken on a new significance, which must be entered into the equation when we analyze the educational status of ethnic minority groups. Over the past one hundred years there has been a shift from an agricultural-based society to an industrial/manufacturing society to our present information-based society with computers and other high technological advances appearing almost daily. In the time when the economy was based largely on agricultural production, there was always a place for those individuals who had not completed their education. This truism continued mostly intact during the industrial/manufacturing era. However, we are beginning to recognize more and more that as our society moves further into the information era, low educational attainment may be more handicapping than ever before (Naisbitt, 1982). Computer literacy is fast becoming essential in every aspect of our daily life. Computers are now commonplace even in our schools at every level and increasingly are being used in the daily curriculum to instruct students in mathematics, science, composition, and foreign languages.

Naisbitt (1982) stated that 75 percent of all jobs in 1985 would involve computers in some way and "people who don't know how to use them will be at a disadvantage." There is no reason to discount the accuracy of this prediction, and our fear is that it may have more relevance for ethnic minority group members who, on the whole, have a lower rate of educational attainment than whites. With less education, ethnic minority students are becoming "disadvantaged" in a new and possibly even more profound way. The final outcome of this new "disadvantage" may be an even greater income differential between the various ethnic minority groups and their white counterparts.

PERSPECTIVES ON ACHIEVEMENT

Our perspectives on the nature of human beings and/or the cultural differences between groups have implications for explaining differences in educational performance. For example, a belief that some racial groups have superior genetic material for intelligence implies that these groups can perform better in intellectual and educational endeavors. A perspective that accepts the genetic equality of racial or ethnic groups in intellectual potential attributes differences in academic achievements to other factors such as opportunities for learning, cultural differences in motivation, etc. In general, four broad perspectives have been used to account for academic and intellectual performances of various groups: (1) genetic inferiority, (2) cultural deficit, (3) cultural mismatch, and (4) contextual interaction. They are used not only to explain differences in achievements, but also to guide educational policies. (For a related discussion of explanations of school performance, see Díaz et al., this volume.) Table 1 shows the four perspectives, the assumptions made, and the solutions proposed.

Table 1

PERSPECTIVES ON FAILURE TO ACHIEVE AND POSSIBLE SOLUTIONS

Perspectives	Attribution of Blame	Primary Solutions
Genetic Inferiority--minorities fail to do well because they are genetically inferior.	The groups themselves, not society, are to blame.	No solutions are possible since little can be done to change heredity.
Cultural Deficit--minorities fail to do well because their culture is viewed as deficient.	The groups themselves, as well as social prejudice and discrimination, are to be blamed.	Train minorities to be less deficient and eliminate prejudice and discrimination.
Cultural Mismatch--minorities fail to achieve because their cultural traits are incompatible with those in the United States mainstream.	No one is responsible since cultures just happen to be different.	Change groups so that they can participate in the mainstream, but also change schools in order to better accommodate and ameliorate the mismatch.
Contextual Interaction--minorities fail to achieve because of an unfortunate interaction of many factors.	No one factor, group, or institution is responsible since outcomes are produced through the interaction of many factors such as circumstances, cultural values, etc.	Change one or more of the factors or the context to alter the interaction and thereby change the outcomes.

Genetic Inferiority

The genetic inferiority perspective assumes that certain racial or ethnic populations do not possess the appropriate genes for high intellectual performance. Thus, they are incapable of achieving to the same extent as whites. In the United States, the four major ethnic minority groups have been, at various times, defined as being genetically inferior to whites. Blacks have been considered genetically inferior intellectually with a limited capacity for mental growth (Thomas and Sillen, 1972). In 1854, the California Supreme Court ruled that Chinese could not testify against a white person because, among other things, the Chinese were considered a race of people whom nature marked as being inferior and incapable of intellectual development (Kitano, 1980). Hispanics and Native Americans have also been deemed genetically inferior in intelligence (Padilla, 1984). While beliefs in a hereditary explanation have waned for Native Americans, Asians, and Hispanics, there is still considerable discussion of the issue in the case of Blacks (Jensen, 1969; Loehlin et al., 1975).

The adoption of a genetic perspective has implications for educational policies and programs. In the past, advocates of this perspective have taken the stance that ethnic minority groups should be denied formal public education or segregated in their own classes because of their intellectual limitations (Thomas and Sillen, 1972). Even though a few educators would argue today for a denial of education or for segregation, notions of genetic inferiority continue to have ramifications for policy. For example, under this perspective, little can be done to alter the differences exhibited between groups considered inferior and those thought to be superior. Educators can only help groups to meet whatever potentials are dictated by nature.

The hereditary approach is based upon three propositions: (1) genetic make-up influences intelligence, (2) adequate measures of innate intelligence exist, and (3) observed differences between groups are best explained by heredity. While there is evidence that heredity influences intelligence, the same cannot be said for the support of the other two propositions. There is considerable debate over intelligence--whether it is best conceptualized as one factor or as several factors--and over the relationship between current IQ tests and innate intelligence. A strong argument has been made that intelligence cannot be distilled into a single aptitude, so that an overall IQ score cannot be used as a measure of innate intelligence (Garcia, 1981). The problem is further complicated when such tests are used to compare culturally different groups. Garcia notes that some groups differ from other groups in motivation and practice when taking IQ tests. Individuals who are highly motivated and who are familiar with the kinds of tasks on the tests have an advantage. Yet, those who believe in the genetic inferiority perspective fail to appreciate the enormous effects of motivation and practice. Mercer (1979) has shown that IQ test performances are directly related to how "anglicized" individuals are. Those Blacks and Hispanics who are similar to Anglos in values, attitudes, social class, and other characteristics have higher IQ scores than their counterparts who are more dissimilar to Anglos. The findings suggest that nurture, rather than nature, may be responsible for IQ test performance and that the tests are inappropriate for ascertaining native intelligence between groups.

It is beyond the scope of this chapter to review the voluminous literature on the IQ controversy. It is important, however, to realize that many ethnic minority groups have at different times been considered genetically inferior. Sarason (1973) notes that even in the case of Jews, there was a popular belief that they were genetically inferior in intelligence. Kamin (1974) also summarizes a similar position with respect to Italians, Greeks, Yugoslavs, and various other groups.

The current focus on Blacks and heredity continues in the same unfortunate tradition. Although the genetic perspective has gained some prominence, it is flawed on at least two counts. The argument for the genetic inferiority of Blacks has been shown to be statistically unfounded, and it does not explain counter examples of successful Blacks. Second, the genetic inferiority view suggests we are powerless to improve the academic performance of certain groups through anything short of genetic engineering.

Cultural Deficit

In contrast to the genetic interpretation, the cultural deficit viewpoint attributes the lower educational achievement of various ethnic minority groups to cultural deficiencies. The deficiencies are viewed as either inherent in the group's culture itself or the result of discrimination against the group. In either case, prejudice and discrimination are at the root of the deficit perspective: A recent immigrant group is prejudged to be deficient, for example, because it has come from a nonliterate, tribal society; discrimination against the group is thought to cause such deficient behavioral patterns as crime, personality disorders, alcoholism, laziness, etc. The essential point about the deficit perspective is that minority group members are viewed as lacking the cultural competence necessary for dealing with academic and social challenges. The groups' supposed weaknesses are emphasized to the detriment of their strengths.

Much of the social science literature on the deficit perspective has come from analyses of Black-white relations. Under the concept of racism, a number of investigators (Jones, 1972; Pettigrew, 1973) have viewed the plight of Blacks as a direct result of societal institutions and practices deriving from a deficit perspective. The history of slavery, segegation, and discrimination, founded on beliefs of genetic and cultural deficits, is thought to produce detrimental consequences to Blacks, such as increased stress, decreased opportunities, and lowered self-esteem. Baldwin (1957) stated, "I can conceive of no Negro native to this country who has not, by the age of puberty, been irreparably scarred by the condition of his life. The wonder is not that so many are ruined by it but so many survive" (p. 71). The deficit view point has assumed that Blacks (and other ethnic groups experiencing discrimination) are culturally deficient, underprivileged, deprived, pathological, or deviant. Studies that are supportive of this view have repeatedly demonstrated the social, psychological, and economic problems of various ethnic minority groups. For example, Blacks have been characterized as having high rates of drug addiction, personality disorders, and crime; Native Americans have been seen as being prone to alcoholism and suicide; Hispanics have been viewed as exhibiting tendencies toward drunkeness, criminal behavior, and undependability. (See Fischer, 1969; Kitano, 1980; Padilla and Ruiz, 1973 for a discussion of these characterizations.) It has been assumed that ethnic minorities experience problems involving self-identity and self-esteem because of exploitation, cultural conflicts, and negative social stereotypes. In the field of education, those subscribing to the cultural deficit perspective have come to expect lower academic performance from ethnic minority students. After all, if these students enter school with a deficient culture compared to Anglos, and have been deprived of opportunities, have low self-esteem, and have been underprivileged, they cannot have the motivation and skills to suceed.

In principle, the cultural deficit perspective suggests two possible solutions: (1) the training and education of ethnic minorities so they are less deficient, and/or (2) the elimination of prejudice and discrimination. We have seen some attempts to alter discriminatory practices and ethnic stereotypes. These have included efforts to integrate schools, to search for gifted students among ethnic minorities, to assign ethnic minority pupils, if justified, to classes for the educable mentally retarded, to avoid ethnic slurs, etc. However, since discrimination and prejudice are embedded within the fabric of society, progress has been slow. Much attention has been placed upon the remediation or prevention of imaginary and real deficits through early intervention programs such as Head Start, compensatory education, tutorial services, and special remediation classes. The goal of these programs has been to make up for the presumed deficiencies in skills and in cultural background. In doing so, the hope has been that ethnics will perform on a par with Anglos and become competitive in American society.

In some respects, the cultural deficit perspective is helpful in furthering the cause of ethnic minority groups. It focuses attention on minorities, school, and societal practices, rather than on ideas about genetic inferiority in explaining the status of ethnic minority groups. The view is somewhat positive in suggesting that all human beings are capable of overcoming their deficits by changing, adapting, and achieving. The view, however, remains prejudicial in its preoccupation with group or individual weaknesses. Educational programs are more soundly conceived when they focus on building upon existing abilities and strengths, a subtle but significant shift from the deficit perspective.

Social and educational change, however, is difficult to achieve since prejudice and discrimination are, and have been, intimately intertwined in institutional practices. Even if massive educational reforms are possible, educational equality is not likely to follow shortly thereafter. Concomitant changes must also occur in other social institutions. While educators can take the lead, other institutions such as the criminal justice system, the political system, mass media, etc., must also practice the ideals of equality. Unfortunately, arguments that ethnics are assisted by changes in institutional policies, while valid, also have the effect of perpetuating an image of ethnic inferiority.

For example, in the 1954 case of *Brown v. Board of Education* (347 U.S. 483), the United States Supreme Court ruled that segregation (the separate but equal argument) was detrimental to Black children. The Court based its decision on social science research, which revealed the educational and psychological problems faced by Blacks in segregated schools. Klineberg (1981), who argued in favor of desegregation, noted how his initial joy over the Court's decision was later tempered by an unexpected controversy. Even though inferiority was no longer attributed to heredity, ethnics were viewed as deficient or inferior because of societal practices. Neglected were the strengths, competencies, and skills found in ethnic families, communities, and cultures. (For more on the cultural deficit view, see Keddie, 1973.)

Cultural Mismatch

The cultural mismatch perspective of achievement is based upon the assumption that cultures vary in the extent to which the skills learned in one culture are adaptive in another culture. The skills learned in Culture A may be highly functional for Culture B. However, another culture-- for example, Culture C--may transmit to its members skills that are non-functional or even maladaptive in Culture B. Thus, a mismatch between the skills possessed by some ethnic minority groups and those required in American society result in poor adaptation. In contrast to the cultural deficit perspective, cultural mismatch proposes that ethnics may have "different," rather than "deficient" skills. That is, outcomes are explained in terms of the match or fit between the traits of the ethnic culture and those of the larger society. When problems arise, an adjustment on one side, or the other, is in order.

One can easily see how the cultural mismatch viewpoint can be used to explain not only low achievement but also extraordinary success. In the case of Chinese- and Japanese Americans, Sue and Kitano (1973) have indicated that many social scientists explain the educational and occupational attainment of these groups as a product of hard work, thrift, family cohesion, and patience. Asians, particularly the Chinese, have been portrayed as being socialized to a Confucian work ethic, which is highly similar to the Protestant work ethic. The congruence of these work ethics has meant that Asians are particularly well-equipped to compete in the American educational system and to be accepted within white middle-class society. In a similar vein, Gordon (1964) has adopted a cultural match perspective to explain the extraordinary achievements of Jews. His position has been that Jews came to America with middle-class values such as thrift, sobriety, ambition, educational aspirations, and ability to delay immediate gratification for long-range goals. However, other ethnic groups that have not fared well in American society lack the appropriate cultural values and traits that would enable them to achieve greater upward mobility. For example, Mexican-Americans have been characterized as fatalistic, dependent, and cooperative in spirit, characteristics that are antithetical to the "rugged individualism" required to be successful in the United States (Ramírez and Castañeda, 1974).

As in the cultural deficit perspective, the mismatch notion posits that those ethnic groups with dysfunctional values should change and become more "Americanized." There is a strong push toward acculturation. Unlike the cultural deficit viewpoint, however, society or schools may also need to change to improve the fit of the two cultures in contact (Labov, 1969; Heath, this volume). Thus, language minority students must learn English to compete successfully in school and later in the work place, but schools may need to use their native tongue in early stages so that they do not fall behind as they are acquiring English.

While intuitively appealing, the mismatch perspective is too simplistic in accounting for the status and achievement levels of ethnic minority groups. In an analysis of the achievements of various white and non-white immigrant groups, Steinberg (1981) has found that: (1) ethnic groups have come from a variety of historical and socio-economic circumstances, (2) they have encountered different opportunities as well as different obstacles to their advancement, and (3) factors that are part of (1) and (2) influence the status of the next generation of ethnics. With Jews, Steinberg (1981) states:

> *In terms of their European background, Jews were especially well equipped to take advantage of the opportunities they found in America. Had Jews immigrated to an industrial society without industrial skills, as did most other immigrants, their rich cultural heritage would have counted for little. Indeed, a parallel situation exists today in Israel, where Jews immigrating from underdeveloped countries in North Africa typically lack the occupational and educational advantages of the earlier settlers, and despite the fact that all share the same basic religion, the recent immigrants find themselves concentrated at the bottom of the Israeli society. Thus, in large measure, Jewish success in America was a matter of historical timing. That is to say, there was a fortuitous match between the experience and skills of Jewish immigrants, on the one hand, and the manpower needs and opportunity structures, on the other. It is this remarkable convergence of factors that resulted in an unusual record of success. (p. 103)*

Suzuki's (1977) analysis of Asian American upward mobility also casts doubt on the cultural mismatch idea as a satisfactory explanation of outcomes. His belief is that after World War II, there was a need for individuals to assume lower echelon white collar positions created by an expanding economy. An education was required for these positions, and here, cultural values of self-discipline and perseverance were quite functional. In essence, Suzuki (1977) agrees with Steinberg (1981) that cultural and societal factors (political, economic, etc.) interact, rather than simply match or mismatch, in influencing the performance of a given group.

The mismatch viewpoint and its assumptions are not only overly simplistic as an explanatory scheme, but also too extreme in the advocacy of acculturation as a solution. As we will discuss shortly, strict acculturation creates a variety of problems and inappropriately asserts the superiority of one culture over another.

Contextual Interaction

The contextual interaction perspective attempts to deal with the criticism directed toward the approaches discussed earlier. It postulates that achievement is a function of the dynamic interaction between the values of the ethnic minority group and the cultural values of the larger American society. Cultural values of the larger society are broadly defined. They include an emphasis not only on rugged individualism, free enterprise, and competition but also on the social, political, economic, and racial climate. Members of ethnic minority groups develop behaviors, beliefs, aspirations, and achievement patterns as a result of an interaction between the influences of the two cultural orientations. Whereas the mismatch perspective conceptualizes cultures as static, the interaction viewpoint proposes that cultures change as they come into contact with each other. The differences between the two perspectives can be seen in the case of the Chinese. The mismatch approach tries to define Chinese culture and then examines the match between Chinese cultural values and those values in American society. If the values are congruent, Chinese are expected to achieve and perform well. If the values do not match, achievement patterns are likely to be inferior, and results are likely to be defined in terms of a cultural deficit.

The contextual interaction approach acknowledges that the values of different groups can be compatible or can clash; however, the key to understanding achievement is the change that occurs because of the interaction between different cultures. For example, many Chinese may have had cultural values that were helpful in achievement such as appreciation of hard work, respect for education, etc. Nevertheless, as hypothesized by Suzuki (1977), the emphasis on education was further stimulated by discrimination against Chinese in occupations that required little education. Thus, Chinese came to value education even more because of the interaction between their culture and the culture of the larger society.

For Blacks, Native Americans, and Hispanics who have had many generations of experience in the United States, it is inappropriate to say that their status is simply due to cultural deficits or mismatches. Rather, colonization, exploitation, and discrimination are also part of their history, which, in turn, influence their behaviors and perceptions. Ogbu and Matute-Bianchi (this volume) indicate that individuals develop "folk theories" about achievement. These are subjective, cause-effect beliefs that evolve as a result of contextual interactions. Whereas many Chinese may develop the folk belief, "education is important if I am to succeed in life," other persons may feel, "education is not worth much. Teachers discriminate against you; tests and curriculum are biased in favor of Anglos; and even with education, employers discriminate against you." In illustrating these folk beliefs, we are not trying to characterize ethnic minority groups or individuals. The point is that depending upon the interaction of cultures, beliefs and behaviors may vary considerably.

We can illustrate this point further by referring to research by Banks *et al.* (1977). These investigators were interested in how Blacks deal with negative feedback from Anglos and other Blacks. When given negative feedback from other Blacks, the Black subjects' self-esteem was lowered; however, when the negative evaluations came from Anglos, the effects upon self-esteem and behavior were negligible. Why did Blacks disregard the feedback from Anglos? Instead of relying upon a strict cultural explanation (e.g., Blacks have always had cultural values that make them distrustful of Anglos), understanding of the interactive relationship between the two groups (e.g., Anglos have oppressed Blacks so that they are considered biased) provides a more meaningful explanation of the results.

Compared to the other perspectives, contextual interaction embraces a broad perspective and a great many interacting factors in the search for explanations and solutions to the differential achievement patterns found among ethnic minorities. The deficit approach suggests that discrimination be eliminated and ethnic deficiencies be mediated. The mismatch approach advocates the changing of those ethnic minority cultural values that are incongruent with those dominant in society, the changing of schools to accommodate cultural differences, or both. In the contextual interaction perspective, however, there is acknowledgement that all these solutions, as well as others, may be helpful. The difference is that this perspective does not confine its search for educational solutions only to eliminating prejudice and discrimination in society. Other aspects of society may require modification such as greater understanding of ethnic groups and an appreciation of the pluralistic nature of society. Moreover, the contextual interaction approach does not view groups as culturally deficient or inferior. Although persons may have to acquire new skills, these skills need not mean a loss of one's ethnic culture. This perspective is much more tolerant of ethnics who espouse a bicultural philosophy as a means of accommodating to the demands of the mainstream as well as their own ethnic community.

In terms of schooling, this approach causes us to focus on the interactions between an ethnic group and the educational system and how those interactions might be altered so that better outcomes are achieved. The system, the group, and the community may all need to change. Banks (1983) believes that reform of the total school is needed to foster multi-ethnic education. These reforms include: teachers' attitudes toward ethnic students and their education; the formal curriculum, teaching strategies, tests and testing procedure; and school-sanctioned languages and dialects. Díaz et al., Heath, and Kagan (this volume) discuss ways to make educational experiences more meaningful for ethnic minority groups. Change may also have to come from ethnic minority individuals and groups as they adapt to institutions. For example, one may need to attain high levels of English language proficiency. However, this change does not necessarily imply the elimination of proficiency in one's native language. Studies on immersion education (Lambert, 1984) suggest that given appropriate educational experiences, the acquisition of a new language need not "subtract" from the proficiency of the native language.

The contextual interaction perspective offers a comprehensive means of conceptualizing the outcomes for ethnic minority groups. It recognizes both the detrimental effects of discrimination and the importance of developing adaptive skills in American society. It also appreciates the fact that cultures are not static--values and cultural practices are ever-changing. The solutions that derive from such a view, such as reform of schools and innovative tactics to enable individuals and communities to function in their ethnic culture as well as in the larger society, are idealistic but possible. It should be noted that Díaz et al. (this volume) offer several perspectives of achievement. Their ideas concerning hereditary deprivation parallel our discussion of genetic inferiority. Their notion of cultural deprivation is similar to the cultural deficit idea we have advanced. Both approaches attribute the lack of achievement to cultural or social class socialization practices that presumably do not match, or are incompatible with, the skills demanded in schools. On the other hand, their context-specific concept deals more with a process rather than outcomes, which we have emphasized in the contextual interaction perspective.

Implications of the Perspectives

To a greater or lesser extent, the four different perspectives present significant challenges when we attempt to translate them into concrete suggestions for educational practices. First, the perspectives provide general directions for intervention, but they do not specify the exact form of intervention. For instance, what precise teaching strategies should be used in order to respond to ethnic minority students? If one is interested in altering cultural values, which values should be changed? Second, individuals actually may adopt more than one perspective. A person may believe that certain ethnic groups are genetically inferior in intelligence but also that society has oppressed these groups. Such a situation may create conflicts over a course of action. Third, we lack research and knowledge on types of intervention that are effective and applicable to a wide range of groups and circumstances. Fourth, even if promising means are found to enhance educational opportunities, the implementation of programs may be difficult. Educational policies are determined by many factors including economic and political considerations. Knowledge of what to do and the power to implement are necessary for programs to develop. Fifth, ethnic minority issues involve conflicting values or paradoxes that obscure the research for solutions. This last point is discussed more fully in the next section of this chapter. While these problems must be acknowledged, we cannot allow them to paralyze efforts to address the needs of ethnic minorities. As mentioned previously, the differential achievement patterns and the growing numbers of ethnic minorities in our schools present a dilemma that must be addressed immediately.

In summary, a major challenge confronts our school system. On several educational and socio-economic indices, ethnic minorities lag behind Anglos. The different ethnic groups also show variability on these measures, with some groups faring better in some areas than others. The challenge for educational practitioners is to explain differences between and within groups and to devise educational programs that can enhance achievement levels. We have suggested that explanations for the differential performance patterns as well as the kinds of strategies proposed to change educational practices depend upon one's perspective. The genetic inferiority perspective is the most detrimental. Not only is it a negative view of the achievement potential of certain ethnic minority groups, but it also fails to acknowledge the viability of more plausible explanations for differential achievement patterns. The other three perspectives vary in subtle but important ways in offering directions to improve academic performances. Díaz *et al.* (this volume) also discuss perspectives used to conceptualize achievement. Although they use different terms, e.g., context-free and context-specific, their analysis also points to the importance of determining one's frame of reference in explaining educational outcomes.

Our presentation of the four perspectives is intended to illustrate how the nature of proposed solutions is dependent upon one's beliefs about the educability of different groups. We also believe that attempts to address these problems are influenced by another sociocultural factor-- namely, the set of values that one holds. From our experience, many of the values relevant to ethnic minority issues are in conflict. In the next section, we discuss the notion of value conflicts and paradoxes and draw implications for educational practice.

CONFLICTS AND PARADOXES

Rappaport (1981) and McGrath (1980) believe that many social issues consist of paradoxes in which two or more positive or cherished values are pitted against one another. Rappaport indicates that some paradoxes consist of antinomies in which two or more laws, principles, or ideals are contradictory. For example, freedom of expression and speech is a strong principle advocated by many Americans. Yet, a large segment of the population also values protection from exposure to unwanted or allegedly harmful materials. Should one, for instance, have the right under the principle of freedom of speech to expose others to pornographic materials or to express racial slurs? It is not uncommon to find individuals endorsing both principles in the abstract. The contradiction or paradox is most apparent when these two equally valid or morally justifiable positions are applied in a concrete situation.

In the case of antinomies or true paradoxes, Rappaport (1981) argues the fruitlessness of using convergent reasoning in an attempt to find the solution, namely, a single and permanent resolution of the paradox. Efforts to find the true solution often obscure the inherent and fundamental nature of the contradiction and lead to the favoring of one principle at the expense of the other. An alternative approach is to engage in divergent reasoning whereby true paradoxes are identified and a number of diverse actions are prescribed. These solutions may require change over time since single, overall solutions may not always fit a changing context. Otherwise, today's solutions may well become tomorrow's problems, as illustrated later.

Our belief is that many educational programs and practices reflect conflicts in which the clashes of values and the fruitlessness of single solutions have not been clearly recognized. Moreover, in trying to resolve issues, one side has been dominant, often to the detriment of ethnic minority groups. Perhaps we can best illustrate this point by noting some value conflicts and the concomitant problems they give rise to in the educational system.

Table 2 shows five value conflicts that often occur in ethnic group relations (Sue, 1983). We provide examples of each side of the conflict and indicate the nature of the conflict. Possible means to approach the paradox of values are also examined. It should be noted that we have presented the value conflicts as dichotomies for the sake of discussion. In actuality, individuals may hold each value to differing degrees along a continuum.

Table 2

VALUE CONFLICTS
AND PARADOXES

Conflicting Elements	Effects	Possible Solutions
1. **Etic**--Human beings are all alike **Emic**--Human beings differ according to culture	Ignores cultural diversity Cannot generalize or compare cultures	Alternation, co-existence
2. **Assimilation**--become American and merge into society **Pluralism**--allow for and appreciate cultural diversity	Loss of ethnic cultures Co-existence of separate and distinct groups	Co-existence, divergent thinking
3. **Equal opportunity**--apply same color blind criteria to all **Equality of outcomes**--see that minorities are proportionately represented	Unequal outcomes Differential treatment (discrimination)	Mediation, alternation, higher level of abstraction
4. **Modal personality**--study between group differences **Individual differences**--study within group differences	Ignores within group variations Ignores between group variations	Divergent thinking, mediation, alternation
5. **Presence of prejudice/discrimination** --minorities are oppressed in society **Absence of prejudice/discrimination**--opportunities are equal for all	Blame society; must eliminate discrimination Blame minorities; up to minorities to achieve	Co-existence

Conflict 1: Etic Versus Emic

John is an 11-year-old Japanese student who was referred by his teacher to the school psychologist. John was excessively quiet and shy in school. Although his grades were slightly above average, the teacher noted that John was extremely anxious when asked to speak in front of the class. The psychologist administered some psychological tests to John and concluded that John was emotionally disturbed, excessively timid, and over anxious. When informed of the test results, John's parents were shocked. They perceived him as being quiet and well behaved, but able to relate to them and his close friends in an appropriate manner. The parents then took John to a psychotherapist. After reviewing the psychological test results and seeing John for several sessions, the psychotherapist indicated that John was not emotionally disturbed. He believed the test results were not valid indicators of John's emotional state, since the tests had not been standardized on Japanese Americans. John was shy but not emotionally disturbed.

The case illustrates a major controversy in ethnic issues that involves the concepts of emics and etics. The concepts are borrowed from the field of linguistics where phon*emics* examines sounds used in one language while phon*etics* refer to the study of sounds that are universal to all languages. The emic approach is culture specific. It studies the behaviors and values in one specific culture and interprets behaviors from within the cultural system. The etic approach forms criteria or standards that are absolute or universal (Brislin *et al.*, 1973). Different cultures can be compared on these standards. In John's case, those who favor emics would argue that his apparent shyness cannot be evaluated by tests that have not been developed or at least standardized on Japanese Americans. Etic proponents would adopt a more universal interpretation arguing that regardless of culture, if a person scores high on a psychological measure, they are disturbed.

Each perspective has validity. There are meaningful core characteristics that are evident in all groups--for instance, the development of language and communication, ability to utilize abstract concepts, or motives to survive. On the other hand, some characteristics are specific to a cultural group, particular patterns of social interaction, attitudes, and values. The problem occurs when one perspective dominates the other. An extreme emic perspective would not allow cross-cultural generalizations or cultural comparisons to be made. A strong etic orientation fails to appreciate the legitimacy of cultural relativity and diversity. As mentioned in the next conflict to be discussed, the problem is that society's standards (which are largely emic and Anglo-oriented) are presumed to be etics or universals. Ethnic minority groups are then inappropriately judged according to these assumed etics. Available research studies have typically taken for granted that ethnic minority behaviors can be judged according to established norms (American Psychological Association Ad Hoc Committee on Minority Affairs, 1979). Deviations from these norms are considered to be indicative of personal problems or maladjustment. For example, our educational system promotes competition and individualism as a means of learning. Pupils are encouraged to compete with one another and to assert their own ideas (see Kagan, this volume). The assumption is that these are effective means of fostering learning and that the incentives provided (e.g., teacher's praise, peer group recognition, grades, etc.) are sufficient motivators for learning. Ignored is the possibility that a competitive atmosphere may not be universally conducive to learning and that incentives in society may not be equally rewarding in a multi-ethnic setting.

In approaching ethnic minority issues, we need to recognize that some standards or criteria assumed to be universal (etics) are actually specific (emics) to American society. Furthermore, in the conflict between emic and etic positions, one must specify the exact standard, criteria, or issue being discussed. If we assume that each position has validity on some particular issues (human motivation, test performance, etc.), by specifying the issue, we may be able to achieve greater consensus. In other words, rather than saying, "human beings are alike," or "you can't compare people from different cultures," one should indicate in what precise ways people are the same or are culturally different. Only when this is done will we know the true dimensions of our multicultural society.

Conflict 2: Assimilation Versus Pluralism

During a PTA meeting, one parent mentioned that he was glad the school was interested in teaching students about ethnic heritage. He believed that by becoming aware of the cultures and rituals of different groups, students could better understand their own heritage and those of other groups. Another parent, however, disagreed. While she believed that students should have knowledge of different cultures, the school's scarce resources should not be devoted to ethnic heritage. She stated that, "Focusing too much on the culture and heritage of different students only causes friction and segregation between groups. We all live in this society and must learn the same skills in order to succeed."

Underlying the positions adopted by each parent is a fundamental conflict of values: assimilation versus pluralism. Assimilation involves the absorption of ethnic minority groups into the dominant group and quite often the loss of the values and behavioral patterns of their ethnic culture. Those who adopt an assimilation philosophy usually want ethnic groups to become "American." On the other hand, pluralism refers to the co-existence of distinct cultural groups in society. Those who encourage pluralism believe that cultural differences should be maintained and appreciated and that different groups with different cultural orientations can peacefully co-exist alongside each other. Thus, the school system in a pluralistic society should expose students to diverse role models (e.g., teachers from different ethnic groups), information on various cultures, and promote educational practices that help students appreciate their own cultural heritage as well as that of other groups.

The dilemma posed by the conflict between assimilation and pluralism has been articulated for many years. In the past, the assimilation or Anglo-conformity of ethnic groups was expected since, among other things, the Anglo-Saxon culture was deemed superior (Gordon, 1978). Even though many persons have now rejected the notion that Anglo-Saxon culture is intrinsically superior, the assimilation push is resurfacing with a more complex face. Its advocates now use practical or functional arguments rather than references to intrinsic superiority. For instance, it is asserted that educational programs for immigrant children should stress learning of English as rapidly as possible, rather than bilingual education since any language other than English is not very functional and may, in fact, be a handicap in classroom learning. As another example, we can look at the controversy over achievement and intelligence testing. Although many investigators no longer take the view that such tests are totally free from cultural biases, they may still advocate for their use since these tests can moderately predict academic performance in school. Since school performance is highly valued, testing is considered useful and an essential part of education. Those who favor pluralism believe that under the notion of educational pragmatism, ethnic cultural patterns are being eliminated when the school forces students to compete academically solely in English. By this English-only policy, the school is asserting the superiority of the dominant group. Again, there is a clash of fundamental values. How can one argue against the acquisition of functional skills, the development of good predictors, and some degree of "Americanization"? Similarly, how can one doubt that the maintenance of pluralism, diversity, and respect for different cultures is also a valid principle?   The one-sideness of the assimilation effort is the problem.

Advocates of assimilation often overlook the fact that consensus may be lacking on what constitutes functional skills or that circumstances may alter what skills are considered useful.   For instance, with an increasing immigrant population, the ability to speak Chinese, Spanish, and so on may be an important asset.   Hodgkinson (1983) indicates that by the end of the 1980s, the motive for working with, and knowing about, different ethnic groups will not be political liberalism or obligation.   Rather, because of our growing multi-ethnic society, the self-interest of all will be served by one's competence in dealing with culturally diverse groups.   Furthermore, maintenance of pluralism does not necessarily imply the inability to acquire functional skills.   Olmedo (1981) suggests that bilingualism does not interfere with the basic ability to learn.   Some experts have even argued that bilingualism enhances cognitive development, creativity, and social awareness (Bain and Yu, 1980; Torrance *et al.,* 1970).

Certain bilingual programs have shown that proficiencies in two languages can be developed and maintained, with an enhancement of educational attainments (Lambert, 1984).   Ogbu and Matute-Bianchi (this volume) suggest the possibility of learning functional skills without relinquishing one's own culture.   Some ethnic minorities are able to participate in two cultural frames of reference for different purposes.   They keep a strong ethnic identity and, at the same time, acquire competencies necessary to advance in school and later in society generally.   The point is that the learning of functional skills required for participation in society at large does not necessarily entail a diminution of ethnic cultural patterns.   Thus, while the positions of assimilation and pluralism are contradictory (since the strengthening of one weakens the other), the assumption underlying assimilation, effective functioning can occur only if one assimilates, is not valid.   The continual challenge before us is to define what is meant by "functional" and to explore ways in which individuals can develop educational competencies without losing the language, values, and identification with ethnic minority cultures.

Confict 3:   Equal Opportunity Versus Equality of Outcomes

In discussing his stance on ethnic issues, a high school principal stated "I believe in equality and do not discriminate against any group. In our hiring of teachers, we are color and ethnic blind. We depend upon applicants' qualifications." An administrator at a small college said, "We are very active in affirmative action efforts to recruit students and faculty from different ethnic groups. We will not be satisfied until the ethnic composition of the college reflects that in our community.''

The statements by the two administrators illustrate a clash of values over the appropriate action to take in addressing ethnic minority group concerns. The first position focuses on establishing a process that ensures that all members of society have the same opportunity. Individuals should be treated equally with respect to education, employment, housing, etc. In contrast, the college administrator is attempting to achieve equality of outcomes (e.g., seeing that there is proportionate representation of ethnics). Through affirmative action procedures, he is attempting to directly influence outcomes. Such procedures may include efforts to increase the pool of ethnic applicants, selection procedures that take into account ethnicity, and different criteria for selecting different groups.

Proponents of equal opportunity want to eliminate discrimination. The goal is to abolish racial or ethnic bias among teachers, intentional patterns of ethnic group segregation in education, and discriminatory admissions or selection procedures so that an ethnic or color blind system is operating. However, even if the goal is accomplished, there is no reason to believe that educational outcomes will be equal for all groups. Although equal outcomes may not be attainable because of between group differences in motivation, interests, and backgrounds, there are other reasons. Because of the long history of ethnic relations in the United States and the cultural interaction patterns that have emerged (as previously described), some ethnic groups will continue to be a step behind.

Realizing these problems, those favoring equality of outcomes have argued for affirmative action and special programs (e.g., compensatory education, bilingual education, educational reforms, multicultural education) in order to narrow the gap between ethnics and whites. In their view, color-blind procedures that are applied to groups already showing disparate educational performances, can only serve to maintain differential achievements. The dilemma here is quite apparent. Advocates of equal educational opportunities and nondiscrimination run the risk of perpetuating unequal outcomes; those who argue for equal outcomes (e.g., seeing that minority groups are as likely to graduate, enroll, or otherwise benefit from education) may have to discriminate by treating some groups differently because of social, cultural, and historial factors. By emphasizing one principle, the other principle may have to be sacrificed.

Unfortunately, the controversy has often been translated into one involving discrimination: "If it is unfair to discriminate *against* ethnic groups, should we now discriminate in reverse in order to favor ethnics (via affirmative action and special programs)?" It is unfortunate in the sense that in focusing on discrimination one cannot see the forest for the trees. The more important and obviously meaningful question is, "What kind of society do we want?" If one values a society in which a primary goal is to maximize the potential of every individual irrespective of color, ethnic group, or sex, then extraordinary measures must be taken. This means that immediate and long-term attempts must be made to correct differential achievement patterns. Only after opportunities become truly equal can a color- or ethnic-blind system have any meaning.

Conflict 4: Modal Personality Versus Individual Differences

One of our colleagues conveyed the following story to us:

> *His daughter's fourth-grade teacher had just returned from a human relations workshop where she had been exposed to the necessity of incorporating "ethnicity" into her instructional planning. Since she had a Japanese-American student in her class, she asked the child to be prepared to demonstrate to the class how the child danced at home. When the child danced in typical American fashion on the following Monday, the teacher interrupted and said, "No! No! I asked you to show the class the kinds of dances you danced at home." When the child indicated that she had done just that, the teacher said, "I wanted you to show the class how you people danced at the* Bon Odori" *(a Japanese festival celebrated in some Japanese American communities at which people perform Japanese folk dances). (Mizokawa and Morishima, 1979, p. 9)*

In this example, the teacher had assumed that the Japanese child knew how to perform a Japanese folk dance. However, the student was quite assimilated and was unable to illustrate Japanese dances.

The conflict involved in the modal personality versus individual differences refers to one's values regarding between and within group differences. The teacher in the above case sought to appreciate ethnic differences (e.g., "Japanese dance differently from Americans"). Since the student was Japanese-American, the teacher believed that the student must know how to perform the ethnic dance. The between-group approach largely ignores individual differences. It typically relies upon the concept of modal personality in describing cultural patterns (Inkeles and Levinson, 1969). In this concept, cultures may vary in the extent to which their members exhibit certain traits. By comparing various groups, one can calculate the average (or modal) characteristics in each group and then determine how different the groups are. For example, suppose that some researchers believe that Chinese and Anglos differ in their cultural emphasis on education. They develop a measure to ascertain cultural values regarding education. The average or modal score on the measure is much higher among Chinese than Anglos, prompting the investigators to conclude that Chinese are educationally oriented. Such a conclusion, of course, does not reflect the individual differences within groups (not all Chinese may value education and not all Anglos lack educational orientation). Carried to an extreme, modal personality has an apparent stereotypic quality to it.

In this book, some of the contributors try to characterize ethnic cultural patterns. For example, Heath (this volume) notes that in families of Mexican-American families, parents expect extended family members to share responsiblity for child-rearing. Díaz *et al.* (this volume) found that Mexican-Americans value education and good writing skills. Kagan (this volume) argues that cooperativeness is a characteristic of Mexican-American and other ethnic minority students in general. Ogbu and Matute-Bianchi (this volume) as well as Heath find that Chinese children acquire a respect for elders and authority. Undoubtedly, in response to these characterizations, some individuals will object by claiming that the findings are stereotypic or that Anglos also have these traits. It should be noted, however, that the *modal* approach is appropriate, depending on the purpose (as will be discussed later).

The individual differences emphasis is interested in within group variations. Members of an ethnic population are quite heterogenous. Some are acculturated, speak no ethnic language, live in ethnically mixed neighborhoods, and are quite different from nonacculturated members of their group who maintain a more traditional orientation. Proponents of individual differences argue that the danger in formulating modal or average personalities for each ethnic group is that stereotypes emerge that detract from the contribution each individual makes to their cultural group. In the case of the Japanese-American student described previously, individual differences advocates state that one cannot assume that she is typically or traditionally Japanese in behavior and values simply by knowing her ethnicity. Although correct in asserting ethnic group heterogeneity, carried to its extreme, the individual differences notion tends to deny commonalities due to culture. It is focused upon individuals and their uniqueness.

The strengthening of one principle (modal personality or individual differences) has the effect of weakening the other. What must be realized, however, is that each may be appropriate in a given context, for a given purpose. Discussions of cultures imply that generalizations and abstractions will be made. Knowledge of cultures provides a background for understanding different groups. However, given the context, it is then appropriate to examine the heterogeneity within groups. For example, Native Americans come from many different tribes with distinct languages, values, and rituals of their own. Chinese and Mexican-Americans are composed of immigrants as well as individuals who may be sixth- or seventh-generation Americans. The challenge for educators is to identify critical differences between and within ethnic minority groups and to incorporate this information into classroom practice.

Conflict 5: Presence Versus Absence of Prejudice and Discrimination

During a workshop on multicultural education, one teacher said, "When it comes down to it, ethnic minorities are still oppressed by direct and indirect forms of discrimination and stereotypes. I can see this in the attitudes of some teachers and administrators, especially when I advocate for changes on behalf of minority groups." Adopting a different point of view, another teacher said, "I disagree. The school I work for does not discriminate. I think a lot of minorities see discrimination when it doesn't exist. Americans have made great strides in race relations--if you visit other countries, you'll see what discrimination is really like."

The final perplexing and complicated issue is that of the current existence of racism. As indicated by Denton and Sussman (1981), national surveys reveals that both Blacks and Anglos believe that race relations have greatly improved and that Anglos believe discrimination has all but disappeared (and now it is up to the Blacks to demonstrate their drive and motivation to take advantage of their opportunities). Blacks see persistent forms of discrimination while admitting to racial improvements. Do discrimination and prejudice exist, or are they phenomena of the past? If ethnic minority groups fail to achieve equality, should we "blame the victims" in view of the belief that equal opportunities are now present for all? One perspective praises society for changes; the other claims that despite changes, society is still implicated in racial and ethnic problems. As in the other four issues, two positions can be taken.

The disturbing fact is that despite the popular belief, the notion that racism has all but disappeared has not received much support. In a review of research studies on prejudice and discrimination, Crosby *et al.* (1980) tried to analyze whether the expression of attitudes of equality actually corresponds to a lack of prejudice and discrimination. They examined three types of unobtrusive studies (i.e., those in which unobtrusive measures were used or in which the experiments included hidden manipulations). The first involved research on whether Blacks or whites in need of assistance received the same amount of help from whites; the second examined whether race of victim is a factor in the extent of punishment meted out by whites in learning tasks; and the third noted whether whites' nonverbal behaviors varied as a function of the race of the person with whom they interacted. The investigators concluded that anti-Black prejudice and discrimination still exist. Blacks tend to receive less than whites, to receive more indirect punishment, and to be treated differently in interactions. The attitude change, although important, reflects more of a change in what people feel they ought to say in response to surveys than in what they truly feel about equality.

McConahay and Hough (1976) also believe that the nature of prejudice and discrimination has changed and is now more subtle. According to their theory of symbolic racism, the old-fashioned, "redneck" variety with overt discriminatory acts and negative racial stereotypes has decreased. This has been replaced by a more complicated form of racism manifested in the belief that minority groups are too demanding and pushy and are getting more than they deserve. Much of this feeling is expressed in symbolic issues such as opposition to welfare programs of one type or another, affirmative action programs, and educational programs such as bilingual education. The theory suggests that direct anti-ethnic sentiments are suppressed; what is expressed is opposition to factors or ideological symbols associated with Blacks and ethnic groups. For instance, Sears and Citrin (1982) have argued that one of the bases of the California tax revolt shown in support of Proposition 13 was symbolic racism wherein non-ethnics maintained that minority group members were getting more than their share of the tax dollar through social service programs and the way to stop this was by supporting Proposition 13.

That racial prejudice may underline opposition to ideological symbols was further tested by Sears *et al.* (1977). The researchers note that opposition to busing to achieve racial desegregation is substantial. Two major explanations have been advanced for this antibusing sentiment--self-interest and symbolic racism. The former assumes that opposition is caused by fears that taxes will rise to support busing, that children may be sent to low-quality and distant schools, social relationships between children will be disrupted, that children may be sent to high-crime areas, and so on. In other words, people may oppose busing because it is not perceived as serving their self-interest. The symbolic racism explanation is that antibusing attitudes are frequently caused by racial prejudice directed toward a symbolic issue--in this case, busing. To test the two hypotheses, Sears et al. (1977) gathered data from a national survey on attitudes toward busing. They reasoned that self-interest in the busing issue would be reflected in respondents who had school-aged children, who had children in public rather than private or parochial schools, who lived in all-white neighborhoods, and who anticipated that busing might occur in their schools. According to a self-interest notion, antibusing sentiments would be strong among those who had the greatest threat. On the other hand, the symbolic racism hypothesis would be supported if antibusing attitudes were related to issues of racial intolerance and lower levels of education, factors traditionally associated with racial prejudice. Analysis indicated that opposition to busing was not related to the measures of self-interest but was related to factors such as intolerance and education.

In describing the work of Crosby et al. (1980) and Sears et al. (1977), we are not suggesting that society has not made significant changes or that all antibusing sentiments reflect a new breed of racism. The main point is that there are opposing views over race relations and that many racial issues involve value clashes. On one side are those who value and praise the great strides made in recent years with respect to civil rights and who point to affirmative action programs as proof of these advances in civil rights. On the other side are individuals who are critical of American institutions such as education who believe that prejudice and discrimination persist in a variety of forms. We acknowledge that progress has been made in ethnic and race relations; however, as indicated in our analysis, prejudice and discrimination still exist and equality has not been achieved. We must confront the fact that positive changes have occurred and that there is still much that needs to be accomplished.

TOWARD SOLUTIONS FOR THE CONFLICTS

From our discussion of value conflicts, it is clear that attempts must be made to find solutions to these value conflicts especially as they affect educators. The conflicts need resolution for several reasons. First, the values or principles involved have some degree of validity. Thus, individuals who argue for one side may feel quite self-righteous over their position. Another problem is that because of the kernels of truth associated with each value or principle, individuals may experience indecision or confusion over the resolution of the conflicts within themselves. The clash of values, therefore, can be seen between individuals who hold different values or within persons who cannot come to terms with the conflicts. Second, dominance of one side of the conflict weakens the other. The possibility exists that the dominant position may blind individuals to the validity of the other position. Third, it is our belief that the dominant position, more often than not, has reflected the majority group stance at the expense of ethnic minority groups. This has paralyzed efforts to respond positively to ethnic minorities in the school settings.

In presenting the conflicts, we have alluded to ways of addressing the clashes of values. At this point, we want to present certain processes that may be helpful in moving toward the resolution of conflicts. The processes involve divergent thinking, mediation, alternation, co-existence, and level of abstraction.

Divergent Thinking

Divergence refers to the act of departing from a set course or norm. In divergent thinking, conflicts are addressed by conceptualizing or redefining issues in innovative ways that may depart from norms or convention. For example, in the assimilation-pluralism conflict, one can diverge from the typical manner in which the conflict is approached. Rather than to deal with the assumption that assimilation is necessary in order to develop functional skills, one could focus on the ever-changing definition of what skills are considered functional or the possibility that development of functional skills does not preclude the existence of pluralism. For example, the classroom teacher can employ multicultural examples when giving lessons in social studies. This can be done at the same time that the teacher discusses emic and etic approaches to studying the United States as well as other cultures.

Divergent thinking can often help to redefine issues. For example, many educators concerned over the reading and writing skills of students have opposed liberal education and have advocated a back-to-basics approach. Fixation over the liberal-basic education debate overlooks a more important issue, namely, effective means for students to learn. By diverging from this debate, Kagan (this volume) is able to focus on innovative means to enhance learning through cooperative strategies, which are applicable to liberal or basic education.

Divergent solution to problems are difficult especially in institutional settings such as schools that foster conformity to a routine. School personnel, together with parents and community leaders, must seek ways to incorporate new strategies in educating ethnic minority and LEP students. American industrialists have looked to Japan for new management strategies to increase the efficiency and productiveness of American factories. Similarly, educators must learn about educational practices in other countries from which most immigrant children originate. Closer coordination between American educators and educators in other countries could prove beneficial in opening up a host of innovative instructional practices that could benefit all students, including ethnic minority children.

Mediation

At times, mediation or compromises may be necessary. In the case of modal personality versus individual differences approaches, one may want to discuss cultural characteristics of groups at an abstract and general level and then spend some time indicating the importance of variation within a culture. Conversely, one can primarily focus upon differences within a cultural group and acknowledge that different groups have distinct core features.

Although we usually equate mediation or compromise with a labor dispute, the terms are equally appropriate in a classroom between different learners and their teacher. Today, the typical classroom in California is made up of students from many strata of society. Different religions, social classes, and ethnic groups are represented in a classroom, and because of such diversity, instruction--without forsaking academic content--must be oriented to the heterogeneous student body. Heterogeneity demands mediation or compromise. It forces the recognition that just as there is variation in student composition, there must be variation in teaching style.

One error that educators have made is the belief that all students learn in exactly the same way. Today we know that students differ by learner style; that is, some students may learn better when cooperative strategies (see Kagan, this volume) are employed, while others may do better with a strategy that promotes individual discovery and problem solving. Whatever the approach favored by an individual teacher, instruction must be conducted to mediate the demands of current instructional approaches with that of the individual and cultural learning styles of a culturally diverse student population.

Alternation

One may alternate by emphasizing one element of the conflict at one particular time or in one context and then by emphasizing the other element at another time or in another context. As noted earlier, we may want to see to it that outcomes for various groups are equal before engaging in equal opportunity or color blind procedures. In this case, we apply one strategy and then change strategies over time. In some circumstances or contexts, one side of the conflict may be more appropriate than another. Discrimination may be present in some situations, but absent in other situations.

It should be clear that these various solutions are not mutually exclusive of each other. Alternation requires a certain degree of flexibility and divergent thinking. The important thing to recognize in value alternation is that both values may be correct and that one can take a position that supports both values for different purposes in the same situation. For instance, equal opportunity, without reverse discrimination, is important, but so is equality of outcome without lessening of standards. For numerous reasons, it is important that higher education be made accessible to ethnic minority students, but equality is not accomplished if these same students are allowed to drop out or to receive a watered-down curriculum. Strategies that ensure both values are essential and equally applicable at all educational levels. (For more on alternation, see Ogbu and Matute-Bianchi, this volume.)

Co-existence

If each side of a paradox has some validity, it is important to realize that both sides must exist. Attempts to abolish the other side, if successful, result in an unbalanced view of reality. For instance, the elimination of an emic approach would result in the dominant view that all human beings are alike and can be judged according to universal standards. Such an extreme view is absurd. The co-existence of conflicting, but valid, positions is necessary in order to reflect reality and to create the tension necessary to find solutions to ethnic issues.

It was once mistakenly believed that American education served as the great melting pot where differences disappeared and where the amalgamation of people occurred. Just as this belief was maintained, the Constitution of the United States held that all men, irrespective of race or creed, had certain inalienable rights, including that of freedom of speech. Today we recognize that this country is not the great melting pot earlier believed. More important, the Constitution guarantees us the right to express our ethnic diversity. Some would go so far as to assert that the celebration of ethnic differences seen everywhere in such diverse forms as ethnic restaurants, media, festivals, enclaves, etc. is what has made this country great. If this co-existence is true of the macrocosm, should it not be true of the school place?

Level of Abstraction

In addressing value conflicts, it may be helpful at times to move to a higher level of questioning about values. For example, proponents of equal opportunity value color blind procedures, while those favoring equal outcomes value results (outcomes) rather than procedures. We noted earlier that the important question may be, "What kind of society do we want?" The answer to this question, which is asked at a higher level of abstraction, may enable both sides of the conflict to find unifying aspects or common goals.

One of the problems we feel with the educational system is that it has become lost in the forest because of the changing nature of the trees! In other words, the world is being transformed at a remarkably fast pace and, in large measure, schools are not keeping pace with these transformations. Today it is entirely possible for a student to be in a classroom in Mexico City, Singapore, or Tokyo one day and the next in Los Angeles or San Francisco. Further, due to multinational corporations, a Harold Robbins best seller is translated into numerous languages simultaneously with its release in English, and Julio Iglesias belts out his records in no less than six languages. Yet, our educational system is organized around a monocultural belief structure that de-emphasizes foreign languages and cultures. Fortunately, several reports have appeared that unquestionably have an impact on the types of questions asked of our educational system. For instance, the National Commission on Excellence in Education (1983), in its report *A Nation at Risk*, has had a profound influence on American education and its role in a global technological society. In their discussion of what has occurred in education and the risk at hand, the commission stated:

> *The risk is not only that the Japanese make automobiles more efficiently than Americans and have government subsidies for development and export. It is not just that the South Koreans recently built the world's most efficient steel mill, or that American machine tools, once the pride of the world, are being displaced by German products. It is also that these developments signify a redistribution of trained capability*

throughout the globe. Knowledge, learning, information, and skilled intelligence are the new raw materials of international commerce and are today spreading throughout the world as vigorously as miracle drugs, synthetic fertilizers, and blue jeans did earlier. If only to keep and improve on the slim competitive edge we still retain in world markets, we must dedicate ourselves to the reform of our educational system for the benefit of all, old and young alike, affluent and poor, majority and minority. Learning is the indispensable investment required for success in the "information age" we are entering. (pp. 6-7)

What this report is forcing us to do is to rethink educational policies and to do so on a higher level in terms of goals and objectives and the means to achieve these objectives. In doing so, we hope our regard for the education of ethnic minority students will also improve.

We have tried to illustrate some to the tactics that might be used in approaching the value conflicts generated by ethnic minority issues. Obviously, the conflicts may be amenable to several different tactics. The main point is that we must continually devise means of balancing elements in the conflicts and find means to enhance the performance of ethnic minority groups.

SUMMARY

Concern for the educational achievements of ethnic minority students is well justified. Their performances in the educational system lag behind those of whites on many different indices. Because of immigration and differential birth rates, our schools in particular and society in general will be confronted with even larger numbers of ethnic minorities.

How can the outcomes between ethnics and whites and between one ethnic group and another be explained? The central thesis in this chapter (and in this book) is that sociocultural factors account for much of the observed variations among groups. We have been especially interested in two sociocultural factors: (1) the cognitive perspective that is used to explain ethnic group differences, and (2) values that underlie minority group issues. Both factors are relevant to how one approaches these issues and what kinds of attitudes and solutions are generated.

Four cognitive perspectives were identified, including genetic inferiority, cultural deficit, cultural mismatch, and contextual interaction. Five conflicts or paradoxes were discussed: etic-emic, assimilation-pluralism, equal opportunity-equality of outcome, modal personality-individual differences, and presence-absence of prejudice and discrimination.

We believe that it is important to recognize the impact of one's perspectives in the educational system and to attempt to resolve the value conflicts. The demographics of tomorrow's and, indeed, today's schools reflect a clientele that few educators and politicians have been trained to accommodate. Linguistic and cultural diversity is becoming more the norm than the exception. It has been said that if we are not aware of history, we will be condemned to repeat it. For decision makers and policymakers to continue to be unaware of the sociocultural factors that affect the lives of everyone in this increasingly pluralistic society is to rob us all of the productive, democratic, and harmonious society that is in our power to create.

REFERENCES

American Psychological Association Ad Hoc Committee on Minority Affairs. *Report to APA Board of Directors.* Washington, D.C.: American Psychological Association, 1979.

Bain, B., and Yu, A. Cognitive consequences of raising children bilingually: "One parent, one language." *Canadian Journal of Psychology,* 1980, *34,* 303-313.

Banks, J. A. Multiethnic education and the quest for equality. *Phi Delta Kappan,* April 1983, 582-585.

Banks, W. C., Stitt, K. R., Curtis, H. A., and McQuater, G. V. Perceived objectivity and effects of evaluative reinforcement upon compliance and self-evaluation in blacks. *Journal of Experimental Social Psychology,* 1977, *13,* 452-463.

Brislin, R. W., Lonner, W. J., and Thordike, R. M. *Cross-Cultural Research Methods.* New York: Wiley, 1973.

Crosby, G., Bromley, S. and Saxe, L. Recent unobstrusive studies of black and white discrimination and prejudice: A literature review. *Psychological Bulletin,* 1980, *87,* 546-563.

Denton, J., and Sussman, B. Race relations: Gains seen for blacks, but what lies ahead? *Seattle Times,* March 29, 1981, 47.

Díaz, Stephen, Moll, Luis C., and Mehan, Hugh. Sociocultural resources in instruction: A context-specific approach. In *Beyond Language: Social and Cultural Factors in Schooling Language Minority Students.* Los Angeles, California: Evaluation, Dissemination and Assessment Center, California State University, Los Angeles, 1986.

Fisher, J. Negros, Whites and rates of mental illness: Reconsideration of a myth. *Psychiatry,* 1969, *32,* 428-446.

Garcia, J. The logic and limits of mental aptitude testing. *American Psychologist,* 1981, *36,* 1172-1180.

Gordon, M. M. *Assimilation in American life.* New York: Oxford University Press, 1964.

————. *Human Nature, Class, and Ethnicity.* New York: Oxford University Press, 1978.

Heath, Shirley Brice. Sociocultural contexts of language development. In *Beyond Language: Social and Cultural Factors in Schooling Language Minority Students.* Los Angeles, California: Evaluation, Dissemination and Assessment Center, California State University, Los Angeles, 1986.

Hodgkinson, H. L. Guess who's coming to college. *Academe,* 1983, *69,* 13-20.

Inkeles, A., and Levinson, D. J. National character: The study of modal personality and sociocultural systems. In G. Lindzey and E. Aronson (Eds.), *The Handbook of Social Psychology.* Reading, Massachusetts: Addison-Wesley, 1969.

Jencks, C., Bartlett, S., Corcoran, M., Crouse, J., Eaglesfield, D., Jackson, G., McClellan, K., Mueser, P., Olneck, M., Schwartz, J., Ward, S., and Williams, J. *Who Gets Ahead: The Determinants of Economic Success in America.* New York: Basic Books, 1979.

Jensen, A. R. How much can we boost IQ and scholastic achievement? *Harvard Educational Review,* 1969, *39,* 1-123.

Jones, J. M. *Prejudice and Racism.* Reading, Massachusetts: Addison-Wesley, 1972.

Kagan, Spencer. Cooperative learning and sociocultural factors in schooling. In *Beyond Language: Social and Cultural Factors in Schooling Language Minority Students.* Los Angeles, California: Evaluation, Dissemination and Assessment Center, California State University, Los Angeles, 1986.

Kamin, L. J. *The Science and Politics of I.Q.* New York: Lawrence Erlbaum Associates, 1974.

Keddie, D. (Ed.). *The Myth of Cultural Deprivation.* Baltimore, Maryland: Penguin, 1973.

Kitano, H. H. *Race Relations.* Englewood Cliffs, New Jersey: Prentice-Hall, 1980.

Klineberg, O. International educational exchange: The problem of evaluation. *American Psychologist,* 1981, *36,* 192-199.

Labov, W. The logic of non-standard English. *Georgetown Monographs on Language and Linguistics,* 1969, *22,* 1-31.

Lambert, W. E. An overview of issues in immersion education. In California State Department of Education (Ed.), *Studies on Immersion Education.* Sacramento: California State Department of Education, 1984.

Loehlin, J. C., Lindzey, G., and Spuhler, J. N. *Race Differences in Intelligence.* San Francisco: W. H. Freeman and Co., 1975.

McConahay, J. B., and Hough J. C. Symbolic racism. *Journal of Social Issues,* 1976, *32*(2), 23-46.

McGrath, J. E. Social science, social action, and the journal of social issues. *Journal of Social Issues,* 1980, *36*(4), 109-124.

Mercer, J. R. In defense of racially and culturally nondiscriminatory assessment. *School Psychology Digest,* 1979, *3,* 89-95.

Mizokawa, D. T., and Morishima, J. K. The education for, by, and of Asian/Pacific Americans. *Research Review of Equal Education,* 1979, *3,* 1-33.

Naisbitt, J. *Megatrends.* New York: Warner Books, Inc., 1982.

National Commission on Excellence in Education. *A Nation at Risk: The Imperative for Educational Reform.* Washington, D.C.: United States Department of Education, 1983.

Ogbu, John U., and Matute-Bianchi, Maria.   Understanding sociocultural factors: Knowledge, identity, and school adjustment.   In *Beyond Language: Social and Cultural Factors in Schooling Language Minority Students*.   Los Angeles, California: Evaluation, Dissemination and Assessment Center, California State University, Los Angeles, 1986.

Olmedo, E. L. Testing linguistic minorities. *American Psychologist, 1981, 36,* 1078-1085.

Padilla, A. M., and Ruiz, R. A. *Latino Mental Health: A Review of the Literature* (DHEW Publication N. 74-113). Washington, D.C.: U.S. Government Printing Office, 1973.

Padilla, A. M., and Ruiz, R. A. *Latino Mental Health: A Review of the Literature* (DHEW Publication No. 74-113). Washington, D.C.: U.S. Government Printing Office, 1973.

Pettigrew, T. F. Racism and the mental health of white Americans: A social psychological view. In C. V. Willie, B. M. Kramer, and B. S. Brown (Ed.), *Racism and mental health*. Pittsburgh, Pennsylvania: University of Pittsburgh Press, 1973.

Ramírez, M., and Castañeda, A. *Cultural Democracy, Bicognitive Department, and Education*. New York: Academic Press, 1974.

Rappaport, J. In praise of paradox: A social policy of empowerment over prevention. *American Journal of Community Psychology*, 1981, *9,* 1-25.

Sarason, S. B. Jewishness, blackishness, and nature-nurture controversy. *American Psychologist, 1973, 28,* 962-972.

Sears, D. O., and Citrin, J. *Tax Revolt: Something for Nothing in California*. Cambridge, Massachusetts: Harper University Press, 1982.

_____. Speer, L. K., and Hensler, C. P. *Opposition to Busing: Self-interest or Symbolic Racism?* Paper presented at the meeting of the American Psychological Association, San Francisco, California, 1977.

Steinberg, A. *The Ethnic Myth: Race, Ethnicity, and Class in America*. Boston: Beacon Press, 1981.

Sue, S. Ethnic minority issues in psychology: A reexamination. *American Psychologist,* 1983, *38,* 583-592.

_____, and Kitano, H. H. L. Stereotypes as a measure of success. *Journal of Social Issues,* 1973, *19,* 83-98.

Suzuki, B. H. Education and the socialization of Asian Americans: A revisionist analysis of the "model minority" thesis. *Amerasia Journal,* 1977, *4,* 23-52.

Thomas A., and Sillen, S. *Racism and Psychiatry*. New York: Brunner/Mazel, 1972.

Torrance, E. P., Gowan, J. W. J., and Aliohi, N. C. Creative functioning of monolingual and bilingual children in Singapore. *Journal of Educational Psychology,* 1970, *61,* 72-75.

United States Commission on Civil Rights. *Civil Rights Indicators for Minority Groups*. Washington, D.C.: U.S. Government Printing Office, 1978.

United States Department of Commerce. *Detailed Population Characterstics: California*. Washington, D.C.: U.S. Government Printing Office, 1983.

UNDERSTANDING SOCIOCULTURAL FACTORS: KNOWLEDGE, IDENTITY, AND SCHOOL ADJUSTMENT

John U. Ogbu
University of California, Berkeley

María Eugenia Matute-Bianchi
University of California, Santa Cruz

The anthropologist may correctly observe that a certain ritual increases community solidarity; but it does not follow that the participants performed the ritual for the purpose of achieving solidarity which they almost surely did not. (Anonymous)

In the United States and other urban industrial societies like Britain and Japan, research has shown that some minority groups do not do well in school (DeVos, 1973; Ogbu, 1978; Parliamentary Select Committee, 1973). In the United States, language minorities, such as Native Americans, Mexican-Americans, Native Hawaiians, and Puerto Ricans, are among the minorities that experience *persistent disproportionate* school failure. There are many competing explanations of the school failure, ranging from genetic deficiency to institutional discrimination. Since the early 1970s, some social scientists have, however, increasingly emphasized the role of language and cultural differences in the minority school failure. Many appear to have concluded that a major part of the problem lies in the cultural and language discontinuities between the minorities and the schools (an institution reflecting the culture and language of the dominant group in society). Public policy has, as a result, moved more or less in the same direction, generating bilingual and bicultural education as "solutions" to the problem of minority school failure.

This chapter is not about the efficacy of blingual/bicultural education solutions, nor is it about the public policy generating and sustaining these solutions. Rather, it is about why some language minorities experience persistent disproportionate school failure. We will be emphasizing the question of *why,* in contrast to some prevailing approaches that generally address the question of *how* minority children fail or how they achieve school failure.

The discontinuities may be language and communication, cognition, social interaction pattern, "culture" or values, depending on the researcher's interests and field of specialization. From this perspective, a researcher may set out to show how the postulated discontinuities produce school failure. It is true, of course, that some people study how minority children acquire their language and communication patterns or learning styles and cultural norms that are different from and in conflict with those of the schools; that they may also study how a mismatch between the two produces minority school failure. However, whether the researcher studies the discontinuities phenomenon at school sites only or studies it at home and in the community, this conceptual framework generally forces him or her to focus primarily on events in small settings: classroom events, including teacher-student interaction; instructional styles; peer-group interaction; language acquisition and use in parent-child dyad; family activities (e.g., family dinner); playground events; and, in rare cases, community groups. Basically, we think that the problem of persistent disproportionate school failure among some minorities has been too narrowly conceptualized in terms of discontinuities between the cultural and language backgrounds of the children on the one hand and the demands of the school milieu on the other. Woolard (1981) aptly sums up the results of such studies with respect to language or communication: "Many investigators have documented the Batesonian schismogenesis produced by the interaction of people with different communication styles" (p. 2). Ogbu (1979, 1981a, 1981b) has pointed out that although these micro-level, process-product studies, have taught us much about *how* minority students fail, there are problems with the paradigm. One major weakness is that the formulation does not and cannot lead to an explanation of *why some minority groups, why some language minorities do quite well in school in spite of cultural and language barriers.* Another weakness is that this conceptual framework either does not recognize or cannot accommodate those broader historical and sociocultural forces that may influence minority educational experiences, perceptions, and practices.

The question of how minority children fail in school is important for both theoretical and policy reasons. However, since some minorities succeed even though they speak a different language and have a different culture, we need a conceptual framework that will enable us to account for the school success of some and the school failure of others. In other words, we need a conceptual framework that not only describes but also explains the reasons for the process of minority school failure: why it happens the way it happens among some minorities. We have not fully developed such a conceptual framework, but we will illustrate how to approach the why aspect of the problem in this chapter. We believe that developing such a conceptual framework requires that we (1) take into account the nature of the linkage between schooling on the one hand and, on the other hand, sociocultural and historical forces; (2) distinguish between types of minority groups who are successful in school from other types of minorities that are not so successful; (3) differentiate between types of cultural discontinuities; and (4) examine each type of minority in relation to the societal and historical forces and schooling. In Part One of this chapter, we start by presenting some cross cultural evidence of variability in minority school performance in order to emphasize the need for a broader conceptual framework. Following this, we discuss the linkage between schooling and sociocultural forces; then we distinguish between types of minorities and suggest why some are not characterized by persistent disproportionate school failure. We will then distinguish between types of cultural discontinuities. In Part Two, we describe two illustrative cases--Chinese-Americans as an example of a successful language minority group, and Mexican-Americans as an example of a relatively unsuccessful language minority group. In the concluding section, we discuss some implications of our approach.

PART ONE

VARIABILITY IN LANGUAGE MINORITIES' SCHOOL PERFORMANCE: A PHENOMENON IN SEARCH OF AN EXPLANATION

Some language minorities do not do well in school; other language minorities do quite well. That is, there appears to be some variability in the academic performance of language minorities. This variability can be seen in local studies (Gibson, 1983; Ogbu, 1974), national studies (Coleman, 1966; Heller *et al.,* 1982; Slade, 1982; Wigdor and Garner, 1982), and cross cutural studies (Ogbu, 1978; Penfold, 1981; Skutnabb-Kangas and Toukoma, 1976; Guthrie, 1983; Mat Nor, 1983; Wan Zahid, 1978; Wollard, 1981).

Ogbu (1986) reported from his research in Stockton, California, that in the 1930s both Asian students (Chinese and Japanese) and Mexican-American students were experiencing difficulties in school because of their limited proficiency in English. However, a study by the school district in 1947 (Stockton Unified School District, 1948) showed that the language problems had disappeared among the Asians but persisted among Mexican-Americans. In fact, Asian students were by this time doing so well academically that their representation at the junior college level (grades 13 and 14) had risen to 250 percent of their expected rate. In contrast, less than five percent of the Mexican-Americans in the seventh and eighth grades made it to junior college. In his own ethnographic study in the same community between 1968 and 1970, Ogbu also found that Chinese and Japanese students did considerably better in school than Black and Mexican-American students (Ogbu, 1974; 1977).

Gibson (1983) did not directly compare Punjabi high school students with Mexican-American students in the same school in Valleyside, California, but the results of her study are instructive. She found that Punjabi students were doing well academically in spite of their cultural and language differences. She says that "almost all Punjabi youths graduate from high school---regardless of how recently they arrived in the United States--Punjabi children raised and educated from first grade in Valleyside (do better than those who came to America later). Many do quite well academically, as well as in fact their mainstream counterpart, or, in the case of boys, even better" (p. 3). She sums up the Punjabi school success as follows:

> *Punjabi youngsters are successful in school, by and large, in spite of sharing group characteristics which many researchers have found to correlate with school failure--parents with low income, low status jobs, little formal education, little or no proficiency in English, and a cultural tradition regarded as "backward" and un-American by some in the larger society. Not all Punjabis in Valleyside fit this description, but enough do that their success strategies merit serious analysis. (p. 3)*

Gibson's study also addresses the issue of cultural discontinuities. Take, for example, the problem of differences in the meaning of "eye contact" between teachers and minority students. Byers and Byers (1972) have used this to explain why Puerto Rican children have learning difficulties in school. According to them, Anglo children are brought up to look at an adult directly when being reprimanded; if they fail to do so, it means an admission of guilt and a sign of disrespect. Among Puerto Ricans, on the other hand, children learn to look respectfully down when they are being chastised. It is suggested then that problems arise for Puerto-Rican children when teachers who are not familiar with their culture interpret their behavior--looking respectfully down--as disrespectful or as an admission of guilt. It is concluded that since what is polite for the Puerto Ricans is considered rude by Anglos, teachers and Puerto Rican children may unwittingly "misinterpret one another's behavior, thus jeopardizing learning transactions."

Punjabi students in Valleyside seem to face similar problems in co-educational classrooms because they are brought up to avoid eye contact with members of the opposite sex. This means that Punjabi girls may experience problems addressing male teachers and male classmates and Punjabi boys may also face similar problems in addressing female teachers and female classmates. Cultural discontinuities also arise for the Punjabis with respect to class discussion. This is because in Punjabi culture children are taught to defer to adult authority. Such a training, it is reasoned, does not prepare Punjabi students to participate in classroom discussions where they have to express ideas different from those of teachers. Other examples of cultural discontinuities include differences between whites and Punjabis in training children in decision-making, wage earning, and financial management. In spite of these and other differences in culture, values and attitudes, Punjabi students are quite successful in school and, as Gibson (1983) reiterates, "in the case of boys, [the Punjabis are even] more successful" than Anglos.

At the national level, Coleman (1966) reports that Asian American students do better than Blacks, Mexican-Americans, Native Americans, and Puerto Ricans in reading, verbal ability, and math tests. As reported by the *New York Times* (Slade, 1982), Asian American students did better than other language minorities on the SAT administered by the Educational Testing Service in 1980-1981.

Cross cultural studies indicate that this variability also exists outside the United States. In Britain, for example, East Asian students do considerably better than West Indian students even though the former are less fluent in English than the West Indians (Ogbu, 1978; Tomlinson, 1982). In New Zealand, the native Maori language minorities do less well in school than immigrant Polynesians who share similar language and culture (Penfold, 1981).

Instances where language minorities do better than the majority groups have also been reported from Spain (Woolard, 1981) and Malaysia (Mat Nor, 1983; Wan Zahid, 1978). According to Woolard, the Catalan language in Spain was repressed and legally banished for a long time from the public domain, including education. She says that Catalan children are "trundled off to Castilian language schools, treated as if they were no other language than Castilian, and [made to learn] to 'speak Christian'" (p. 10). Yet, in spite of this traumatic treatment,

> *Catalan speakers are by and large successful in school. For example, at the University of Barcelona, 60 percent of the students are native Catalan speakers. This group is over-represented here, and clearly has greater access to higher education than the Castilian speakers. (p. 10)*

Mat Nor (1983) reports that the educational reforms in Malaysia have centered around language issues. The English language has been eliminated as the medium of instruction in the public schools and replaced at all levels with Malay, the language of the dominant group or numerical majority. Malay has been also introduced as the medium of instruction in higher education with the establishment of the National University of Malay in 1970. In spite of this language policy and the practice of the educational system, Chinese and Indian students--the language minorities--continue to do better in school than native Malay speakers. Mat Nor (1983) reports, for example, that at the 1983 graduation ceremony at the National University of Malaysia, Chinese students won 9 of the 15 academic prizes in the social sciences, in spite of the fact that they faced language problems since the medium of instruction was in Malay and the majority of the professors were Malay.

Many more examples of this variability in minority academic performance can be found in other parts of the world. However, we have given enough examples to show that the relative minority school failure is not caused primarily by the fact that minority children speak a different language or come from a different cultural and language background, i.e., that they do not speak the same language or come from the same culture as the dominant group in society whose language and culture are reflected in instruction and cultural practices of the schools. This conclusion is reinforced by two other observations. One is that in some instances the minorities who are more different in language and culture from the dominant group are the ones who are more successful in school. For example, some have reported that in the United States, Mexican students appear to be more successful than Chicano students (Fernandez and Nielsen, 1984; Woolard, 1981). In Britain, East Asian students who are more different from the British in language and culture do considerably better in school than West Indian students who are more similar to the British in language and culture (Ogbu, 1978).

The second observation is that in some instances a minority group does poorly in school in the country of its origin where its language and culture are more or less similar to the language and culture of the dominant group. However, when members of the same minority group migrate to another society, they tend to do quite well in school even though their language and culture are now less similar to the language and culture of the dominant group controlling their schools. A good example of this phenomenon is the case of the Japanese Buraku outcast. In Japan itself, Buraku students continue to do poorly in school when compared with the dominant Ippan students. In the United States, however, the Buraku do as well as the Ippan immigrants (DeVos, 1973; Ito, 1967; Shimahara, 1983). Another example is the case of the Japanese Koreans. In Japan, where they went originally as colonial subjects in forced labor, the Koreans do very poorly in school. However, in the United States, Korean students do quite well like other Asian students (DeVos, 1983; DeVos and Lee, 1981; Rohlen, 1981). Finally, West Indians are reported to be poor students in Britain (Ogbu, 1978; Tomlinson, 1982), but they do quite well in the United States (Fordham, 1984) and in St. Croix (Gibson, 1982), where they consider themselves immigrants.

We have no satisfactory explanation yet for this variability in minority school performance. Classroom studies of language and cultural differences as well as studies of the mismatch caused by these language and cultural differences do not even begin to address the question of the variability. We believe, however, that one step toward explaining the variability is to show the connection between education and other societal institutions and events that may influence the school perceptions and behaviors of the minorities or their responses to schooling. The next related step is to distinguish between different types of minorities and explore how their different or similar experiences, perceptions, and responses affect the outcomes of their schooling.

STATUS MOBILITY SYSTEM OR
FOLK THEORY OF SUCCESS AND SCHOOLING

Consider the following questions for a moment: Why does a society, any society, go to the trouble of providing formal schooling for its children? Why do American parents send their children to school? Why do children, as they get old enough to make their own decisions, continue to go to school? Our observations of Americans and our review of

studies in the United States and other industrial societies lead us to conclude that a society builds schools to train future adult members to carry
out social, economic, and other tasks that the powers consider important
for the well-being of society. The type of schooling provided by a given
society depends on what and how the powers define the essential tasks.
Furthermore, in contemporary urban industrial societies like the United
States, economic considerations, or tasks, are primary.   That is,
although education is influenced by political and ideological needs and
issues (Cohen, 1975) and by religious beliefs and tradition, the most important source of influence shaping formal education today appears to
be the industrial economy and its perceived needs. As for clients of
education, i.e., parents and students, we suggest that their perceptions
and responses are also highly influenced by economic considerations.
Furthermore, we suggest that even though some Americans idealize the
pursuit of education for its own sake, in reality schooling in the United
States has usually been structured and perceived in terms of training in
marketable skills and credentialing for labor force entry, renumeration,
and advancement.   Therefore, we further suggest that the study of
minority education or the education of any segment of American society
has to consider this wider context and meaning of schooling.

Let us examine a number of specific linkages between schooling and
the economy and other opportunities in society in order to show what
light such linkages shed on the problem of academic performance among
caste-like minorities.

Economic Influence on   Structure and Content of Schooling: Some
Current Examples

Education is linked to the economy through the influence of the
perceived needs of the economy on the content of education. We will use
current changes in American economy to illustrate how the perceived requirements of the economy influence education or schooling. We begin
by noting that current competition among the United States, Japan, and
other industrial nations for high-tech economy, as well as the growing influence of computer industry and technology on American economy are
at the heart of the new economic forces reshaping American education
from kindergarten through graduate education. Within the public
schools, the economic influence is mediated through pressures from state
and federal governments as well as from industrial leaders. For example,
in 1982 California provided extra funds in its education budget for

strengthening math and science curriculum in the public schools. Furthermore, in almost every issue *Education Week* carries an account of one or more states considering some school reforms to strengthen math and science curriculum or basic skills in the public schools.

Industries' efforts for the same purpose are frequently reported in local and national newspapers and magazines. For example, the *San Francisco Examiner-Chronicle* of February 14, 1982 (Franklin, 1982) reported that the powerful "1900-member Industrial Education Council of California" was seeking ways to attract more students to math and science and also ways to provide training for teachers. Ultimately, it was seeking to bring more qualified people into the state's rapidly expanding high-technology industry. The Executive Vice-President of the Council stressed during an interview with the paper's reporter that the Council wanted to make parents understand that future graduates with strong backgrounds in math and science would have good employment prospects. It was evident from the remarks of the Executive Vice-President of the Council that industrial leaders are explicit about their intention, namely, to restucture public school and college education to serve industries more effectively. As the Executive Vice-President put it, it is "not a question of having kids come out (i.e., graduate) with math and science skills, it's a question of California economy. Will we have people who are functional and can produce?" To achieve their objectives, industries are conducting summer internship programs for high school students as well as for public school and college teachers. Some firms in Santa Clara County have gone further and sent computers to elementary schools or have adopted some public schools through industry-school partnership programs (Rutowski, 1985).

How Schools Support the Economic System

Whether schools realize it or not, they support the prevailing economy by trying to teach children the beliefs and know-how the industrial leaders and other powers think are essential or good for the economic well-being of society. In general, schools support existing economic system by preparing young people to accept the system, to join its labor force, and to become consumers of its products. Specifically, schools teach children the beliefs, values, and attitudes that support the economic system and other societal institutions and some practical skills that make the economic system work. Schools enhance children's development of some personal attributes compatible with those required at the workplace and credential people to enter the labor force.

Evidence that the public schools teach children beliefs, values, and attitudes that support American economy can be found in analysis of school textbooks. The best example of such an analysis is the study by Elson (1964). In her analysis of nineteenth century textbooks, Elson found repeated statements, emphases, and pictures portraying the American economic system as the best in the world; the textbooks conveyed the message that the American economy was the best because of "American liberty and industry" (p. 246). School books advised children on how to succeed in this economic system. They were taught that they "could anticipate a perpetual glorious future in which man's control over nature would steadily be extended" (p. 247). The school books also stressed that children would get ahead merely through personal efforts and hard work rather than by joining labor unions or through collective bargaining. On the whole, the books extolled the acceptance of American labor conditions and hard work as the best way to get ahead; they taught children that poverty was the result of idleness, wealth the fruit of hard work, and private property a sacred right whose accumulation deserved universal and unquestioned approval. Analyses of contemporary school books (Harty, 1979; Adams and Laurikietis, 1977; Frazier and Sadker, 1973) indicate that they continue to teach children those beliefs, values, and attitudes that support the American economic system. The same beliefs, values, and attitudes are reinforced by "field trips" to industries sponsored by local business establishments and by presentations in public schools by representatives of corporations (Franklin, 1982).

Schools teach children practical skills essential to make the industrial economy "work." The most obvious are reading, writing, and computation. Consider for the moment how the American banking system would "work" if its employees and clients did not learn to read, write, and compute. Currently, schools are responding to the belief that future generations of American workers need high-tech and computer knowledge and skills by acquiring and teaching computers. In some school districts, there is now in place or a plan to introduce computers in almost every classroom, from kindergarten through twelfth grade (Holt, 1982). In 1983, it was reported that a school district in Minnesota that was worried about lack of funds for its regular education budget and about declining student enrollment had put together "a $150,000 arsenal of more than 200 Apple, Commodore, and Atari microcomputers for the district's remaining 6,000 students; [and] 20 more computers [would] arrive soon" (Scheinin, 1983, p. C-3). At a meeting of a school PTA in Oakland, California, attended by one of the authors in the fall of 1982, the school's principal informed parents that introducing computers as early as kindergarten is the proper way to prepare children more effectively for future employment in an economy that will be dominated by computers. In another school, the coordinator of a volunteer program said that some affluent families in the school district were reinforcing schools' efforts with home computers. This was subsequently confirmed in a conversation with some parents at another PTA meeting. Indeed, it has been observed by some that just as more affluent families are quickly passing on the advantages of the new education to their children, also more affluent schools are restructuring their curriculum quickly to emphasize the requirements of the emerging economic order. They add that poorer families and schools are "training a whole generation of computer illiterates who are doomed to be a social underclass" (Scheinin, 1983, p. C-3). Similar changes are also taking place at the college level; that is, the colleges are undergoing changes in order to emphasize training for the requirements of the emerging economic order (Ogbu, 1983).

How schooling enhances the acquisition of other personal attributes required by the urban industrial economy has been documented in a number of studies. For example, LeCompte (1978) and Wilcox (1978) have examined the structure and process of classroom tasks and concluded that they appear to teach children personal habits like conformity to schedule, conformity to authority, keeping busy, maintaining order, and that these parallel the habits of punctuality, obedience, dependability, perseverance, differing gratification, predictability, and other attributes valued by employers (Cohen, 1972; Scrupski, 1975; Waller, 1967).

Finally, schools credential young people to enter the workforce. The importance of school credentials is illustrated by Ogbu's finding (1977) in Stockton where he interviewed two groups of informants. One group consisted of United States citizens who claimed to know how to do certain things, such as boat repair and carpentry, but could not practice these trades as professions because they did not have "papers to show for it." That is, they had not been "credentialed" or licensed by some educational agency in the state. The other group was made up of immigrant professionals, especially dentists from the Philippines. Although these people had trained in some of the best institutions in their countries of origin and had practiced there, they could not practice in Stockton without first receiving credentials from California educational agencies.

In summary, then, from a societal point of view, schools are structured to' prepare citizens to support the economic system as producers, workers, and consumers, and to believe in the system. Schools try to accomplish this task in several ways, though they do not necessarily recognize or acknowledge that they do so.

Why People Go to School: Folk Theory of "Making It"

Neither the political nor the economic interests of society, nor the changing requirements of the economic system, not even the efforts of the school can guarantee that schools will succeed in "educating" a client population. Schools' success depends, in part, on the role of schooling in people's folk theory of success. Schooling is but one of several factors shaping the folk theory. Others include the overall status of members of an indentifiable group, especially in a stratified society, their economic niche, their historical experiences, and their cultural values. The extent to which education or schooling is emphasized and practiced depends on the people's experiences in the labor force.

A concept that enables us to understand people's educational attitudes and efforts, given their labor market experience, their history and cultural values, is the concept of *status mobility system* or *folk theory of getting ahead*. Every society or population has its own theory of getting ahead; each folk theory tends to generate its own ideal behaviors and its own ideal successful persons or role models--the kinds of people who are widely perceived by members of the population as people who are successful or people who can get ahead because of their personal attributes and behaviors. Parents usually try to raise their children to be like these people and as children grow older they, too, strive to be like them.

Thus, in a population in which a significant number of people of varying backgrounds are perceived or known to have become successful or to have "made it," especially through wage labor (broadly defined) because of their school success, people will tend to believe strongly that the way to get ahead is through education. In such a population, people will also develop appropriate behaviors enhancing school success. In general, if school success is perceived by members of a population over a reasonable period of time to make people successful, people will incorporate the pursuit of education into their status mobility system or folk theory of success. In other words, where there is a stong connection between school success and later economic and societal success in adult life, people will develop a positive image of schooling, value going to school, and learn to persevere or work hard to do well in school. Eventually, what makes people succeed academically will become a common knowledge and may even become a part of their folklore. People, thus, will develop shared beliefs, values, attitudes, and behaviors that support both wanting school credentials, persevering, and working hard in the pursuit of credentials. Eventually, these perceptions, beliefs, values, and practices enhancing academic success will become institutionalized in the culture and manifested at appropriate times and places as categorical and instrumental values and behaviors.

When this situation develops in a population, parents and other childrearing agents teach children consciously and unconsciously the categorical beliefs, values, attitudes, and behaviors promoting striving for academic success; they also guide and supervise children in ways that ensure that the latter actually conform to expectations of school success. For their part, children tend to respond positively to schooling. By positive response we mean that children accept and internalize the beliefs, values, and attitudes that support striving for school success, including those supporting the economic system and other societal institutions; that children make concerted efforts to learn what schools teach; and that as they get older they even take initiatives to search out those qualities essential for future participation in the labor force and how to acquire them. However, it is not sufficient for parents and schools to encourage children to respond positively to schooling. The children themselves must also observe that among adult members of their community, *there is* a reasonable connection between school success on the one hand and, on the other, success in getting jobs, wages, and other societal benefits. Or, the children must believe that such a connection can be reasonably expected when they finished school. To reiterate, children's positive responses are reinforced when shared cultural knowledge and "folklore" of their community about the relationship between school success and success in adult life, based on collective experience, are not too discrepant with verbal encouragement of parents and other adults.

From what children learn in the community and from direct and indirect teachings of the schools themselves, children acquire the "facts" and "beliefs" that enable them to form appropriate "cognitive maps" or mental pictures of their community's status mobility system and how schooling fits into it. That is, the children eventually develop a cultural conception of how to get ahead or how to "make it" and what role schooling plays in getting ahead. Where schooling facilitates getting ahead, children are taught and they learn and believe, consciously or unconsciously, that school success requires a reasonable degree of conformity to schools' rules of behavior and practices for academic achievement, i.e., conformity to schools' requirements and expectations.

Children learn how to go to school and how to succeed. However, as we will later argue, immigrant minority children can also learn how to go to school (i.e., to conform to schools' requirements and expectations) and to succeed, even though they have not been brought up in a community where schooling has served as a traditional route to success in adult life; in contrast, caste-like minorities do not learn quite so successfully or easily how to go to school.

Alternative Strategies and Schooling: What Happens When School Success and Adult Opportunities Do Not Fit

There are some situations where discrepancies exist between schooling and adult opportunity structures, producing folk theories that may or may not support striving for academic success. One is when a group is engaged in a *voluntary* principal economic activity or way of life that does not require schooling. The Amish in the United States are a good example; they do not stress school success as defined by the white middle class because Amish do not need white middle-class school credentials to succeed in the Amish economy and status system (Hostetler and Huntington, 1971). Another kind of situation was the case of earlier non-white immigrants to the United States, such as the Chinese and Japanese immigrants in the nineteenth and early twentieth centuries. These immigrants were not adequately rewarded in the United States for their school success; yet, they maintained folk theories that supported conventional school success in America. This was partly because the immigrants expected to be rewarded for their American school success elsewhere--in their home country. (We will discuss the Chinese case later in this chapter.) A third situation of discrepancy is found among caste-like minorities who has been *involuntarily* incorporated into society and *involuntarily* relegated to menial occupations or ways of life that do not require and do not reward school success. Such minorities tend to develop folk theories and coping strategies that do not necessarily enhance conventional school success. Furthermore, they seem, perhaps for this reason, not to develop a strong tradition of academic orientation and effort. In the next section, we will elaborate on the distinction between immigrant and caste-like minorities to explain why they respond differently to schooling with different outcomes.

TYPES OF MINORITY STATUS

As pointed out earlier, some language minorities do well in school; others do not. Moreover, some language minorities do well in school even when American society does not reward them adequately for their school success. It is clear, then, that language minority status *per se* is not always associated with *persistent* low school performance. To distinguish those who do well in school from others who do not and to explain the differential success rates, we suggest classifying minorities into *autonomous, immigrant,* and *caste-like minorities* (Ogbu, 1974; 1978; 1983). We will show later that persistent disproportionate school failure is experienced mainly by caste-like minorities.

Autonomous language minorities are probably not found in the United States. Yet, they exist in other parts of the world, especially in developing nations in Africa and China. Nonlanguage minorities who are autonomous, however, can be found in the United States; they include the Amish, Jews, and Mormons. Autonomous minorities are minorities mainly in a numerical sense. They are integrated totally in political or economic domain. They are not distinguished from their fellow citizens by denigrated specialized economic, political, or ritual roles. If they possess distinctive racial, ethnic, religious, language, or cultural identification, it is usually guaranteed by national constitution or by tradition. Autonomous minorities may be victims of prejudice, but not of subordination in a system of rigid stratification. They are not characterized by persistent disproportionate school failure. Rather, they often have a cultural frame of reference that enhances and demonstrates success.

Immigrant minorities are people who have moved more or less *voluntarily* to their host or new society for economic, social, or political reasons (Mabogunje, 1972; Ogbu, 1978; Shibutani and Kwan, 1965). Examples of immigrant minorities in the United States are Chinese-Americans, Cuban-Americans, Filipino-Americans, Japanese-Americans, and "West Indians." The immigrants may be subordinated and exploited politically, economically, and socially. For example, they may be denied political representation directly or indirectly as well as denied proper channels to express their grievances. Their economic exploitation may include lower wages and exclusion from certain desirable jobs. Also, they may be forced into denigrated menial roles. The immigrants may be segregated residentially and their children given inferior education. In spite of such treatment, children of immigrants are often successful in school. Their school success is partly the result of several factors influencing how they respond to their treatment and how they perceive and respond to schooling.

Immigrants tend to respond to similar treatment differently from caste-like minorities. For example, immigrants are not highly influenced by the dominant group's denigration and rationalization of their subordination and exploitation, partly because they do not consider themselves a part of the stratification system prevailing in their host society; they see themselves as "strangers" or "outsiders." Therefore, even if the immigrants initially occupy the lowest rung of the occupational ladder, lack political power, and have low prestige, it does not follow that they have a low opinion of themselves. Indeed, immigrants may not even stand their host's status system or accept it. Some immigrants may actually consider their menial position in America *better* then what they had "back home," i.e., prior to immigration to America (Shibutani and Kwan, 1965). Furthermore, during the first generation, immigrants have not really had time to internalize the negative effects of discrimination or to have those effects become an ingrained part of their culture.

Another distinctive factor is that the immigrants' reference group is located in their "homeland" or neighborhood. That is, immigrants do not evaluate their success by comparing themselves with the elite members of their host society. Rather, immigrants, at least initially, measure their success or failure by the standards of their homeland and compare themselves with their peers there or in their own immigrant neighborhood. By such comparisions, they often find much evidence that they have made some progress and that there are good prospects for their children to make even greater progress because of "better opportunities" (Shibutani and Kwan, 1965). We should point out that in the past some nonwhite immigrant minorities came to America primarily to accumulate wealth with which to return to their homelands for status advancement; in recent times, however, nonwhite immigrants and refugees have come to stay in America permanently and to seek self-advancement in America. In either case, self-advancement is uppermost in their minds and this acts as a strong incentive to overcome obstacles that might hinder success.

Immigrant minorities have an option to return to their "homeland" or reemigrate elsewhere if they find conditions in their host society intolerable. This means that the immigrants can export their school credentials and other skills elsewhere for greater benefits (Ogbu, 1983; Sung, 1967). The prospects for better employment and wages with American school credentials in their homeland allow the immigrants to develop and maintain folk theories of success that support schooling even when they are denied jobs in the United States. Of course, reemigration is not always possible even for all nonpolitical emigres; but this option is more available to the immigrants than to caste-like minorities.

Finally, diplomatic and economic ties between the immigrants' country of origin and their host society can substantially affect their status. For example, worsening ties between the two countries can result in harsher treatment; but friendly diplomatic or economic relations can vastly improve their perceptions and opportunities and influence their education.

The overall effects of these features are that they enable the immigrants to adopt and maintain attitudes toward schooling that enhance strong desire for and pursuits of school credentials; they also enable them to adopt attitudes and behaviors that help them overcome cultural, language, and other barriers in pursuing education. In general, the immigrants perceive school credentials as a key to advancement, especially advancement for their children. Education to the immigrants is an important investment. That is, their folk theory or status mobility system stresses the pursuit of education for future rewards. Morever, the immigrants make a distinction between behaving in a manner that enables them to obtain school credentials for employment and material benefits on the one hand and, on the other, behaving in a manner that would lead them to abandon their own culture and identity and adopt the culture and identity of the dominant group of their host society. The immigrants, in other words, *do not equate* schooling with a one-way, linear acculturation or assimilation into the white culture in America. They adopt, instead, what is essentially an alternation model of behavior toward schooling (Gluckman, 1960; Lebra, 1972; Mayer, 1962).

The essence of the alternation model is that is is possible and acceptable to participate in two different cultures or two different languages, perhaps for different purposes, by alternating one's behavior according to the situation. However, as noted above, the immigrants' participation in the culture of the dominant group is selective. Immigrant minorities do not necessarily want to become "Americanized" or behave like the white middle class, in general. In fact, they may disdain many aspects of white middle-class way of life. As Gibson (1983) found in Valleyside, Punjabi immigrants show no reticence in speaking out against many aspects of mainstream American culture. The weaknesses, from the Punjabi perspective, "relate to use of money, attitudes about work, social relations, sexual propriety, and family" (p. 72). At the same time, immigrant parents admonish their children to adopt those aspects of school culture or white middle-class culture they think enhance academic success. Thus, Punjabi parents emphasize for their children the importance of acquiring job-related skills; proficiency in English; basic skills in reading, writing, and math; and the importance of getting and following advice of teachers, school counselors, and other school personnel about rules of behavior and practices for school success.   Immigrants recognize and experience prejudice and discrimination in school and society but do not appear discouraged partly because they rationalize their experiences by contending that as ''guests in a foreign land they have no choice but to tolerate prejudice and animosity'' (Gibson, 1983, p. 66).   Parents impress this attitude on their children and place the responsibility of doing well in school on the children themselves.   Thus, in the case of the Punjabis, Gibson (1983) reports that:

> *Punjabis rarely blame the educational system, or the teachers, for a child's difficulties. Responsibility for learning rests, in the Punjabi view, with the individual. Punjabis are not naive about institutional and societal barriers to their success. They simply persevere, seeking ways to overcome obstacles in their path. Punjabi children are taught to do their best and to hold themselves accountable for their failures.   If children fool around, squandering educational opportunities, they bear the consequences. (p. 149)*

This means that immigrant children are taught to accept schools' rules of behavior and practices for achievement.   Children should behave at school according to school expectations, and at home and community according to home and community expectations.   Immigrant children generally learn to switch back and forth between the school and ethnic cultural frames of reference, i.e., they learn to cross cultural boundaries. This ability to alternate between the two cultural frames of reference without affective dissonance enhances their ability to transcend barriers of language and culture and perform well in school.

Caste-like minorities are minorities that have become *incorporated* into a society more or less *involuntarily* and *permanently* through slavery, conquest, or colonization and then relegated to menial status. Blacks are a good example, having been brought to America as slaves and restricted to menial roles through legal and extra-legal devices after emancipation (Berreman, 1960; Davis *et al.*, 1965; Myrdal, 1944). Native Americans, the original owners of the land, were incorporated by conquest and then forced into reservations (Siegel, 1955; Spicer, 1962).   Mexican-Americans in the southwestern United States were also incorporated by conquest; people who later immigrated from Mexico were accorded the subordinate status of the conquered group (De Leon, 1983; Balderrama, 1982; Grebler *et al.*, 1970; Weber, 1973).   Membership in a caste-like minority group is permanent and often acquired at birth. However, this is less true for Native Americans, Mexican-Americans, and Puerto Ricans than it is for Blacks because of the wide range of color differences within the other three groups that range from pure white to pure black (Nava, 1970; Senior, 1972).

What distinguishing features characterize caste-like minorities? One major feature already mentioned is that caste-like minoriites become minorities involuntarily and permanently. Other features lie in their exploitation by the dominant group and in the pattern of the responses the minorities make to that exploitation.

The dominant group's exploitation of the minorities is usually rationalized by the former by what DeVos and Wagatsuma, 1967; DeVos, 1984 call "caste thinking," or the belief that there is some unalterable biological, religious, social, or cultural inferiority that sets the minorities apart from the rest of the society. Because of the strong emotional belief that such an indelible mark exists among the minorities, dominant-group members usually take steps to protect themselves from contamination by instituting appropriate barriers against the minorities, like formal and informal prohibition of intermarriage, residential segregation, and the like. Both immigrant (e.g., Chinese-Americans) and caste-like minorities may experience this kind of treatment; but the two kinds of minorities interpret the treatment differently.

Dominant-group exploitation is both instrumental and expressive. Instrumental exploitation takes many forms, but in the context of schooling, denial of equal educational opportunity and institutionalization of a job ceiling against the minorities are most important. Educational exploitation includes diversion of funds from minority education by assigning to predominantly minority schools inferior, untrained, inexperienced, or low-paid teachers; or by providing lower nonteaching operating expenses, such as clerical and maintenance, supplies, textbooks, and the like, to predominantly minority schools. This type of exploitation has been most fully documented in the case of Blacks. Educational exploitation leads to inadequate preparation of the minority youths for joining the labor force (see Bond, 1966; Hughes and Hughes, 1973).

Economic exploitation takes the form of a *job ceiling*. A job ceiling consists of formal statutes and informal practices used to limit the minorities' access to desirable occupations, truncate their opportunities, and narrowly channel the potential returns they could expect to get from their education (Mickelson, 1983; Ogbu, 1978). A job ceiling describes three aspects of the employment experiences of minorities: that they are not permitted to *compete freely as individuals* for any type of job to which they aspire and for which they are *educationally qualified;* as a group, members of a caste-like minority are not allowed to obtain their proportionate share of highly desirable jobs solely because of their membership in a subordinate group; and, as a result, they are largely confined to the least desirable jobs below the job ceiling (Ogbu, 1978).

The job ceiling usually permits Anglos to compete more easily and freely for the more desirable jobs on the basis of education and ability. It benefits Anglos because the job ceiling allows even less qualified Anglos to obtain jobs they might not have obtained if qualified minorities were allowed equal opportunity. The job ceiling also benefits white corporations or white businesses. Consider the case of AT & T that was settled in 1974. An investigation by the Equal Employment Practices Commission found that the giant company "saved" $362 million a year by not paying Black, Hispanic, and female employees what they would have earned on the basis of education and ability if they were white males (DeWare, 1978).

The dominant group also exploits the minorities expressively through scapegoating. They project onto the minorities alleged inborn and societal traits they themselves do not like. According to DeVos and Wagatsuma (1967), such projections vary from one caste-like society to another. Thus, in Japan the dominant Ippan consider the Buraku outcastes as reprehensible, violent, aggressive, and disease-ridden. Anglos emphasize the supposed primitive sexuality of Blacks (Dollard, 1957) and the "dirtiness" and "indolence" of Mexican-Americans (De Leon, 1983; Weber, 1973). Scapegoating and other projections serve to relieve intrapsychic stresses experienced by dominant-group members, especially in times of social, political, and economic crisis. Consider, for example, the rise in violence and antagonisms against minorities in California in the early 1980s during worsening economic conditions. It should be noted that the projections and scapegoating may outlive the crises that brought them about and take on a life of their own, thus becoming a part of the cultural beliefs and practices of the dominant group (DeVos, 1984).

Apart from the forced incorporation of caste-like minorities, none of the treatment by the dominant group described thus far--overarching ideology of inferiority and denigration, instrumental and expressive exploitations--applies exclusively to caste-like minorities. They can also apply to immigrant minorities. What distinguishes caste-like minorities is how they perceive, interpret, and respond to the treatment. Their differential response is, in part, the result of their different history of involuntary incorporation and subsequent barriers to true assimilation.

Caste-like minorities do not accept the dominant group's rationalization of their subordination and exploitation, namely, that they are biologically, socially, or culturally inferior. However, the thinking and behaviors of caste-like minorities are very affected by the rationalization and denigration of the dominant group (Berreman, 1967; Tuden and Plotnicov, 1970). Furthermore, the minorities usually react by developing their own rationalization or explanation of the existing social order and their place in it. Their epistemology often includes what may be called *an institutionalized discrimination perspective* (Lewis, 1981; Ogbu, 1974). That is, caste-like minorities tend to believe more or less that they cannot advance into the "mainstream" of society through individual efforts in school and society or by adopting the cultural practices of the dominant group. The belief that they cannot "make it" by following the rules of behavior and practices for achievement that "work" for Anglos often lead caste-like minorities to adopt "survival strategies" to cope with their economic, social, and political subordination and exploitation. Blacks, for example, have developed several survival strategies to *circumvent, raise,* or *break the job ceiling* against them. (We shall describe the strategies used by Mexican-Americans later.) Other caste-like minorities adopt survival strategies appropriate to their situation. These survival strategies eventually become institutionalized cultural practices and beliefs, requiring their own norms, values, and attitudes as well as competencies or skills that may or may not be congruent with striving for school academic success (Ogbu, 1986).

The job ceiling and related exploitation weaken the connection between schooling and adult economic opportunities among caste-like minorities, thereby shaping their folk theory of success or status mobility system. Their instrumental responses to the job ceiling--collective struggle, clientship, and the like--are true expressions of their evolved folk theory of success under the job ceiling. Moreover, the folk theory of success under this circumstance may deemphasize striving for academic success.

The expressive responses made by the minorities may also lead them to deemphasize striving for academic success. Two expressive responses will be described to illustrate this. The first is the formation of collective oppositional identity; the second is oppositional or ambivalent cultural frame of reference developed by the minorities.

Caste-like minoriites tend to form a sense of peoplehood or collective social identity in opposition to the collective social identity of the dominant group. The collective oppositional identity arises from the minorities' feeling of and experience with collective oppression. Members of the group eventually come to realize and believe that regardless of their place of origin, place of residence, individual ability and training, individual economic status and physical appearance, they cannot expect to be treated exactly like members of the dominant group; nor can they easily or freely escape their birth-ascribed membership in a subordinate and disparaged group. They know that the door of true assimilation is not as open to them as it is to white ethnic immigrants; they do not really have a "homeland" to return to like some nonwhite immigrants, and their experiences and inferior status are not due to anything inherently wrong with them. Even those individuals who try to "pass" often suffer discouraging social and psychological costs. For these reasons, caste-like minorities respond by what DeVos and Wagatsuma (1967) calls "an ethnic consolidation" or a collective sense of identity (Castile and Kushner, 1981; Spicer, 1966, 1971).

Second, the formation of collective oppositional identity system is usually accompanied by *an evolution of an oppositional cultural system or cultural frame of reference* that contains mechanisms for maintaining and protecting the group's social identity. The content of the oppositional cultural frame of reference may vary. It may include deviant behaviors (as defined by dominant-group members), collective hatred for the dominant group and collective distrust, as well as cultural inversion. We suggest, however, that the term "cultural inversion," should be understood in both a broader sense and a narrower sense. In its broader meaning, cultural inversion designates various ways in which the minorities try to show their opposition to the dominant group. In a narrower sense, it is the tendency for minorities to regard certain forms of behaviors, events, symbols, and meanings as *not appropriate* for them because they are characteristic of Anglos; at the same time, the minorities claim other forms of behaviors, events, symbols, and meanings as appropriate for them because they are not a part of the Anglo's way. That is, what is appropriate or even legitimate for the minorities is defined in opposition to the practices and preferences of Anglos.

Cultural inversion serves a number of functions. It is used to repudiate negative stereotypes or derogatory images. It is sometimes used to "get even" toward Anglos or to "turn the table against whites" (Holt, 1972). Cultural inversion varies in form: hidden meanings of words and statements, different notions of time and its use (Weis, 1985), different language use and communication styles, or outright rejection of Anglo's behaviors and preferences.

The point to stress is that cultural inversion and other coping behaviors and attitudes of caste-like minorities *result in the coexistence of two opposing cultural frames of reference or two opposing cultural ideals orienting behaviors.* One is considered appropriate for Anglos, the other is appropriate for minorities. The minorities' cultural frame of reference is strongly associated with their sense of identity and emotional state. Therefore, members who try to behave like Anglos, i.e., cross cultural boundaries, may meet with opposition from their peers or other members of their community. Individuals who try to behave like Anglos may also experience internal discouragement because of their shared sense of identity with peers and because of uncertainty as to whether Anglos would accept them or not. We should point out, however, that cultural inversion is practiced selectively; we do not know why some areas are selected for inversion while others are not.

What are the educational consequences of these responses of caste-like minorities to their subordination and exploitation? Generally, the experience of a job ceiling leads them to develop a folk theory of making it that differs from that of the dominant group and that does not stress school academic success. This does not mean that caste-like minority informants are always able to explain their folk theories or what they do from this perspective. In fact, they often respond with the "abstract" theory of the larger society when questioned about how to get ahead. However, a researcher learns what the minorities' folk theories are by studying how the minorities attack directly and indirectly the criteria and procedures of selection for employment and societal rewards, from the alternative or survival strategies the minorities develop to cope with the job ceiling, and from explicit statements they make about competing with Anglos for jobs and other situations (Ogbu, 1986).

Furthermore, the various ways in which the minorities respond to their treatment tend to become institutionalized as a part of their cultural beliefs and practices and these in turn, give rise to other cultural beliefs and practices as well as personal attributes that may not necessarily support attitudes and behaviors enhancing academic success. For instance, the job ceiling and the minorities' efforts to cope with it may give rise to disillusionment about future opportunities. The competencies that are needed and promoted by the minorities' survival strategies may, for example, not necessarily be congruent with those required to do well in school. Moreover, the incongruence or "culture conflict" that arises in this situation is not as temporary as the culture conflicts that arise from the fact that immigrant minorities bring to American schools different cultural features and behavior patterns they had acquired to meet the needs of the situations in their countries of origin. The incongruent competencies of caste-like minorities arose as a part of coping and oppositional mechanisms under conditions in American and are more resilient.

PRIMARY AND SECONDARY CULTURAL DIFFERENCES

One other distinction that has to be made has to do with the type of cultural differences that characterize immigrant and caste-like minorities. This distinction is important and should not be ignored, as has been the case. Although both immigrants and caste-like minorities differ in culture and perhaps language from the dominant group, immigrants are characterized by *primary* cultural differences, while caste-like minorities are characterized by *secondary cultural differences* (Ogbu, 1982).

Primary cultural differences are those different cultural features that existed *before* two populations came in contact, such as those brought by immigrant minorities from their countries of origin to the United States. Primary cultural differences cause *primary cultural discontinuities* in formal education, and the resulting educational problems are often of a temporary nature. We can summarize the distinguishing features of primary cultural differences as follows: (1) the differences existed *before* the minorities came in contact with the dominant group; (2) the cultural differences are quite specific in nature and are usually a matter of content; they are, therefore, easily identified through ethnographic research; (3) the minorities or bearers of primary cultural differences recognize the differences and the problems they generate in school and the workplace, and they are usually willing to learn how to overcome the cultural discontinuities in order to succeed in school and in the workplace. Thus, immigrants from non-English-speaking countries want to learn English because it is the language of the public schools; those who came without appropriate mathematical concepts want to learn these and how to use them as required by the schools; and (4) immigrants and other bearers of primary cultural differences do not seem to suffer from *affective dissonance* or emotional crisis and ambivalence when they try to learn the cultural features of the dominant group they need to know in order to participate effectively in school and in the workplace. That is, they experience relatively little affective dissonance when they try to cross cultural boundaries.

Secondary cultural differences are, on the other hand, those different cultural features that came into existence *after* two populations have come in contact, especially in contact involving the subordination of one population by the other. For caste-like minorities, secondary cultural features are products of reponses to subordination and exploitation by the dominant group. They are also results of reinterpretations of pre-contact, pre-conquest, or pre-subordination cultural features. This is evident in many studies of "acculturation" problems among Native Americans and Mexican-Americans in the southwestern United States. (See Siegel, 1955 for a review of this group of acculturation studies.) Secondary cultural differences are, then, a part of boundary-maintenance mechanisms or oppositional process between the minorities and the dominant group. They are emotionally charged and resistant to change. Secondary cultural differences lead to secondary cultural discontinuities in school, and the educational problems caused by the latter are often lingering.

Distinguishing features of secondary cultural differences and discontinuities include the following: (1) the secondary cultural differences arose *after* the minorities had been subordinated by the dominant group; (2) secondary cultural differences and discontinuities are usually more a matter of "style" than "content." The majority of the studies of secondary cultural difference situation focus on "style," not "content," in contrast to studies of primary cultural differences among immigrant minorities. Examples of the former include studies of differences in cognitive style (Ramírez, and Castañeda, 1974; Shade, 1982), communication style (Gumperz, 1981; Kochman, 1982), interaction style (Erickson and Mohatt, 1982), learning style (Boykin, 1980; Philips, 1983, 1972), and parental teaching style (Laosa, 1982); (3) bearers of secondary cultural differences are reluctant to accept or learn certain features of dominant group culture as well as some behavioral norms and assumptions and practices in the institutions like the schools controlled by the dominant group. That is, they are reluctant to cross cultural boundaries; (4) in school, bearers of secondary cultural differences may refuse not only to cross cultural boundaries, but also to organize themselves in opposition against the teacher (Foster, 1974; Philips, 1972, 1983). Finally, those individuals who try to cross cultural boundaries may experience both affective dissonance or social identity crisis and negative peer pressures to conform (Petroni, 1970; Philips, 1983; Wax, 1971; Wax, 1970).

The difference between the distinctive cultural features of the immigrants and those of caste-like minorities is traceable to the difference in the history of the relationships between each type of minority and the dominant group. The two types of cultural differences and discontinuities have different educational implications. Primary cultural differences permit the immigrants to cross cultural boundaries without much affective dissonance. Hence, the immigrants can alternate between school required behaviors and the normative behaviors of the immigrants' community. Immigrants experience some problems in learning the dominant-group or school way of behaving, but the difficulties are of a temporary nature. Secondary cultural differences do not encourage their bearers to cross cultural boundaries. Learning the standard behaviors of the school and the school attitudes is not clearly distinguished by them from linear acculturation or assimilation into the dominant group culture. Therefore, caste-like minorities tend to experience affective dissonance in school learning.

The linear acculturation model assumes that it is not possible or appropriate or both to participate in the culture of the dominant group (or school culture) and in the culture of the minorities by the same individual. This is either because the schools have been designed by Anglos to teach the culture and language of Anglos to the minorities so that the latter are deprived of their own culture, language, and identity or because one inevitably loses one's culture, language, and identity by going to school that is based on the culture, language, and identity of others. The linear acculturation model of schooling is bound up with the idea of replacement of minority culture, language, and identity, hence, with the idea of conflict (Lebra, 1972). Given the oppositional identity and oppositional cultural frame of reference that caste-like minorities maintain, the linear acculturation model of schooling is problematic for them. Thus, there appears to be conscious and unconscious opposition or ambivalence toward school learning as "acting white." The dilemma for caste-like minority students is that the individual has to *choose* between behaving in a way that promotes academic success ("acting white") and behaving in a way considered appropriate for a good member of his or her group. That is, unlike the immigrants, caste-like minorities do not appear to make a clear distinction between those behaviors that result in academic success and school credentials for employment and other material benefits and those behaviors that result in the replacement of the minority culture and identity with Anglo culture and identity to linear acculturation. The two case studies that follow--Chinese-Americans and Mexican-Americans--will illustrate the differences between immigrant minorities and caste-like minorities and their consequences for school performance.

PART TWO

CASE STUDIES

In preface to these two case studies, we call attention to our earlier presentation of a typology of minority groups and the application of this typology to various minority groups in the United States. We wish to underscore the fact that both the Mexican-descent and Chinese-descent populations in the United States are large and extremely diverse. As a result, in applying the typology to the Mexican-American and Chinese-American populations, it is important to remember that not all members of either group can be categorized as caste-like or immigrant, nor would all members of either group identify with the caste-like or immigrant orientation. Within these populations is a range of sociocultural forces at play in dynamic interaction, yielding a variety of psychological, emotional, and cultural adaptations to life in the United States.

CHINESE-AMERICANS:
AN IMMIGRANT LANGUAGE MINORITY GROUP

Historical Background

Chinese immigrants began to arrive in the United States about 1847 and reached a total of 105,465 by 1880 (United States Department of Commerce, 1970). The immigrants were made up of three distinct groups: *laborers* who came to work in gold mines or do other labor on the west coast (some later tried to become farmers); *merchants and shopkeepers* who settled primarily in San Francisco and neighboring cities like Oakland (ARC Associates, 1982; Guthrie, 1983) and Stockton (Litherland, 1978); and *temporary visitors,* including state officials, teachers, and students.

Anti-Chinese sentiments, especially among Anglo workers, who were experiencing difficulties because of bad economic conditions, and various attempts to limit Chinese immigration and rights in California, culminated in the passage of federal exclusion laws beginning in 1882. These laws did not stop Chinese immigration entirely, however, because of data indicate that up to 1943, when the exclusion laws were repealed, some Chinese continued to arrive in the United States almost every year

(Sung, 1967). Beginning in 1944, the Chinese were allotted an immigration yearly quota of 105; this number increased when the passage of the War Brides' Act of 1946 permitted the Chinese to bring their wives from China. Later, immigration laws, like the Displaced Persons Act of 1948 and the Immigration and Nationality Act of 1952 further increased the number of Chinese immigrants. However, the immigration of 1944 to 1965 was selective, favoring the most highly educated, professional, and technically skilled Chinese. It was stipulated in the 1944 law, for example, that 50 percent of the Chinese annual quota had to be people with higher education technical training, specialized experience, or exceptional ability *as determined by the Attorney General of the United States.*

The number of Chinese immigrants has increased and their composition changed dramatically since Congress passed a more liberal immigration law in 1964 (Sung, 1967). The amendment of the Immigration and Naturalization Act in 1964 gave annual quotas of 20,000 immigrants for each country and a total annual quota of 170,000 immigrants for Asian countries. This liberalization of the immigration law has led to an influx of new Chinese immigrants with little or no ties to older immigrants; also, the new immigrants do not readily fit into established Chinese-American community social organization. Further, it is reported that many of the new immigrants do not speak English and are not well trained. Those that are trained have difficulty using their skills due to a lack of English proficiency and familiarity with the American cultural context (ARC Associates, 1982; Sung, 1975). It was also reported that the new immigrants have brought to Chinese-American communities new vitality.

Exploitation by the Dominant Group

Anglos have subjected Chinese immigrants to instrumental and expressive exploitations from the initial arrival of the Chinese. Anglos generally looked down upon the earlier immigrants as inferior people. In some states, intermarriage between Anglos and Chinese was illegal; where intermarriage was permitted, the offsprings of such unions were usually defined as Chinese, accorded the same inferior status given to their Chinese parents, and made to affiliate with the Chinese community (Sung, 1967). This can be seen from the refusal of San Francisco Board of Education to allow a 10-year-old girl to enroll in the city's public schools because one of her parents was Chinese (Melendy, 1972). Chinese immigrants were also residentially segregated in San Francisco (Coolidge, 1969), Oakland (ARC Associates, 1982; Guthrie, 1983),

Stockton (Litherland, 1978), and other California cities. One result of the residential segregation was the formation of "chinatowns," which followed the same process that produced Black ghettos in American cities.

The Chinese faced a job ceiling throughout California and in various sectors of the economy. In general, the early immigrants were relegated to such menial jobs as miners, cooks, laundry workers, and domestic servants. They were paid wages lower than were given to Anglos doing comparable work. Those who attempted to become farmers or branch into occupations considered in the Anglo domain met with opposition (ARC Associates, 1982; Litherland, 1978). The job ceiling against the Chinese is well illustrated by the research conducted in Oakland by ARC Associates. In Oakland, Chinese merchants and shopkeepers suffered from restrictive competition. For example, Anglo businesses organized a Merchant Exchange and Free Market in 1878 to lobby for a city ordinance to bar peddling and to persuade local residents not to patronize Chinese shops. Furthermore, until World War II, educated Chinese had little prospect for employment in positions commensurate with their education and ability throughout the United States, nor did they expect good wages if employed. Consequently, earlier Chinese immigrants (up to World War II) received very few rewards in America for their educational efforts (Chiu, 1967; Coolidge, 1969; Sung, 1967).

Anglo treatment of the Chinese began to change during World War II. Chinese immigrants were angered by Japan's invasion of northern China in 1937. During World War II, some trained as pilots and mechanics and volunteered with China or the United States to fight against Japan. As for Anglos, their perceptions of the Chinese began to change after Japan attacked Pearl Harbor in 1941 and China and the United States came to fight on the same side of the war. They then redirected their anti-Asian sentiments toward the Japanese and came to view the Chinese as "faithful allies, heroic fighters, and tragic victims" (Lyman, 1970, p. 124). With the new image of the Chinese, the earlier exclusion laws were repealed in 1943. Furthermore, the Chinese in the United States became more employable because of their new image and the shortage of workers during and after the war. Anglo employers began to hire Chinese-Americans for high-level jobs, thus raising the job ceiling against them. This resulted in the growth of the proportion of the Chinese professional workers from 2.9 percent in 1940, to 18 percent in 1960, to 26 percent in 1970 (Sung, 1975). Other barriers against the Chinese also began to relax. For example, real estate agents started to sell homes outside chinatowns to Chinese-Americans and in predominantly white areas. This led to residential dispersion. However, the residential dispersion has affected mainly professional American-born Chinese and immigrants who can afford to buy homes in the suburbs; a large segment of the Chinese still reside in crowded chinatowns because they cannot afford to move out. The latter includes particularly the new immigrants who lack capital to open up businesses or buy homes outside chinatowns.

Chinese-American School Performance

Chinese immigrants have achieved a high degree of academic success in America even though, as described above, they have faced a job ceiling and other barriers; have been subjected to segregated and inferior education; and have language, cultural, and learning styles that are very different from the language, culture, and learning styles of American public schools. We will return to the issues of language and cultural differences later.

What is the evidence that substantiates that Chinese-Americans are successful in school? We may begin to demonstrate this with Ogbu's study in Stockton, California (Ogbu, 1974), in which he found that Chinese students did better than Black, Mexican-American, and Anglo students in the same junior and senior high schools. This is true when he compared the groups in terms of grades received for classroom work or on the results of the state-mandated tests in reading and math.

The academic success of Chinese students in the public schools can also be seen in their disproportionate representation at Lowell, a college preparatory high school in San Francisco that draws its students from the city's public junior high schools. The Chinese are a small proportion of the total public school population in San Francisco, but they made up 25 percent of Lowell's students in 1965, 35.8 percent in 1972, and about 50 percent in 1976 (Ow, 1976). A high proportion of Chinese-American students go on to college and earn college degrees. Thus, in 1960 about 16.7 percent of Chinese males (compared to 8.0 percent of Anglo and 2.2 percent of Black males) had completed four or more years of college. Among the females, the comparable figures were 12.3 percent, 5.3 percent, and 2.8 percent, respectively (Sung, 1967). The figures for completion of four or more years of college, according to a 1970 census, are 25 percent for Chinese males and 15 percent for Chinese females (United States Department of Commerce, 1970).

Conventional Explanations of Chinese Immigrants' School Success

Why are Chinese immigrants, a language minority group, academically successful? Two kinds of conventional explanations have usually been offered. One is that the Chinese brought a cultural tradition to America that stresses respect for learning and value for education as a means to achieve self-advancement. Sung (1967) says, for example, that the "Chinese respect for learning and for scholars is a cultural heritage" (pp. 124-125). She goes on to argue that "even when a college degree led to no more than a waiter's job [in America], the Chinese continued to pursue the best education they could get, so that when the opportunities developed, the Chinese were qualified and capable of handling the job" (pp. 124-125). This *cultural value explanation* is only true to some extent. The trouble with it is that it does not distinguish between the values and behaviors of Chinese peasants and those of higher classes. Earlier Chinese peasant immigrant children and nonpeasant children were successful in school. However, in China itself at the time (and now), the children of the peasants were not necessarily successful in school. We have no reliable study on Chinese peasant educational attitudes and values *in* China prior to World War II, but we do have some information about the relative illiteracy rates. Pepper (1970) stated that it was estimated in the 1930s that about 84 percent of the rural population of China could not pass very simple literacy tests. Approximately 69.3 percent of the males among the peasants and 98.7 percent of the females surveyed in all regions of China in the late 1930s were illiterate. According to Snow (1961) in northwest China, almost no one, except a few landlords, merchants, and officials could read before the arrival of the communists. The illiteracy rate was about 95 percent. Most earlier immigrants who came as laborers were illiterate peasants. The point to stress, however, is that if the children of the sojourners did so well in American schools, why did their peers in China continue to be illiterate?

The second conventional explanation may be called the *family influence hypothesis;* it takes two forms. One version argues that the moral obligation to support aging parents acts as an incentive to succeed in school and later in one's job. Specifically, there is a reciprocal obligatory relationship between parents and children that promotes school success. Chinese parents are said to support and encourage their children to grow up as successful adults who would support them in old age. Children have a moral obligation to repay their parents' sacrifices by being successful and supporting them in old age. Chinese immigrants are said to bring this cultural practice to America where parents make all kinds of sacrifices to educate their children and bring them up as successful adults. Children reciprocate by working hard in school in order to succeed academically, obtain good employment, and earn good wages to fulfill their filial obligations.

The other version of this family influence hypothesis is that the Chinese family has an authority structure, especially in parent-child relationships, similar to that of teacher-pupil relationships in the public schools. The family authority pattern leads to the socialization of Chinese children into submission, obedience, and respect for elders and other people in authority. The attitudes, values, and behavior learned by Chinese children in the home are later transferred to their relationship with teachers and other school personnel. The latter, in turn, reward the children with good grades not only for their academic efforts but also for their good behavior, obedience, and responsibility (Coolidge, 1969; Fong, 1973; Tow, 1923).

Ogbu (1983) has pointed out that the family influence hypothesis, while plausible, is not sufficient to explain the academic success of Chinese-Americans. The hypothesis, for example, does not account for the failure of children of the peasants to succeed in school in China like their counterparts in America. It is true that the immigrants' experiences in a socialization process that stresses submission, obedience, and respect for authority helps them behave well as defined by school personnel and thus achieve positive stereotypes that may enhance their school success. It has been long and well-documented that teachers generally see Chinese students as well-behaved, intelligent, and hardworking. Teachers and counselors are said to convey these perceptions and expectations to the students in several ways. The students, in turn, respond by trying to conform to the model student role to get good grades, according to Sue and Kitano (1973). Chinese students have been reported from the early days to achieve this positive and functional academic identity (Coolidge, 1969; Fong, 1973; Sue and Kitano, 1973; Tow, 1923).

Considered together, the cultural value and family influence hypotheses suggest that the Chinese immigrants are successful in American schools because their culture is compatible with the culture of the school. However, this would ignore other important considerations. For example, as we have mentioned, other immigrant groups like the Punjabis, behave at school more or less like the Chinese even though they may not have family structure or socialization patterns that are similar to the Chinese. They behave the way they do at school because they have deliberately decided that such behaviors are necessary for them

to do well in school. Moreover, language differences and Chinese traditional learning style can conceivably be seen as a serious threat to the immigrants' school success.   Chinese language is quite different from
English so that Chinese students may have difficulty mastering English.
An informal study by a student of one of the authors shows that at the
University of California, Berkeley, Chinese students are overrepresented
in remedial English programs (Ino, 1982). The language differences have
not prevented the Chinese immigrants from doing well in school. With
regard to learning style, we should point out that Chinese immigrants
came with a traditional learning style quite different from the learning
style emphasized by American schools. For example, the Chinese traditional style emphasizes external forms and rote memorization, rather
than observation, analysis, and comprehension. However, this, too, has
not prevented the immigrants' children from succeeding academically in
American schools. Finally, the authority structure of the Chinese family
described earlier does not promote qualities like independence and
autonomy that Western psychologists suggest are beneficial for developing achievement motivation which, in turn, promotes academic success
(McClelland, 1961; Rosen, 1969; Katz, 1967). We conclude that the
Chinese school success, like the school success of other immigrant
minorities, does not depend necessarily on cultural and language compatibility. Rather, it depends more on how the immigrants perceive and
respond to schooling in relation to their perceptions of opportunity
structure. It also depends on the willingness and ability of the immigrants to modify their culture and language in order to learn and practice the behaviors that enhance school success.

The Chinese Immigrants' Perceptions and Responses

   Our main argument is that because Chinese immigrants came more or
less to America voluntarily to seek means, including their children's
education, to enhance their status "back home" in their country of
origin, or (in the case of more recent immigrants) in America, they have
generally adopted attitudes and behaviors that enable them to overcome
language, cultural, and institutional barriers to the extent within their
capabilities in order to achieve their objectives. These attitudes and
behaviors are both manifested in adult behavior and impressed on
children with respect to their school work.

   As we indicated earlier, it is partly because of the overriding goal of
advancement and partly because the immigrants' culture, identity, and
language are not a part of an oppositional system, that the immigrants

tend to adopt what is essentially *an alternation model of schooling*. Chinese immigrants distinguish clearly between how they ought to behave in order to do well in school and obtain school credentials for employment and other material benefits from how one behaves in order to assimilate into the Anglo culture. Therefore, they are not afraid to adopt the instrumental behavior that "works" for the Anglo middle class, i.e., Anglo instrumental behavior that leads to school success and other benefits; they do not perceive behaving like Anglos in this respect as necessarily replacing their own culture, language, or identity. We wish now to describe some of the Chinese immigrants' perceptions and responses and the reasons behind them in order to show how they influence the academic attitudes and behaviors of the immigrants.

1. *Self-advancement as a primary goal objective.* To understand why Chinese immigrants responded to job ceiling and other barriers the way they did and why they perceived and responded to schooling the way they did, it is necessary to understand *why* they came to America. The main objective of the immigrants was at first to make money with which to return to China to improve their status there, as defined by Chinese culture. The laborers, for example, came to make money with which to buy land upon return, a traditional strategy for gaining entry into the gentry class (Sung, 1967). They also intended to use some of the money to build a family house, provide a dowry for a daughter's marriage, or arrange a suitable marriage for a son (Shibutani and Kwan, 1965). There is some evidence that the immigrants intended to return to China. For example, they were mostly single males or husbands who left their families in China; they used members of their families as collateral for passage money advanced by Chinese merchants; they explicitly said they were sojourners; and before the Communist takeover of mainland China, they had their bones sent back to China for burial if they died in America (Barth, 1964; Lyman, 1970; McCleod, 1947; Shibutani and Kwan, 1965; Sung, 1967). United States government records show that many re-emigrated *before* and *after* the passage of the Exclusion Acts of 1882 (Sung, 1967). Immigrants since World War II, of course, have come to seek advancement in the United States.

2. *Rejection of invidious distinctions made by Anglos.* Because earlier immigrants were sojourners, they did not define their status like Anglos did, and they reacted to discrimination and prejudice differently than Blacks and other caste-like minorities. Although the immigrants were relegated to largely menial jobs, denied political rights, and segregated in chinatown ghettos, they did not accept these as indicators of their racial

or cultural inferiority, nor did they define themselves by the kinds of jobs they performed or the place they lived, both of which they regarded as temporary. They did their menial jobs well and set up language schools beginning in 1886, with the help of the Imperial Government of China. One major purpose of the language school was to teach their children Chinese language, history, civilization, and important contributions they believed China had made to the world. In so doing, the immigrants were able to counteract the assertions by Anglos about Chinese inferiority and to reinforce their identity.

3. *The immigrants' response to prejudice and discrimination.* Chinese immigrants did not eschew entirely prejudice and discrimination against them. For example, it is reported that when a discriminatory ordinance was passed in Oakland in 1889, designed to close down laundries owned by the Chinese, the latter went to court, which ruled in their favor (ARC Associates, 1982). However, in general, the immigrants were not actively concerned about improving their "civil rights." They shared the attitudes already described for the Punjabis in Valleyside who expected some loss of civil rights because they are aliens. In the case of the Chinese, Shibutani and Kwan (1965) report that "before the Communist Revolution a Chinese sojourner was not concerned with civil rights; he took it for granted that he was an alien and did not consider the possibility of gaining equal status [with Anglos]" (p. 517). The immigrants were pragmatic and accommodative in civil rights matters, housing, and employment because their main objective was to accumulate resources to take back to China where they would seek advancement in status and better treatment.

4. *The reference group of the immigrants was located in China, not middle-class America.* Another reason the immigrants were not concerned about "civil rights" is that they did not come to America to seek equal status or equal treatment with Anglos; they did not try to compete for status with them. Rather, they sought to be able to do those things that demonstrated successes in their own country, such as being able to buy land to enter the gentry class, obtaining education in America to enter civil service in China, and so on. We have already cited Shibutani and Kwan (1965) who report that the immigrants found that they had made progress beyond their peers back home. For contemporary immigrants and refugees, the reference group still consists of peers "back home," but the goal is self-advancement in America where they have come to stay more or less permanently.

5. *Alternative opportunities to benefit from American education.* We mentioned earlier that until World War II, there was a great deal of employment discrimination against educated Chinese Americans. Sung (1967) reports, for example, that the Second Californian Constitutional Convention of 1879 specifically forbade all corporations in the state to employ Chinese and that Stanford University placement service report of 1928 stated that it was almost impossible for a first- or second-generation Chinese or Japanese to find any jobs in the engineering, manufacturing, or business fields.

Chinese immigrants were not discouraged from pursuing academic success by this situation. This was partly because of increasing use of Western-type education for civil service examination and for political and economic advancement in China. American education made these new opportunities accessible and the opportunities made American education more and more attractive. The incentive to succeed in obtaining American education for status advancement in China was particularly strong before the repeal of the exclusion laws of 1943. Not ony did educated Chinese return to China where they were more fully rewarded for their American education, but also many immigrants came to America because they wanted to provide their children with the opportunity of obtaining American education for positions in China. As Sung (1967) explains:

> *Though his own life in the United Sates was wretched, he [the immigrant] had hopes for the future. If by "serving a term" in the United States he could save enough money to buy several parcels of land in China, he could raise himself to the gentry class. His sons would have a chance to get an education that would open doors to other opportunities. If his sons were in this country, they were urged and prodded into getting as much education as possible, for though the occupational outlook for them was bleak, they could always go back to China to practice as doctors, engineers and scientists. (p. 240)*

There are no statistics about the number of Chinese-American doctors, engineers, and scientists who returned to China because of employment barriers in the United States or for other reasons. We do know that American education was highly valued in China during that period. One indirect evidence of the value of American education is that the immigrants remitted large sums of money to be used to build American-type schools in their homeland. We learned, for example, that through such remittance the immigrants had made the Toishan district, from which most of the immigrants came, one of the most educationally endowed by 1940: It had, by that time, 7 high schools, 2 normal schools, 2 trade schools, 167 consolidated schools, and 824 grade schools (Sung, 1967). Educated Chinese-Americans who did not return to China and did not find employment in the wider society, took the only other alternative route--withdrawal into the Chinese-American business sector--self- or family employment in a laundry, restaurant, or grocery store (Sung, 1967).

6. *Diplomatic influences on opportunity structure and schooling.* Changes in the United States-China relations, beginning during World War II, expanded employment opportunities and lowered other barriers for educated and other Chinese-Americans. Changes in the diplomatic relations between the two countries, which we reported earlier, coupled with shortage of skilled manpower in the United States during and after the war, raised the job ceiling for high-level professional and technically trained Chinese. This resulted in the increase in the proportion of Chinese-Americans in such job categories from 2.9 percent in 1940 to 26 percent in 1970. This kind of change, no doubt, encouraged the immigrants not only to work hard for possible rewards outside the United States but also for achieving new opportunities in America.

Opportunity Structure, Alternation Model, and High Academic Effort Syndrome

People work hard and do well in school because they see a connection between school success and success in getting jobs, good wages, and other societal benefits. When such an experience is widespread and long enough, members of a society or social group develop cultural beliefs and practices that support school academic success of children. Immigrants and others who are not brought up in such a cultural situation *can* learn to behave in a way that helps them succeed, however, *provided* they think that they will be rewarded with jobs, wages, and other societal benefits in their host society or outside it. The latter was initially the case of Chinese immigrants but, of course, opportunities for jobs, wages, and other societal benefits of education also began to open up as a result of the World War II period. The immigrants have generally believed that American education offered a good opportunity to advance their status. As one Chinese student reported in a class project (Ong, 1976):

The immigrants viewed free public education of their children as the hope of the future. Education became the chief means to raise their economic status and social conditions and to get out of Chinatown ghetto. The Chinese were motivated to use education to advance themselves. (p. 8)

She then went on to add, "As a matter of fact, one of the major reasons for immigration was the quest for a better life for their children through American free public education." Consequently, these immigrants tend to exert considerable pressures on their children *to study hard and succeed in school according to Anglo middle-class criteria or standards of school success.*

The extent to which the academic behavior of Chinese students and other immigrant groups are based on pragmatism can be seen from the result of a survey of Asian students at the University of California, Berkeley in the mid-1970s (Ong, 1976). The survey found that these students were under considerable pressures from their parents to do well in school for the same reasons that earlier Chinese immigrants wanted their children to succeed. Four reasons are most frequently given by the students for attending college: to make money, to get a better job (than their parents have), because it is difficult to find menial jobs, and because other avenues for advancement (in the United States) are closed to Asians (Ong, 1976). This pragmatic attitude extends also to fields of study in college. A number of Chinese informants have told one of the authors that the disproportionate representation of Chinese students in science and mathematic fields is a kind of insurance against employment discrimination. They point out that even if an Anglo employer is prejudiced against Chinese, the one with the technical skills will be hired. The disproportionate representation is borne out in three surveys of major fields of studies of Chinese students at Berkeley (Ow, 1976). In one survey, it was found that between 1961 and 1968, about 74.3 percent of the males enrolled were majoring in engineering and physical sciences. In another survey in 1971, some 75 percent of the males were in engineering, physical, and biological sciences. Still a third survey in 1976 found that among the males, 73.6 percent (and among the females, 53.1 percent) were in the same three fields--engineering, physical, and biological sciences (Ow, 1976).

It is this pragmatic attitude of the immigrants that enables them to develop an alternative model of schooling. By making a clear distinction between those Anglo middle-class or school behaviors that facilitate academic success and others not essential for academic success, they are able to conform to school rules of behavior for achievement without cultural and identity conflicts. For the same reason they are able to over-come barriers arising from cultural and language differences through in-vestment of efforts necessary to learn the "alien" cultural, communica-tion, and behavioral repertoires essential for school success and to avoid fields that are either impossible to overcome the barriers or not very pro-fitable in terms of employment prospects.

MEXICAN-AMERICANS:
A NONIMMIGRANT LANGUAGE MINORITY GROUP

Historical Background

Mexican-Americans did not initially become a minority group in the United States through voluntary immigration, but by conquest. They were in what is now the southwestern United States for about 150 years before the "Anglos" arrived, conquered, and annexed their territory--acts completed by the Treaty of Guadalupe Hidalgo in 1848 (Acuña, 1981; Knowlton, 1975; Weber, 1973). In addition to the conquered Mex-icans, others have immigrated both legally and illegally from Mexico into the Southwest and Midwest, particularly since the first decade of the twentieth century.

Given the interdependence of the United States and Mexican economies, as well as the stresses of poverty, hunger, and uneven development in Mexico, migration from Mexico is a national United States phenomenon, manifesting differing patterns over time (Mines, 1981). Earlier immigrants were young males with relatively little school-ing and low skills and tended to be concentrated in low-grade jobs. In re-cent decades, immigrants have included many women and children as well as people with more schooling and higher skills. Moreover, evolving migratory tendencies reflect binational kinship networks operating in Mexican village communities which have become migrant-dependent. These migratory networks function to locate settlers in the Southwest, although some migrate to the Midwest and the east coast (Dinerman, 1982; Mines, 1981; West and Macklin, 1979).

Technically, the people who have come from Mexico since the annexa-tion to work or settle in the United States are immigrants. During the first generation, Mexican immigrants tended to behave like immigrants from other countries (Zarrugh, 1979), although the interdependence of the United States and Mexican economies and the geographical propin-quity that stimulates migration indicate that there are significant differences in the options exercised by Mexican immigrants. However, the immigrants from Mexico are identified with and treated like native Mexican-Americans and in the course of time, come to identify with the latter and think of themselves and their descendants as Mexican-Americans (Mines, 1981). In this way, they, too, become incorporated into the Anglo Mexican-American caste system.

Exploitation by the Dominant Group

Like the Chinese immigrants, Mexican-Americans in the Southwest have suffered both expressive and instrumental exploitation. Mexican-Americans were generally regarded by Anglos as offspring of mixed matings between the Spaniards and Indians or between Spaniards and Blacks. They were, therefore, not really "white" but "colored" and "inferior" people (DeLeon, 1983). This belief that Mexican-Americans were biologically inferior to Anglos has persisted into the twentieth century. Later, the basis of Mexican-American inferiority has shifted and has now become mostly cultural (Carter, 1970; Grebler *et al.,* 1970). However, whether Anglo caste thinking is based on biological or cultural considerations, the essence is that Mexican-Americans are inferior to Anglos. As Simmons (1971) points out on the basis of this study in Border City: "Despite variations, the Anglo Americans' principal assumptions and expectations emphasize the Mexicans' presumed inferiority. In its most characteristic patterns, such inferiority is held to be self-evident" (p. 62).

Anglo stereotypes reflect an attitude that Mexican culture, as derivative of an "uncivilized" Indian past, was so dissimilar from Anglo culture that assimilation was virtually impossible and that because of this, Mexicans faced difficulties that were of their own making. Such notions continue to this day and are a prominent feature of popular culture, as well as in the social science literature that describes Mexicans as disadvantaged because of their presumed passivity, inability to delay gratification, indolence, present-time orientation, and poor self-esteem (Carter and Segura, 1979).

Scapegoating, as a manifestation of expressive exploitation, is a recurring phenomenon in the Mexican experience in the United States, especially with respect to Mexican immigration. During periodic cycles of economic retrenchment and the failure of United States economic enterprise and governmental strategies to ameliorate these conditions, Mexican workers have been blamed for high unemployment, low wages, increasing crime, disease, and high welfare costs. During times of economic crises, the news media highlighted stories of the "silent invasion" (Rios-Bustamante, 1981). The Immigration and Naturalization Service issues monthly statistics regarding arrests and deportations, linking its estimates of undocumented residents in the United States with unemployment figures. City and county health care authorities often decry the drain on local funding created by undocumented Mexicans (Cornelius and Montoya, 1983; Mines, 1981; Rios-Bustamante, 1981).

The exploitation of Mexican-Americans has included unequal access to housing, education, political power, and economic resources and rewards (Acuña, 1981; Almaguer, 1975; Barrera, 1979; Grebler *et al.*, 1970; Griswold del Castillo, 1979; Romo, 1983; Stoddard, 1973) based upon a sharply segmented dual labor force that has been organized along racial lines into primary and secondary segments.

The displacement of Mexican-Americans from economic power began with the appropriation of their land holdings after the annexation (Acuña, 1981; Barrera, 1979; Estrada *et al.*, 1981). The Treaty of Guadalupe Hidalgo, which formally transferred the Southwest to the United States, recognized the legitimacy of the land grant rights acquired by Mexican-Americans under previous Spanish and Mexican rulers. However, the office of the United States Surveyor General subsequently rejected the legal status of the land grants and this caused both groups and individuals to lose their land holdings (Acuña, 1981; Barrera, 1979; Grebler *et al.*, 1970; Knowlton, 1975; Rosenbaum, 1981). With the loss of the land holdings and other economic assets, most Mexican-Americans were relegated to the status of wage laborers under a job ceiling (Barrera, 1979; Camarillo, 1979; Griswold del Castillo, 1979; Romo, 1983).

Both Blair (1971, 1972) and Schmidt (1970) have studied the job ceiling against Mexican-Americans, at least through the period of the 1960s. Blair studied the phenomenon in Santa Clara County in California; Schmidt's study covered the entire Southwest. Schmidt found clear evidence of a job ceiling against minorities in general and against Mexican-Americans in particular. He found that the exclusion of Mexican-Americans and other minorities from more desirable white-collar jobs was not due to lack of qualifications and further noted that Mexican-Americans were overrepresented in the operative jobs, especially in the less desirable operative jobs.

Blair's study of the job ceiling against Mexican-Americans in Santa Clara County, California, is even more pertinent because he analyzed the relationship among education, jobs, and earnings in terms of investment of resources and efforts. Since the 1960s, economists and policy makers have argued (see Dore, 1976; Harrison, 1972; Weisbrod, 1975) that a disproportionate number of minorities like Blacks, Mexican-Americans, Native Americans, and Puerto Ricans are poor because they do not have adequate education to enable them to get more desirable jobs with better wages. Consequently, social policy has been directed toward providing these minorities with more education. According to this economic theory of human capital, education or schooling is an investment that is expected to yield reasonable returns in terms of jobs and wages (Becker, 1964; Blair, 1972; Dore, 1976).

Blair (1971) asked if this human capital model applied to all segments of American society, specifically to minorities like Mexican-Americans. He found that in Santa Clara County, Anglos and Mexican-Americans did not get equal jobs or equal pay for similar educational attainment. The gap in earning was greater when Anglos and Mexican-Americans obtained high school diplomas or college degrees than when they dropped out of high school or dropped out of college before getting diplomas or degrees. The wage differential between Anglos and Mexican-Americans with similar education was about $800 a year if both lived in the barrio, and about $1,713 a year if they lived in the suburb. Blair called this wage differential a "schooling penalty" for Mexican-Americans (i.e., a type of fine paid by a Mexican-American for staying in school longer to obtain a high school diploma or a college degree). He also found that the schooling penalty was greater for younger Mexican-Americans than for older members of the group. These findings led Blair to suggest that Mexican-Americans youths probably realized, albeit unconsciously, that continuing their education or graduating from high school or from college brought them little reward compared with their Anglo peers; consequently, they frequently dropped out of school (Ogbu, 1978).

Since the mid-1960s, the pattern of employment and earning opportunities has improved for some segments of the Mexican-American population, especially for the more educated, because of deliberate government policy and encouragement given to private businesses, backed by legislation. We note in this connection the role played by affirmative action in the public and private sectors. The opportunity structure for Mexican-Americans has probably also improved because of demographic changes. Barrera (1979) noted that there has been a steady percentage gain in the representation of Mexican-Americans in the professional and technical fields since 1930. However, these changes have favored mainly college-educated Mexican-Americans; among the latter, for example, the linkage between school credentials on the one hand and jobs and earnings on the other is probably now more similar to the linkage found among Anglos. For the Mexican-American masses and for similar segments of other caste-like minorities, such changes in job and earning opportunities have not yet occurred. As Barrera (1979) argued, the segmentation line has become weaker over time for a certain segment of the Mexican-American population, but not for the majority of the group that remains stratified at the bottom of the occupation structure. For them, there has been no affirmative action or other comparable programs (Ogbu, 1983), and they continue to face a job ceiling (Poston *et al.,* 1976; Santos, 1977). The job ceiling and other instrumental barriers against Mexican-Americans are ultimately a significant source of the sociocultural factors that cause their persistent disproportionately poor academic performance.

Mexican-American School Performance

Although Chinese-Americans faced a job ceiling and other instrumental barriers, they have been quite successful in school. A contrasting situation exists among Mexican-Americans. Their disproportionate and persistent academic failure and the academic gap between them and Anglos has been documented by several researchers. (See Carter, 1970; Carter and Segura, 1979; Coleman, 1966; Grebler *et al.,* 1970; Ogbu, 1975, 1978, 1984b; United States Commission on Civil Rights, 1971a, 1971b, 1972a, 1972b, 1973, 1974; The Achievement Council, 1984; Brown *et al.,* 1980.) Carter (1970) reported that Mexican-Americans attending the same schools as Anglos have a lower grade point average, and the gap between the two groups widens as they progress through school. Ogbu (1974) found a similar pattern in Stockton. Mexican-American students do less well when their performance in specific subject areas such as a language arts, science, and math is considered. Mexican-American children are said to begin school doing as well as Anglo children; but by the third or fourth grade, their school performance begins to diverge increasingly. Many do not complete the twelfth grade. By the fourth and fifth grade, many Mexican-Americans become psychological drop-outs, appearing to withdraw mentally from school. This withdrawal is characterized by boredom, failure to work, inattentiveness, and behavior problems (Carter and Segura, 1979). Those few Mexican-Americans who manage to reach the last years of high school are indeed similar to Anglos; the low achievers in the group have long since departed (Carter and Segura, 1979).

In spite of various efforts to close the academic gap through various programs (e.g., bilingual education, compensatory education, etc.), there is evidence that the academic gap is not narrowing. According to a report by the Achievement Council (1984), Mexican-American students are likely to lag behind Anglo students in virtually all subject areas at all grade levels, as measured by the *California Test of Basic Skills;* the gap also widens as students progress through school. Moreover, elementary schools with high proportions of Black, Hispanic, or poor students consistently perform at the bottom of the achievement distribution as measured by the California Assessment Program Survey of Basic Skills. The average percentile rank for elementary schools with more than 70 percent Hispanic students was below 20 for all CAP tests, except for one category for grades 3 and 6, in the 1982-1983 tests.

Conventional Explanation of Mexican-Americans' School Failure

Conventional explanations of the relative school failure of Mexican-American children include those emphasizing culture conflict (Ramírez, and Castañeda, 1974, cultural deprivation (Burma, 1970; Padilla, 1971), inadequate IQ (see DeAvila and Havassy, 1975 for review; United States Commission on Civil Rights, 1974), institutional barriers (Carter, 1970; Carter and Segura, 1979; United States Commission on Civil Rights, 1974), language conflicts (Gumperz and Hernandez-Chavez, 1972; United States Commission on Civil Rights, 1972a), and so on. Most of these explanations simply cannot withstand the test of cross-cultural comparisons (Ogbu, 1978). This is the case, for example, of the explanations based on language or cultural differences. While we recognize that these explanations may have some merit, we believe that none of them has paid sufficient attention to the contributions of sociocultural factors to the school failure of Mexican-American students.

Mexican-Americans' Perceptions and Responses to Caste-Like Forces that Influence Their School Performance

The way in which direct and indirect discriminatory educational practices of the dominant Anglo society have affected Mexican-American education has been described (see Carter, 1970; Carter and Segura, 1979; United States Commission on Civil Rights, 1971a, 1971b, 1972a, 1972b, 1974). We recognize the importance of these sociocultural factors (Ogbu, 1978), but we do not intend to deal with them here. Instead, we will consider *how the job ceiling and other forms of subordination shape Mexican-American perceptions of schooling, and how, in turn, these perceptions affect Mexican-American striving or effort to do well in school. An important part of our argument is that the school failure of*

Mexican-Americans, especially among the older children, is due, in part, to inadequate effort or low academic effort syndrome, resulting from sociocultural factors created by caste-like barriers.

We will show how the subordination and exploitation of Mexican-Americans produces certain sociocultural forces within the Mexican-American population which, in turn, affect the academic achievement of a *disproportionately large number* of Mexican-American children, *but by no means all.* First, we will show that Mexican-American experiences with the job ceiling and other opportunity barriers have generated certain folk models of self-advancement that influence their instrumental behaviors. Our second task is to show that the subordination and exploitation of Mexican-Americans led many of them to develop an ambivalent or oppositional identity and an ambivalent or oppositional cultural frame of reference, both of which make practicing certain "Anglo" behavior--including academic behaviors--problematic. Third, we will argue that under these developments, Mexican-American children acquire certain cultural beliefs, attitudes, competencies, and an identity that adversely affect their school efforts.

Job Ceiling, Secondary Cultural Differences, and Folk Theory of Success

Mexican-Americans have experienced a history of job ceiling and related barriers. From this experience, many within the group believe that they do not have the same opportunity to get ahead as Anglos do. They have responded to this perceived limitation of opportunity in a number of ways, including feelings of bitterness, frustration, resentment, and mistrust, and with various efforts to circumvent, raise, or eliminate the job ceiling.

Bitterness, frustration, resentment, and mistrust. It is not sufficient to show statistically that Mexican-Americans have faced a job ceiling or that they have discriminated against in employment and wages [as Blair (1972) and Schmidt (1970) did in the studies discussed earlier]; it is important that we also try to learn how Mexican-Americans *feel* about their experiences and respond to such experiences. It is equally important to ascertain the extent to which they are aware of their economic and political exploitation. We believe that their knowledge of their exploitation, and their understanding of how their subordination was developed and maintained, have led to bitterness, resentment, and distrust of Anglos. As Acuna pointed out (1981), the conquest of 1848 left a legacy of hate, which has exerted a powerful influence in shaping contemporary Mexican-American responses to their subordinated status in society.

Grebler *et al.* (1970) note that another consequence of the land dispossession and economic subjugation brought about by the conquest was "...widespread and lingering mistrust and suspicion of the new, dominant population by the indigenous settlers and their descendants" (pp. 50-51). Recent studies document cultural or ethnic knowledge of exploitation (Kanellos, 1979; Grebler *et al.,* 1970) and how it is reflected in the *corridos* (ballads) surviving from earlier times, which record the Mexicans' struggle against racism and injustice (Paredes, 1958).

In a study of Mexican-Americans in Los Angeles and San Antonio, Grebler *et al.* (1970) examine "directly the perceptions of discrimination or the 'problems' Mexican-Americans face in competition with Anglos" (p. 389). They found that "...more than half of the respondents in Los Angeles and an overwhelming majority in San Antonio felt that Mexican-Americans have to work harder, especially in politics" (p. 389).

Survival strategies. Survival strategies are mechanisms used by Mexican-Americans and similar minorities to circumvent, reduce, or eliminate economic, political, and other barriers against them; among the most common are passing, clientship, caste leakage, collective struggle, and deviant behavior.

1. *Passing.* Passing for Anglos is an instrumental response to the job ceiling and, therefore, related to opportunity barriers. It has been used by Mexican-Americans to achieve upward social mobility throughout their history in the United States (Acuña, 1981; Grebler *et al.,* 1970; Moraga, 1983; Nava, 1970; Rosenbaum, 1981; Stoddard, 1973; Vigil, 1980). Although Mexican-Americans are defined officially as "white," the population includes people who are "pure white," *Mestizos,* other "mixed bloods," and even "pure Indians" (Forbes, 1970; Nava, 1970; Ogbu, 1978). Forbes has suggested, therefore, that Mexican-Americans should be regarded as "a racial as well as a cultural minority, and [that] the racial differences which set them apart from Anglos cannot be made to disappear by the 'Americanization' process carried on in the schools" (p. 15).

Mexican-Americans have several ways of passing, including descent claims, change of ethnic identification, and personal name changes. The use of descent dates back to the second half of the nineteenth century. At that time, according to Acuña (1981), Rosenbaum (1981), and Stoddard (1973), *"Manitos"* or Hispanos with Indian ancestry, who became affluent with rewards from Anglos whom they helped to displace the original Hispano families, claimed "Spanish purity." With such claims came Anglos approval, and many became "Spanish" rather than "Mexican'' or ''Mexican-American'' if they had ''appropriate'' physical features like white skin. Grebler *et al.* (1970) state:

> *It is far from surprising, therefore, that upwardly mobile Mexican Americans should have called themselves "Spanish" in places where Mexican Americans were considered untouchable. As community studies (even of the recent past) unmistakably indicate, to be a Mexican was to be stigmatized. This assumption of "Spanish" identity made it possible to move from a stigmatized caste into a neutral position. This was a status jump that was totally impossible for Negroes....(p. 322)*

Although one can become ''Spanish'' and, therefore, raise one's status without changing one's name, as Grebler *et al.* (1970) suggest, some elect to pass by actually changing their personal surnames. Vigil (1980) said that many Mexican-Americans have changed their names in order to make it into the Anglo middle-class world. For example, a person might change his or her surname from Martínez to Martin, Ramírez to Raymer, Valenzuela to Valen, or Flores to Flowers.

2. *Clientship.* Patron-client relationship, or clientship, is another strategy that Mexican-Americans have used to *circumvent* the job ceiling and related barriers. It dates back to the preconquest period in the form of peonage (Acuña, 1972; Gómez-Quiñones, 1982; Rubel, 1966; Rosenbaum, 1981; Vigil, 1980). In the economic sphere, the patron-client relationship survived into the American period and to some extent into contemporary urban environments.

Among Mexican-American farm workers, a patron-client relationship often exists between farm laborers and farm owners or between the laborers and labor contractors or labor supervisors. Mines' (1981) study on the development of permanent migrant settlement networks in the United States in the evolution of a community tradition of migration from Mexico shed some light on this kind of relationship, as did Kannellos' (1979) study of Mexican-American folk theater in the Midwest. Lipschultz (1974) described the docility and subservience of Mexican-American laborers in their relationship with Anglo patrons or employers in the early part of this century.

In small towns, generally, Mexican-Americans depended on Anglo go-betweens to secure services from the local government for their communities (Grebler *et al.,* 1970; Rosenbaum, 1981). In some communities, the Anglo go-between is replaced by a Mexican patron or boss (Mines, 1981). According to Grebler *et al.* (1970), "the patron usually owed his economic status to the local Anglo powers, and one of his functions was to enlist the Mexican-American voters on the right side" (pp. 556-557). This kind of rural *patronismo* has been carried over into urban centers like Fresno, San Jose, and Riverside in California, "where Mexican-American agricultural workers depend on ethnic bosses for work and favorable treatment by growers" (p. 557). A similar form of this patronage is described by Mines (1981) in his discussion of the binational kinship networks and how they function for Mexican migrants in the United States. According to Mines, for many Mexican migrants who become successful (i.e., are able to establish long-term, stable employment in the United States) in the United States, such kinship networks have replaced the labor contractor as the preeminent link for the migrant in locating employment, housing, and access to essential services while in the United States (Mines, 1981). Spicer (1975) has described another form of urban patronage; the patron are usually the more affluent members of the community--both Anglos and non-Anglo--who induce poor Mexican-Americans into a relationship that orients them to the direction of the cultural values of the patron. One of the authors has described elsewhere the influence of the clientship in local school politics (Ogbu, 1974; 1981a; see also Carter, 1970).

3. *Caste leakage.* Another strategy used by Mexican-Americans to circumvent the job ceiling after World War II was "caste leakage" (Grebler *et al.,* 1970; Moore, 1968). This occurred in the caste systems of small towns where there were very few middle-class positions within the Mexican-American communities. Instead of remaining to compete for the limited positions or resigning themselves to menial positions, the potentially upwardly mobile Mexican-American migrated to cities in the Midwest and California. This strategy did not alter the job ceiling or the caste system, but it enabled some individuals to circumvent the job ceiling and other barriers (Barrera, 1979) and to find better paying, more stable work.

4. *Collective struggle.* The concept of collective struggle includes those activities that Anglos legitimate as "civil rights" activities, but it also includes other activities not so legitimated, which, nevertheless, are used by minorities to increase their pool of jobs and other resources.

Students of Mexican-American history have observed that there was resistance to Anglo exploitation after the annexation of the Southwest (Acuña, 1981; Barrera, 1979; Estrada *et al.,* 1981; Hernandez, 1983;

Knowlton, 1975; Rosenbaum, 1981). For example, the social banditry of Tiburcio Vasquez and Joaquin Murietta in the nineteenth century in California, the revolt of *Las Gorras Blancas* (White Caps) in San Miguel County in New Mexico in the 1890s, the revolt of Juan Chema Cortina in Texas in 1860, the early *mutualistas* (voluntary associations), the labor organizing struggles in the 1920s and 1930s, and the efforts of the *Congreso de los Pueblos de Habla Español* in the 1930s, figure prominently in the history of Mexican-American collective struggle prior to World War II (Acuña, 1981; Barrera, 1979; Hernandez, 1983; Rosenbaum, 1981). These efforts were not particularly successful in making permanent or far-reaching changes, but they represent, nevertheless, very visible, prominent collective efforts to oppose Anglo domination among the poorest segments of Mexican-American communities across the Southwest.

From 1910 to the end of World War II, the Mexican-American middle class formed several secular organizations that encouraged Mexican-Americans to conform to American values and American ways of life. Among the organizations were the Order of Sons of America formed in San Antonio in 1921; the League of United Latin American Citizens (LULAC), organized in 1929; and The Good Neighbor Clubs. These organizations stressed learning English, adopting traditional American values, training members and poorer immigrants for citizenship, and mobilizing a solid front against vigilante groups such as the KKK (Stoddard, 1973). Working class organizations also tried to fight against Anglo exploitation, and their efforts were manifested in the organized protests and strikes among field laborers, railway workers, pecan shellers, coal miners, and sheepherders between 1903 and 1930. Such efforts, however, were usually unsuccessful.

The strategy of collective struggle became more successful in dealing with the job ceiling and other barriers *after* World War II. The experience of Mexican-American war veterans changed the situation. When the veterans returned from the war, they refused to continue to live under caste-like barriers, excluded from social clubs, professional associations, and fraternal orders. The veterans were frustrated by the persistence of the job ceiling that confined them to mostly menial and manual labor. Consequently, Mexican-American veterans organized the American G.I. Forum of the United States to fight for equal rights. Since that time, there has been a proliferation of Mexican-American civil rights organizations (Acuña, 1981; Knowlton, 1975; Santiestevan, 1975). Through these collective efforts, Mexican-Americans have won redresses of various kinds and in some areas have actually changed their political status. However, the fact remains that for the most part, Mexican-Americans are still cemented to the bottom of the occupational ladder.

5. *Deviant behavior.* The final strategy employed by Mexican-Americans to circumvent the caste barriers is incorporated into a variety of activities labeled deviant by society: The use and marketing of narcotics, gang memberships, and violent behavior. In her study of gangs, drugs, and prisons in the barrios of Los Angeles, Moore (1978) examined the persistence and influence of Mexican-American youth gangs, the use of heroin and barbiturates in Mexican-American neighborhoods, the growth of these markets for such drugs, and the enduring influence of barrio norms among the men of the barrios who are incarcerated in California prisons and who return to these barrios upon their release. Such deviant behavior, according to Moore, is firmly rooted in the limited opportunity structure that is mediated by the segmented labor market, providing an environmental context of limited opportunities with legitimate jobs generally offering little prospect for lifetime satisfaction. The street gangs are an adaptive response to the limited structure of the primary job market and in this respect the segmented labor market is an essential factor in understanding the structure and context of gang affiliation, the use and marketing of illegal drugs and stolen goods, and the prison connections of the residents of barrios (Moore, 1978). Sweeney's study (1980) of East Los Angeles gangs, and Davidson's (1974) study of Chicano prisoners in San Quentin, underscore the point that a segment of the Mexican-American population is indeed very alienated from the success goals of the larger society, and are, in fact, simply not attached to conventional norms of success. The phenomenon of Mexican-American deviant behavior is best understood as an attachment to what is explicitly an alternative survival system that provides peer acceptance, a set of core values to live by, a compatible frame of reference, an identity, and a purpose that is more satisfying than what is possible to achieve in the larger society.

Mexican-American Folk Theory of Making It or Status Mobility System

When asked about how one gets ahead, most Americans respond with the abstract societal beliefs about getting an education and working hard. Most members of a given population do not have an explicitly formulated folk theory of getting ahead that is readily reproducible to an inquirer. Therefore, we shall not derive a Mexican-American folk theory of getting ahead primarily from responses to direct questions about getting ahead, but rather from observing what Mexican-Americans actually do to get ahead.

In general, we derive a Mexican-American folk theory of success by studying: (1) what they think about competition with Anglos; (2) their direct and indirect attacks on selection criteria, or procedures for jobs and other societal positions; and (3) their alternative strategies.

Many Mexican-Americans do not believe that they have an equal chance when they compete for positions with Anglos who have the same educational qualifications. More than half of the Mexican-Americans interviewed in Los Angeles, and an overwhelming majority of those in San Antonio, said that to get ahead, especially in politics, they have to work harder (Grebler *et al.*, 1970).

One of the ways by which Mexican-Americans and other minorities indicate that they do not believe that the rules of behavior for achievement that work for Anglos work for them is that they exert a great deal of time and effort trying to change the criteria or selection procedures for employment, appointment, or election through activities such as protest marches and boycotts against employers who discriminate (Ogbu, 1986).

We also gain some knowledge of the folk theory of getting ahead among Mexican-Americans when we examine the survival strategies or mechanisms by which they cope with the job ceiling. These include passing, caste leakage, and clientship. The fourth strategy, collective struggle, and the fifth strategy, deviant behavior, are used primarily to raise or break the job ceiling. The message from these survival strategies is that the rules of behavior for self-advancement or upward social mobility that work for Anglos do not necessarily work for Mexican-Americans; that to advance in status, Mexican-Americans must either follow a different path, acquire additional qualifications (e.g., Anglo patronage), or "fight the system." These are elements of a Mexican-American folk theory of success, a shared cultural knowledge and belief system.

Mexican-American Oppositional Identity, Cultural Frame of Reference, and Low Academic Effort Syndrome

Like other disparaged indigenous minorities, the social identity of Mexican-Americans has been affected by their subordination and exploitation by the dominant Anglos. Unlike some other minorities, however, Mexican-American social identity appeared to be, until recently, characterized more by ambivalence than opposition. According to Forbes (1968) and Morner (1967), the *Mestizos* in Mexico had learned to repudiate their Indian ancestry and to emphasize their Spanish or white lineage. Indeed, there was a kind of "pigmentocracy" of status levels based on skin color that rewarded light skin color (Stoddard, 1973); Vigil, 1980). To get ahead in Mexico, they had to repudiate their Indian ancestry (Stoddard, 1973).

Among Mexican-Americans, what developed initially was an ambivalent social identity, partly because of the preconquest identification with European or white heritage, which was reinforced by Anglos' preferential treatment of light-skinned Mexican-Americans. Some Mexican-Americans did not, in fact, want to identify with Mexican or Indian heritage under Anglo rule. Instead, they tried to manipulate their descent so as to claim "Spanish" identity or "white" identity. The Anglo caste system provided a strong incentive for people to want to renounce their Mexican-American identity and assume Spanish identity. The claim to Spanish identity increased among upwardly mobile and light-skinned Mexican-Americans as immigration from Mexico increased at the turn of the century (Grebler *et al.,* 1970; Stoddard, 1973).

Since the option to assume Spanish identity benefited primarily light-skinned Mexican-Americans, what about the dark-skinned ones? The latter continued to face a job ceiling, social rejection, and other barriers "no matter how refined in speaking English or stylishly dressed" (Vigil, 1980, p. 177). Those who desire or sought to be accepted as Spanish or white, but were rejected because of their appearance, often faced problems of conflict and marginality.

Prior to World War II, and to some degree after the war, the option to pass or assume Spanish or white identity also had some effects on Mexican-American identity at the group level. It appeared to have prevented the emergence of a truly collective oppositional identity to Anglos and, instead, encouraged community dissension and an ambivalent identity. Even though Mexican-Americans resented those who "passed" (Grebler *et al.,* 1970; Vigil, 1980), the cultural orientation toward a preference for European or white identity over Mexican or Indian identity made the option of passing appealing to those who could not pass.

A significant change toward a preference for Mexican-American identity, and toward an oppositional identity, began to emerge after World War II because of the events described earlier, which gave rise to the formation and activities of the American G.I. Forum and other post-war organizations of Mexican-Americans. The roots of this identity--and its use as a tool of resistance--are rooted in the adversarial, antagonistic, and subordinate relationship of Mexican-Americans to the larger society. As such, this post-World War II identity is a response formed *in opposition* to the dominant society and must be understood in terms of three factors: (1) the geographical concentration of Mexican-Americans in the Southwest, within segregated barrios, and outside the mainstream of American cultural, economic, and political developments; (2) continuing and increasing immigration from Mexico, providing a constant source of cultural renewal for the preservation of language and cultural forms; and (3) continuing racial discrimination in employment, housing, education, the courts, and other institutions, which have isolated Mexican-descent people and prohibited their integration into the society.

These three factors combine to provide the context for the Mexican presence in the United States, promoting intensive intra-group reliance and interaction in developing a collective identity as a disadvantaged, disparaged minority group. Moreover, this discrimination and exclusion has reduced their sociocultural contact with the Anglo mainstream. Mexican-Americans in the barrios in the Southwest have lived in a world apart, with the barrio serving as an "urban village" facilitating a continuance of the lifestyle and social interaction patterns of small-town dwellers in Mexico (Laird, 1975), with continuing immigration (legal and undocumented) reinforcing these basic institutions. The barrio is a cultural haven, absorbing new residents and sheltering the residents from the complexities and difficulties of the Anglo world. In this respect, Mexican immigration and settlement patterns across the Southwest and Midwest bear little resemblance to the "uprooting" experience which noted sociologist, Oscar Handlin, depicted as characteristic of the European immigrant experience in the United States. Rather, the barrio provided a context that promoted continuity rather than the social disorganization, marginality, and uprootedness of other immigrant experiences in the United States. As such, the barrio has provided a stable source of essentially Mexican elements in the working-class Mexican-American identity system. Given the continuing segregation and racial discrimination in the post-World War II period, the Mexican culture and its reconstruction into an oppositional identity marks a new era of collective social identity.

Just as many Mexican-Americans in the post-World War II period have emphasized Mexican identity in opposition to an Anglo-based identity, they have also opted for a cultural frame of reference that stresses the maintenance of Mexican-American culture and language. In the new cultural frame of reference, they appear to resist orientations and practices they perceive as detrimental to the integrity of their culture.

The new cultural frame of reference has been reinforced by the "Chicano Movement" beginning in the 1960s (Arce, 1981; Gómez-Quiñones, 1977; Sanchez, 1983). Among the younger generation, the emphasis is on resisting acculturation and assimilation as well as on conforming to Mexican-American cultural norms and practices. The increasing acceptance of a distinct Mexican-American or Chicano identity has led to increasing stress on a distinct Mexican-American cultural frame of reference. Within this Mexican-American cultural frame of reference, orientations and practices suggesting assimilation or linear acculturation into the Anglo cultural domain are perceived as threatening to Mexican-American integrity and are, therefore, opposed. While not everyone espouses this cultural frame of reference, the oppositional cultural framework of reference apparently receives the tacit support of a large segment of the population. Such support is no doubt continually infused by recurrent waves of immigration from Mexico. Hence, there is a continual intermingling of specifically Mexican (i.e., primarily cultural differences) as well as Mexican-American elements (i.e., secondary cultural differences) into this frame of reference.

Evolution of Sociocultural Factors as a Practical Solution to Problems

The affective state and folk model of Mexican-Americans have led them to develop certain cultural practices (e.g., survival strategies, cultural inversions) that do not simply reflect their value orientation or subculture; rather, these are practical solutions to perceived problems of living as a minority group under caste-like stratification. Some of these practical solutions meet their instrumental needs (e.g., upward social mobility), others serve to confirm, maintain, and protect their identity (e.g., as "Spanish" and "white" or as "Mexican" or "Mexican-American"). Whereas the cultural frame of reference associated with "Spanish" or "white" identity was ambivalent for reasons discussed earlier, the cultural frame of reference accompanying emphasis on "Mexican" and "Mexican-American" identity is more oppositional. The cultural practices generated by the oppositional cultural frame of reference serve as a boundary-maintaining mechanism between Mexican-Americans and Anglos. Although individual Mexican-Americans live and act out these solutions to problems of getting ahead, the solutions are a group or cultural solution. That is, they embody group or cultural logic, beliefs, attitudes, and practices that are not necessarily the same as those of individual Mexican-Americans.

Low Academic Effort Syndrome Among Mexican-Americans

How does an oppositional identity and a distinctly Mexican-American cultural frame of reference influence the academic performance of

Mexican-American children? To understand the nature of this influence, one must recognize that the sociocultural factors we have described are a part of the culture into which Mexican-American children are born and reared. That is, they are a part of the folk system or cultural repertoire (attitudes, knowledge, beliefs, and practice) that are transmitted to Mexican-American children by socializing agents in Mexican-American communities and in the wider society, and that the children acquire as they get older. For example, Mexican-American children learn shared cultural knowledge about the job ceiling as well as attitudes and coping strategies associated with it. They also learn about various identity choices with their communities and the lifestyles of folk models associated with them. We will briefly describe a number of ways through which these sociocultural attitudes, knowledge, beliefs, and practices affect the school performance of Mexican-American children.

Distrust and academic efforts. Although Mexican-Americans began actively to fight for better educational opportunities after World War II, they do not feel that the problem is over. The conflict between Mexican-Americans and the schools has involved not only the dispute about segregated and inferior education but also their treatment in the formal curriculum and in textbooks, and in counseling, discipline, and use of language. We suggest that one consequence of this persistent conflict with the schools and general mistrust of Anglos is the mistrust of the schools themselves. Under this circumstance, it becomes increasingly difficult for Mexican-American children to accept, internalize, and follow school rules of behavior for achievement.

Disillusionment, ambivalence, and academic effort. The job ceiling has traditionally weakened the relationship between Mexican-American academic efforts and subsequent employment and earning status (Blair, 1972; Schmidt, 1970). Thus, even though Mexican-American parents and other adults may admonish the children to work hard and get a good education for future employment and self-advancement, the actual texture of the lives of these parents and of other barrio adults may communicate a powerful contradictory message to the children. This message is that Mexican-Americans do not receive equal rewards with Anglos for their education because of a job ceiling. The message is communicated to the children subtly and unknowingly when parents and other adults talk about their experiences and frustrations or when they talk about similar experiences and frustrations of relatives, friends, neighbors, and Mexican-Americans in general. With knowledge of Mexican-American employment, unemployment, and underemployment history, even young children will begin to form their image of the connection or lack of connection between school success and future employment or self-advancement. As the children get older and encounter personal failures and frustrations as they try to get part-time and summer jobs, these perceptions and frustrations discourage them from maximizing their academic efforts.

Survival strategies and incongruent competencies. The survival strategies Mexican-Americans develop to cope with the job ceiling (passing, clientship, caste leakage, collective struggle, and deviant behavior) enable them to increase their access to better jobs, wages, or other societal resources by circumventing the job ceiling or by trying to raise or break it. These strategies tend to require and promote special attitudes, skills, or competencies and behaviors that are not necessarily compatible with those required for classroom work.

Passing for Spanish or white probably promotes attitudes, competencies, and behaviors that enhance academic success. Those who pass must adopt attitudes and cultural frames of reference that go with their assumed Spanish or white status. Vigil (1980) notes that in some instances, assimilation efforts that go with passing:

> ...reach extremes in which [those who are passing] become flag-waving superpatriots and worked to master perfect English. They socialize their children/offspring to this end. [And] in their efforts to rid themselves of Mexican-American culture--they often aroused the wrath of their fellow Mexican. (p. 161)

Clientship or *tio tomasing* tends to convey the message that although education may be necessary, it is not enough. It also involves manipulative attitudes, skills, and behaviors that parents and other barrio adults use in dealing with Anglos and the institutions they control. Carter (1970) has even suggested that the barrio school principal tends to act out this patron-client relationship with the community, thus providing immediate and ample opportunities for students to learn this coping strategy from their parents' responses. The point to stress is that the dependent, manipulative attitudes, skills, and behaviors the children learn from this coping strategy are not necessarily those that promote Anglo-type school success.

Collective struggle in one sense can encourage more school effort. This is particularly the case when Mexican-American children see that the strategy is helping to open up more and better opportunities for them in education and jobs. On the other hand, collective struggle also teaches Mexican-American children that "the system" or "Anglo society" are to blame for the high unemployment and other problems that face people living in barrios. Eventually, children learn to blame the system for their own academic failure and discount the value of educational effort in achieving adult success.

Deviant behavior is a reflection of the destructiveness of enduring subordination and relegation to a perpetual caste-like status in society. Pervasive and enduring social and economic deprivation have transformed traditional values into negative, embittered, self-destructive behavioral patterns, frequently of a violent nature. These and other types of behavioral orientations must be understood as adaptive responses to a particular ecological context. Deviant behavior is a part of a complex adaptation to barrio life, which is itself an attachment to a collective sense of peoplehood as an alternative system complete in and of itself. Those who follow a strategy of deviant behavior have not internalized the success goals of the larger society. Doing well in school is not part of the code of conduct for those attached to a deviant lifestyle. Ultimately, this particular strategy will only be neutralized as a viable alternative coping mechanism with the elimination of caste barriers, particularly the job ceiling, and the opening up of many more *legitimate* opportunities to achieve success, sense of purpose, and self-worth.

We said earlier that the shift in emphasis from Spanish or white identity to Mexican and Mexican-American identity has also led to a cultural frame of reference behavior that emphasizes Mexican-American cultural practices or styles rather than Anglo practices and styles. While we are not suggesting any homogeneity in current identity systems and cultural frame of reference--the group is extremely heterogenous--we do believe that among both, Mexican-American pragmatists and idelogists, the schools are perceived as agents of assimilation or linear acculturation into the Anglo cultural system. Also, since linear or one-way acculturation is considered detrimental to the integrity of Mexican-American identity, culture, language, school policies, and practices are viewed as things to be resisted, challenged, and changed.

Some students go as far as asserting that doing school work is doing "the white people's thing" or doing "the Anglo thing." They may complain that the schools are teaching only Anglo language or English and not their own language, Spanish. There is, thus, an element of opposition or resistance that is not always conscious and overt. Often, it takes the form of mental withdrawal (Carter, 1970; Carter and Segura, 1979), lack of serious academic attitudes, high absenteeism from school, reluctance to do classwork when present, and disruptive behavior in the classroom. The factors described earlier combine with these oppositional tendencies to discourage many Mexican-American children from maximizing their academic efforts to learn what they are taught or to demonstrate what they have already learned when called upon to do so.

IMPLICATIONS

The foregoing discussion has been necessarily thorough and detailed in order to explore systematically the variability in academic performance observed in language minority children. "Not all minorities are alike" is a refrain frequently heard but rarely explained beyond superficial traits or cultural stereotypes. The analysis presented in this chapter is comprehensive and exhaustive precisely because *it is essential to contextualize* the historical and structural conditions that shape the sociocultural factors influencing school performance. The detail in the analysis is provided so that we can readily understand why and in which ways "minorities are not all alike."

What, then, are the implications of the foregoing analysis for classroom teachers and educators? What can they gain from this analysis that can stimulate the development of more effective classroom practices for ethnic and language minority students? There are a number of implications, from the more general to the specific, that emanate from the analysis. First, let us turn our attention to the general implications.

1. *We must understand cultural phenomena without stereotyping individuals within groups.* We wish to reiterate the cautionary note stated at the beginning of part two of this chapter: *Not all Mexican-descent people in the United States can be categorized as caste-like or non-immigrant, nor do all members of the group identify with the caste-like or non-immigrant orientation.* The analysis presented here is concerned with those Mexican-Americans who *do* manifest a caste-like or non-immigrant orientation and who, therefore, do not succeed in school. An incomplete assessment of the foregoing analysis might lead some to utilize the typology of minority status (immigrant vs. caste-like) as a way of generalizing to entire groups of people, thus stereotyping individual language minority students as either "caste-like" or "immigrant" in their behavioral orientation to school. The typology utilized in this chapter is merely a heuristic device to assist in ordering a multitude of observations and facts into categories for analysis. *It is essential to remember that these categories are merely analytical concepts.* They are

not reified material realities existing within the psyches of "immigrant" Chinese, Punjabi, or Korean students, or in "caste-like" Mexican-American or Puerto Rican students. *We caution against identifying individual students as either "immigrant" or "caste-like" in their schooling orientation, thus restricting expectations of academic performance to a generalized analytical category.* Additionally, it would be a tragic misapplication of the analysis to develop separate curricular response for "caste-like" and for "immigrant" students. A much more productive response lies in the area of developing cooperative small group teaching methods that include both group rewards and individual accountability. Such approaches show tantalizing potential to increase academic performance among a range of ethnic and language minority students. Cooperative methods may also improve student self-esteem, attitudes toward school and fellow classmates, while mobilizing peer support for constructive classroom behavior, e.g., reinforcing the alteration model discussed in this chapter. (See Kagan's chapter in this volume for more discussion of cooperative learning.)

2. *Not all Mexican-American students exhibit a caste-like mentality in their behavioral response to the demands of schools.* Just as it is important to remember that not all immigrant students succeed in school, it is equally important to remember that many Mexican-American students do, in fact, perform well in school. Despite historical and structural conditions that have constrained opportunities for Mexican-descent persons as a group in the United States, there are some Mexican-Americans who have developed a folk theory that *does* embody serious academic attitudes, which *does* emphasize perservering academic efforts. Although this chapter has been about the persistence of chronic, disproportionate school failure among many Mexican-American students in the United States, it would be a gross mistake to ignore or misunderstand the academic achievement of those Mexican-American students who have performed well in school.

3. *Change begins with a different way of conceptualizing the problem.* Our analysis provides teachers and educators with an opportunity to rethink how schooling functions in a larger sociocultural context, i.e., how what has gone on outside the school walls influences and shapes what goes on in the classroom. The analysis assumes that academic performance and classroom behavior are, to some degree, a function of how much effort people invest in doing academic work and how that such efforts are influenced by sociocultural forces. At one level, the sociocultural forces determine the strength of the connection between

school success and decent adult opportunities or employment possibilities. The existence of this connection, in turn, promotes positive perceptions of schooling and persevering academic efforts on the part of members of a given population. At another level, the sociocultural forces promote positive perceptions of schooling and persevering academic efforts by creating a context in which people can learn appropriate academic attitudes and school behaviors or cross cultural boundaries without affective dissonance. In order for teachers and educators to adapt classroom strategies and practices to the variability within a diverse language minority student population, it is important to understand the way in which schooling is linked to the larger society, particularly economic institutions. Once this linkage is understood, it is then important to underscore the fact that different language minority groups perceive the linkage in different ways, developing different cultural strategies in response to these perceptions. Differences in cultural strategies are observed not only between groups but also *within* groups, e.g., within the heterogenous Mexican-descent population.

4. *Sociocultural factors are not immutable or impervious to change.* An incomplete reading of the foregoing analysis might lead others to conclude, "The conditions that produce a caste-like mentality and poor school performance are beyond my control, and therefore, what can I possibly do in the classroom?" Rather than throw one's hands up despairingly, it will be more productive to ask, "Given these historical and structural conditions, and given the development of specific sociocultural factors outside the school, what can I do as a classroom teacher or teacher trainer to promote school learning and to reduce affective dissonance experienced by some language-minority students in the classroom? Given these outside forces, what strategies need to be developed to ameliorate the effects of primary cultural discontinuities? Of secondary cultural discontinuities? What are the important differences to remember about primary and secondary cultural discontinuities that have a bearing on what is done in the classroom? What classroom conditions need to be nurtured so that the alternation model of classroom learning can be effectively, and affectively, realized for all language minority-students?"

5. *Increasing opportunities for school success of caste-like minorities.* What does this analysis of the influence of sociocultural forces mean for increasing the school success of caste-like minorities? Let us begin by reiterating the central message of our chapter. First, at the level of the

process of schooling, one important contributing factor, but by no means the only one, to the low academic performance of caste-like minority children is their relative lack of serious academic attitudes and persevering efforts, coupled with reluctance to adopt school rules of behavior and practices for academic achievement. However, caste-like minority students' academic attitudes and behaviors, which are not subject to the students' conscious and rational analysis, are products of historial and structural experiences of subordination and exploitation of their group at the hands of the dominant group.

Given the twin nature of the influence of the sociocultural forces on the academic achievement of caste-like minority children, a sound policy for increasing their academic performance *must* include ways to eliminate caste-like barriers in minority youth and adult opportunity structures, including school "reforms" and classroom practices as well as how to change the minority students' academic attitudes and efforts. A promising area of innovative classroom instructional strategies that may well be compatible with the elimination of societal caste-like barriers in employment and opportunity structures is cooperative learning. Cooperative small group learning methods exhibit marked potential for improving academic achievement and, at the same time, provide self-enhancing psychological benefits for participants and a positive impact on intergroup relations.

However, prior to the development of such policies and strategies, there are at least two prerequisites. One is to recognize that a caste-like stratification has existed and, in many respects, still exists in the United States, with all the implications for the minorities that we have described in this chapter. Another prerequisite is to recognize that real change depends on opening up decent youth and adult futures, not just on patching up the supposed deficiencies of individuals. Still a third prerequisite is for caste-like minorities themselves to recognize that their school performance will greatly improve when they themselves adopt appropriate academic attitudes and learn to persevere in their academic pursuits. In this regard, the role of the minority teacher--*and other minority leaders in the community*--can assume greater clarity and importance as "cultural brokers" to the minority community, especially to minority parents. There is a greater linkage to be forged between minority-group teachers and minority community leaders in relationship to minority communities. These individuals can serve to maintain the vitality and identity of the minority community at the same time that appropriate academic attitudes are championed and instilled. A prerequisite for minorities to develop appropriate academic attitudes and persevering efforts is for them to separate the process of schooling from that of assimilation into the dominant-group culture. Such attitudes and efforts can be developed through a carefully formulated plan forged by communities in collaboration with minority teachers and community leaders.

REFERENCES

Achievement Council, The. *Draft Report*. Oakland, California: Mills College, 1984.

Acuña, R. *Occupied America: A History of Chicanos*. 2nd Ed. New York: Harper and Row Publishers, 1981.

_____. *Occupied America: The Chicano's Struggle Toward Liberation*. San Francisco, California: Canfield Press, 1972.

Adams, C., and Laurikietis, R. *The Gender Trap: A Closer Look at Sex Roles, Book 1: Education and Work*. London, England: Virago, Ltd., 1977.

Almaguer, T. Class, race, and Chicano oppression. *Socialist Revolution,* July-September 1975, *5*(25), 71-91.

ARC Associates, Inc. *Bilingual Education in a Chinese Community: Final Research Report*. Contract Grant No. 400-80-0013. Washington, D.C.: National Institute of Education, 1982.

Arce, C. A reconsideration of Chicano culture and identity. *Daedalus,* 1981, *110*(2), 177-191.

Balderrama, F. E. *In Defense of La Raza: The Los Angeles Mexican Consulate and the Mexican Community, 1929-1936*. Tucson, Arizona: University of Arizona Press, 1982.

Barrera, M. *Race and Class in the Southwest: A Theory of Racial Inequality*. South Bend, Indiana: University of Notre Dame Press, 1979.

Barth, G. *Bitter Strength*. Cambridge, Massachusetts: Harvard University Press, 1964.

Becker, G. S. *Human Capital*. New York: National Bureau of Economic Research, 1964.

Berreman, G. D. Concomitants of caste organization. In G. A. DeVos, and H. Wagatsuma (Eds.), *Japan's Invisible Race: Caste in Cultural and Personality*. Berkeley: University of California Press, 1967.

_____. Caste in India and the United States. *The American Journal of Sociology,* 1960, *66*, 120-127.

Blair, P. M. Job discrimination and education: Rates of return to education of Mexican Americans and Euro-Americans in Santa Clara County, California. In Martin Carnoy (Ed.), *Schooling in a Corporate Society: The Political Economy of Education in America*. New York: David McKay Co., 1972.

_____. *Job Discrimination and Education: An Investment Analysis*. New York: Praeger, 1971.

Bond, H. M. *The Education of the Negro in the American Social Order*. New York: Octagon, 1966.

Boykin, A. W. *Reading Achievement and the Sociocultural Frame of Reference of Afro-American Children*. Paper presented at an NIE Roundtable Discussion on Issues in Urban Reading, Washington, D.C., November 19-20, 1980.

Brown, G., Rosen, N., Hill, S., and Olivas, M. *The Condition of Education For Hispanic Americans*. National Center for Educational Statistics. Washington, D.C.: U.S. Government Printing Office, 1980.

Burma, J. H. A comparison of the Mexican American subculture with the Oscar Lewis culture of poverty model. In J. H. Burma (Ed.), *Mexican-Americans in the United States: A Reader*. Cambridge, Massachusetts: Schenkman Publishing Co., 1970.

Byers, P., and Byers, H. Nonverbal communication and the education of children. In C. B. Cazden, Vera P. John, and Dell Hymes (Eds.), *Functions of Language in the Classroom*. New York: Teachers College Press, 1972.

Camarillo, A. *Chicanos in a Changing Society*. Cambridge, Massachusetts: Harvard University Press, 1979.

Carter, T. P. *Mexican Americans in Schools: A History of Educational Neglect*. New York: College Entrance Examination Board, 1970.

————, and Segura, R. *Mexican Americans in School: A Decade of Change*. New York: College Entrance Examination Board, 1979.

Castile, G. P., and Kushner, G. (Eds.) *Presistent Peoples: Cultural Enclaves in Perspective*. Tucson, Arizona: University of Arizona Press, 1981.

Chui, P. *Chinese Labor in California*. Unpublished manuscript, Department of History, University of Wisconsin, Madison, 1967.

Cohen R. School reorganization and learning. In S. T. Kimball and J. H. Burnett (Eds.), *Learning and Culture*. Seattle, Washington: University of Washington Press, 1972.

Cohen, Y. A. The state systems, schooling, and cognitive and motivational patterns. In N. K. Shimahara and A. Scrupski (Eds.), *Social Forces and Schooling*. New York: David McKay Co., 1975.

Coleman, J. S. (Ed.). *Equality of Educational Opportunity*. Washington, D.C.: U.S. Government Printing Office, 1966.

Coolidge, M. R. *Chinese Immigration*. New York: Arno Press, 1969.

Cornelius, W., and Montoya, R. A. (Eds.) *America's New Immigration Law: Origins, Rationales and Potential Consequences*. San Diego: Center for U.S.-Mexican Studies University of California, San Diego, Monograph Series, 11, 1983.

Davidson, R. T. *Chicano Prisoners: The Key to San Quentin*. New York: Holt, 1974.

Davis, A., Gardner, B. B., and Gardner, M. R. *Deep South: A Social Anthropological Study of Caste and Class*. Chicago, Illinois: University of Chicago Press, 1965.

DeAvila, E. A., and Havassy, B. E. Piagetian alternative to IQ: Mexican-American study. In Nicholas Hobbs (Eds.), *The Future of Children, Vol. 2: Issues in the Classification of Children*. San Francisco, California: Jossey-Bass, 1975.

DeLeon, A. *They Called Them Greasers: Anglo Attitudes Toward Mexicans in Texas, 1821-1900*. Austin, Texas: University of Texas Press, 1983.

DeVos, G. A. *Ethnic Persistence and Role Degradation: An Illustration From Japan*. Paper prepared for the American-Soviet Symposium on Contemporary Ethnic Processes in the USA and USSR, New Orleans, Louisiana, April 14-16, 1984.

————. Achievement motivation and intra family attitudes in Korean immigrants. *Journal of Psychoanalytic Anthropology*, 1983, *6*(1), 25-71.

————. Japan's outcastes: The problem of the Burakumin. In Ben Whitaker (Ed.), *The Fourth World: Victims of Group Oppression*. New York: Schocken, 1973.

————, and Lee, C. *Koreans in Japan*. Berkeley, California: University of California Press, 1981.

_____, and Wagatsuma, H. (Eds.). *Japan's Invisible Race: Caste in Culture and Personality.* Berkeley: University of California Press, 1967.

DeWare, H. Affirmative action plan at AT & T is permitted. *The Washington Post,* July 4, 1978, A1, A7.

Dinerman, I. R. *Migrants and Stay-At-Homes: A Comparative Study of Rural Migration from Michoacan, Mexico.* San Diego: Center for U.S.-Mexican Studies, University of California. Monograph Series, #5, 1982.

Dollard, J. *Caste and Class in a Southern Town.* (3rd ed.). Garden City, New York: Doubleday, 1957.

Dore, R. P. *The Diploma Disease.* Berkeley: University of California Press, 1976.

Erickson, F., and Mohatt, J. The cultural organization of participant structure in two classrooms of Indian students. In G. D. Spindler (Ed.), *Doing the Ethnography of Schooling.* New York: Holt, 1982.

Elson, R. M. *Guardians of Tradition: American Schoolbooks of the Nineteenth Century.* Lincoln, Nebraska: University of Nebraska Press, 1964.

Estrada, L., Garcia, C., Macias, R., and Maldonado, L. Chicanos in the United States: A history of exploitation and resistance. *Daedalus,* 1981, *110*(2), 103-132.

Fernandez, R. M., and Nielsen, F. *Bilingualism and Hispanic Scholastic Achievement: Some Baseline Results.* Unpublished manuscript, Department of Sociology, University of Arizona, 1984.

Fong, S.L.M. Assimilation and changing social roles of Chinese Americans. In S. Sue and H.H.L. Kitano (Eds.), *Asian Americans: A Success Story. The Journal of Social Issues,* 1973, *29*(2), 115-127.

Forbes, J. D. Mexican-Americans. In John H. Burma (Ed.), *Mexican-Americans in the United States: A Reader.* New York: Schenkman, 1970.

_____. Race and color in Mexican-American problems. *Journal of Human Relations,* 1968, *16*, 55-68.

Foster, H. L. *Ribbin', Jivin', and Playin' the Dozens: The Unrecognized Dilemma of Inner City Schools.* Cambridge, Massachusetts: Ballinger Publishing Co., 1974.

Franklin, R. *Corporations, Consumerism, and Education: The Linkage of School and the Economic Structure of American Capitalism.* Unpublished research project, Department of Anthropology, University of California, Berkeley, 1982.

Frazier, N., and Sadker, M. *Sexism in School and Society.* New York: Harper and Row, 1973.

Gibson, M. A. *Home-School-Community Linkages: A Study of Educational Equity for Punjabi Youths.* Final Report. Washington D.C.: The National Institute of Education, 1983.

_____. Variations in school performance in St. Croix. *Anthropology and Education Quarterly,* 1982, *13*(1), 3-24.

Gluckman, M. Tribalism in modern British Central Africa. *Cahiers d'etudes africaines,* 1960, *2*.

Gómez-Quiñones, J. *Development of the Mexican Working Class North of the Rio Bravo: Work and Culture Among Laborers and Artisans, 1860-1900.* Popular Series No. 2. Los Angeles, California: Chicano Studies Research Center Publications, University of California, Los Angeles, 1982.

_____. On culture. *Revista Chicano-Riquena,* Spring 1977, *5*(2), 29-47.

Grebler, L., Moore, J. W., and Guzman, R. C. *The Mexican-American People: The Nation's Second Largest Minority.* New York: The Free Press, 1970.

Griswold del Castillo, R. *The Los Angeles Barrio, 1850-1890: A Social History.* Los Angeles: University of California Press, 1979.

Gumperz, J. J. Conversational inferences and classroom learning. In J. Green, and C. Wallat (Eds.), *Ethnographic Approaches to Face to Face Interaction.* Norwood, New Jersey: ABLEX, 1981.

_____, and Hernandez-Chavez, C. E. Bilingualism, bidialectalism, and classroom interaction. In C. B. Cazden, V. P. John, and Hymes, D. (Eds.), *Functions of Language in the Classroom.* New York: Teachers College Press, 1972.

Guthrie, G. P. *An Ethnography of Bilingual Education in a Chinese Community.* Unpublished doctoral dissertation, College of Education, University of Illinois, Urbana-Champaign, 1983.

Harrison, B. *Education, Training, and the Urban Ghetto.* Baltimore, Maryland: Johns Hopkins University Press, 1972.

Harty, S. *Hucksters in the Classrooms.* Washington, D.C.: Center for Study of Responsive Law, 1979.

Heller, K. A., Hotzman, W. H., and Messick, S. (Eds.). *Placing Children in Special Education: A Strategy for Equality.* Washington, D.C.: National Academy Press, 1982.

Hernandez, J. A. *Mutual Aid for Survival: The Case of the Mexican American.* Malabar, Florida: Robert E. Krieger Publishing Co., 1983.

Holt, D. M. Schools adjusting to computer use. *The Tribune,* October 25, 1982, A-9.

Holt, G. S. Stylin' outta the Black pulpit. In T. Kochman (Ed.), *'Rappin' and Stylin' Out: Communication in Urban Black America.* Chicago: University of Illinois Press, 1972.

Hostetler, J. A., and Huntington, G. E. *Children in Amish Society: Socialization and Community Education.* New York: Holt, Rinehart, and Winston, 1971.

Hughes, J. F., and Hughes, A. O. *Equal Education: A New National Strategy.* Bloomington, Indiana: Indiana University Press, 1973.

Ino, D. *Language Barriers for Immigrants, Refugees and Foreign Students at the University of California, Berkeley.* Unpublished Research Project, Department of Anthropology, University of California, Berkeley, 1982.

Ito, H. Japan's outcastes in the United States. In G. A. DeVos and H. Wagatsuma (Eds.), *Japan's Invisible Race: Caste in Culture and Personality.* Berkeley, California: University of California Press, 1967.

Katz, I. The socialization of academic motivation in minority group children. In D. Levine (Ed.) *Nebraska Symposium on Motivation.* Lincoln, Nebraska: University of Nebraska Press, 1967.

Kanellos, N. Folklore in Chicano theater and Chicano as folklore. In S. A. West and J. Macklin (Eds.), *The Chicano Experience.* Boulder Colorado: Westview Press, 1979.

Knowlton, C. The neglected chapters in Mexican American history. In G. Tyler (Ed.), *Mexican Americans Tomorrow: Educational and Economic Perspectives.* Albuquerque, New Mexico: University of New Mexico Press, 1975.

Kochman, T. *Black and White Styles in Conflict.* Chicago: University of Chicago Press, 1982.

Laird, J. F. *Argentine, Kansas: The Evolution of a Mexican American Community, 1905-1940.* Unpublished doctoral dissertation, University of Kansas, 1975.

Laosa, L. *Families as Learning Environments for Children.* New York: Plenum Press, 1982.

Lebra, T. S. Acculturation dilemma: The functions of Japanese moral values for Americanization. *Council on Anthropology and Education Newsletter,* 1972, *3*(1), 6-13.

LeCompte, M. D. Learning to work: The hidden curriculum of the classroom. *Anthropology and Education Quarterly,* 1978, *9*(1), 21-37.

Lewis, A. Minority education in Sharonia, Israel, and Stockton, California: A comparative analysis. *Anthropology and Education Quarterly,* 1981, *12*(1), 30-50.

Lipschultz, R. J. Attitudes toward the Mexican. In M. S. Meier and F. Rivera (Eds.), *Readings on La Raza: The Twentieth Century.* New York: Hill and Wang, 1974.

Litherland, R. H. *The Role of the Church in Educational Change: A Case History of a Feasible Strategy.* Unpublished doctoral dissertation, San Francisco Theological Seminary, 1978.

Lyman, S. M. *The Asian in the West.* Reno Nevada: Western Studies Center, Desert Research Institute, University of Nevada System, 1970.

Mabogunje, A. L. *Regional Mobility and Resource Development in West Africa.* Montreal: McGill-Queens University Press, 1972.

Mat Nor, Hasan. *The Malay Student Problems: Some Issues on Their Poor Performance.* Unpublished research project, Department of Anthropology, University of California, Berkeley, 1983.

Mayer, P. Migrancy and the study of Africans in towns. *American Anthropologist,* 1962, *64,* 576-592.

McClelland, D. *The Achieving Society.* New York: Van Nostrand, 1961.

McCleod, A. *Pigtails and Gold Dust.* Caldwell, Idaho: Caxton Printers Ltd., 1947.

Melendy, H. B. *The Oriental Americans.* New York: Twayne Publishing Co., Inc., 1972.

Mickelson, R. *Race, Gender, and Class Differences in Youth Academic Achievement Attitudes and Behavior.* Unpublished doctoral dissertation, University of California, Los Angeles, 1983.

Mines, R. *Developing a Community Tradition of Migration: A Field Study in Rural Zacatecas, Mexico and California Settlement Areas.* Center for U.S.-Mexican Studies, San Diego, California: University of California, San Diego, Monograph #3, 1981.

Moore, J. W. Social class, assimilation and acculturation. In J. Helm (Ed.), *Spanish-Speaking People in the United States.* Seattle: University of Washington Press, 1968.

_____. *Homeboys: Gangs, Drugs, and Prison in the Barrios of Los Angeles.* Philadelphia, Pennsylvania: Temple University Press, 1978.

Moraga, C. La guera. In *Loving in the War Years.* Boston, Massachusetts: South End Press, 1983.

Morner, M. *Race Mixture in the History of Latin America.* Boston, Massachusetts: Little, Brown & Co., 1967.

Myrdal, G. *An American Dilemma: The Negro Problem and Modern Democracy.* New York: Harper, 1944.

Nava, J. Cultural backgrounds and barriers that affect learning by Spanish-speaking children. In John J. Burma (Ed.), *Mexican-Americans in the United States: A Reader.* New York: Schenkman, 1970.

Ogbu, J. U. *Language Minorities.* Unpublished manuscript. New Haven, Connecticut: Carnegie Council on Children, 1975.

_____. *Understanding Community Forces Affecting Minority Students' Academic Effort.* Paper prepared for the Achievement Council, Mills College, Oakland, California, 1984b.

_____. Stockton, California, revisited: Joining the labor force. In K. M. Borman (Ed.), *Becoming a Worker.* Norwood, New Jersey: ABLEX Publishing Corporation, 1986.

_____. Variability in minority school performance. In G. D. Spindler (Ed.), *Education and Cultural Process: Toward an Anthropology of Education.* New York: Holt, Rinehart, and Winston, 1974.

_____. Minority status and schooling in plural societies. *Comparative Education Review,* 1983, *27*(2), 168-190.

_____. Cultural discontinuities and schooling. *Anthropology and Education Quarterly,* 1982, *13*(4), 290-307.

_____. Societal forces as a context of ghetto children's school failure. In L. Feagans and D. Clark (Eds.), *The Language of Children Reared in Poverty: Implications for Evaluation and Intervention.* New York: Academic Press, 1981b.

_____. Education, clientage, and social mobility: Caste and social change in the United States and Nigeria. In G. D. Berreman (Ed.), *Social Inequality: Comparative and Developmental Approaches.* New York: Academic Press, 1981a.

_____. Social stratification and socialization of competence. *Anthropology and Education Quarterly,* 1979, *10*(1), 3-20.

_____. *Minority Education and Caste: The American System in Cross-Cultural Perspective.* New York: Academic Press, 1978.

_____. Racial stratification and education: The case of Stockton, California. *ICRD Bulletin,* 1977, *12*(3), 1-26.

_____. *The Next Generation: An Ethnography of Education in an Urban Neighborhood.* New York: Academic Press, 1974.

Ong, C. *The Educational Attainment of the Chinese in America.* Unpublished Research Project, Department of Anthropology, University of California, Berkeley, 1976.

Ow, P. *The Chinese and the American Educational System.* Unpublished Research Project, Department of Anthropology, University of California, Berkeley, 1976.

Padilla, A. M. Psychological research and the Mexican Americans. In M. Mangold (Ed.), *La Causa Chicana.* New York: Family Service Association of America, 1971.

Paredes, A. *"With His Pistol in His Land": A Border Ballad and Its Hero.* Austin, Texas: University of Texas Press, 1958.

Parliamentary Select Committee on Immigration and Race Relations, Session 1972-73. *Education, Vol. 1: Report.* London: Her Majesty's Stationery Office, 1973.

Penfold, V. B. *Personal Communication.* Education Officer, Maori and Island Education, Auckland, New Zealand: Department of Education, 1981.

Pepper, S. Education and political development in communist China. *Studies in Comparative Communism,* July-October, 1970, *3*(3 and 4), 132-157.

Petroni, F. A. Uncle Tome': White stereotypes in the Black movement. *Human Organization,* 1970, *29*(4), 260-266.

Philips, S. U. *The Invisible Culture: Communication in Classroom and Community on the Warm Springs Indian Reservation.* New York: Longman, 1983.

————. Participant structure and communicative competence: Warm Springs children in community and classroom. In C. Cazden, Vera P. John, and Dell Hymes (Eds.), *Functions of Language in the Classroom.* New York: Teachers College Press, 1972.

Poston, D. L., Alvirez, D. and Tienda, M. Earnings differences between Anglo and Mexican American male workers in 1960 and 1970. *Social Science Quarterly,* 1976, *57,* 618-631.

Ramírez, M. and Castañeda, A. *Cultural Democracy, Bicognitive Development and Education.* New York: Academic Press, 1974.

Rios-Bustamante, A. J. *Mexican Immigrant Workers in the U.S.* Los Angeles: Los Angeles Chicano Research Center, University of California at Los Angeles, 1981.

Rohlen, T. Education: Policies and prospects. In C. Lee and G. A. DeVos (Eds.), *Koreans In Japan: Ethnic Conflicts and Accommodation.* Berkeley: University of California Press, 1981.

Romo, R. *East Los Angeles: History of a Barrio.* Austin, Texas: University of Texas Press, 1983.

Rosen, B. C. Race, ethnicity, and the achievement syndrome. In B. C. Rosen, H. J. Crocket, and C. Z. Nunn (Eds.), *Achievement in American Society.* Cambridge, Massachusetts: Schenkman, 1969.

Rosenbaum, R. J. *Mexicano Resistance in the Southwest: The Sacred Right of Self-Preservation.* Austin, Texas: University of Texas Press, 1981.

Rubel, A. J. *Across the Tracks: Mexican Americans in a Texas City.* Austin, Texas: University of Texas Press, 1966.

Rutowski, P. *School-Industry Partnership.* A doctoral research proposal, University of California, Berkeley, 1985.

Sanchez, R. *Chicano Discourse: Socio-Historic Perspectives.* Rowley, Massachusetts: Newbury House Publisher, Inc., 1983.

Santos, R. *An Analysis of Earnings Among Persons of Spanish Origin.* Unpublished doctoral dissertation, Michigan State University, 1977.

Santiestevan, H. A perspective on Mexican-American organizations. In G. Tyler (Ed.), *Mexican-Americans Tomorrow: Educational and Economic Perspectives.* Albuquerque: University of New Mexico Press, 1975.

Scheinin, R. Schools graple with the issues of computers in the classroom. *The Tribune,* February 2, 1983, C-3.

Schmidt, F. H. *Spanish Surnamed American Employment in the Southwest: A Study Prepared for the Colorado Civil Rights Commission Under the Auspices of the Equal Employment Opportunities Commission.* Washington, D.C.: U.S. Government Printing Office, 1970.

Scrupski, A. The social system of the school. In N.K. Shimahara and A. Scrupski (Eds.), *Social Forces and School.* New York: David McKay Co., 1975.

Senior, C. Puerto Ricans on the mainland. In F. Cordasco, and E. Bucchiono (Eds.), *The Puerto Rican Community and Its Children on the Mainland.* Metuchen, New Jersey: Scarcrow Press, 1972.

Shade, B. J. *Afro-American Patterns of Cognition.* Madison, Wisconsin: Wisconsin Center for Educational Research, 1982.

Shibutani, T., and Kwan, K. M. *Ethnic Stratification: A Comparative Approach.* New York: The Macmillan Co., 1965.

Shimahara, N. K. *Mobility and Education of Buraku: The Case of a Japanese Minority.* Paper presented at the Annual Meeting of the American Anthropological Association, Chicago, Illinois, November, 1983.

Siegel, Bernard (Ed.). *Acculturation: Critical Abstracts, North America. Stanford Anthropological Series, No. 2.* Palo Alto, California: Stanford University Press, 1955.

Simmons, Ozzie G. The mutual images and expectations of Anglo-Americans and Mexican-Americans. In N. N. Wagner and M. J. Haug (Eds.), *Chicano: Social and Psychological Perspective.* St. Louis, Missouri: J. V. Mosby, 1971.

Skutnabb-Kangas, T. and Toukoma, T. *Teaching Migrant Children's Mother Tongue and Learning the Language of the Host Country in the Context of the Socio-cultural Situation of the Migrant Family.* Helsinki: The Finnish National Commisssion for UNESCO, 1976.

Slade, Margot. Aptitude, intelligence or what? *New York Times,* October 24, 1982.

Snow, Edgar. *Red Star Over China.* New York: Grove Press, Inc., 1961.

Spicer, E. H. Patrons of the poor. In J. Friedl and N. J. Chrisman (Eds.), *Cityways.* New York: T.Y. Crowell, Co., 1975.

_____. Persistent cultural systems: A comparative study of identity systems that can adapt to contrasting environments. *Science,* 1971, *174,* 795-800.

_____. The process of cultural enclavement in Middle America. *36th Congress of International de Americanistas, Seville,* 1966, *3,* 267-279.

Stockton Unified School District. *Community Survey: In-School Youth.* Unpublished manuscript, Research Department, Stockton Unified School District, 1948.

Stoddard, Ellwyin R. *Mexican Americans.* New York: Random House, 1973.

Sue, S., and Kitano, H. H. L. Stereotypes as a measure of success. In S. Sue and H.H.L. Kitano (Eds.), *Asian Americans: A Success Story?* Special Issue, *The Journal of Social Issues,* 1973, *29*(2), 83-98.

Sung, Betty Lee. *Chinese American Manpower and Employment.* Washington, D.C.: United States Department of Labor, Manpower Administration, 1975.

_____. *Mountain of Gold: The Story of the Chinese in America.* New York: Macmillan, 1967.

Sweeney, T. A. *Streets of Anger, Streets of Hope: Youth Gangs in East Los Angeles.* Glendale, California: Great Western Publishers, 1980.

Tomlinson, Sally. *A Sociology of Special Education.* London: Routledge and Kegan Paul, 1982.

Tow, J. S. *The Real Chinese in America.* New York: The Academy Press, 1923.

Tuden, A., and Plotnicov, L. Introduction. In A. Tuden and L. Plotnicov (Eds.), *Social Stratification in Africa.* Pittsburgh, Pennsylvania: University of Pittsburgh Press, 1970.

United States Commission on Civil Rights. *Report I: Ethnic Isolation of Mexican Americans in the Public Schools of the Southwest: Mexican-American Study Project.* Washington, D.C.: U.S. Government Printing Office, 1971a.

_____. *Report II: The Unfinished Business: Mexican-American Study Project.* Washington, D.C.: U.S. Government Printing Office, 1971b.

_____. *The Excluded Student: Educational Practices Affecting Mexican Americans in the Southwest: Report III.* Washington, D.C.: U.S. Government Printing Office, 1972a.

_____. *Mexican-American Education in Texas: A Function of Wealth: Mexican-American Education Study Project: Report IV.* Washington, D.C.: U.S. Government Printing Office, 1972b.

_____. *Teachers and Students: Report V: Mexican-American Study, Differences in Teacher Interaction with Mexican American and Anglo Students.* Washington, D.C.: U.S. Government Printing Office, 1973.

_____. *Toward Quality Education for Mexican Americans: Report VI: Mexican-American Education Study.* Washington, D.C.: U.S. Government Printing Office, 1974.

United States Department of Commerce, Bureau of Census. *Special Tabulations, Public Use Sample Data.* Washington, D.C.: U.S. Government Printing Office, 1970.

Vigil, James Diego. *From Indians to Chicanos: A Sociocultural History.* St. Louis, Missouri: The C.V. Mosby Co., 1980.

Waller, W. *The Sociology of Teaching.* New York: Wiley, 1967.

Wan Zahid, N. *An Analysis of Malay Educational Failures.* Unpublished doctoral dissertation, University of California, Berkeley, 1978.

Wax, M. L. *Indian Americans: Unity and Diveristy.* Englewood Cliffs, New Jersey: Prentice-Hall, 1971.

Wax, R. The warrior dropout. In H. M. Lindquist (Ed.), *Education and the Process of Cultural Transmission.* Boston: Houghton Mifflin, Co., 1970.

Weber, David J. (Ed.). *Foreigners in Their Native Land: Historical Roots of the Mexican Americans.* Albuquerque, New Mexico: University of New Mexico Press, 1973.

Weis, L. *Between Two Worlds: Black Students in an Urban Community College.* Boston, Massachusetts: Routledge and Kagan, 1985.

Weisbrod, Burton A. Education and investment in human capital. In D. M. Levine and M. J. Bane (Eds.), *The "Inequality" Controversy: Schooling and Distributive Justice.* New York: Basic Books, 1975.

West Stanley A., and Macklin, June (Eds.). *The Chicano Experience.* Boulder, Colorado: Westview Press, 1979.

Wigdor, A. K., and Garner, W. R. (Eds.). *Ability Testing: Uses, Consequences, and Controversies.* Part I: Report of the Committee; Part II: Documentation. Washington, D.C.: National Academy Press, 1982.

Wilcox, Kathleen. *Schooling and Socialization for Work Roles.* Unpublished doctoral dissertation, Harvard University, 1978.

Woolard, Kathryn, A. *Ethnicity in Education: Some Problems of Language and Identity in Spain and the United States.* Unpublished manuscript, Department of Anthropology, University of California, Berkeley, 1981.

Zarrugh, Laura. Home away from home: The Jacalan community in the San Francisco bay area. In Stanley A. West, and June Macklin (Eds.), *The Chicano Experience.* Boulder, Colorado: Westview Press, 1979.

SOCIOCULTURAL CONTEXTS OF LANGUAGE DEVELOPMENT

Shirley Brice Heath
Stanford University

Catherine, a six-year-old Chinese-American, listens attentively to the teacher's instructions; whenever the teacher asks the children to respond in chorus, she chimes in. When the teacher talks individually to Catherine, she speaks in short sentences in a quiet voice. At play, she watches the other children, joining in games that do not require that she talk. At home, she speaks primarily Chinese with her parents, except when she replays parts of the script from her teacher's role at school. By mid-year of the first grade, Catherine also speaks English as she plays with her dolls, responds to books her older brother reads in English, and plays with her brother's friends. Her first use of English in extended talk with other children at school occurs when she tries to involve them in dramatic play.

Jesus, son of a recently arrived migrant from Mexico, whose father works in the kitchen of a big city hotel and whose mother works in an electronics plant, had two years of schooling in Mexico. There he had been an enthusiastic student and an amusing jokester and storyteller among his friends. In the United States, he entered a third-grade classroom, where he was assigned to the lowest reading group; the bilingual coordinator explained to his parents that as Jesus began to use more English, he would be able to do better work in school. Jesus' parents began English lessons through a community social program and tried to speak only English to Jesus at home. On the school playground, Jesus quickly became a popular figure, imitating English phrases he heard from other children and throwing himself eagerly into their games. In the classroom, Jesus was reluctant to volunteer answers, and during reading, he often did not answer the teacher's questions about the story in the basal reader. When the teacher asked him to write a story about a set of pictures she gave him, he moved his desk over to join his friends and started talking excitedly in Spanish. His teacher reminded him that he must work alone on his story.

Ralph, son of a Vietnamese merchant who came to the United States in the first wave of refugees, is a senior in high school. He speaks relatively little in mixed groups of students, but answers when called on in class, writes carefully crafted essays, and excels in math and science. He has for three years been a student government leader. In his community, he works for his father and uncle, and he plans to go to the local community college and transfer to a state university in two years.

Similar vignettes of students in the schools of California could include children from many other groups--Filipinos, Samoans, Hmong, Guatemalans. In the past, children of all these groups have had to enter school with little or no English. To meet the expectations of teachers and testing specialists, they have had to learn not only the vocabulary and grammar of English but also the ways of using English the school expects. Their cultural and linguistic backgrounds differ from those of their native-speaking classmates, and the school has tried to meet their language needs by placing them in bilingual classes or English-as-a-second-language (ESL) classes that have focused primarily on providing English vocabulary and practice in grammar. Some schools have encouraged parents to enroll in English classes, and on occasion, school personnel have visited their homes to explain school policies and to clear up problems with attendance or academic performance.

INTRODUCTION

The aim of this chapter is to consider how children from some of the different language minority groups in California learn ways of using language in their homes and communities. The two-part message of this chapter is simple:

1. For all children, academic success depends less on the specific language they know than on the ways of using language they know.

2. The school can promote academic and vocational success for all children, regardless of their first-language background, by providing the greatest possible range of oral and written language uses.

This chapter opens by contrasting two views: first, the social science view that language learning is cultural learning and thus variable across sociocultural groups; and second, the educator's view that language learning for all children follows the single developmental model that schools reflect in the scope and sequence approach of the curriculum.

Ethnographers have helped answer the question of how we can gain knowledge about how children of different language minority groups learn to use language and have identified three major factors in language socialization: (1) parents' assumptions about child-rearing and their role in teaching language; (2) range of types of language uses available to children at home; and (3) extent of exposure young children have in their communities to a diversity of speakers, languages other than their own, and ways of using language that differ from those of their homes. The chapter closes with suggestions for ways in which increased knowledge about the sociocultural contexts of language learning in the homes and communities of language minority children can enable school personnel to promote and sustain children's facility in the widest possible range of using oral and written language to share and build knowledge.

LANGUAGE LEARNING AS CULTURAL LEARNING

Educators know relatively little about how children from families and communities of language minorities learn to use language. It is not possible to generalize to these children the findings of current research on children from middle-class English-speaking families, which posit a unilinear developmental path of language acquisition for all children. Yet, behind language arts curricula in schools stands an image of a "natural" path of development in language learning for all children. Educators' ideas about the pace and direction of children's movement along this path have depended heavily on studies reporting the language learning of mainstream middle-class first-born children, either inter-acting at home with their parents or in a laboratory setting with props provided by researchers. These scholars have given much more attention to how children learn the structures of their language than to ways in which they learn to use language to accomplish social and cognitive goals (Snow and Ferguson, 1977; Fletcher and Garman, 1979). In recent years, however, the research of ethnographers in language minority com-munities has expanded our knowledge about not only the strucutres of different languages but also the variation of language socialization pat-terns and the wide range of language uses different communities enjoy and foster in their children's early learning.

The sociohistorical, religious, and socio-economic contexts of families and communities of language minorities often differ markedly from the home life derived from mainstream patterns that dominate the thinking of school and human services personnel, such as social workers and guidance counselors. I argue in this chapter that all language learning is cultural learning: Children do not learn merely the building blocks of their mother tongue--its sounds, words, and order; they also learn how to use language to get what they want, protect themselves, express their wonderings and worries, and ask questions about the world. The learning of language takes place within the political, economic, social, ideological, religious, and aesthetic web of relationships of each community whose members see themselves as belonging to a particular culture. Thus, as children learn their language and how to use it, they also learn about the roles people, who are given certain names--such as mother, father, oldest, youngest--play in their lives. They learn how decisions are made and enforced; what to eat and drink; how to define and respect that which is called beautiful or good; and how to identify, ignore, avoid, or destroy that which is called ugly, bad, or worthless.

Cultural learning includes all the learning that enables a member of a family and community to behave appropriately within that group, which is critical to one's self-identification and whose approval is necessary for self-esteem. The family and others, such as friends who interact face-to-face on a regular basis with the child, form the primary social group from whom a sense of "who am I and what am I worth?" initially derive. It is little wonder, then, that caregivers' ways of using language guide children's fundamental language performance for accomplishing successful and satisfying social interactions.

For some children, the primary group provides the major learning environment for the preschool years. For other children, contexts for learning language extend beyond the family and immediate community into secondary social groups or institutions, which provide educational, medical, religious, and recreational services. In these secondary networks, children find uses of language--oral and written--that differ to a greater or lesser degree from those that sustain their daily life at home. For some children, these settings provide occasions for using a language other than their home language and for using language to exchange information drawn from written sources or authorities who are not intimately known to the children. For all children, these settings introduce the kinds of encounters that permeate much of formal schooling and allow individuals to obtain the attention, services, and evaluations of the teacher (Merritt, 1982).

Most of these secondary social groups, such as churches, daycare programs, and neighborhood libraries and recreational programs, expect to provide services in English and to use a certain number of written materials to support their daily operations. For example, registering a child for daycare, obtaining a doctor's appointment, clearing a parking ticket, requesting pastoral visits, and signing out library books require oral communication that is linked in part to some written materials. Just as important as the written language of these documents are the uses of oral language that surround them and underlie the daily activities of these secondary social groups (Shuy, 1984). Successful handling of the forms, instructions, and informational texts these institutions give out requires certain ways of talking. Individuals must know, for example, how to ask for clarification about content and procedures and must understand that written texts are often given with the assumption that their readers will take certain actions after reading them. Furthermore, individuals have to learn to recognize the importance of some written materials as permanent records either to be kept by the owner or passed on to others.

The smooth operation of secondary institutions depends on certain uses of oral and written language; and the more frequent and intense the occasions for young children to participate in such institutions, the greater the chance that they will learn before they begin school many of the uses of language that help ensure academic success. Some of these uses are compatible with the habits of talk that surround written materials within primary institutions, such as the home; certainly, some families practice uses of language that are highly compatible with some of those valued in school, work, and bureaucratic negotiations. However, an underlying premise of language use in secondary institutions is that the interactions of individuals are not based on intimate knowledge, extensive shared backgrounds, or the expectation of a long and sustained relationship. Thus, oral and written language must be depersonalized and able to stand somewhat autonomously from certain types of extensive knowledge that are not stated explicitly.

Some primary groups are open--admitting and even encouraging the involvement of secondary or outside social institutions in the child's early socialization; others open themselves less to outsiders and depend on familiar institutions and closely-linked community members for almost all daily support. It is often the case that language minorities, particularly those in low or threatened socio-economic positions, such as migrant workers, illegal aliens, or refugees, neither seek extensive interactions with outside or mainstream institutions nor create and manage analogous institutions within their own communities. Hence, the children from these groups often come to school bringing language uses and cultural beliefs supporting ways of using language that differ greatly from those of the classroom.

USING LANGUAGE IN SCHOOL

Strangely enough, though the common expectation is that the school prepares the young for life in the "real world" gradually and with compassion, school personnel rarely recognize that some fundamental notions that lie behind the language arts curriculum represent harsh demands for language minority children (Heath, 1982a). Not only is there the general expectation that all children will learn to speak English, but also the assumption that they have internalized *before* they start to school the norms of language used in academic life. Schools expect all children to have learned how to do, at least, the following with language before they begin their formal schooling:

1. Use language to label and describe the objects, events, and information that nonintimates present them. The most common form of request for such labels and descriptions is the "known information" question, one for which the teacher already knows the answer ("Can anyone tell me today's date?" "What's the name of the main character in the story?").

2. Use language to recount or recast past events or information shared with or given by nonintimates in a predictable order and format. Teachers request such recountings by questions ("Where have we heard this term before?" "What happened the other day when someone didn't follow the rules for putting books away?") and shape answers by correcting facts and their ordering as the student offers the recount ("Did Ann really make her book from construction paper, or was it something else? Think hard for a minute." "But wait, tell us about what happened when we were leaving the playground; don't jump ahead so fast.").

3. Follow directions from oral and written sources without needing sustained personal reinforcement from adults or peers ("Let's get ready for lunch." "Turn to page 65.").

4. Use language to sustain and maintain the social interactions of the group. Individual or personal goals or desires are acceptable only so long as they do not disrupt the harmony and balanced working relations of other group members ("If you want to use the scissors, Jenny, ask Tammy politely.").

5. Use language to obtain information from nonintimates. Children should know how to request and to clarify information, and they should view such information as extending beyond the authority of a particular person or specific occasions to either general use or transfer

to similar situations ("Why didn't you ask?" "Remember the other day when we worked a problem like this one on the board? If not, open your books, and find the example.").

6. Use language on appropriate occasions to account for one's unique experiences, to link these to generally known ideas or events, and to create new information or to integrate ideas in innovative ways ("My uncle has geese on his farm; I could bring some feathers"--said in response to teacher's query in a science lesson about why goose down repels water and provides such a warm covering; "Somebody once gave my mom an African violet; now they're all over the house. Is that propagation?"--said in response to introduction of Biology unit on plant propagation.).

Those students who achieve academic success either bring to school all of these language uses, and the cultural norms that lie behind them, or they learn quickly to intuit the rules of these language uses for both speaking and writing. Those who ultimately succeed in the highest academic lanes acquire or bring with them the facility for using oral and written language for multiple purposes and in varying styles; those who would go on to higher education must learn to use not only English but also at least one other language in their academic pursuits. (For a full review of the studies of classroom discourse from which these genres were derived, see Cazden, 1985; since the seminal work of Sinclair and Coulthard, 1975, and Mehan, 1979, studies have consistently demonstrated the narrow range of language uses rewarded in classrooms. This narrowness is especially evident for producing written language; see Applebee, 1981 and Langer, 1986; see Heath, 1986a for a discussion of the relation of genre uses to academic success.)

School personnel depend on these uses of language because they believe they promote learning and ensure harmonious classroom interactions. In general, schools expect those who do not come to school fluent in these language uses to learn them in the developmental order given above; e.g., learning to label and describe is expected before learning to use language to seek out or test information, and certainly before offering orally or in writing integrated or innovative ideas. Moreover, as students move higher in grade levels or advance in the study of a particular subject, they find more opportunities for using language to obtain, test, and create information than they had in their early years of schooling or in their introductions to subject matter. The curricula of both primary and secondary levels of schooling are based on the assumption that both the range of occasions for these language uses and their sequencing, in oral and written forms, represent a "normal" pattern of development for all children.

A SINGLE DEVELOPMENTAL MODEL

The primary social groups of working-class English-speaking groups and language minorities may not share the school's expectations about when, where, and how children learn language. (This chapter will discuss only language minority groups; however, native English-speaking groups may, as a result of historical, racial, or class factors, as well as separate cultural identities, develop sociocultural patterns that differ from those of the mainstream and the school. See Heath, 1983b for a full-length discussion of the widely different language socialization patterns of Black and white working-class communities in the Piedmont Carolinas.) The school expects children to follow a single developmental model in acquiring uses of language. Yet, educators' developmental models have, in large part, come from psychologists or linguists who have either studied their own children or children of similar primary social group membership. Much of the research of those who have described language acquisition and posited universals has been carried out with what we term "mainstream children" whose families are school-oriented, nuclear, and open to numerous types of involvement with secondary social groups such as Boy Scouts, Sunday school, camps, swimming clubs, and nursery schools. These mainstream homes offer toys and books bought and used by caregivers, usually parents, with young children. Parents surround their children with a future orientation and encourage the development of a self-image, which is reinforced as the child grows older by fellow members of secondary social groups, such as Scouts, athletic coaches and team members, and fellow summer campers. Fundamental to developmental models is the expectation that children have experience in such future-oriented groups both before and during the school years and that they absorb norms for listening, following rules, asking clarification questions, and expecting adults to lead them in their activities (Heath, 1983b). Developmental models assume a linear progression for learning in which earlier stages will not normally be repeated, and behaviors characteristic of later stages will not precede or appear in the place of those behaviors judged as simpler or more fundamental than others.

Those scholars who argue against a single developmental model and set learning in sociocultural contexts admit a universal base of potential for all neurologically normal human beings. However, they argue that an individual's potential will be played out in different patterns in accordance with factors in the language socialization of an individual's primary social group (Schwartz, 1976; Leiderman *et al.*, 1977; Wagner and Stevenson, 1982). Interactions with members of the primary social group; the extent of involvement outside this group; the number and types of toys, books, and other objects especially designed for children in the home; and expectations of appropriate roles for children will heavily influence the order and combination of language skills and uses the child learns (Schieffelin and Ochs, 1986).

Certain aspects of the grammar of the native tongue may even condition certain perceptual or meaning categories children create for themselves. For example, children whose first language contains morphemes that mark objects as long, flat, rigid, or flexible, will choose shapes over color before children whose first language does not contain morphemes marking such refined categories of shape. However, if a language group whose native tongue did not mark such categories were to train their children to attend to shape before color, their children could learn to select out and name such properties. We must bear in mind that the cultural learning of each primary social group is only a relatively small and arbitrary selection of the possible sets of behaviors (including ways in which language is used) of which the human infant is capable. Similarly, developmental models endorsed by schools represent an arbitrary and limited set of choices that can match the choices made by primary social groups to greater and lesser extents. For many language and culture groups, there is little fit between the kinds of language uses chosen by the school and those developed in the family and community.

WHO CAN TEACH AND WHO MUST LEARN?

If different language groups demonstrate different ways of talking, writing, and valuing patterns of using language in their primary social groups, how are we to know these patterns? Social scientists (mostly anthropologists and psychologists) who want to gather such information within homes and communities learn the language of the group, spend long periods of time with group members, and try to record as much as possible of their daily habits (Schieffelin, 1979). Though the appearance of a stranger in a primary social group alters some daily patterns, if social scientists remain long enough, their presence becomes less disturbing, and they can record the natural daily patterns of communication. They record the people and props that surround children as they learn to talk, as well as the occasions and extent of different kinds of language uses such as questions, proverbs, stories, explanatory monologues, and directives.   These researchers also note the values adults want their children to have, the extent to which they talk of their children in future roles, the ways they discipline and control their children, and the extent to which they bring outside institutions into the lives of the young. In addition, such researchers check their perceptions of ideals of behaviors and actual events with members of the social group, accepting as data the responses of the natives to the analysis of their actions and beliefs by an outsider.

These descriptions are especially valuable for comparison with the behaviors, judgments, expectations, and discipline procedures of other cultural groups, as well as with those of mainstream institutions, including the school. It is possible, then, to identify behaviors expected in schools that are missing in the child's home, differ in frequency, valued differently, or appear only in coordination with certain participants, topics, settings, and purposes. Such comparison involves accepting that there is a vast universe of possible behaviors, including language uses; and each cultural group or institution, unaware of this range of possible behaviors, transmits and reinforces only a very few to the young of their social group.

The particular array of language uses within any social group depends in large part on how the cultural group or institution views the roles of its members (Spindler, 1974). Are roles strictly segregated by age and sex? Where does the primary responsibility for the successful transmission of knowledge rest, with learner or instructor? To what extent is the young learner responsible for acquiring knowledge as an individual or for paying attention to adults who may see it as their responsibility to impart knowledge? Can roles shift across settings and situations, or does the playing of certain roles, such as that of caregiver for a young child, rest only with the parents and immediate family or with the community to which the child belongs? Role relationships result in specific kinds of language uses. For example, do parents expect a child to ask questions of them? Do they ask a child to answer questions to which they already know the answer? In school and in mainstream families, adults surround children with questions ("Where is your nose?" "What's your name?" "What does the donkey say?" "What's the story about?" etc.), and the school views it as "normal" for adults to ask children questions to which adults already know the answers. Mainstream adults see the asking of questions as a way to determine what the child knows or understands. The underlying assumption here is that the child can show what he or she knows primarily through verbalization and not display or demonstration of appropriate action in a relevant context. This view of learning differs greatly from that which prevails in cultural groups or institutions, which depend on apprenticeship or demonstration as the major modes of transmitting knowledge and testing to see whether knowledge has been acquired.

ETHNOGRAPHY AND THE STUDY
OF LANGUAGE DEVELOPMENT

The purpose of anthropological research on the learning of language in different primary social groups is not to label some groups as more "developed" or better than others; a given set of expectations for development does not guide the research of these social scientists. Instead, the usual goal is to describe what exists within these groups and to compare these descriptions with those of other groups in order that we may begin to know the range of human possibilities. Each group's ways are limited in terms of the full range of possibilities. Knowing the ways of other groups offers the possibility of expanding the abilities of all groups to create and learn new information and to adjust and adapt to new circumstances. Applied anthropologists often use information gathered through ethnographies--long-term studies of the daily habits of a particular social group in which researchers both observe and participate in the lives of those they are studying. These ethnographic studies can be used to help national or regional institutions who are planning social change for such groups. The goal behind the sharing of ethnographic information with social planners is to adjust plans for social change to local conditions, expectations, and cultural habits, so that change can occur with as little disruption as possible to the daily habits of the group (see Díaz *et al.*, this volume).

There are several dangers in the localized work that social scientists such as ethnographers do; the greatest is the overgeneralization of their work. The public at large uses inclusive labels for groups of people: Chicanos, Native Americans, Indo-Chinese, Asians, Blacks, Hispanics, etc. Little attention is given to historically or socially accurate definitions of such terms, or to the fact that members of some social groups do not agree on names for themselves (Lampe, 1984 on Mexican-Americans). The report of a study on one group of recently arrived migrants from Mexico is overgeneralized to all those of Mexican origin, regardless of their period of residence within the United States or of their sense of self-identification. A research finding reported for one group of Blacks is erroneously extended to all Blacks. A newspaper account of the academic prowess or gang organization of one Asian group is overextended to all who even "look like Asians."

Human beings have an overwhelming tendency to generalize information about social groups other than their own; stereotypes, ethnic jokes, racism, national pride, and denigrations of the language of others are all forms of this kind of generalization. Every social group is ethnocentric--and "linguacentric"--viewing its own ways of behaving and talking as better than all others and as appropriate for establishing the standards by which all others will be judged.

It is important, therefore, to recognize that patterns reported for one group of Blacks or one neighborhood of Spanish speakers or one Chinese-American community may not occur in other communities that will, on the surface, seem to be similar. Historical background, socioeconomic class, regional location, religious membership, and the extent of racial prejudice a group encounters are only some of the major influences that lead to different patterns of behavior and language use for groups speaking the same language or coming from the same national origin. The school and many other institutions within the United States have the goal of changing people's values, skills, and knowledge bases. Hence, teachers, social welfare agents, policemen, doctors, and ministers overlook group differences and urge people to change in the direction of the majority or the mainstream. The question is, then, "How might information from local communities, which may be generalized only with caution to similar communities, be used by the school and other institutions of social change?" (We will return to this question again after discussion of language development in three language-minority groups.)

FIRST- AND SECOND-LANGUAGE DEVELOPMENT IN A COMMUNITY PERSPECTIVE

The immediate primary social group--the family and intimate friends--judge a speaker's first-language competence and may also facilitate second-language competence. For example, if a primary social group uses Spanish as the language of everyday interactions, family members and friends will judge young children as linguistically competent on the basis of skills exhibited in Spanish. If, by the age when other children are talking clearly and transmitting content accurately, an individual child is still not communicating needs and desires effectively, community members will assess the child as linguistically incompetent. Similarly, if the child uses language in ways that are inappropriate within certain situations of that cultural group--picks up swear words and insults and flings these at adults, for instance--parents and other caregivers will assess the child as socially incompetent.

Also, the primary social group can often facilitate second-language competence. In an environment in which the learning of English is seen as part of the skills the language-minority child will need, adults may provide models and occasions for exposure to English. The distribution of English-speaking models may vary widely across language-minority communities and families (see Sawyer, 1976; Laosa, 1980 for discussion of these varieties for Spanish-speaking families). In some households, adults may, in the desire to have their children learn English, speak only English to the children, though the adults' knowledge of English may not be such that they can handle the language for a wide variety of topics or occasions. In other families, the parent who is more proficient in English than the other may choose to speak only English at home, while the other parent speaks a minority language. In still other cases, while the parents retain the minority language, the older children who have learned to play games, exchange taunts, and talk about school and their social concerns in English may speak English among themselves and speak their native tongue to their elders.

Children growing up in communities in which such models are available within the family may have few occasions for hearing English spoken by intimates for a wide variety of purposes and in a range of styles. Their knowledge of the uses of English may then be said to be "limited," or "limited English proficient" (LEP). For example, they may hear enough English to gain only a receptive knowledge and to understand what is being said. Later, they may develop a productive knowledge of English, but the extent of their productive knowledge will depend on the degree to which they have been exposed to models who use English for a full range of uses. If they hear English used in limited functions, such as in play or for talk on only some topics by a few models in their primary group, they are likely first to learn set phrases or chunks of language, such as greetings or the language of play ("time out," etc.), and only later to manipulate the components of the language system productively (Wong Fillmore, 1976). In particular, the range of uses of English associated with written materials, or the exchange of information not directly related to daily interactions, is likely to be narrower than that found in families using English for multiple purposes in writing and speaking.

Individuals need not be the only direct channel for the introduction of English in language-minority communities. Institutions, such as the church, health clinic, library, Scout groups, or nursery schools, may create situations in which English speakers interact with non-English speakers. If the language-minority community is not large enough to support its own grocery stores, small shops, and services such as laundries, adults must leave the community and negotiate with English speakers to maintain their daily home life. Preschoolers who accompany parents on these excursions outside their community learn English from these exchanges, though initially a receptive knowledge only. Later, as they are old enough to go for errands on their own, they must have productive skills or recruit someone who does. Perhaps as important as these occasions for hearing English is the fact that language-minority speakers come to know directly (rather than simply through the media) that there is a range of occupations in which English speakers work. There are English-speaking shopkeepers, grocery clerks, and postal clerks, just as there are English speakers in what are often more threatening occupations--such as medicine, law enforcement, and schooling.

Later, school success need not depend on preschool exposure to English; the child's exposure to and participation in the widest possible range of oral and written uses of any language is more critical than the particular language of this exposure and participation. Children who live in communities large enough to support their own shops and a range of job types in a language other than English can provide direct models of a wide range of language uses for children. The language of negotiation in the corner laundry, community health clinic, church nursery school, and legal aid office differs in structure, vocabulary, and intent from that generally used in the home. The greater the opportunities for experiencing language uses across a variety of contexts, the greater the language repertoire the children of the language-minority community will learn. To the extent that this repertoire includes uses of language similar to those of schools, workplaces, and bureaucratic agencies, children will have in place knowledge that will facilitate their learning these functions in English when they get to school. All occasions that demand explanation of facts and assumptions not shared by others provide practice in the kind of decontextualized impersonal language that the school and other mainstream institutions value. For instance, a child who listens to a bank teller tell his mother the rules for opening a savings account learns something about how to present information to someone who does not share it.

However, what of events and occasions for language learning in the homes of language-minority communities? Let us become more specific and consider some of the work that is available on the primary social groups in such communities. Because full ethnographies of communication in language-minority communities in the United States are very rare, we must draw from research by psychologists sensitive to cultural differences, general anthropological and historical accounts, and ethnographic research now in progress, as well as interviews with spokespersons for some of these language groups. For communities of Chinese-Americans, Mexican-Americans, and Indo-Chinese-Americans, we will consider: (1) parental assumptions about their role as teacher, (2) genres of uses of oral and written language, and (3) links between the home and community and outside institutions. Researchers now see these as the major sociocultural influences on children's language development.

Parental Assumptions

Parents can relate to their children in many different ways, and some communities promote certain relationships over others. Some parents may believe they are responsible not only for nurturing their children but also for training them and acting as their primary teachers. In this view, the responsibility for the child's development rests with the parent as an active force in the child's training. Yet, another parental view is one that sees the child as having the greatest active role in his or her development; self-development is expected, as long as parents provide basic nurturing and caregiving for the very young. Yet another view is that which emphasizes communal responsibility for the young. Infants belong to their families as well as their communities, and child-rearing is too precious a task to be given over completely to two individuals, the physical parents. Thus, the social, moral, and religious development of the child rests with the community; parents provide basic needs and reinforce the communal values in the home. Other variants of parental assumptions of responsibility depend on the family structure--extended or nuclear, the segregation of tasks according to age or sex, and the presence of dysfunctional influences, such as alcoholism, drug abuse, and severe poverty. Fundamental in examining cross-cultural patterns of language socialization, however, is the acknowledgment that parents can and do play widely varying roles in their children's language learning.

Chinese-American Families. Within those Chinese-American families for which we have data derived from historical accounts, interviews, or ethnographies, parental roles are closely linked with communal member-ship and values.   Historical studies of traditional Chinese family life reinforce this view and document the long-standing esteem for age, authority, perfection, restraint, and practical achievements (Hsu, 1949). For a comparison of the mainstream "American" family and Chinese family norms, see Hsu, 1983; Ogbu and Matute-Bianchi, this volume. Every individual in the Chinese-American family is expected to fulfill his or her role, regardless of personal characteristics.   The family and com-munity have a strong commitment to maintaining role relations and hierarchical status categories; rights and duties are unequally distributed because individuals are expected to conform to particular role and status duties.   Role behaviors, along sex and age lines especially, are pre-dictable because members of the community have a high degree of con-sensus and reinforce required behaviors through rituals and other established systems of interaction, such as family business parties (Cheng, 1948; Hsu, 1955; Stover, 1962; Ogbu and Matute-Bianchi, this volume).

Children are expected to learn to acknowledge these guiding mandates for behavior and to assume responsibilities according to their age and sex.   Moreover, they are expected to play roles and perform duties in-dependently of their personal feelings or goals. Parents see themselves as primary agents in directing children to assume in appropriate fashion the roles that the community expects of boys and girls, and later young men and women.   Children must defer to adults, who determine what their children can do and tell them when they should do it. Children are en-couraged to model themselves after authorities, to listen to authorities and watch what they do, and finally to practice again and again to achieve perfection. Learning is centered on the situation rather than the individual, because the individual must center on the situation in order to adjust to both the familiar environment and new circumstances. The at-tention to role autonomy and to situation rather than self as individual encourages mutual adaptation and dependence among those sharing a situation (Mead, 1951; Hu, 1960; Stover, 1962).

In conversational exchanges, parents control topics, length of time for talk by children, and the direction of the conversation. Parents initiate conversation with children, ask them factual questions, talk about steps they are following as they go about tasks, and monitor their children's talk and activities through verbal correction, explication, and evaluation. (Compare Hu, 1944 and Liu, 1959 with Stover, 1962 and Cheung, 1986, the latter two studies are based on participant observations of families in the United States and show strong continuities in verbal and other face-to-face behaviors with forms described in earlier literature.)

Parents have the goal of providing the very young with a secure environment that meets physical and emotional needs. They monitor their children's behavior with attention and follow-up by punishment or praise to reinforce children's behaviors regarded as acceptable and proper for children of a particular age. Catherine, the Chinese-American child of our opening vignette, showed her acceptance of the teacher's authority by responding in chorus with other children and in interacting with the teacher individually. She did not volunteer to try out her English until she had practiced at home--first, by repetition of the teacher's words, then through self-talk in solitary play with her dolls, and gradually through dialogue in cooperative play with other children. At school she first tried out her English among her peers when she had perfected the kind of talk in which she could play an authority figure--the director of dramatic play. Though a single child's pattern of learning to use English does not stand for the generalized pattern of all children in her community, this child's behavior--in the context of her family and community background--seems to reflect her parents' teachings regarding respect for authority, practice to achieve perfection, and accomplishment of practical goals. Catherine's parents and others in her community expect Catherine to retain Chinese and to learn English; in both languages, they expect her to take on increasingly complex and important tasks as she gets older. For her younger brothers and sisters, she is to serve as a model, encouraging them to assume responsibilities appropriate for their ages, to respect persons in authority, and to live up to the expectations of the community.

Parents and other family members in Catherine's primary social group provide children with special toys and books, expect them to take care of these items, to learn to use them appropriately, and to read to learn. The extent of reinforcement of school norms and the provision at home of books and other items that support school activities vary along class lines. However, families across classes see their role as complementing that of the school; they tell their children to listen to the teacher, to obey, and to recognize that practicing habits rewarded by the school will help ensure their future job opportunities. Particularly in middle- or upper-class families, specific practical skills at school--such as writing, reading, mathematics, and science--exceed in important areas of study, which they may regard as having no value for occupational or personal goals of the future. Within the family and the community, however, these same parents may emphasize aesthetic and historical skills and knowledge, as well as perfection in the practice of more mundane activities. In short, Chinese-American parents see themselves as active agents in their children's language learning; and it is not at all unusual for them to expect their children to continue speaking Chinese along with English because of the practical values of both languages and the communal identification values of Chinese. Children who leave aside their native tongue as they grow older may also feel they have to leave behind strong identity linkage to the roots of their community.*

Mexican-American Families.   We have laid out reasons why generalizations across communities, regions, and historical periods for any language minority often bear little resemblance to specific actual realities. This warning about overgeneralization applies especially in the 1980s to Hispanic populations--the fastest growing and perhaps most diverse language minority group in the United States. Descriptions of the number and variety of Hispanics in the United States abound, and there is growing public recognition of the variation among Hispanics (Ford Foundation, 1984) and their diverse attitudes and approaches toward acculturation or assimilation (Montgomery and Orozco, 1984). Scholarly research must acknowledge this variability and admit that far too many studies still report information about only impoverished or lower-class Hispanics, regional representatives of certain groups, or Hispanics of a certain national origin, drawing broad-sweeping conclusions about Hispanics in general. (For a critique of research, see Peñalosa, 1975 and Heath, 1986c.)

---

* Discussion of language socialization in the homes of Chinese-American and Mexican-American children in this chapter have benefited greatly from research-in-progress and unpublished research carried out by students at both the University of California, Berkeley, and Stanford. All errors of fact and interpretation remain, of course, my own. Of particular help has been the research of Lucinda Alvarez, who has studied two bilingual preschoolers of working-class families at home and at school. Her research (1986) documents the kinds of speech events available to children and the nature of the language uses of their parents who migrated to the United States from rural Mexico. Davida Desmond (1986), Ann Eisenberg (1982), Eli Pardo (1984), and Cynthia Prince have taken part in discussions of the materials presented here on Mexican-Americans and provided complementary and substantiating data. Olga Vasquez and Yolanda de la Cruz, Mexican-American teachers of bilingual children, have read portions of this chapter to assess accuracy and relevance. Christinia Cheung has provided substantial data on the language learning environments of mainstream and working-class Chinese-American families. Genevieve Lau, a Chinese-American teacher and school administrator, has not only provided data, but has also assessed the chapter's account of Chinese-American families and their children. Within the next few years, the publications of research currently underway by these and other scholars will, no doubt, both alter and greatly augment these beginning efforts to describe the sociocultural foundations of language development among the language minorities of California.

The discussion following here focuses only on communities of those Mexican-American families of relatively recent (within the past two decades) arrival in the United States. These families, though comparatively more economically stable in the United States than they were in Mexico, are lower- or working-class and may not have access to regular routes to upward socio-economic mobility and occupational choice. Many are confined to work in service jobs (hospitals, hotels, restaurants, and large office buildings), factory work in the garment and electronics industries, and agribusiness. (See Chavez, 1984; Connor, 1986; Heath, 1986c for discussions of patterns of identification, occupational choice, and movement out of the migrant stream for Mexican-Americans, as well as comparisons between the patterns of choice for recent Mexican migrants to the United States and earlier waves of immigrants from Mexico.)

Among families of recent migrants from Mexico, parents have been able, in their years before migration, to depend on extended family members to share responsibility for childrearing; circumstances after migration to the United States often alter these family patterns somewhat. The ideal remains, however, that parents, especially mothers, have primary caregiving responsibility while children are young; but the entire extended family accepts the child as a member at birth, and parents may therefore expect other family members to share some responsibilities for childrearing (Laosa, 1984). Seasonal rituals that accompany baptism, choice of godparents, confirmation, and reaching the age of 15 reinforce the membership of any child in the extended family, which includes not only kin but also close family friends.

Parents model behaviors their children are to learn, and children observe and repeat actions others have demonstrated. Adults do not usually accompany their actions with step-by-step directions, nor do they monitor children's actions by giving sequential orders or asking children to verbalize what they are doing as they work. They seldom ask questions that require children to repeat facts, rehearse the sequence of events, or foretell what they will do. Children ask questions of parents primarily when they seek information relevant to a task or decision at hand. Parents and older siblings tell young children what to do, and as they carry out tasks, adults reinforce good behaviors by evaluating them as "good" or "right" or denounce inappropriate responses as "bad" or "wrong." Older children are expected to entertain younger ones and see that when they have needs, the mother or some other maternal figure is informed.

Interpersonal behaviors in these families can perhaps be characterized as divided into a public world when members from outside the family are present and a private world reserved only for family members and occasionally for close and trusted friends. The social and linguistic content of interactions in each of these worlds appears to be quite different (Sanchez, 1984). Though researchers in such homes and communities can report only language behaviors--such as those noted above--that may be more public than private, they do note that older children talk about times such as bedtime, when parents come into their rooms to bless them and talk, or when young children climb into bed with their parents for periods of quiet accounts or eventcasts (Desmond, 1986). These occasions are surely times when children tell their parents about things they have learned to do, places they have been, victories and frightening experiences they have had, and plans they have for tomorrow, next weekend, or next summer. Because of strong norms of politeness and respect that may cause these families to appear to be authoritative or "neutral" with respect to their children's language contributions in the presence of outsiders, researchers must be alert for sources of information that suggest that there are some extended occasions for children to report their feelings, knowledge, and plans to adults (Delgado-Gaitan, 1982; Pardo, 1984; Alvarez, 1986; Desmond, 1986).

It is impossible to generalize about the views of either Mexican-American families or communities regarding whether or not their children should keep their Spanish and learn English. Some families, who have come from Mexico to find temporary work that will enable them to return to Mexico with cash for purchasing their own land or paying off debts, may not see English as a definite part of the future of their children. Others who plan to remain in the United States, with frequent visits to Mexico, assume their children will keep their Spanish, but recognize that they must learn enough English to meet school expectations and to have a wider choice of job opportunities. Still other families link Spanish symbolically and instrumentally to their self-identification and daily survival, and they promote Spanish, while encouraging their children to learn English as well. Within families who have older children, both Spanish and English may be used on a daily basis--parents and younger children speaking Spanish and older children using English among themselves, but Spanish with their parents and younger siblings.

The reasons and patterns for retaining Spanish and acquiring English are infinitely varied, and their attitudes toward one or the other language or the use of both not only are different across communities of different regional origin, occupational level, and location after migration, but also can be highly unstable. Return migration, the constant supply of new migrants, and the existence of models of Spanish/English bilinguals in the mainstream institutions of education, law, and medicine change attitudes rapidly. (See Aguirre, 1977 for a review of studies of language maintenance among Chicanos; see Hakuta, 1985 for a review of the role of bilingual education in language retention.)

Recent Mexican-American arrivals usually choose to settle in communities where there are either family members or close friends who share responsibilities for caregiving. Younger children are almost never alone with only one adult; they are surrounded by adults and children. Adults intervene in children's play when there are major disruptions, to praise or scold certain behaviors or language uses, and to tease children. Teasing requests from adults usually ask children about the personal names or qualities of those around them (e.g., "You're my little mama, aren't you?"). Nicknames, songs, and rhymes affectionately call attention to particular characteristics of little girls and boys, and are often subtle invitations from adults for play with young children (Schieffelin and Ochs, 1986). Playful exchanges are accompanied with strong positive reinforcement by the teaser and by the audience. Young children grow up in a rich verbal environment filled with talk from a wide variety of speakers, and though relatively little of this talk is directed specifically to preschoolers, they hear language from old and young used for many functions; and they are pulled into adult talk through directives, correctives, teasing language play, and occasions when adults want to teach them to do something. Visits to relatives and participation in festivals and celebrations of holidays bring these children into contact with family and friends from distant communities.

Before children become adolescents, the dictum that children are not equal conversational partners with adults is played out in daily interactions as well as special social occasions. To the extent possible, adults talk together and children and young people talk to each other; gatherings rarely include children and adults talking together. Adults tell children to offer food or drink to guests, not to interrupt adults when they are talking, and to be responsive to the calls of adults or older children. Good manners require that children be respectful of their elders, answer talk directed to them, and not initiate social conversations with elders. Adolescents in the presence of adults are expected to listen; on such occasions, adults may tell stories about themselves, other individuals known to all present, or characters remembered by a particular adult. These stories sometimes are accounts of behaviors that are unacceptable, and stories may end with a value-laden summary statement that assesses the wrongdoer. Stories may also tell of fictional or real-life heroes and herolines, "old times," and escapades of relatives or friends. A favorite theme of such stories is the wayward behavior of the young, but children who are present are not addressed directly; indirectly, they hear admonishments and warnings regarding their possible future actions.

In short, Mexican-American working-class families of relatively recent arrivals to the United States seem to consider their children active agents in their own language learning. Adults see themselves as teachers of only specific types of language uses--especially those through which children show their respect for and politeness toward elders. In general, however, adults expect children to learn to use the language of most everyday interactions without specific instruction from their elders. Adults are models in a supportive social community. Though primary nurturing responsibilities rest with mothers, the extended family carries broad moral and social obligations. Adults expect children to go further in life than they have gone, but they rarely suggest specific future careers for their children or seek out opportunities for their children to observe, talk with, or be apprenticed to adults in particular careers. The family of Jesus (the Mexican-American child of our second vignette) expects that he will not have to be kitchen help when he grows up, but he has heard little specific talk of how to envision himself in other work settings.

Indo-Chinese-American Families. Generalizations about Indo-Chinese refugee groups are especially untrustworthy, because almost no long-term social science research has been carried out in their communities. From the few descriptions involving intensive interactions with family and community members, we can glean only bits and pieces about parent responsibilities in language development (Reder *et al.,* 1983 and Reder, 1981). Across all the Indo-Chinese refugee groups, including Vietnamese, Hmong, Laotians, and Cambodians, fairly strict age and sex divisions of labor and role expectations exist (Finnan, 1980). Men and women carry out different tasks and serve different roles with outsiders, and the young are expected to respect age and to look to their elders as models for their future development. The linguistic and cultural adaptation by these groups seems to be conditioned by: (1) their prior social class membership and urban experience, (2) the period of time spent in refugee camps before arrival in the United States, and (3) conditions of initial entry into the United States.

The earliest groups of Vietnamese refugees were from the middle and upper classes, who had had extensive experience with cross-national business, urban life, and formal schooling. Many were fluent in French, were highly literate, and brought institutions with them (or adopted American ones) to provide mutual support for their group members. They developed organizations similar to chambers of commerce or other business support groups, created family businesses, and built a secure network and firm financial base for the academic efforts of their young. Those who came later were, in some cases, helped by those who had become established, and the intact community has been a stable support unit for the return of individual students after the pressures of trying to adapt to new academic settings. (See Hume, 1985; compare these descriptions with those of Tepper, 1980.)

Other groups, such as the Hmong, Laotians, and Cambodians, have come from refugee camps in Thailand; have had considerably less experience in urban settings; and are often unfamiliar with institutions such as the school, factory, public hospital, and employment office. Many of the Hmong had little or no experience with written forms of their language, and though some had learned basic reading and writing skills in the refugee camps in Thailand, they had few literates among them who could lead their adaptation to American life. However, within the camps, some had begun to learn English; and those who had sufficient English served as cultural brokers with representatives of federal and state agencies when they arrived in the United States. The Hmong, organized through a traditional clan membership, have an acknowledged leader within the United States, and distantly scattered communities have kept in touch through audio cassettes. Their members have preferred argicultural occupations and have worked as cooperative groups to secure large blocks of land to establish their own farms from Minnesota to California.

Early language learning opportunities for many of the Indo-Chinese refugees came in their initial sponsorship by individual families or churches. In their first months in the United States, they lived in close contact with mainstream American families who modeled not only the sounds, lexicon, and sentence structures of English but also ways of using language with children to reinforce those habits valued in schools. In some locations, the adoption of Christianity and participation in church life have provided occasions not only for using English in a wide variety of functions but also for seeing firsthand the teaching strategies that surround written texts.

In short, though we do not have the data to allow analysis of specific parental assumptions about learning among Indo-Chinese refugees, we can outline the extent to which these families have had compatible support systems helping them acquire English and habits of using English that would be acceptable in school. Adoption by churches and individual families helped provide extended, intense, and immediate observation and participation with academic and social uses of English. The prior adaptation by earlier families of Vietnamese and the establishment of support institutions helped facilitate knowledge about English language classes, business opportunities, and services available from state and federal agencies. Strong tendencies both to accept guidance from those among their own members who could act as cultural brokers and to work cooperatively to pool resources and labor have enabled most of these groups to build stable supportive communities for their young. Ralph, subject of our third vignette, knows he will remain in the United States, and he will someday take his father's place in the family business. Most Indo-Chinese groups entertain little or no hope of returning to their homeland, and they are thus driven by a future mental image of life in the United States. Therefore, occupational choices, self-identification as family and community members, and expectations of sustaining strong links between their communities and outside institutions drive them to learn English and to see the school as essential in their success.

Genres of Languages Uses

The term "genres" is one we usually think of in association with written forms of language. However, we use the term here to refer to the first level of discourse for language learners; genre refers to the type or kind of organizing unit into which smaller units of language, such as conversations, sentences, lists, or directives may fit. Each cultural group has fundamental genres that occur in recurrent situations; and each genre is so patterned as a whole that listeners can anticipate by the prosody or opening formula what is coming--a joke, a story, or a recounting of shared past experiences. Moreover, each sociocultural group recognizes and uses only a few of the total range of genres that humans are capable of producing.

Within the bureaucratic world and workplaces of every society, institutions require expertise in only some arbitrarily chosen genres. We may think of genre as synonymous with form, schema, or mold; we recognize each distinctive genre because it contains organized patterns for combining speech acts (such as requests, directives, etc.) and signaling what is to come within the stretch of discourse identifiable as a particular genre. Each genre is governed by its own set of rules. Though there may be certain fragments (such as questions, affirmations, declarations, and evaluations) existing outside the frame of genres, all genres that we can identify are internally organized to accommodate these fragments.

Genres are, then, maps or plans for stretches of discourse. They may carry within them certain relationships between writer and reader or speaker and listener, a representation of the observable physical world, and some form of affective or emotional assessment by the individual. Readers and listeners understand these stretches of discourse in large part because they associate them with others they have known; the opening line of a joke sets up expectant associations of what will come. One sentence of a set of directions for putting together an exercise bicycle is enough to create an image of what is to come. The extent to which children can gain access to both models and direct practice of oral and written genres that are valued within the school determines in large part their future school success; repeated and multiple experience with these genres ensure that individuals learn their forms and structures--the molds from which they are made.

Thus, of each cultural group, we ask questions such as: What is the extent of parroting of genres vs. substantive engagement with and practice in speaking, reading, and writing certain genres? What is the range of genres used in the home, solicited from children, and allowed from children? How do these match those of the school, the workplace, and other institutions outside the family and community? What are the driving values behind certain genres? How do these values relate to those underlying ways of using language at school? These are the questions that will guide our discussion of Chinese-American and Mexican-American family patterns. (At present, we lack sufficient information on Indo-Chinese American families to allow us to describe specific genres for these groups.)

Before discussing patterns from language-minority groups, we will review the patterns existing in mainstream school-oriented communities and in school activities. Linguists, sociologists, psychologists, and anthropologists have provided data that support the following school patterns; the first two--label quests and meaning quests--are language activities that ground school learning; the latter four are genres in which these activities become integrated as the learner becomes fully skilled in a repertoire of genres.

1. Label quests. These are language activities in which adults either name items or ask for their names. With very young children, adults name the item, usually pointing to it or holding it in front of the child. As children learn to say words, adults ask "What's this?" "Who's that?" Label quests include not only the names of items but also their attributes. While feeding a young child, the mother may say "potato, hot potato," as she prepares to feed the child. When the child can talk, he or she is asked questions about clothes, foods, toys, and books: "What color is that?" "Where is the big spoon?"

Throughout school, but particularly in the primary grades, teachers ask students to give them the names and attributes of items used in the classroom, read about in books, and discussed in class. Textbooks rank questions that ask "what" and "what kind of" as their easiest. Throughout schooling, teachers and curriculum-designers assume knowledge of labels and attributes precedes "higher order" knowledge, such as that required to answer "why," "how," and "when" questions.

2. Meaning quests. Within this language activity, adults either infer for the young child what he or she means, interpret their own behavior or that of others, or ask for explanations of what is meant or intended. The mother may say of the baby's cry, "You're hungry," or may explain away an action by saying "Mother didn't mean to...," or may speak of a book's character as intending to be good or bad, secretive or open. Adults make inferences about the meaning of children's statements as they restate, "Up, mama, up," into "You want to get up on my lap, don't you?"

In school, teachers and tests ask students to explain the meanings of words, pictures, combinations of events, and their own behaviors. It is not sufficient to say what something is; one also must learn to say what it means--how it was intended, what action will be its result, and how it is to be interpreted or valued. From basal readers to twelfth-grade Shakespeare classes, teachers ask the meaning of passages and require students to infer from a written text what an author meant.

3. Recounts. Within this genre, the speaker retells experiences or information known to both teller and listener. As children retell, they may be questioned by the listener who wants to scaffold the telling in a certain way. For example, adults ask children to repeat stories they have heard read to them or to tell third parties about an outing they have gone on with a parent. The prompt for such recounts is usually a question--"Can you tell Daddy what happened to you and Mommy today?" and questions correct the recount when it begins to veer off the chronological path.

Teachers ask children to provide summaries of material known to teacher and fellow students, to recount facts known to all class members, and to display their knowledge through oral and written recounts almost daily. Tests ask questions that depend upon a strict recounting of the passage the student has read.

4. Accounts. Unlike recounts, which depend upon a power differential, one party asks another to retell or perform for the sake of performance; accounts are generated by the teller. Thus, power resides initially in the teller rather than in another person who serves as judging audience. Accounts provide information that is new to the listener or new interpretations of information that the listener already knows (e.g., a reinterpretation of why the hot water heater is leaking again). Examples include children telling parents about an afternoon spent at a friend's birthday party or at a neighborhood backyard swimming pool. Accounts are judged not only by their truth value--"could this have happened?"--but also by the organization of the telling. If the teller follows what the audience expects as a "logical" telling, the account will be accepted; if the organization of the telling seems chaotic and unpredictable, the listener will discount the event and the teller (Michaels, 1981).

Schools allow the general stream of students few occasions for accounts. Show-and-tell, in the primary grades, and creative writing, in the upper grades, are the major occasions in which students may tell about their own experiences and be held accountable to the content and the form of the telling. However, at the highest levels of ability grouping and in higher education, teachers ask students for their interpretations, their valuation of events or materials read on the basis of their experiences, their integration of the knowledge of others, or their creation of knowledge (initially in creative writing and later in reports of experiments and other types of research).

5. Eventcasts. In this genre, individuals provide a running narrative on events currently in the attention of the teller and listeners (as in sportscasts or in giving directions) or forecast events to be accomplished in the future (as in developing plans). The narrative may be simultaneous with the events or precede them. A mother may narrate as she changes a child's diaper the events that will ensue: "We'll get dressed, then we'll have our bottle, and then we'll go see if we can take a ride to pick Daddy up from work." As children grow older, they provide eventcasts during their solitary play, talking aloud to themselves about what they are doing, and in dramatic play, as they tell their friends who will play certain roles, what identities certain objects will assume, and how the script for the dramatic play in the pretend kitchen, battle field, or doctor's office

will go. Adults model eventcasts as they talk about plans for the future and the sequenced steps they will take on a family trip. Making jello in the kitchen or changing a tire are accompanied by running narratives that detail steps being taken in the process.

In school, teachers often begin the day or the class hour by telling students what will take place. Mathematics and science teachers explicate for students the steps they are to take as they work out problems and experiments; eventually, they expect students to be able to explain these steps themselves. The outline for an essay or the study plan for a group project are eventcasts--explication of sequential steps to be taken to accomplish a current or future goal.

6. Stories. This is perhaps the most familiar genre because of our customary associations with the written stories read to children and requested of children's imagination. The mold of these fictional accounts is such that they must include some animate being who moves through a series of events with goal-directed behavior (Stein, 1982). Children hear their parents tell stories about their youth, have stories read to them, and listen to Bible stories at church. Parents elaborate factual accounts to make them fictional stories that will entertain young children at bedtime or cajole them into taking foul-smelling medicine. Peers create and elaborate on ghost tales, and parents embellish real events or possible events to teach lessons.

In school, from basal readers to senior-class history texts, fictional stories supplement factual or expository prose. Stories of fantastic adventures by animate creatures abound in basal readers; pseudo-biographical accounts embellished with morals and summative lessons give human interest to details of political and military accomplishments. Brief stories serve as epigraphs to invite readers into expository prose, and students learn to listen to stories and read fictional literary accounts in order to draw morals and thematic statements, as well as to learn how to craft their own writing.

These language activities and genres do not exhaust all the possibilities in the universe of discourse, but they are the most valued in formal education and those most commonly reported by researchers who have studied how children in mainstream school-oriented families learn language. (For a review of such studies, see Heath, 1984.) Some of these genres, such as the eventcast, ask the child to separate himself or herself from the here and now and project plans, possible sets of circumstances, and events into the future. In eventcasts, recounts, accounts, and stories, children must interpret, describe events chronologically, and propose problems and solutions. In mainstream homes and in school, much of the activity surrounding these genres is focused on books or the accomplishment of particular tasks. For example, adults reading a child's book that has only pictures and no storyline may ask children to label items and then to tell the meaning of actions taking place in the pictures. Once they have read a book, children are asked to recount its contents or to compare it with accounts they have given of their own experiences. As children draw, they are asked to provide eventcasts of their drawing; when they build with blocks, tinker toys, or other combinations of objects, they become accustomed to questions such as, "What are you making?" "What are you going to do when you run out of blocks?" (For a review of mainstream families' language behaviors surrounding bookreading and play, see Heath, 1982b; 1983a.)

In language-minority homes, some or all of these language activities and genres, as well as others, can and do occur; many others, besides those valued by the school, also occur. Critical to school success, however, is the extent to which all these school-valued genres occur in the home--in either the minority langauge or in English--repeatedly, around written materials, and with strong positive reinforcement. It is important that members of the child's primary and secondary social groups model these genres, ask questions about them, and guide their elaboration and extension. The frequency and intensity of occasions both within and outside the home that call for these genres is critical. In mainstream communities, voluntary associations, church schools, nursery schools, and baseball teams support these genres; language-minority children need similar repeated reinforcement and occasions for practice both within and outside their homes.

Chinese-American Families. In Chinese-American families, label quests are embedded in on-going action and often used as corrections for children's mistakes in language. For example, if a child asks for juice and then refuses it, making it clear he or she wanted soda instead, adults will offer the correct name of the item wanted. Correction of the name for the item will occur before an expression of the belief that the child should prefer juice to soda. Especially in homes where the mother does not work outside the home, mothers may spend time reading to young children and helping them in creative art projects or constructing toys. During these activities, books and even the writing of Chinese characters may be the focus of label quests.

Meaning quests frequently center on discussion of roles--what boys do, how old one has to be to do a particular activity, and expectations about behavior in certain roles. Adults use statements about the meaning of certain behaviors (e.g., a whining tone) to comment on the appropriateness of such an action for a child of a particular age. ("Boys your age don't need to do that to get what they want; just ask.") These meaning quests become increasingly common as children approach school. Current behaviors are assessed for their appropriateness to school norms, to growing older, and to becoming a "big boy." Meaning quests from parents to children do not usually include expressions of emotional evaluations. Displays of sadness, temper, or excitement are not solicited or rewarded by adults; when such displays occur, parents scold, tease, or ignore children, chiding them for not restraining their emotions (Stover, 1962). Adults' comments about books or acquaintances do not model meaning interpretations based on emotions; for example, parents are not likely to say of a storybook character who has lost his way in the forest, "He's probably very sad and wishing he were home with his mother right now." They are much more likely to say, "He's lost in the forest. How could that happen to a little boy?"

Accounts occur far more frequently in Chinese-American homes than recounts. Children's actions and knowledge are considered appropriate for discussion in the home, and adults often ask children about events of their day. Outside the home, or when strangers are present, however, children are expected to be quiet unless addressed by adults and to listen to adult conversation without interrupting. Requests for accounts can also focus on inappropriate behaviors. ("Where have you been? You were not supposed to leave the yard.") Summative comments after such accounts usually focus on the appropriateness of the behavior for the role ("Brothers have to take care of their sisters."), age ("You're too old for that."), or sex ("Girls don't do that.") than on general warnings.

Eventcasts occur during on-going activities in Chinese-American homes. Mothers provide eventcasts as they go about tasks they model for their children. Such eventcasts may also be punctuated with assessments of certain steps: "You put his shirt on first, that's good, he may be cold. Now where are his pants?" The sexual division of labor exposes girls to more eventcasts than boys, since girls are expected to learn to help their mothers in the kitchen and around the house. Boys run errands, watch younger children, retrieve the laundry from the laundromat, and repair small items; but if fathers are available in the home for less time than mothers, boys receive fewer eventcasts than girls. However, on family outings or during family preparations for a future event, children of both sexes hear their parents talk about plans, sequenced actions, and solutions to problems.

Storytelling occurs during bookreading and in tales about historical events and people. Talk around books may include analogous stories, in which a character or a set of events is similar to that in the story just read.

Mexican-American Families. In the homes of the relatively recent migrants from Mexico, on which our discussion in this chapter focuses, adults use label quests focusing on parts of the body, family members' names, immediate activities, and only rarely on distant or secondary items, such as the names of items on television or in books. Adults are far less likely to ask a child to label his or her shoe than they are to ask the name of a cousin or to show an adult guest where his or her nose is. The occasions for such label quests usually take place with very young children at large family gatherings, and they are not usually part of the daily patterns of interactions between just mothers and their children. Meaning quests occur in teasing exchanges with older children, and they may be directed toward a third party. For example, an adult teasing a four-year-old may tell his older brother, "Tell him I'm only teasing, I'll bring his teddy bear back." Children hear adults talk about the meanings of actions and emotional responses to events, but in mixed adult-children groups, adults rarely ask children to express their interpretations of events or their emotional evaluations.

If parents know what has happened, they believe they do not need to ask a child who also knows to recount the event. Thus, adults rarely request recounts of children, except of special events that should be told to an unknowing third party; for example, a mother may ask her young son to tell a visiting aunt about his sister's birthday party. Adults ask for accounts from children often, especially in intimate family gatherings, and particularly when they sense that something unusual has occurred. When invited to talk, children can tell what they saw or did, and parents may question them about the account. Older children, and occasionally younger children, are asked to give accounts for visiting family members or friends. For example, if an older son is home from college, and friends are visiting, his mother may ask him to tell about his first year at school. Adults may then add moral summations to benefit younger children or to transmit directly a message to the older son (Desmond, 1986).

Eventcasts almost never occur around daily tasks in Mexican-American families. Modeling and close observation, supplemented by reinforcement through praise or caution, surround the teaching of most tasks in the home. However, family members talk together to plan future events, such as a shopping trip in a friend's borrowed car, a visit to Mexico, or plans to bring a relative from Mexico to live. Cooperative talk among several people create these eventcasts, and they are rarely handed down or delivered as mandates from a single individual. Family members use talk to form plans, consider alternatives, pose problems, and reach solutions. Stories fill many hours in Mexican-American homes; young and old tell scary *bruja* (witch) tales, as well as stories about real events embellished with new details and about historical figures and events. Children have books in the home, sometimes bought by parents, but often brought from school by older siblings who may read stories aloud occasionally. Children tell stories during dramatic play, such as when they "play school," and the telling of stories and accounts consumes the majority of time of single-sex groups formed by pre-teens.

Jesus, our Mexican-American child of the second vignette, read stories in Spanish books in his small rural school in Mexico, but he could not bring his schoolbook home. In Mexico, publishing companies and commercial establishments have not promoted children's literature as a literary genre; *"cuentos,"* comic books, and collected stories of national heroes can be found in some stores of large cities, but the extensive commercial promotion of children's literature found in the United States and some European nations does not exist in Mexico. Thus, the absence of books for children in the homes of most Mexicans should not be regarded as an indication of neglect of children's preparation for school by individual families. In the United States, Jesus sees neighbor children doing their homework, occasionally is invited to "play school" with older neighborhood children, and sometimes goes to a reading group in the neighborhood library, but he must learn how to respond in classroom situations focusing on the individual. In Mexico, the teacher asked the children to read in chorus; here, the teacher asks direct questions of him, and he is expected to do his seatwork on his own without help from his friends. In Mexico, he had been a reader; in his community he knew what stories were and he could tell them. In his new school setting, definitions of reader and storyteller do not include his ways of recognizing or telling stories.

Links Between the Home and Community

We have argued that students who come from homes in which English is not the native language must have--in either their mother tongue or English--multiple, repeated, and reinforced access to certain language uses that match those of the school. The language activities (label quests

and meaning quests) and genres (recounts, accounts, eventcasts, and
stories) noted here function as the primary language uses through which
students demonstrate the academic, cognitive, and linguistic proficiency
required by the school.   [See Cummins' (1981) discussions of
Cognitive/Academic Language Proficiency (CALP).] It is through these
language uses that students in school display their knowledge. The extent to which children have access to these uses of language and to which
such occasions of access revolve around written texts determine, in large
part, success in school and in many mainstream institutions beyond the
school.

We may ask why it is that some studies show that children from homes
that have continued to use their mother tongue rather than English tend
to perform better in school than children from homes where children
have some exposure to English from older siblings or parents who try to
use only English with their children (Dolson, 1984). No doubt there are
many factors that bear on this question. However, when parents and
older siblings use English but do not have a strong command of it across
varieties of genres, the language modeled and the occasions of access for
children may be limited to instrumental needs of daily living. Thus,
children in such homes learn some vocabulary, grammatical structures,
and forms of discourse, but they have not had extensive practice in a
variety of genres focusing on topics that cannot be known through direct
personal experience. For example, they may be able to handle questions
focusing on labels, but they will lack the skills to create eventcasts or they
may have had insufficient experience in responding to questions that
probe the meaning or intention of what they have said (Saville-Troike *et
al.,* 1984).   On the other hand, children who acquire sufficient competence in English to act as translators for their parents have opportunities to hear and speak genres that may not be characteristic of their
home language uses.

In homes that continue to use their native tongue, there is a strong
likelihood that there will be a a wide range of genres including some or all
of those valued in school as well as others valued within the primary
group but not in institutions beyond the family and community. These
children will have had multiple, repeated, and reinforced occasions to
practice naming, describing, explaining, planning, summarizing, and
creating in their native tongue. When they learn English in school, they
have to learn the sounds, vocabulary, and syntactical system of another
language, but they do not have to learn a new set of uses for language as
well (Escobedo, 1983). Consequently, when they come to school, they

not only have the basic interactional skills needed for social exchange but also they are conversant with the types of genres school personnel expect students to use to display their cognitive and academic skills.

If all the genres noted here as valued in the school are not available in the home, can institutions within the community provide them? Yes. Retail and service institutions give children the opportunity to interact and watch their parents communicate with individuals who are not intimates. Thus, in the exchange of goods and services, children have to explain their meaning, ask for clarification, and recognize that what they say is not always understood as they intended. Whether in English or in their native tongue, children need extensive practice in having to explain themselves to those who do not share their specific home experiences, assumptions about meaning, and expectations of outcomes. Church activities, especially those focusing around discussion of written texts, provide opportunities for practice of genres similar to those used in school. Participation in voluntary associations, such as sports teams, Scout groups, and music lessons give added practice in uses of language similar to those of the school.

It also may be that even when such groups from beyond the community are not available for direct participation by children, activity by adults in these groups can affect children's language learning. For example, when adults participate in labor unions, political action groups, benevolent societies, or church Bible study groups, they bring home printed texts and talk about them. In addition, such groups may bring outsiders into language-minority communities for meetings, and children will then have exposure to uses of language that do not focus around here-and-now daily activities, but around future, distant, and often abstract goals that are not linked to specific roles.

A major theme through much of the early scholarly research on language minorities was the suggestion that their lower-class and working-class families "lacked a future orientation." Current researchers find that parents do consider carefully the future of their children as they anticipate it; that is, they may think of family roles before occupational niches. Thus, they may encourage young women to learn skills related to housekeeping and child care, because they expect them to marry and become wives and mothers. This is not to say that such families do not also expect children to grow up and take jobs. However, they may consider the family's responsibility to rest primarily with the preparation of the young for roles of the private and not the public world of the future.

Increased involvement of language minorities with secondary groups representing mainstream educational, medical, legal, and occupational institutions can help provide families with information that may help them expand their role in preparing their children for the future. With specific reference to language, if the language-minority community itself does not contain business, religious, and political institutions in which varieties of genres reflecting different language uses exist, then mainstream institutions need to provide such opportunities within the community. For example, in our third vignette of Ralph, his Vietnamese business community gave him occasions to hear at home talk about the oral and written language of retailing. Once he was old enough, Ralph began to work in his family's business, gaining experience in public language, keeping written records, negotiating with representatives of mainstream institutions, and planning for future goals.

The public media, whether in English or the minority language, also provide models and occasions for interaction around a wide range of language uses. Television and radio programs may: (1) be watched or listened to in silence, (2) serve as a topic of conversation, (3) prompt questions and other kinds of discourse from children, or (4) be mere background noise for talk unrelated to the programs. By age two, children from all kinds of socio-economic and cultural backgrounds can look at television in an active, goal-oriented way (Rice, 1986). Many of the programs most frequently chosen by children, such as "Sesame Street," provide dialogue appropriate for young children and issue questions inviting children to see themselves as part of the group participating on screen. Children learn vocabulary, formulaic language (especially the language of commercials), and intonation patterns from television; they use characters on television to create their own verbal routines, dramatic play, and story embellishments.

However, since much of television and most radio programming offer fast, abstract, and unsimplified discourse about settings, objects, and persons that children do not know in their primary social community, children may view or listen to information without becoming engaged with it as a participant (see Kagan, this volume). The greatest proportion of the public media does not invite the child in as an interacting conversationalist; instead, the media expect children to be passive viewers and listeners. One dramatic exception is rock music; pre-teens and teenagers learn the lyrics of rock songs. Their fascination with and knowledge of this entertainment realm often aid their assimilation into a generalized peer culture (Garcia *et al.,* 1985). Although radio programming in

English and other languages has included an increasing number of opportunities for adults to "call in" and become a part of the program,
children are usually excluded from this type of direct interaction with the
distant medium (Kagan, this volume).

Even in the midst of adults' conversations, however, children may
break in with questions about what they see on television. Thus, television in some homes becomes a prop for talk, just as books do in other
homes (Rice, 1986). Children ask, "What happened to the motorcycle?"
"Where did Spider man go?" "Can big bird come to my house?"
Not only do adults respond to questions from their children but also they
may initiate conversation around the mutually-shared scene or action of
a program: "Look, he's falling." "What's that?" "Remember
Manuel's motorcycle like that?" Thus, in homes that do not include
adult-child bookreading as a regular routine, television can serve as a
source of uses of language similar to those in reading activities in the
primary years of schooling.

A CONTEXT FOR CHANGES IN
CLASSROOM LANGUAGE USES

I asked earlier how information about local communities might be
used by the school and other secondary institutions. I reiterate here the
caution against overgeneralization of information on language-minority
communities. Such information must be received with the dictum that
the presence of a single behavior noted as characteristic of a particular
group is never sufficient evidence that other behaviors described in the
research literature in connection with that behavior are also present.
Thus, if a Mexican-American child does not tell stories about flat line
drawings, then teachers should not jump to the conclusion that he or she
comes from a home in which adults do not read books to children.
However, if several behaviors co-occur, that is, if the child does not easily explain what is occurring in a science project in which he or she is participating, is weak on vocabulary that does not relate to here-and-now
familiar daily objects, and does not recount summaries with accuracy,
then teachers should consider the need for explication and practice of
these uses of language. The work of DeAvila *et al.* (1981) with MICA
(Multicultural Improvement of Cognitive Abilities) illustrates the
dramatic improvement in academic achievement of language-minority
children who are allowed in their study of math and science to work
either individually or in small groups with extensive verbal interaction,

which includes many types of accounts and eventcasts (Kagan, this volume).

Eventcasts during on-going activities, label quests focusing on distant abstract items, and recounts of information known to students and listeners have to be learned in school; if the child's English skills are weak, these should first be learned in the native tongue. In this way, the complexities of concepts underlying certain grammatical constructions (such as coordination with temporal connectives--"we can do that when we have finished this"--necessary in eventcasts) can be mastered in the native tongue before they are transferred to English. Thus, the kind of knowledge presented here about the sociocultural environments of language learning that may lead to facility with certain types of language uses favored by the school, but not other types, can help guide teachers to expand language uses to benefit all students. Clearly, the school should not decide to teach what may be regarded as genres most characteristic of Mexican-American homes to Mexican-American children in school; the point of studying language uses across sociocultural groups is to enable teachers to expand the oral and written language uses of all children. Thus, it is important that those who have had few opportunities to give accounts in their home settings be able to do so at school, but it is also necessary for those who have much home experience in handling eventcasts help other students learn to talk about strategies for the future and detail events going on in the present. Vocational and academic success depend on a wide range of functions, forms, and ways of using both oral and written language, and it is the responsibility of the school to facilitate expanded language uses in English and other languages for students from all sociocultural and class backgrounds.

To accomplish these goals of expanding learning through increasing facility in language uses, teachers can explain the language activities and genres noted above and accompany instruction in content matter with references to the types of languages uses certain activities call for. Language arts curricula can expand to include not only materials in basal readers but also other types of materials with which children may be familiar in their daily environments--jokes, synopses of movies or television shows, *cuentos,* etc. Within the classroom, many of the forms of children's home language uses are appropriate if teachers do not expect the unilinear developmental model of languages uses. The "talk story" adopted by some teachers of Hawaiian children illustrates one such successful incorporation, which facilitates the adaptation of these children to the school's language uses and helps them succeed in reading (Au,

1980; Au and Jordan, 1981). The adaptation of home language uses by teachers of working-class Black and white children in the Piedmont Carolinas is yet another model of ways in which expanding classroom genres promoted increased academic performance of minority children. (See Heath, 1982b; Heath, 1983b for a discussion of anthropological work that has enabled teachers to alter classroom language uses while improving minority children's academic performance; see also Cazden, 1983.)

A major benefit of teacher's and children's attention to the wide variety of language uses outside the classroom is increased language awareness on the part of all. The range of language uses within classrooms is amazingly small and does not begin to measure up to the range of uses many occupations require. Current research suggests strongly that the greater the extent to which the school can foster metalinguistic awareness (or attention to language *per se* in children), the greater the chance that children will transfer any language-related instruction beyond the immediate instructional setting (Wilkinson *et al.,* 1980; Olson, 1984; Goelman *et al.,* 1984; Heath, 1986b). Through such talk about language and attention to how language is used in a wide variety of oral and written context, students learn not just literacy skills (e.g., how to alphabetize, recognize letters and clusters, etc.), but also much more important literate behaviors (e.g., comparing the theme of one story to that of another, assessing the style and factual content of written materials) that are critical for success in academic environments (Heath, 1986c).

Information from local communities may be used to alter practices in the school so that they might include explication of, as well as opportunities for, practice of certain critical genres. Comparative information from across language-minority communities also helps emphasize the value of multiple, repeated, reinforced practice of different language uses; a brief explanation and two weeks of coverage in class is no match for the hundreds of thousands of times certain children may have practiced such language uses in their preschool experience. Thus, certain language skills cannot be seen as appropriate for one brief portion of the sequence of skills to be covered and thereafter assumed to be acquired as the basis for the development of other skills viewed as higher order. The ideal way to accommodate children across a variety of language-minority backgrounds is to give them redundant, reiterative, and interdependent occasions for practice along a wide range of genres of language uses. Of those named here as important in school, none is inherently more elementary than another. All are necessary at all stages of schooling and all can be incorporated into the curriculum of any grade level or subject area. Teachers must, however, be culturally and linguistically sensitive to the kinds of language uses they are offering students and the cognitive and academic, as well as linguistic, demands they are making of students.

Mainstream institutions beyond the school--the workplace, bureaucratic office, and marketplace--require all the genres named here, and many others as well; thus, all children will benefit from an expansion of types of language uses. As the institution expected to prepare the young for successful participation in a wide variety of secondary institutions, the school can benefit from such expansion. Success in all types of work, from wage labor to professional services, depends on asking and answering questions, acknowledging the authority of written texts (and knowing when to question them), working within roles, and producing and understanding a variety of oral and written languages uses. Moreover, adaptability and flexibility for movement from one role to another depends on being able to use language for a variety of functions; the manager or foreman's job requires different language functions than that of the lineworker.

Must the school bear the major burden for preparing language-minority children for the kinds of performances in English that the world of work requires? Yes. Though it is possible that other mainstream institutions such as the church, labor union, voluntary associations, and the public media may play some role in modeling and giving practice for the genres noted here, communities tolerate the intrusion of these secondary institutions only to a certain extent. As noted earlier, some primary social groups are relatively closed, choosing to keep their socialization practices primarily in the hands of language-minority members. Others are either more open to external influences or model their own community institutions after those of the mainstream. Most language-minority communities are reluctant to accept parent education from outsiders; rearing children is a private or community responsibility, and rare is the group that freely allows strangers to tell them how to socialize their young to language or anything else. Thus, parent education programs that set out to teach parents how to raise their children so they will be linguistically prepared for school have relatively little chance of achieving far-reaching influence. The desire for change in such a core value as how one socializes the young must come from within a group; trying to impose external values on preschool home life is not likely to bring any significant internal change to families.

Further research is certainly required in language-minority communities before we know the answers to many of our questions regarding sociocultural environments of language development or the varied types of genres possible within each community.   However, we now know enough to be assured that both cultural ways of life and the social relationships of language-minority communities to the larger society combine to shape children's early language experiences.   The extent of attention language minorities give to creating images of the future for children and linking past and present experiences to these images, as well as their tolerance for questions from children, help determine how prepared children are for the cognitive and academic demands of the school. Microanalysis of longitudinal data set in broad descriptions of specific language-minority communities in different regions, of different occupational levels, and of different national origins will enable researchers to identify key factors that affect points of connection between language at home and at school.   This knowledge will then help teachers, administrators, and developers of commercial textbook and testing materials expand their ways of using language and of making cognitive demands through certain types of genres.   Such research, we might hope, will lead to a wider understanding of how a single developmental and unilinear model of learning language in school currently limits and distorts our judgments of academic potential and achievement not only for language-minority children but also for all children.

REFERENCES

Aguirre, A. Review as social commentary. *Language in Society,* 1977, *6*(3), 391-402.

Alvarez, C. *Home and School Context for Language-Learning: A Case Study of Two Mexican-American Bilingual Preschoolers.* Unpublished doctoral dissertation, Stanford University, 1986.

Applebee, A. N. *Writing in the Secondary School: English and the Content Areas.* Urbana, Illinois: National Council of Teachers of English, 1981.

Au, K. Participation structures in a reading lesson with Hawaiian children. *Anthropology and Education Quarterly,* 1980, *11,* 91-115.

_____, and Jordan, C. Teaching reading to Hawaiian children: Finding a culturally appropriate solution. In H. Trueba, G. Guthrie, and K. Au (Eds.), *Culture and the Bilingual Classroom.* Rowley, Massachusetts: Newbury House, 1981.

Cazden, C. Can ethnographic research go beyond the status quo? *Anthropology and Education Quarterly,* 1983, *14,* 33-42.

_____. Classroom discourse. In M. C. Wittrock (Ed.), *Handbook of Research on Teaching* (3rd ed.). New York: Macmillan, 1985.

Chavez, J. *The Lost Land: The Chicano Image of the Southwest.* Albuquerque New Mexico: University of New Mexico Press, 1984.

Cheng, D. *Acculturation of the Chinese in the United States: A Philadelphia Study.* Foochow, China: Fukien Christian University Press, 1948.

Cheung, C. *The Tao of Learning: Socialization of Chinese American Children.* Unpublished doctoral dissertation, Stanford University, 1986.

Connor, W. (Ed.). *Mexican Americans in Comparative Perspective.* Washington, D.C.: The Urban Institute Press, 1986.

Cummins, J. The role of primary language development in promoting educational success for language minority students. In *Schooling and Language Minority Students: A Theoretical Framework.* Los Angeles, California Evaluation, Dissemination and Assessment Center, California State University, Los Angeles, 1981.

De Avila, E., Cohen, E. and Intili, J. K. *Interdependence and Management in Bilingual Classrooms.* Palo Alto, California: Center for Educational Research, 1981.

Delgado-Gaitan, C. *Learning How: Rules for Knowing and Doing for Mexican Children at Home, Play, and School.* Unpublished doctoral dissertation, Stanford University, 1982.

Desmond, D. *Language in a Mexican American Community.* Unpublished doctoral dissertation, Stanford University, 1986.

Díaz, Stephen, Moll, Luis C., and Mehan, Hugh. Sociocultural resources in instruction: A context-specific approach. In *Beyond Language: Social and Cultural Factors in Schooling Language Minority Students.* Los Angeles, California: Evaluation, Dissemination and Assessment Center, California State University, Los Angeles, 1986.

Dolson, D. *The Influence of Various Home Bilingual Environments on the Academic Achievements, Language Development, and Psychosocial Adjustment of Fifth and Sixth Grade Hispanic Students.* Unpublished doctoral dissertation, University of San Francisco, 1984.

Eisenberg, A. *Language Acquisition in Cultural Perspective: Talk in Three Mexicano Homes.* Unpublished doctoral dissertation, University of California, Berkeley, 1982.

Escobedo, T. H. (Ed.). *Early Childhood Bilingual Education: A Hispanic Perspective.* New York: Teachers College Press, 1983.

Finnan, C. *Community Influence on Occupational Identity Development: Vietnamese Refugees and Job Training.* Paper presented at American Anthropological Association Meetings, 1980.

Fletcher, P., and Garman, M. (Eds.). *Language Acquisition.* Cambridge, England: Cambridge University Press, 1979.

Ford Foundation. *Hispanics: Challenges and Opportunities.* New York: The Ford Foundation, 1984.

Garcia, M., Kim, K., Veyna-Lopez, L., and Romero, A. *Case Studies of Native Spanish and Korean-Speaking Children in the Longitudinal Language Development Project.* Working Paper. Los Alamitos, California: National Center for Bilingual Research, 1985.

Goelman, H., Obert, A., and Smith, F. (Eds.). *Awakening to Literacy.* Exeter, New Hampshire: Heinemann Educational Books, 1984.

Hakuta, K. *Mirror of Language: The Debate on Bilingualism.* New York: Basic Books, 1985.

Heath, S. B. Questioning at home and at school: A comparative study. In G. Spindler (Ed.), *Doing the Ethnography of Schooling: Educational Anthropology in Action.* New York: Holt, Rinehart & Winston, 1982a.

————. What no bedtime story means: Narrative skills at home and school. *Language in Society,* 1982b, *11*(2), 49-76.

————. A lot of talk about nothing. *Language Arts,* 1983a, *60*(8), 999-1007.

————. *Ways with Words: Language, Life, and Work in Communities and Classrooms.* Cambridge, England: Cambridge University Press, 1983b.

————. *Linguistics and Education. Annual Review of Anthropology* (Vol. 13). Palo Alto, California: Annual Reviews, Inc., 1984.

————. Being literate in America: A sociohistorical perspective. In J. A. Niles (Ed.), *Thirty-fourth Yearbook of the National Reading Conference.* Rochester, New York: National Reading Conference, 1986a.

————. Intelligent writing in an audience community. In S. W. Freedman (Ed.), *The Acquisition of Written Language: Revision and Response.* Norwood, New Jersey: Ablex Publishing Co., 1986b.

————. Language policies: Patterns of retention and maintenance. In W. Connor (Ed.), *Mexican Americans in Comparative Perspective.* Washington, D.C.: The Urban Institute, 1986c.

Hsu, F. *Under the Ancestors' Shadow.* London: Routledge & Kegan Paul, 1949.

————. *American and Chinese.* London: The Cresset Press, 1955.

————. Chinese kinship and Chinese behavior. In F. Hsu (Ed.), *Rugged Individualism Reconsidered.* Knoxville, Tennessee: The University of Tennessee Press, 1983.

Hu, C. *China: Its People, its Society, its Culture.* New Haven, Connecticut: Human Relations Area Files Press, 1960.

Hu, H. The Chinese concepts of face. *American Anthropologist, 1944, 46,* 45-64.

Hume, E. Vietnam's legacy: Ten years after: A series. *The Wall Street Journal.* March 21, 1985, 1 and 15.

Kagan, Spencer. Cooperative learning and sociocultural factors in schooling. In *Beyond Language: Social and Cultural Factors in Schooling Language Minority Students.* Los Angeles, California: Evaluation, Dissemination and Assessment Center, California State University, Los Angeles, 1986.

Lampe, P. E. Mexican American labeling and mislabeling. *Hispanic Journal of Behavioral Sciences,* 1984, *6*(1), 77-85.

Langer, J. *Children Reading and Writing: Structures and Strategies.* Norwood, New Jersey: Ablex, 1986.

Laosa, L. Maternal teaching strategies and cognitive styles in Chicano families. *Journal of Educational Psychology,* 1980, *72,* 45-54.

————. Sociocultural diversity in modes of family interaction. In R. W. Henderson (Ed.), *Parent-Child Interaction: Theory, Research, and Prospect.* New York: Academic Press, 1984.

Leiderman, P. H., Tulkin, S. R., and Rosenfeld, A. (Eds.). *Culture and Infancy: Variations in the Human Experience.* New York: Academic Press, 1977.

Liu, H. The traditional Chinese clan rules. *Monographs of the Association for Asian Studies VII.* Locust Valley, New York: J. J. Augustin, 1959.

Mead, M. Columbia University research in contemporary cultures. In H. Guetzkow (Ed.), *Groups, Leadership and Men.* Pittsburgh, Pennsylvania: Carnegie Press, 1951.

Mehan, H. *Learning Lessons: Social Organization in the Classroom.* Cambridge, Massachusetts: Harvard University Press, 1979.

Merritt, M. Distributing and directing attention in primary classrooms. In L. C. Wilkinson (Ed.), *Communicating in the Classroom.* New York: Academic Press, 1982.

Michaels, S. "Sharing time": Children's narrative styles and differential access to literacy. *Language in Society,* 1981, *10*(3), 423-442.

Montgomery, G. T., and Orozco, S. Validation of a measure of acculturation for Mexican Americans. *Hispanic Journal of Behavioral Sciences,* 1984, *6*(1), 53-63.

Ogbu, John U., and Matute-Bianchi, Maria E. Understanding sociocultural factors: Knowledge, identity and school adjustment. In *Beyond Language: Social and Cultural Factors in Schooling Language Minority Students.* Los Angeles, California: Evaluation, Dissemination and Assessment Center, California State University, Los Angeles, 1986.

Olson, D. "See! Jumping!" The antecedents of literacy. In H. Goelman, A. Orbert, and F. Smith (Eds.), *Awakening to Literacy.* Exeter, New Hampshire: Heinemann Educational Books, Inc., 1984.

Pardo, E. *Acquisition of the Spanish Reflexive: A Study of a Child's Over-Extended Forms.* Unpublished doctoral dissertation, Stanford University, 1984.

Peñalosa, F. Sociolinguistic theory and the Chicano community. *Aztlán,* 1975, *6*(1), 1-11.

Reder, S. *A Hmong Community's Acquisition of English.* Research report. Portland, Oregon: Northwest Regional Educational Laboratory, 1981.

————, Green, K. R., and Sweeney, M. *Acquisition and Use of Literacy in the Hmong Community of Newton.* Portland, Oregon: Northwest Regional Educational Laboratory, 1983.

Rice, M. *Television as a Talking Picture-book: A Prop for Language Acquisition.* Unpublished manuscript, University of Kansas, 1986.

Sanchez, R. *Chicano Discourse: Socio-historic Perspectives.* Rowley, Massachusetts: Newbury House, 1984.

Saville-Troike, M., McClure, E. and Fritz, M. Communicative tactics in children's second language acquisition. In F. R. Eckman, L. H. Bell, and D. Nelson, (Eds.), *Universals of Second Language Acquisition.* Rowley, Massachusetts: Newbury House, 1984.

Sawyer, J. *The implications of Passive and Covert Bilingualism for Bilingual Education.* Paper presented at the Southwest Areal Language and Linguistics Workshop, San Antonio, Texas, 1976.

Schieffelin, B. Getting it together: An ethnographic approach to the study of the development of communicative competence. In E. Ochs and B. Schieffelin (Eds.), *Developmental Pragmatics.* New York: Academic Press, 1979.

————. and Ochs, E. (Eds.). *Language Socialization.* Cambridge, England: Cambridge University Press, 1986.

Schwartz, T. (Ed.). *Socialization as Cultural Communication: Development of a Theme in the Work of Margaret Mead.* Berkeley, California: University of California Press, 1976.

Shuy, R. Linguistics in other professions. In *Annual Review of Anthropology,* Vol. 13. Palo Alto, California Annual Reviews, Inc., 1984.

Sinclair, J., and Coulthard, M. *Towards an Analysis of Discourse: The Language of Teachers and Pupils.* New York: Oxford University Press, 1975.

Snow, C., and Ferguson, C. (Eds.). *Talking to Children.* Cambridge, England: Cambridge University Press, 1977.

Spindler, G. The transmission of culture. In G. Spindler (Ed.), *Education and Cultural Process: Toward an Anthropology of Education.* New York: Holt, Rinehart & Winston, 1974.

Stein, N. What's in a story? Interpreting the interpretations of story grammars. *Discourse Processes,* 1982, *5,* 319-336.

Stover, L. E. *"Face" and Verbal Analogues of Interaction in Chinese Culture.* Unpublished doctoral dissertation, Columbia University, 1962.

Tepper, E. L. (Ed.). *Southeast Asian Exodus: From Tradition to Resettlement--Understanding Refugees from Laos, Kampuchea and Vietnam in Canada.* Ottawa: Canadian Asian Studies Association, 1980.

Wagner, D. A., and Stevenson, H. W. (Eds.). *Cultural Perspectives on Child Development.* San Francisco, California: W. H. Freeman & Co., 1982.

Wilkinson, A., Barnsley, G., Hanna, P., and Swan, M. *Assessing Language Development.* London: Oxford University Press, 1980.

Wong Fillmore, L. *The Second Time Around: Cognitive and Social Strategies in Second Language Acquisition.* Unpublished doctoral dissertation, Stanford University, 1976.

SOCIOCULTURAL RESOURCES IN INSTRUCTION: A CONTEXT-SPECIFIC APPROACH

Stpehen Díaz
University of California, San Diego

Luis C. Moll
University of California, San Diego

Hugh Mehan
University of California, San Diego

INTRODUCTION

A few days after we had videotaped children reading in a Spanish and English language classroom, we returned to have the Spanish-language teacher view and comment on both sets of tapes. She had never seen the children during English reading lessons, and we were especially interested to hear her comments. We selected an English reading lesson that included the students from her "highest ability" reading group. They were the "stars" of her class, students who were reading at an advanced level and who regularly and independently wrote book reports as part of their reading activities.

We started the tape and sat back, coffee in hand, to view the English reading lesson. After only a few moments of viewing, however, the teacher leaned forward, and exclaimed, "Those can't be my kids. Why are they doing such low level work? They are much smarter than that!" What prompted the Spanish-language teacher's outburst was her surprise at the fact that the children's behavior in the English lessons did not match the reading skills they displayed in *her* classroom. In English they were only practicing word sounds, while in Spanish they were reading at advanced levels.

This scenario, which occurred as part of the research we report later in this chapter, illustrates a paradox that needs to be resolved as we pursue our discussion of sociocultural effects on the education of language minority children. The paradox as stated by Cicourel and Mehan (1984) is this:

> *All children are said to inherit or acquire the same linguistic and cognitive capabilities necessary for literacy and school achievement. Yet by the time children are in school, vast differences in ability and performance are reported. (p. 8)*

A wealth of empirical research supports this universalist claim that all children in all cultures normally exhibit roughly the same capacities for early language acquisition and cognitive development. Studies of cognitive growth and language acquisition rediscover the same family of general capabilities that we assume children must possess in order to display normal literacy skills and academic performance. The capacities identified should enable all children exposed to a formal environment of schooling to become literate in their native language and succeed in school. Yet, vast differences in ability and performance are noted when children enter and go through school. Children are immediately classified into ability groups that reflect the stratification system of the larger society and remain in tracks or special programs through much of their life in schools.

We want to achieve a number of goals in this chapter: (1) Address the discrepancy between children's universal capacity for development and the wide range of performance levels of language minority students, (2) Describe an interactional approach to schooling for language minority students that both helps to explain the discrepancy in performance levels and also presents intervention strategies to redress the discrepancy, and (3) Provide examples of intervention strategies in which both teachers and language minority students mutually direct their behavior toward the goal of academic success without sacrificing cultural integrity.

PART I
ACCOUNTS OF SCHOOL SUCCESS AND FAILURE

The gap between universal development and students' failure in school has been explained in different ways. We divide the explanations into two main groups: (1) those that provide context-free interpretations of school success and failure, and (2) those that provide context-specific interpretations. The former were covered in some detail by Sue and Padilla (this volume). We will summarize them quickly here, and then provide a more detailed account of the context-specific interpretations.

CONTEXT-FREE INTERPRETATIONS OF SCHOOL PERFORMANCE

Biological determinism

One proposed solution to the "development paradox" (Cicourel and Mehan, 1984) has been to postulate the existence of genetic differences in intelligence (Jensen, 1969; Herrnstein, 1974). Such "nativists" emphasize the role of heredity over environment in the determination of life chances. They argue that genetic factors are the most important determinants of intellectual growth, and this phenomenon is variously referred to as "hereditary deprivation" or "genetic inferiority." Like a hothouse, the enrichment of environment may speed up the rate of growth, but the final product of growth will not exceed genetically programmed capabilities. Nativists cite studies that compare the differences in IQ between twins reared apart, cross generation studies, migration studies, and studies of Head Start programs to support the claim that heredity accounts for the greatest proportion of the variance in measures of intelligence.

The nativist position on the role of heredity in intelligence and school performance is, in essence, a version of biological determinism. Biological determinism, in turn, is the view that social and economic differences among races, classes, and sexes arise from inherited, inborn distinctions (Gould, 1981). In all its manifestations, biological determinism seems to incorporate two fallacies: *reification* and *ranking*. The concept of "intelligence" has been used to characterize this complex, multifaceted set of mental human capabilities. This shorthand symbol is then reified and "intelligence" achieves a dubious status as a unitary thing. Ranking requires a criterion for assigning all individuals to their proper slots in a single series of slots. The common denominator of all nativist accounts of intelligence and school achievement has been quantification, i.e., the measure of intelligence as a single number for each person. A number of unitary measures have been made in recent history, including skull size, brain size, or an intelligence quotient (Gould, 1981).

Biological determinism has not been supported by basic research on language acquisition and cognitive growth. Studies of language acquisition and cognitive development in western countries have not sustained the thesis that inherited differences in intelligence account for observed differences in the way in which children process information. Instead, studies of linguistic and cognitive development have emphasized the uniformity of acquisition by the time the child enters school (Chomsky, 1965; Piattelli-Palmarini, 1980; Lennenberg, 1966; Brown, 1973; Brown *et al.,* 1969; Slobin, 1973).

Cultural Determinism

Differences in social class or ethnic group experiences are said to expose children to different linguistic and cognitive environments. These differences, in turn, are said to be differentially incompatible with the academic demands of the school.

The documentation of social class differences in speech (Bernstein, 1971) was an important first step in alerting us to the idea that such differences can affect school performance. According to some readings of Bernstein (1971), lower class youth in England fail in school because they fail to master and use the language of mainstream society, the so-called "elaborated code." The "restricted code" of lower class youth restricts their ability to communicate with and understand others.

While Bernstein (1973) says he never intended his elaborated/restricted code distinction to be an explanation of differential school performance, his position was imported to the United States (Hess and Shipman, 1965) and became an influential explanation of the school failure of lower class and ethnically diverse children. For example, Bereiter and Engleman (1966) characterized the language of ethnically diverse and lower class children as "inadequate for expressing personal or original opinions, for analysis and careful reasoning, for dealing with anything hypothetical or beyond the present or for explaining anything very complex" (p. 32). They are saying that lower class and ethnic minority children have a gap or a deficit in their linguistic or cognitive apparatus that is *general,* that is, not bound by context. This general linguistic or cognitive deficiency is said to be the basis of the poor performance of poor children.

Differences in the school performance of these children also have been explained in terms of differences in cognitive styles, which are the result of cultural adaptations to environmental and social contraints (Witkin and Berry, 1975; Berry, 1976). The argument here is that language minority students have cognitive styles that differ from those necessary for success in school and society. Although these styles are adaptations that may be positive within the constraints of a given group's situation, these learning styles are dysfunctional in classrooms. Attempts to change children's cognitive styles have been largely unsuccessful because they are seen as long term, general, and pervasive modes of functioning (Witkin *et al.*, 1962). Some researchers have suggested that the school curriculum be changed and teachers be trained to teach ways to accommodate to the children's stylistic differences (Ramírez and Castañeda, 1974; Ramírez, 1979). This strategy has not been widely implemented and it is difficult to assess the effectiveness of these approaches (Díaz, 1983).

Cultural deprivation is the extreme form of cultural determinism; in this form, the view that the socialization practices of lower income families do not prepare their children for the demands of the classroom is, at first glance, appealing. However, the studies that have linked the poor performance of low income children to their class origins (Coleman *et al.*, 1966; Jencks *et al.*, 1972; Bereiter and Engleman, 1966) were not based on descriptions of day-to-day family life patterns and parent-child interactions. The design of these studies made it impossible to determine the extent to which socialization practices or other culturally-based experiences such as motivation or a counter school/ counter culture (Willis, 1977) were responsible for testing and classroom performance. The cultural deprivation view ignores the social organization of instructional goals and the practices of the school. The concept of "cultural deprivation" presumes universal criteria for referencing culture, language, or dialect against which all other language use and cultural practices are judged to be deficient or inappropriate.

CONTEXT-SPECIFIC INTERPRETATION*

A number of investigators have gone beyond the assumption of uniform cultural arrangements within cultural deprivation explanations of the school difficulties of lower income and ethnically diverse children. These studies compare linguistic and cognitive performance across different types of situations. Before reviewing some of the actual studies, we will review the theoretical base of this line of investigation.

The Theoretical Base of the Context-Specific Approach

At the heart of the context-specific approach is the study of the actual *process* of interaction between individuals and their environments, *not*

---

* Please see Cortés and Sue and Padilla (this volume) for related discussions of interaction in context.

just a measure of the products of interaction. In most cases, particularly in classrooms, these interactions consist of communications between people for the specific purpose of problem solving. In addition, the activity we call learning or problem solving always involves the achievement of many partial goals that require joint activity by teacher and students. Each of these goals, in turn, is reached by performing some act (Leont'ev, 1973; Talyzina, 1978). Hence, in the study of any learning activity, the unit of analysis becomes the act or system of acts of which learning is composed, as seen in the context of the classroom, the school, and the community. Consequently, a critical task in the analysis of educational interactions becomes the careful and detailed description of the learning activity (e.g., a reading lesson) and its constituent sequence of acts. These sequences of acts are jointly produced or collaboratively assembled by the teacher and students. Some sequences include the initiation of questioning by the teacher, the complementary answering of questions by the students, and the distribution and use of educational materials. This line of work operates on the premise that social events such as classroom lessons, testing encounters, or counseling sessions are interactional accomplishments (McDermott and Roth, 1979; Mehan, 1978). Hence, a primary goal of these studies is to describe lessons or other important educational events by characterizing the interactional work of the participants that assemble the structures (McDermott, 1976, 1977; Erickson and Shultz, 1977; Shuy and Griffin, 1978; Cole *et al.,* 1979; Mehan, 1979; Shultz *et al.,* 1982; Au, 1980).

There are two interrelated features of this work that make it particularly relevant and useful for the study of language minority students' discourse and writing. One is the attention paid to context (McDermott, 1976; Erickson and Shultz, 1977); the second is the emphasis on the functions of language (Shuy and Griffin, 1978; Mehan, 1979).

Context is a major determinant of human behavior. By context we do not mean the physical location or circumstances of the interaction. Context is meant in interactional terms. It is constituted by what the participants are doing, which is only partly conditioned by where and when they are doing it (Hymes, 1982; Gumperz, 1971; Erickson and Shultz, 1977; McDermott and Roth, 1979). Contexts are not to be equated with the physical surroundings of settings such as classrooms, kitchens, and churches. They are constructed by the people present in varying combinations of participants and audience (Erickson and Shultz, 1977). As McDermott and Roth (1979) have explained it, contexts are constituted by what people are doing as well as when and where they are doing it.

That is, people in interaction serve as social environments for each other. These interactionally constituted environments are embedded in time and change from moment to moment. In dynamic settings such as schools, interactional contexts may shift rapidly from one moment to the next; the important analytic task, therefore, is to integrate the participants' interactional activities within the particular context of their occurrence.

Language has multiple functions. Probably more than any other instructional efforts, the teaching of limited-English proficient students focuses attention on the development of language proficiency. The emphasis, however, has been on a general or global language proficiency usually as assessed by standardized tests. Because it is treated as a self-contained, scorable ability, language proficiency is commonly analyzed independently of its role or function in specific academic or lesson domains (Shuy and Griffin, 1978). Within the present approach, we describe distinct *communicative activities* that make up lesson environments of which language is a part, rather than deal with language as an abstract formal system.

Teaching and learning are distinct forms of culturally organized communicative processes in which mental and external, practical activity are closely connected. Vygotsky (1978) proposed that psychological functioning grows out of social interactions in the service of practical activity. He held that the intellectual skills that children acquire are directly related to how they interact with adults and peers in specific problem-solving environments. He argued that children internalize the kind of help they receive from others and eventually come to use the means of guidance initially provided by the others to direct their own subsequent problem-solving behaviors. That is, children first perform the appropriate behaviors to complete a task under someone else's guidance and direction (e.g., the parent or the teacher) before they can complete the task competently and independently of outside direction or help.

Activities go through a series or transformations as they are moved from the level of social experience to that of individual experience. These transformations are the result of a number of developmental events. These events occur in learning situations, which Vygotsky (1978) called the "zone of proximal development." He describes this zone as:

> ...*the distance between the actual developmental level as determined by independent problem solving and the level of potential development as determined through problem solving under adult guidance or in collaboration with more capable peers. (p. 86).*

In its application to the study of formal learning environments such as classroom reading lessons, the student's entering skills as perceived by the teacher are a major determinant of the starting point of the zone. The kinds of skills that teachers want the child to master define the farther end point of the zone. The activities that the teacher uses to organize the necessary practice to move the child from the initial, aided level to the final, independent level are the focus of our attention.

Methodological Elements

The overall methodological framework of the context-specific approach to the study of human behavior is ethnographic. In the broadest terms, ethnography can be defined as a *description of the culture of a community or society*. The work in schools we report here was ethnographically informed in the ways illustrated by the following discussion. Additional detail regarding such methodology can be found in Spindler (1963) and Cole *et al.* (1971).

Despite differences of opinion about the scope and specific meaning about the culture that is to be described, ethnographies have many methodological features in common. First, is the shared belief among ethnographers that a cultural description requires a long period of intimate study and residence among members of the community being studied. Since ethnography has traditionally been constructed in communities that are foreign to the researcher, a knowledge of the spoken language and subtle patterns of behavior of the community members has been considered a requisite. Indeed, a sign that an ethnography is proceeding well is that the researcher is acceptable to the participants themselves. This aspect of ethnography places a special burden on researchers studying scenes in their own culture. The ethnographer working in a foreign land is attempting to make the strange familiar in order to understand it, while the ethnographer in local scenes must reverse the process and make the familiar strange in order to understand it.

Instead of relying on documentary evidence supplied by official agencies, or survey data gathered by brief, formal interviews, ethnography is characterized by a wide range of observational techniques, including prolonged face-to-face contacts with members of the local group, direct participation in some of that group's activities, and intensive work with a few informants.

The open-ended character of ethnographic data gathering avoids the limitations imposed by research categories determined in advance.

Ethnographic research becomes self-correcting during the course of the inquiry, because questions posed at the outset are changed as the inquiry unfolds, and topics that seemed essential at the outset are replaced as new topics emerge (Hymes, 1982).

Hence, an ethnography is vigorously naturalistic. It is richly detailed and fine grained. The description is formulated on the basis of extensive unstructured research settings, although a number of "experimental ethnographers" (notably Cole *et al.*, 1971) have applied controls to ethnographic data by the use of ecologically valid experiments in conjunction with detailed field observation.

Yet another distinguishing characteristic of ethnography is its comparative or contrastive feature. The cultural system is not studied in isolation, but in relation to known systems of organization. A delicate matter in this desire for a comparative component is "cultural imposition"-- employing the cultural arrangements of one system is an inappropriate explanatory device for another. A commitment to prolonged face-to-face contacts with members of the community under study is an attempt to ensure that the description of the culture is consistent with the perspective of the participants inside the setting. Categories imported to the setting from the outside are avoided. Instead, the goal of the ethnographic research is to allow the reality of the situation to impinge upon the investigator's subjectivity until the categories for description are determined by the scene itself (Doyle, 1978).

Ethnographers have now taken advantage of technological developments in the audiovisual field. Most notably, videotape and film have been used to collect and analyze data. It is important to point out that tape and film have been used as a data base, not simply as fancy illustrative material. The social organization of naturally occurring events such as classroom lessons and test sessions in institutional settings has been investigated piece by piece, from beginning to end, and from top to bottom.

When audiovisual materials are used, it is possible to retrieve the grounds of an analysis from the data source. Furthermore, as we did in the case studies that follow, participants studied in social scenes can be shown film or tape and asked for their account of what is happening (Erickson and Shultz, 1982; Cicourel *et al.*, 1974; Florio, 1978; Mehan *et al.*, 1985). When researchers check their interpretation of events with participants, a sophisticated check on the validity of the research becomes possible.

Perhaps the most important contribution that the introduction of audiovisual equipment makes to the ethnographic research process is making the reflexive reports explicit. Researchers are often described as passive vehicles, "open windows" (Gusfield, 1981) through which the objective facts of a scene being studied pass unaffected. Viewing videotape and assembling transcripts reminds us that the researcher plays an active role in the research process by organizing the scenes to be studied, assembling materials, and interpreting data. The inclusion of this reflexive aspect (Hymes, 1982; Jules-Rosette, 1978) in ethnography is one of the important features that distinguishes this line of investigation from simple participant observation.

Case Studies of Context-Specific Behavior

When students' linguistic and cognitive performance has been compared across types of social situations, variation in students' performance has been reported. This cross-context variation has led to a "context-specific" view of cognitive performance. (See Laboratory of Comparative Human Cognition, 1982, 1983 for more details.) The context-specific view proposes that intelligence displays and language use are dependent on the circumstances and situations of their assessment. They are not general abilities that appear uniformly in all types of situations. They are specific skills that vary from one type of situation to another.

Labov (1972) was influential in countering the context-free linguistic deficiency interpretation of school failure inherent within cultural deprivation theory with a context-specific view of language use. His analysis of the verbal performance of Black youths from New York City in different testing situations provides one of the most provocative examples of situational variability in linguistic performance.

Labov found that the length and pacing of Black children's speech in testing situations conducted by white adults made them appear extremely dull and linguistically deprived. However, having knowledge of these children and their peers in other situations, Labov surmised that the reasons for the youths' inarticulateness were to be found in the social situation, not personal characteristics or language. His hypothesis was given support when he repeated the testing exercise with a Black adult, and the children's verbal production remained much the same, but became quite elaborate when a Black interviewer transformed testing situations into more informal conversations.

In this social context, one in which the power relations between adult and child have been changed, children who had previously responded in monosyllables eagerly entered into the conversation. Rather than using language in a minimal, defensive way, they now employed it productively to compete actively with friends for the floor, to defend reputations, and to set the record straight regarding other topics.

Hall *et al.* (1977) extended Labov's (1972) interpretation of language use in different kinds of testing situations to a school and a community setting. Dowley, one of Hall's coauthors, took three- and four-year-olds enrolled in a New York City Head Start program to the local supermarket where they discussed the food they saw. Upon returning to the classroom, they were asked to tell the teacher about the trip. Speech in the supermarket was compared to the retelling of the event in school.

The language the students used in the two situations was qualitatively similar in several respects: Neither the form of utterance (questions, commands, statement/assertions), nor the content they expressed differed drastically across the two situations. However, in the informal supermarket setting, the average number of words was greater, the percentage of questions attended to was greater, and the average number of words in response to a question was higher.

A companion set of studies examined patterns of interaction at home with patterns of interaction at school (Philips, 1972, 1982; Erickson and Mohatt, 1982; Au and Jordan, 1978). In the hallmark study in this tradition, Philips (1972, 1982) compared the patterns of classroom interaction among Native American reservation children and among Anglo children in the same community.

A reason given for the difficulties that Native American children face in school is that they lack communicative skills and are nonverbal, i.e., suffer from a linguistic deficit fostered by a deprived cultural environment (Dumont, 1972; John, 1972). Philips (1972, 1982), too, found evidence of "quiet Indian children," but she did not find a *generalized* linguistic deficit. Instead, she found that the patterns of communication of Native American children were *context-specific*, i.e., varied systematically from one type of situation to another.

Philips (1972, 1982) found that the Native American children performed very poorly in those classroom contexts that demanded individualized performance and emphasized competition among peers, and they performed more effectively in those classroom contexts that minimized the obligation of individual students to perform in public contexts. The classroom contexts in which Native American students operated best were similar in organization to local Native American community contexts, where *cooperation* and not *competition* was valued, and *sociality* and not *individuality* was emphasized. Philips (1972, 1982) attributes the generally poor performance of Native American children to differences in the structures of participation normatively demanded in the home and in the school. It seems that the patterns of participation normatively expected in conventional classrooms create conditions that are unfamiliar and threatening to Native American children (see related discussion in Kagan, this volume).

Building on the logic inherent in the work reviewed above, Cazden (1979), Anderson and Teale (1981), and Heath (1982), have compared the structure and function of discourse at home and school of middle-income and lower-income families. These comparisons enable us to see if there is a relationship between language use, language socialization, and differential school performance.

Heath (1982) compared the way white middle-income teachers talked to their Black low-income elementary school students in the classroom with the way in which these teachers talked to their own children at home in a community she calls "Trackton." She found that the teachers relied heavily on questions and language games like peek-a-boo (Cazden, 1979) when they talked to their children at home. The most frequent form of question was the "known information" variety so often identified with classroom interaction (Sinclair and Coulthard, 1975; Shuy and Griffin, 1978; Mehan, 1979). By contrast to "information seeking" questions in which the questioner seeks knowledge presumably held by the respondent (when people, notably teachers and testers, ask a "known information" question), they have knowledge of the information they seek and are testing or examining the respondents' knowledge. Heath (1982) reported that the children of the middle-income teachers were, thus, taught to label and name objects and to talk about things out of context.

These same teachers talked to the students in their classrooms in ways that were very similar to the ways in which they talked to their own children at home. They instructed students primarily through an interrogative format using known information questions and taught students to label objects and identify features of things.

However, this mode of language use and language socialization was not prevalent in the homes of low-income students. Low-income adults only seldom addressed questions to their children at home. Where Trackton teachers would use questions, the parents would use statements or imperatives. For example, when talking about a child's poor health, a low-income Trackton mother might say, "Something is the matter with that boy." By contrast, a Trackton teacher would say, "Is something the matter? What is the matter?"

When questions *were* asked of Trackton children by their parents, they were much different than the types of questions asked by teachers. Questions in low-income homes called for nonspecific comparisons or analogies as answers. They were not the known information or information-seeking questions associated with the classroom.

Heath (1982) concluded that the language use in Trackton homes did not prepare children to cope with three major characteristics of the language used in classrooms: (1) they had not had practice in responding to utterances that were interrogative in form but directive in pragmatic function ("Why don't you use the one on the back shelf" vs. "use the one on the back shelf"), (2) they did not have much familiarity with known information questions, and (3) they had little experience with questions that asked for information from books.

Summary

Studies of children's language in different contexts had led to a different interpretation of the language of lower class and ethnic minority children. Instead of being perceived as having general language deficits, a context-specific approach investigates the concrete conditions under which children learn and are asked to perform. As such, this approach is "pedagogically optimistic." By assigning a major role to specific teaching and learning conditions, as opposed to the general internal properties of children, we can take positive action to create effective learning environments.

The ideas we have just reviewed influenced our observation of the development of language minority children's skills in at least three important ways: (1) we look for the origins of intellectual skills within the child-adult interactional system; (2) these interactions are studied in relation to the content and the objectives of specific teaching and learning situations, because it is the relationship between interactions, content, and the child's actual developmental level that creates effective zones of proximal development; and (3) we look for evidence that these zones of proximal development make a difference, i.e., that the assistance we provide helps children to read more complex text or to write more sophisticated prose.

PART II

CONTEXT-SPECIFIC PERFORMANCE, BILINGUALISM, AND IMPROVED SCHOOL PRACTICE

Context-specific studies have been important in countering cultural and biological determinist interpretations of the school performance of low income and ethnically diverse students. For the most part, however, previous research neither dealt with learning in two languages nor intervened to create educational change. In this section, we present two case studies that combine cross-context analysis and pedagogical intervention. Three questions guide our efforts: (1) What is the relationship between teaching reading in different linguistic and pedagogical contexts? (2) How do current pedagogical practices constrain children's academic advancement? and (3) How can we create better teaching-learning environments?

The two case studies address issues of reading and writing in bilingual settings. The research is also characterized by the participation of teachers as co-researchers. Teachers participated in the preparation and conduct of the studies and in the analysis of data.

STUDY 1: READING INSTRUCTION IN A BILINGUAL SETTING: LEARNING IN SPANISH AND LEARNING IN ENGLISH

We conducted the reading research in third and fourth grade classrooms in a school south of San Diego. This school features a bilingual education program that emphasizes academic development in Spanish and English from first to fourth grade. In this program the students spend part of the day receiving instruction (e.g., reading lessons) in a Spanish-language classroom and then go to an adjacent classroom for instruction in English. As a consequence, we were able to observe and videotape the *same* children participating in reading lessons in separate language and instructional settings (Moll and Díaz, in press, 1986).

This particular instructional arrangement allowed us to unpackage for analysis different components of a bilingual program that are often confounded in more typical self-contained classrooms. Observations in the Spanish-language classroom provided us with information on the organization of reading instruction and on the children's reading abilities in their first language. A contrast of these observations with the reading lessons in the English-language classroom permitted us to address issues of assessment and placement. This contrast, in turn, helped us engineer new teaching/learning situations. We transformed English language lessons into new learning environments, ones focused on reading comprehension with social and linguistic resources provided to help students respond at conceptually higher levels.

We will first contextualize the anecdote we used to begin this chapter in order to explore the relationship between English and Spanish instruction and the resulting underassessment of the children's abilities in the English-language classroom. The underassessment was most striking, as attested to by the teacher's exclamation, with students from the high group, whom we knew to be good readers in Spanish and conversationally fluent in English. In the examples provided, this underassessment takes the form of a gap in the children's activities when going from Spanish to English reading. We then turn to a detailed description of our lesson manipulations to show how we successfully bridged this gap.

Table 1 contrasts the focus of instruction for the different reading ability groups within and across classrooms. When the children shifted from one language setting to another, they did not encounter similar learning environments. The instruction in English was focused primarily on the mechanical tasks of practicing decoding skills, word sounds, or lexical meaning. Complex inferences were not called for. Almost entirely absent from the English-language lessons are key activities that promote reading *comprehension* and help the students learn how to *communicate their knowledge* of content. In short, we did not find the types of activities related to reading that occurred in the more advanced Spanish setting.

Table 1

**FOCUS OF INSTRUCTION BY READING ABILITY GROUP
IN SPANISH AND ENGLISH CLASSROOMS**

English	Reading Group	Spanish
Decoding, word sounds, grammar, comprehension (recall)	High	Comprehension (text-free), book reports, decoding
Decoding, work sounds (recall)	Middle	Comprehension (text-bound), forming appropriate responses, decoding
Decoding, word sounds, grammar	Low	Decoding, comprehension, how to extract information from text

Sources of Difficulty

Why were these lessons organized differently in these classrooms? We identified at least three factors that contributed to the discrepancies in lesson organization.

Lack of coordination. The English-language teacher was unaware of the children's level of ability and performance in Spanish reading lessons. When the teachers did "compare notes," it was usually regarding an individual student's progress or behavior. That is, their discussions were at the level of individual students, not at the level of general lesson organization. As a result, lessons in English were organized and implemented *independently* of information of the children's performance in Spanish. We should emphasize that this observation is in no way meant as an indictment of these teachers. Rather, it points precisely, as we shall explain, to restricted communicative resources among teachers generally, which leads to restricted teaching situations.

Language as the basis of ability grouping. The primary criterion for grouping students in the English-language classroom was the children's oral language proficiency. Children with varying reading skills were routinely grouped together and received a simplified curricular treatment designed to match their assessed level of English language proficiency. One result of this grouping practice is that children who demonstrated advanced reading skills in Spanish were stuck in low-level reading lessons in English for prolonged periods of time. When an oral language problem is treated as a general reading problem, such students fall further behind in the development of English reading skills until they reach a point where they cannot advance academically because of their low reading levels.

Confounding pronunciation and decoding. Pronunciation problems and decoding problems are confounded in the English-language setting. Teachers often assume that decoding is a prerequisite to comprehension and correct pronunciation is the most obvious index of decoding (Goodman *et al.*, 1979). Consequently, the teacher who does not speak Spanish organizes lessons to provide the children with the necessary practice in phonics and other aspects of language learning to be able to go on to advanced comprehension. To make an accurate differentiation between a child's inability to decode and a lack of ability to pronounce English words accurately, the teacher needs to access reading comprehension directly. However, activities permitting a display of reading comprehension rarely occurred in the English reading lessons.

Reorganizing the Reading Context

We tested the influence of this complex of the three factors noted above by designing a two-stage "experiment." In the first stage, we asked the English-language instructor to teach a regular lesson to the children in the "low" reading group. The lesson concentrated on correcting or remediating the difficulties in decoding, vocabulary, and verbal expression that the children displayed during the lesson.

Immediately after the lesson, one of the researchers took the teacher's place with the children and asked them comprehension questions in Spanish about what they had just read in English. In reviewing the videotapes of the lesson, it is clear that the children could understand much more about what they were reading in English than they were allowed to display during the lessons in English. Therefore, the problem could not be located solely in the children's lack of language or reading skills in English. Instead, it appeared that the problem arose from the social organization of reading and speaking in these lessons. The lessons in English presupposed a lack of both oral and reading competence. This presupposition was reinforced by the children's pronunciation problems and expositional difficulties in English reading contexts. As a consequence, the children were restricted to lower level work. The orientation of the reading lessons in English was below the children's ability level as displayed in Spanish. Once we learned about the discrepancy, the question became: How could we organize English reading lessons to take advantage of the skills the children had developed or were developing in Spanish?

This question led us to the second phase of our experiment. We intervened to create more advanced English reading/learning environments for these limited English proficient (LEP) students. We started this second phase by using the available information about the students' level of reading in *Spanish* as a close estimate of their ability to read and comprehend text. We made the assumption that Spanish reading specified the top of the children's "zone of proximal development" and set out to see if this level could be achieved in *reading* English. To do this, we first asked the teacher to provide us with stories in English that were equivalent to the children's fourth-grade reading level in Spanish. This shift required a change in the content of the lesson from phonics and text-specific responses to inferences based on a good understanding of the text typical of more advanced levels.

Second, we changed the structure of interactions surrounding reading in English to establish comprehension as the higher order goal of the lesson. The lower order elements of the process (decoding individual words, correct pronunciation) were now taken for granted and supported by us in an informal manner. The new structure of interaction emphasized our knowledge that children could *process* English text for comprehension, but were inhibited in their *production* of well-formed English sentences to externalize this understanding. Therefore, we used Spanish to teach English reading. We allowed the children to manifest their higher order understanding in a mixed Spanish/English oral interactional medium. Thus, in this second phase of the project, we addressed the students' reading skills but did so *as part of a different teaching-learning system.*

The lesson described below became one of the key moments in the investigation. It contains incidents that established that the children could comprehend at the fourth-grade reading level in English. As part of the lesson, we chose to ask comprehension questions contained in the text because these were the same questions that regular English-speaking students had to answer but had difficulty answering. This is a key point, because the students had problems when they made the "jump" to fourth-grade level reading. However, it turns out that these difficulties are similar to those all fourth-grade Egnlish-speaking students have with the more abstract, subtle information in comprehension questions.

Let us turn to an actual transcript of a lesson to provide concrete examples of what we mean. The story is a fable called "Sr. Coyote and Sr. Fox." We shall call the girls in the lesson Sylvia [S], Delfina [D], and Carla [C]; Esteban Díaz [ED] and Luis Moll [LM] were the instructors. Although the lesson was taught in English, Spanish was allowed in discussing the story. After the story had been read once, Sylvia provided a fair summary of the plot in Spanish (17), showing that she grasped the literal meaning of the story she had read in English.

I. 1. LM: [To Carla] Huh? Should we do it in Spanish first, and then switch to English afterwards?

2. C: Yes. [laughs]

3. LM: OK. Bien, este, cuenta un poquito de, de que se trata la historia, el Señor Coyote y el Señor Fox.

4. C: Um, es que el Señor Coyote se quería comer a, al, um, al Señor Fox, en, de, entonces,

5. LM: Mhm. Ese es el principio. El Señor Coyote vio al Señor Fox y da la casualidad que al Señor Coyote tenía hambre.

6. C: Mhm.

7. LM: Y dijo "Mmm. Este Señor Fox, me lo voy a com-
          er." Bien, y entonces ¿que? Delfina. [Delfina
          laughs and looks in the book.]
8. LM: Mhm? Ayúdala, Sylvia. Ayúdala, Sylvia.
9. ED: ¿Que estaba haciendo el Senor Coyote? En el prin-
          cipio.
10. S: ¿El Senor Coyote? Estaba caminando.
11. ED: Mhm. ¿Y luego, que pasó?
12. S: Se encontró al Senor Fox.
13. LM: Mhm.
14. ED: OK.
15. S: Y el Señor fox supo que el se lo queria comer.
16. LM: Mhm.
17. S: Entonces, entonces, este, le, el dijo que, que le
          ayudara a detener la piedra grande. Que porque si
          no le ayudaba, la piedra les iba a caer encima de
          los dos. Entonces el Señor Coyote dijo que, el pe,
          el miró para arriba y penso y dijo que, que lo iba a
          ayudar. Entonces, le ayuda y el ese el, el Señor
          Fox dijo, el pensó que, que hay, no es una mentira
          de que iba a ir a, a pe a pedir ayuda y que le iba a
          traer comida.

The lesson continued with Delfina summarizing haltingly (#2) what
happened when the Fox left the Coyote "holding up" the hill. We then
get to the key of the story, the Coyote's realization that he has been
fooled by the Fox (#3-12):

II. 1. ED: Mhm, OK, y, y mientras, OK, what happened after
2. D: that, when, when the fox said, "OK." ----- foolish.
3. ED: When the fox said, um, "OK, I'm going to go get
4. D: some chicken and tortillas." What happened
5. LM: after...?
6. ED: He went around, ahy, he was lying, lying and he
7. LM: was, el Señor Coyote was holding every time up all
8. ED: the time the, the hill.
9. LM: All right, and what was he thinking?
10. C: That he, he, he, um, the....
11. LM: Hm? What was el coyote thinking? When he was
12. C: holding, as, as he was holding up the hill.
          Mhm.

13. LM: What do you think?
14. ED: ----- en el español o en inglés.
15. LM: ¿Sylvia o Carla?
16. C: Que...
17. LM: ----- a Carla
18. C: Que le ha echado mentira.

In the next example (III), Sylvia continued with a more coherent description of the ending of the story:

III. 1.   S: Y si luego no le cayó nada en, porque el, el Señor
                Fox le había dicho que, que es, que si es y luego si
                suelta cuando el Señor Fox se iba, le dijo que no la
                soltara porque si la soltaba no va a alcanzar a cor-
                rer y le iba a caer encima.
      2. ED: Mhm.
      3.   S: Y luego, por eso, el, el agarraba y agarraba....
      4. LM: Exacto ----- exacto.
      5.   S: Entonces, el dijo que iba a intentar a ver si no le
                caía. Cuando el, y, a, el Señor Coyote cuando el
                se iba allá. El, um, dijo que iba a ver si no se le
                caía y ya cuando corrio muy recio y miró que la, la
                piedra, um, no se le caía, el dijo que le estaba
                echando mentiras el Señor Fox y entonces se enojó.
      6. LM: Entonces ----- se dió cuenta, mhm. -----
      7.   S: Aha, que, que era mentira lo que estaba cayendo la
                piedra.
      8. LM: Exacto. Exacto. Este, muy listo Señor Fox, ¿ver-
                dad?
      9.   S: Uh huh.
     10. LM: Pensó muy rápido. ¿Y si no piensa rápido?
     11.   S: Se lo come el coyote.

After Sylvia's summary, we turned to the questions included in the textbook. The first question is typical of the types of inference expected of children at this reading level. It asks why the Fox changed the way he addressed the Coyote from "Mr. Coyote" to "Brother Coyote." The answer to this question must be inferred from the story; it is not explicitly answered in the text. Note that Delfina attempted to provide an explanation in English and, in fact, gave us a glimpse that she can answer. Before we could extend what she said in English, she clarified it in Spanish; we then expanded what she said and Sylvia then succinctly gave an appropriate answer to the question.

IV. 1. LM: Um, why do you think, what do you guys think that the fox started calling Señor Coyote "brother coyote"? He says here, "How about it, brother coyote?"

2. S: ¿En que página?

3. LM: En la página, en las dos, en la dos, dos noventa y nueve.

4. C: -----

5. LM: He says, "What do you say?" asked Señor Fox. "How about it, brother coyote?"

6. D: Oh!

7. LM: "I won't be gone more than half an hour." Why did he start calling him brother coyote?

8. D: Oh, because he, only said that to try lying because he wanted to...

9. LM: Right.

10. ED: Mhm.

11. LM: You know he, he was...

12. D: Ay, para que él crea que nada más que haya a venir rápido

13. LM: Claro, cambio de señor a, a, a, a brother coyote para hacerse más el amigo de la, como si fuera amigo.

14. S: Mhm.

15. D: Mhm.

16. ED: El hermano

17. LM: -----

18. S: Para que le creyera lo que iba a hacer.

19. LM: Exacto. Very good. Excellent. That is why. Good point.

We continued the lesson by asking other comprehension questions. The students answered with varying success. Although they needed some help before providing a reasonable answer to the questions, we were confident at the conclusion of the lesson that the students could perform at a fourth-grade level in reading.

The next day, we briefly reviewed their understanding of the story. Their interactions indicated that they understood the text. For example,

Clara, the poorest reader, willingly answered a request to provide a reason why the Fox was able to trick the Coyote. She responded by explaining that maybe the Coyote had overestimated his own intelligence and underestimated the intelligence of the Fox. Further, she was able to formulate her response with minimal help from us. Shortly afterward, Carla and Sylvia jointly clarified a point that Delfina had misunderstood. In response to our questions, the group established that the cleverness of the Fox was reflected in the fact that he used his mind to avoid a physical confrontation that he could not win.

Conclusion

We coordinated aspects of reading lessons in Spanish and English to integrate previously separate lesson components into a unified whole. In so doing, we transformed the English reading lesson for both the teacher and the students into a qualitatively new teaching-learning environment. The new environment made reading comprehension the lesson's goal. Social and linguistic resources were strategically provided to assist Spanish-language students to operate at conceptually higher levels in English. This procedure contrasts with prevailing lessons that subordinated reading comprehension to practice in oral English skills. The teachers concentrated on comprehension as the primary goal at a level comparable to the students' Spanish reading skills, while directly addressing language-related difficulties in the service of that goal. By creating this zone of proximal development for reading, the children were able to comprehend in English at a level that approximates their comprehension in Spanish. This improved performance represents a three-year jump in participation in English reading.

STUDY 2: SECOND LANGUAGE WRITING INSTRUCTION: WRITING IN THE COMMUNITY AND CLASSROOM

The goal of our second study was to explore ways of using data on writing from community settings to inform classroom practice (Trueba, *et al.,* 1982). Twelve secondary school teachers and their twenty-seven students participated in the study for approximately six months. To facilitate the study, we placed our research operations in a local residence in the heart of the communty. From this centrally located field office, we hired and trained local residents, including teachers and graduate students, as researchers to collect home and community observations. The same field office became the place where we conducted all meetings with teachers, as well as where we housed all the data collected during the study. This field office facilitated interactions between the people conducting the ethnography and the teachers responsible for implementing instructional innovations. We were able to create and implement--in collaboration with teachers--writing activities that attended to both the teachers' and students' writing needs, while making contact with community issues and concerns.

We sought not only to foster instructional change but also to document the teaching practices that make such changes possible. Every teacher agreed to implement a minimum of six writing "modules." These modules consisted of a series of relatively well-specified instructional activities intended to facilitate the use of community ethnographic data. These modules were the vehicle for linking community information with teaching-learning practices. In addition, we asked teachers to keep journals. These journals provided researchers and teachers with data on the organization of instruction in the writing modules and with a running log of the teaching practices in the project, a way to contrast the teachers' thinking and teaching over time. When we present an example of a module, we will include excerpts from teacher journals to illustrate our points.

School and Community Characteristics

Our intervention was shaped by the characteristics of the students and teachers who participated in the study. We selected three ethnically diverse junior high schools in the south San Diego area to participate in the study. We concentrated our observations on 27 students from 8 different families in the area. Most of the families are poor. The parents have a low level of education; most did not receive more than three to five years of schooling in Mexico. The language background of these families is predominantly Spanish; some family members are fluent bilinguals. In general, the families communicate in Spanish at home and maintain many of the traditional Mexican customs.

As a group, the students scored among the lowest on tests of writing achievement. Not only were the students considered poor writers, but most teachers reported that they themselves had received little or no formal training in the teaching of writing. For the most part, they felt unprepared to teach writing. In addition, the majority of the teachers reported that writing instruction was an infrequent classroom activity. Most classroom writing was in response to tests or homework assignments with the teacher as the primary audience and evaluator. Writing was rarely used as a broader tool of communication--to convey opinions and ideas or to analyze and explore the world.

Because of the way in which writing appeared in classrooms, we needed to provide the teachers with specific techniques for teaching writing that they could practice, learn, and adapt to various subjects areas. As long as writing was subordinated to other curricular demands, there would be few opportunities for instruction in which students and teachers interacted with the information generated by the ethnography.

Despite the obvious bilingual character of the surrounding community, the schools had excluded Spanish from the curriculum. No bilingual classes were offered, thereby eliminating the possibility of using the students' Spanish-literacy skills as a bridge to English-language literacy. In addition, most teachers were English monolingual speakers and lived outside their teaching community, putting them out of touch with everyday community dynamics. This fact of life pointed out the need to familiarize teachers with community issues on a regular basis.

Our field observations revealed the diversity that characterizes social life in the community. Several factors, especially immigration patterns, constantly mold the specific social configuration of the community. This diversity is most evident in family organization. Field observations documented the different social arrangements as families attempt to adjust to the social and economic realities of life in the community. These arrangements range from the so-called "traditional" families, with clearly demarcated roles and responsibilities for the family members, to families where the father is missing and one of the offspring must assume the adult role. More important for our purposes, family roles and responsibilities were often assigned on the basis of English-language fluency. The children took responsibility for conducting transactions that involved literacy in English in families with fluent English-speaking children where the parents were Spanish monolingual speakers. Although the parents monitored what went on, the transactions were conducted by the children. Since the children mediated the family's communication with important social institutions (e.g., paying bills or answering school-related queries), they assumed control and power within the family system usually reserved for adults (Anderson and Teal, 1981; Anderson and Stokes, 1984). Thus, the social, economic, and linguistic demands of life in the community are met with familial flexibility. Adjusting roles and responsibilities are necessary for survival.

Writing in the Home and Community

Most of the writing observed in home and community settings was functional and practical. It included shopping lists, phone messages, an occasional letter, and most frequently, students' homework assignments. The practical writing seemed to be less demanding in several respects than the writing required of students in classrooms. Phone messages and shopping lists did not look like a promising base from which to *raise* classroom writing skills. Homework became the important vehicle for creating opportunities for family literacy practice because most of the literacy events observed were organized around school-related matters.

Despite the lack of observable extended writing events in community life, parents and other community members expressed repeatedly their belief in the great value of education and their concerns about the education of the young. They viewed the development of writing as an essential element of a good education and of being cultured (*bien educado*). So, although not much writing *was observed* in the home and the community, it was clear that writing in particular and literacy in general *was valued* as an important component of schooling. From the parents' point of view, writing and schooling are inseparable and vital for educational and personal advancement (Ogbu, 1977).

A different and important aspect of community life became clear during initial home visits. Parents, students, and others all impressed us with their concern for social issues that permeate community life. Virtually every conversation that began as a discussion of writing eventually turned to the problems of youth gangs, unemployment, immigration, the need to learn English, and the like. It became clear to us that writing, schooling, and social issues are complexly *related* phenomena in the community.

We organized instructional interventions in relation to the complex social order we were encountering. We organized writing instruction that was responsive to community dynamics and addressed the teachers' training needs and the students' writing problems.

Writing Activities Connecting Community and Classroom Practices

The modules organized classroom circumstances to connect with community information. The key to the initial modules was success. The teachers and students experienced immediate success in producing texts. This success established the credibility of using community information to teach writing. Because of the parents' overwhelming concerns about their children's education, we emphasized expository writing that is useful for school advancement. We provided the teachers with state-of-the-art teaching strategies (Cooper and Odell, 1978) for implementing writing activities systematically. These strategies included pre-writing discussions to generate and clarify ideas about writing and about the community, the production of drafts, evaluative feedback from teachers and peers, revisions of drafts, and final copy.

Along with the teaching strategies, we introduced teachers to our theoretical notions in order to maximize their understanding of and participation in our research activities. We encouraged the teachers to use theory to shape the design of the writing activities and interpret their teaching efforts. Throughout the project, we emphasized the following notions derived in part from the work of Cooper (e.g., Cooper and Odell, 1978) and Graves (1982):

1. Writing as communication. Writing is essentially a communicative activity and should be taught and understood as such.

2. Writing as a tool of analysis. Writing activities can be used as a way for the student to explore or examine social and academic issues and issues that are relevant to them; otherwise, writing is reduced to a mechanical and trivial (not to mention boring) task for students and teachers.

3. Writing for intellectual development. The higher order goal of classroom writing is the elaboration of thinking; the mechanics of writing should be taught in the service of this goal. These mutually complementary activities should be combined as part of the same framework.

4. Writing performance before competence. Teaching involves establishing levels of performance in advance of what the students can do by themselves. These levels are sustained by the way the teacher structures (organizes) help, and this teacher help is eventually appropriated by the students to become part of their writing strategies. A key to successful instruction is establishing conditions (including goals) for writing that are, in a sense, "futuristic," provide guided practice to help students perform under these conditions, and monitor how students move toward performing independently what they can initially only do with help.

This move from other regulation to self-regulation is reflected in the students' acquisition of the writing process, accompanying changes in the type of help the teachers provide, and the improvement of the writing product. Our evaluation of success was based on evidence for these changes in the students' writing.

We found that students' homework assignments created the most frequent opportunities for writing to occur in homes. With this knowledge at hand, we structured homework assignments that not only produced literacy-related interactions in the home but also involved parents and other community members in the development and conduct of the classroom writing activities.

Module Implementation*

We will now review a module conducted in one of the ESL (English as a Second Language) classrooms. We selected this particular module to describe in detail because it illustrates one good way, given the school's unfortunate lack of curricular emphasis on Spanish literacy, to support English literacy development, and to capitalize on extra-curricular sources to help develop the English writing of limited-English proficient students. From our perspective, individual differences in the writing needs of limited-English proficient and fluent-English proficient (FEP) students require attention to the different levels at which students enter the writing activity and the nature of the help they need to perform at the most advanced level possible. In our program, whether they are fluent in English or not, instruction is organized for students to engage in the same basic educational activity: writing for communication and intellectual advancement.

Given their English-language difficulties, LEP students may contribute differentially to the completion of the activity than FEP students, and the teacher may have to provide more structured help. However, both sets of students participate *in comparable activities that are intellectually demanding.* In the module cited, the concern was with information gathered from sources other than the students themselves. (The students had previously written papers expressing their own opinions about bilingualism.) The teacher introduced the idea of surveys and questionnaires as methods for getting other people's opinion on issues. As she notes in her journal:

> *I told them the [next] module was going to be concerned with information, opinions, feelings, etc., that would be gleaned from other sources besides themselves. They looked at me with blank faces. Then I started to discuss and probe the meaning of "survey" and "questionnaire" with them. They loved that! I gave examples of TV polls, of Cola tests, etc. Jorge and Lisa called out, "Does that mean we're going to do that?" They all were kind of excited or at least interested when I said "yes."*

---

* Details about the development and implementation of all modules can be found in Trueba *et al.* (1982) and Moll and Díaz (in press, 1986).

I "fed" them the beginning questions for their question-naires, ones I wanted to make sure all asked. I gave them three they had to use, and two more samples they could choose. The assignment was explained as follows:

These three questions *all* must ask:

- A. What language do you speak best?
- B. What language do you read and write best?
- C. Do any members of your family who live with you speak another language besides English?

Two other questions were optional:

- D. Would you be willing to take classes to become bilingual?
- E. What career do you foresee in your future in which you would benefit by being bilingual?

Each student was required to ask:

- A. Two adults not working on campus.
- B. Two adults who do work on campus.
- C. Three students whose first language is English.
- D. Three students whose first language is other than English.

Homework for tonight was to invent three additional questions related to bilingualism and people's opinions about it.

The module continued the next day as the teacher got the students to generate additional questions to use in the survey. Following are ten questions selected by the class for possible inclusion in their questionnaires:

1. Would you prefer to live around bilingual people in a bilingual community?

2. Are your closest friends bilingual?

3. a. Would you like to go to the university?
   b. Do you know that the best university requires four years of second-language training?

4. Which language do you like the best of the ones you don't speak?

5. What language do you speak with your friends? Why?

6. How many teachers do you have that speak some Spanish?

7. Do you think you would like to return to live where you learned your first language?

8. Which language does your closest friend speak with you?

9. Do you think speaking another language is important?

10. Is it comparatively hard for you to learn another language?

Knowing her students would need further guidance in conducting the survey, the teacher spent part of the next lesson clarifying examples and general concerns. She was particularly surprised at the interest generated by the students interviewing adult respondents:

The students were buzzing when they came in and they buzzed all along! Some had never had occasion to speak to adults other than their teachers here, and a few, especially Hector C. and George [come to mind] were itching to show me Dr. S's responses.

The teacher structured some more help to move the students along and to maintain their interest in quite an involved writing activity.

> *The projects are shaping up and they seem to have a clear idea of what they are doing at this step, so I decided today to introduce the next step. Most had time in class to start formulating a "Results" page. I just put a suggested format on the board and explained after they had gotten their results, they could fill in the results chart.*

The teacher spent a lot of time on the module and at each step of the way, she made sure that the students were in contact with the goal of the lesson. That is, the several tasks necessary to complete the module were done to accomplish a specified and mutually understood goal; at no time were the students relegated to doing writing exercises unrelated to the purpose of the writing activity that makes up the module.

As the module continues, the students show signs of taking over the activity without the need for highly structured supervision. Noticing this change, the teacher decides to be less directive and have the students assume most of the responsibility for completing the necessary tasks. This shift in the control of the task is alluded to in the next excerpt.

> *In class, there was a lot on constructive communicating going on--students asked each other "How to say" this and that, and asked me [usually] "how do I do it?" After I had already explained the questions, they had a difficult time getting going, but I decided not to hand-feed them this time, but instead to let them muddle through. I answered specific questions today, but I didn't volunteer the questions, if you know the difference. I sent them home to finish by Monday.*

The students returned Monday with their papers in different stages of completion. The teacher selected one of the more complete papers and placed it on an overhead to show it to the class. They then proceeded to edit the paper together and to clarify the type of paper required in the module. The balance of the class time was used to write more drafts and to revise those already turned in.

Writing samples.   Below are three unedited examples of students' writing in their second language. Despite obvious errors, these essays initiated exceptional opportunities for teaching that otherwise would not have occurred.

Student A:

The people in my cummunity think that being bilingual is very important for several good reasons. Firts, I felt very proud doing the Survey. the people in our commuinity feel very proud at them self that they speak Spanish and Eanglish because they can talk with there friends in any of those two lenguages. Secondly, the people I ask   Some were bilingual students and adults 60% were bilingual people and 40% weren't bilingual people. Also, I ask a teacher and a student if they would be wiling to work as a bilingual person and they said no and than I ask a Student this qiestion Do you think Speaking Another lenguage is important and he said no that amazed me because I never herd one person that thinks that speaking another lenguage ain't important. finally, I ask a teacher that What career was he interested in that would require a second language and he said no common and he told this I don't know What lauguage I'm interestes that would require a 2nd lenguage because I don't know it and I ask two Students this question what career are yo interested in that would require a 2nd lenguage and 50% said Fransh 10% said Germen 10% said Italian and 20% said no coman as you can see I was having fun.

Student B:

I found that people in our community feel good about belingualism for several good resaons. They think it it very important because they can communicate with other people. The people I ask are 60% students, 40% adults, 70% are Spanish speakers, 20% were English speakers, 70% can write and read English, 20% can write and read Spanish well. Most of the people told me that in there house can speak English and Spanish. The people I ask the questions, answers me very polite and they said the questions were very interesting. Some person said that these project was very good for me and interesting for him. When he said that I feel very good about the work I was doing. The most interesting thing that I found wat that the people like the project. Most of the people said that they were willing to take classes to become totally be-

lingual because it could help them right now and in the future. The students I ask said that they have only friends that speak only Spanish and English not othey language. The adults I ask said that been belingual is very important for them because they can communicate with more people and they can have more opportunitis for some jobs that othey people do I fee very good about the way people answer me.

Student C:

First, In my school, I asked some students and aduls. If they are bilinguals, some people are bilingual and someones are not in my school.   Some of them tall me they are bilinguals. somea_____they're not bilinguals about the 50%. Seconly, In my community some people is don't intersting about to be bilingual because they think, they don't need toher lenguage because they are in America and in America only speak English. Thirth, I don't felt good, because I think they are a little dum people because they think to be a bilingual person is waste them time. Also, I think the people who's don't interesting to be them selfs bilingual are going to the wrong way because the persons who speak two languages or more have the opportunity to know other culture and lenguage. Finaly, In my family think to be a bilingual is to important because they learn other culture and language, And we speak spanish and we need speak English because we live in U.S.A. but like in diferent countries is important to know other lnguages for we can talk with other persons.

This ESL teacher, as well as the others, used formula paragraphs to get the students writing. Most believed, and we agreed, that the added structure facilitated participation and performance in writing activities that the students otherwise could not do because of their oral language limitations. Of course, the idea is that as the students gain fluency in English, they start relying less on the tight structure of the formula paragraphs, and move toward more flexible and independent writing.

Summary

The idea of creating zones of proximal development for writing is to motivate shifts in the control of the task from teacher to student. A major role of any teacher should be to tap those skills that the students have developed in their first language and to put them to good use in the service of academic goals in their second language. In the "regular" classrooms, prewriting, free writing, and response groups were combined in several ways to get the students actively engaged in writing and prepared for more advanced efforts. In the ESL classrooms, the same strategies were used to bring into the classroom the students' experiences and skills; the formula paragraphs were used as the crutch to get and keep the students on task. Obviously, the students' difficulties in English verbal expression, reading, and vocabulary development needed remedy; but the trick was to organize lessons in ways that accommodated these difficulties and minimized their constraining influence, while maximizing the use of the tools that the students did possess, such as knowledge of the topic and other experiences. As the examples above illustrate, this goal was being accomplished; students who would otherwise do little or no classroom writing were writing essays in their second language that incorporated information collected from the community.

EDUCATIONAL IMPLICATIONS:
A MODEL OF MUTUAL ACCOMMODATION

Cazden (1983) pointed out that most ethnographically informed studies of schooling describe existing conditions, but only a few suggest change. She praised two projects, the Kamehameha Early Education Project and Heath's work in Appalachia (Heath, 1983) because researchers worked with educators to produce concrete change. This researcher-educator collaboration, particularly in the incorporation of community data to implement changes in teaching practices, was also a characteristic of the case studies we conducted. We are also aware of the work of Richard Morris and his collaborators in Philadelphia (Morris and Louis, 1982) and Hymes (1982) and his colleagues at the University of Pennsylvania. There is a model for educational change in these studies that has significance for educators of language minority students.

Teacher-Researcher Collaboration

A close collaboration between researchers and teachers is an essential element of this model for social change (Florio and Walsh, 1981; Erickson and Mohatt, 1982; Smith, 1982; Moll and Díaz, in press, 1986; Mehan *et al.*, 1985). Teachers participate in collecting data and analyzing teaching practices with researchers. Through their participation in research, teachers are not simply recipients of research results that may be relevant for their teaching, but collaborators in the development of the research and in exploring how to connect aspects of the students' lives with educational practice.

The Use of an Ethnographic Base

The use of information gathered from ethnographic observation of the local community is a second important element of a model for social change. With the exception of our work, all studies had available an existing ethnographic data base before the onset of the classroom research. The community information need not come from a new research project. Kamehameha Early Education Program (KEEP) Researchers had conducted the ethnography in the native Hawaiian students' community; they used this information gathered previously to organize and interpret classroom changes (Au, 1980; Tharp, 1982). Heath (1981) had been collecting ethnographic data in her research community before she implemented the classroom studies and capitalized on this previous work in deciding how to proceed. Our case studies did not work from an existing data base, but moved progressively from classroom-specific analysis to the collection of community data. We then used the community data selectively to influence the specific educational conditions we were analyzing.

Transforming Community Events for Pedagogical Use

We are not recommending a general solution for all educational situations. Instead, we are recommending a *procedure* to be used to find a specific solution to local circumstances. The idea is to identify local conditions and relate information from the local community to local educational practice. KEEP and Heath (1981) placed particular emphasis on sociolinguistic events that could be transferred for pedagogical use. The incorporation of the "talk story" in KEEP reading lessons is the most famous example of teachers changing classroom practice to accommodate relevant cultural elements.

The KEEP reading program has two additional aspects, however, that may have also contributed to its success (Au, 1980; Tharp, 1982). One is a shift in the focus of instruction from decoding to comprehension and another is the inclusion of the children's experiences as part of the lesson's reading discussions. This combination of elements facilitated comprehension by making the children's experiences relevant to their understanding of reading content. In the KEEP experience, ethnographic information about a specific speech event in the community was used to *interpret* a key aspect of lesson changes that occurred without explicit researcher intervention. Community information was not transported into the classroom to modify lessons; instead, the lessons were transformed by the teachers themselves, and then the community data were used to make sense of the effectiveness of the new reading experience.

Heath (1982) worked cooperatively with parents and educators to modify the learning environment for Trackton students in ways that were mutually beneficial. In order to increase the students' verbal skills in naming objects, identifying their characteristics, providing descriptions out of context, and responding to known information questions, Heath instructed the Trackton teachers on ways to adapt to the community's ways of asking questions. For example, teachers began social studies lessons with questions that ask for personal experiences and analogic responses, e.g., "What's happening there?," "Have you ever been there?," and "What's this like?" These questions are similar to the questions that parents asked their children at home. The use of these questions in early stages of instruction were productive in generating active responses from previously passive and "nonverbal" Trackton students. Once the teachers increased the participation of the students in lessons using home questioning styles, they were able to move them through a zone of proximal development toward responding to questions cf the styles commonly demanded in school.

Heath (1982) talked about the process as collecting *credible* data from both classrooms and community. In doing research on their own families and in classrooms, the teachers explored and discovered "how and why data on everyday behaviors--their own and that of others--can be useful in bringing about attitude and behavior changes" (p. 126). The teachers' collection of data from the community "led them to ask questions of their own practices and to admit other practices which would not necessarily have emerged otherwise" (p. 127). The subsequent lesson interventions were influenced by the ethnography only insofar as the findings were considered pedagogically relevant and useful by the teachers.

Heath (1981) also demonstrated the utility of pedagogically credible data in her writing project. After discovering that job and community settings were not productive settings for generating writing information for use in lessons, the researchers turned to the boys' own social network. In pool halls, clubs, and local gathering places, the researchers found various types of writing and for different purposes, ranging from protest messages to advertisements and announcements. These everyday writing activities served as the basis for organizing classroom writing lessons and for extending classroom writing. For example, students discussed the writing of others, such as social service agencies, which created problems for them or their parents and then were asked to review, revise, and clarify these documents as part of writing lessons. They also produced a "script" to narrate a videotape they prepared for use in senior citizens' centers; wrote brief spots used in local radio programs; created "ethnographic readers" for students to use in elementary classrooms; and a number of other interesting, innovative activities.

In short, when writing was made relevant to their interests and communities, the students wrote. However, Heath (1981) reported that the range of writing practiced in the classrooms was limited by the functions of writing that the students valued. For example, reports of their opinions or events and accounts about experiences they enjoyed, such as shooting pool, were valued. In contrast to these activities, letter writing or creative writing had limited appeal. Therefore, those writing activities associated specifically with schooling (e.g., essay writing and creative writing) or with academic work were not practiced frequently.

Note that Heath (1981) used community information to motivate students to write by making the lessons relevant to students interests, and in so doing, implemented procedures to facilitate the students' writing. In contrast to KEEP, which used the community information to establish the cultural congruence of the classroom changes, and in contrast to Heath's (1981) own work with preschoolers, where she used specific sociolinguistic behaviors to modify the conduct of lessons, here she used ethnographic data to establish the relevance of writing. Through ethnography, the researchers explored social and community settings for information that would make sense to transfer to the classroom for instructional purposes. In addition, as Heath (1982) reported, the lessons themselves became "ethnographic" in nature:

> The approach to turning these students on to writing was based on ethnographic techniques employed by teachers and students. This approach enabled students to become writers and translators for their own communities, for an audience of readers whose abilities they knew and could identify precisely. (p. 43)

Our case studies contain elements similar to those mentioned above, but were adapted to the specific conditions of the local community. In the Moll and Díaz writing research (in press, 1986), a strength was their status as "insiders" in the community where they studied. They tried to capitalize on this strength by moving their base of operations from the university to a locale situated in the heart of the community. This move to ground research activities in the community's realities had important consequences on both the field and the classroom components of the study. The insider stance they assumed heavily influenced their identification of "credible data," in Heath's terms, for their research purposes and pedagogically useful interventions.

More specifically, the insider's perspective led them to emphasize the social realities of the community and the content of students' and families' interactions, as opposed to any specific ways of interacting as in KEEP and Heath's work. The study did not find any literacy practices specific to "Chicanos," nor for that matter, any social conventions similar to the Hawaiian talk-story or to Heath's forms of questioning. It is not that similar sociolinguistic patterns did not occur in this specific community, but that it is unclear, given the teachers' characteristics and the concerns of the community, whether these sociolinguistic data would have become "credible" information for the English monolingual teachers to use readily in their classrooms. Therefore, instead of focusing primarily on interactional processes in the community data collection, it was more profitable, given the specific study population, to focus on social content: the substance of the discourse, parents' educational values, life history, and conditions of our sample families. In other words, the community and classroom realities the researchers encountered, as well as the goals of the study, dictated their methodology and what counted as data for classroom application.

Mutual Accommodation

Regardless of the type of community data employed, information imported into the classroom modified the social organization of educational practice. The goal is to change qualitatively the way lessons are conducted to increase the children's participation. In KEEP's ongoing work, the goal is to improve the students' reading performance by rearranging how they participate in lessons. In Heath's Trackton study, the goal was to elicit responses from otherwise uninvolved students to the teachers' questions. In Heath's writing study, the goal was to get the students to write, and in so doing demonstrate the relevance of writing. In the Moll and Díaz (in press, 1986) efforts, the goal was to use knowledge about the children's Spanish literacy and community data as the basis for reorganizing instruction. Increased student participation in lessons was then associated with improvements in student performance.

Once lessons were changed, similarities between the structural properties of the lessons and sociolinguistic behaviors in nonschool contexts became evidence of the cultural congruence of the lessons or the cultural relevance of the interventions. KEEP's changes in the lesson interactions and in the implementation of a small-group format to encourage cooperation were found to be compatible with Hawaiian cultural norms. In Heath's study, teachers incorporated forms of questioning found in the Black community into lessons to make them culturally relevant for the Black students. In Heath's writing study, the cultural contact was made by contextualizing the writing in community activities. This contextualization changed the meaning of writing for the students. As Heath (1981) put it, linking writing to community activities made "functional literacy truly function in the social context of [the students'] culture" (p. 43). In our work, the objective is to make the link between community and classrooms *through* classroom-specific academic activities. In the reading work, we showed how Spanish, the children's home language, was extremely useful in improving English reading instruction; in the writing research, we showed how social content can be used legitimately to improve classroom writing instruction.

In addition to establishing the cultural relevance of the interventions, instructional changes also had to be pedagogically justifiable. Increased student academic achievement and classroom participation are the main educational outcomes that made the use of community data in classrooms educationally acceptable. Changes on pedagogical grounds were the starting point of KEEP's interventions. Heath reported that in exploring how to make the community questioning fit into the lessons, the teachers found that several types of questions used (in the Black community) could be considered what education textbooks called "probing questions." The type of community information the teachers were asked to use as part of their lessons was therefore "justifiable in terms of good pedagogy" (Heath, 1981, p. 124). If used in the classroom, these types of questions taken from the community data would potentially benefit all students. In Heath's writing study, the pedagogical utility of the changes became readily apparent when students, who were otherwise apathetic to writing instruction, took an interest and started writing in a variety of ways. Similarly, in our case studies we established credibility by producing immediate, practical, and effective changes in instruction. The most convincing argument is success: Demonstrating repeatedly and in different contexts that sociocultural data is a powerful resource to achieve academic goals mutually desired by parents, teachers, and researchers.

Summary

With the mutually beneficial modification of teaching and learning environments based on the collaboration among people from community, university, and school settings, we have model of change that stands in stark contrast to those proposed by the proponents of linguistic and cultural deprivation theories. Instead of denying the coherence and relevance of the language, culture, values, and knowledge of the community, these teacher-researcher-community collaborations propose a model of mutual accommodation in which both teachers and students modify their behavior in the direction of a common goal: academic success with cultural integrity.

CONCLUSIONS

The implication of the context-specific perspective for the sociocultural context of linguistic minority students is clear: It shifts the responsibility for school failure away from the characteristics of the failing child and toward more general societal processes (Gumperz, 1971). This line of research is showing that school failure cannot be explained merely by considering the child's linguistic code or cultural background. The source of students' problems in school is not to be found solely in their language; it is to be found in the social organization of schooling. The problems that linguistic minority children face in school must be viewed as a consequence of institutional arrangements that ensnare certain children by not capitalizing on the fact that these children display skills differently in different types of situations. Instead of instructional rigidity, our finding suggest the need for organizational flexibility to create varying instructional circumstances that take full advantage of students' ample resources.

Although we have addressed many issues in these studies, one issue is of particular significance: Our work suggests that English-language educational programs, as presently structured, systematically underestimate the capabilities of language minority students. As a result of this underestimation, these children are relegated to lessons that do not facilitate their educational and intellectual advancement.

Our research also shows, however, that the present state of affairs can be changed. In the course of this chapter, we have indicated how it is possible to capitalize on children's social, linguistic, and academic strengths to change teaching and learning situations. To do so, we need to view the students' background and lifestyles, not as a hindrance to educational advancement that must be corrected or circumvented, but as legitimate and powerful resources for improving students' performance in schools and, as a consequence, improving the process of schooling itself.

REFERENCES

Anderson, A. B., and Stokes, S. J. Social and institutional influences on the development and practice of literacy. In F. Smith, H. Goelman, and A. Oberg (Eds.), *Awakening to Literacy*. New York: Heineman, 1984.

————, and Teale, W. H. *Literacy as Cultural Practice*. Paper presented at Simposio Internacional: Nuevas Perspectives en los Procesos de Lectura y Escritura, Mexico City, Mexico, July, 1981.

Au, K. H. Participation structures in a reading lesson with Hawaiian children: Analysis of a culturally appropriate instructional event. *Anthropology and Education Quarterly*, 1980, *11*(2), 91-115.

————, and Jordan, C. T. Talk story in Hawaiian classrooms workshop. *Ethnographic and Sociolinguistics Research in Classrooms Symposium*. Los Angeles, California: American Anthropological Association, 1978.

Bereiter, C., and Engleman, S. *Teaching Disadvantaged Children in the Preschool*. Englewood Cliffs, New Jersey: Prentice-Hall, 1966.

Bernstein, B. (Ed.). *Class, Codes and Control: Theoretical Studies Toward a Sociology of Language*. (Vol. 1). London: Routledge & Kegan Paul, 1971.

————. *Class, Codes, and Control: Toward a Theory of Educational Transmissions*. (Vol. 3). London: Routledge & Kegan Paul, 1973.

Berry, J. W. *Human Ecology and Cognitive Style*. New York: Sage-Halsted, 1976.

Brown, Roger. *First Language: The Early Stages*. Cambridge, Massachusetts: Harvard University Press, 1973.

Brown, R., Cazden, D. B., and Bellugi, U. The child's grammar from I to III. In J. P. Hill (Ed.), *1967 Minnesota Symposium on Child Psychology*. Minneapolis: University of Minnesota Press, 1969.

Cazden, C. B. Language in education: Variation in the teacher-talk register. *Thirtieth Annual Georgetown University Round Table on Languages and Linguistics*. Washington, D.C.: Center for Applied Linguistics, 1979.

————. Can ethnographic research go beyond the status quo? *Anthropology and Education Quarterly*, 1983, *14*(1), 33-41.

Chomsky, N. *Aspects of the Theory of Syntax*. Cambridge, Massachusetts: MIT Press, 1965.

Cicourel, A. V., Jennings, S. H. M., Jennings, K. H., Leiter, K. C. W., MacKay, R., Mehan, H., and Roth, D. R. *Language Use and School Performance*. New York: Academic Press, 1974.

————, and Mehan, H. Universal development, stratifying practices, and status attainment. *Research in Social Stratification and Mobility*, 1984, *4*, 3-27.

Cole, M., Gay, J., Glick, J. A., and Sharp, D. W. *The Cultural Context of Learning and Thinking*. New York: Basic Books, 1971.

We would like to acknowledge the help of Daniel Holt and his coworkers at the Bilingual Education Office. Special thanks are expressed to Norman Gold for his patience and excellent editorial recommendations.

_____, Griffin, P., and Newman, D. *They're All the Same in Their Own Way.* San Diego, California: University of California, Laboratory of Comparative Human Cognition, 1979.

Coleman, J. S., Campbell, E. Q., Hobson, C. J., McPartland, J., Mood, A. M., Weinfeld, F. D., and York, R. L. *Equality of Educational Opportunity.* Washington, D.C.: U.S. Government Printing Office, 1966.

Cooper, R. C., and Odell, L. C. *Research on Composing: Points of Departure.* Urbana, Illinois: National Council of Teachers of English, 1978.

Cortés, Carlos E. The education of language minority students: A contextual interaction model. In *Beyond Language: Social and Cultural Factors in Schooling Language Minority Students.* Los Angeles, California: Evaluation, Dissemination and Assessment Center, California State University, Los Angeles, 1986.

Díaz, S. *Cognitive Style Influence: Pervasive or Specific?* Unpublished doctoral dissertation, Harvard University, 1983.

Doyle, W. Classroom tasks and student abilities. In P. L. Peterson and H. J. Walberg (Eds.), *Conceptions of Teaching.* Berkeley, California: McCutchen, 1978.

Dumont, R. V., Jr. Learning English and how to be silent: Studies in Sioux and Cherokee classrooms. In C. Cazden, V. John, and D. Hymes (Eds.), *Functions of Language in the Classroom.* New York: Teachers College Press, 1972.

Erickson, F., and Mohatt, G. Cultural organization of participant structures in two classrooms of Indian students. In G. D. Spindler (Ed.), *Doing the Ethnography of Schooling.* New York: Holt, Rinehart & Winston, 1982.

_____, and Shultz, J. J. *The Counselor as Gatekeeper.* New York: Academic Press, 1982.

_____, and _____. When is a context? Some issues and methods in the analysis of social competence. *The Quarterly Newsletter of the Institute for Comparative Human Development,* 1977, *1*(2), 5-10.

Florio, S. *Learning How to Go to School.* Unpublished doctoral dissertation, Harvard University, 1978.

_____, and Walsh, M. The teacher as colleague in classroom research. In H. Trueba, G. Pung Guthrie, and K. H. Au (Eds.), *Culture and the Bilingual Classroom: Studies in Classroom Ethnography.* Rowley, Massachusetts: Newbury House Publishers, 1981.

Goodman, K., Goodman, Y., and Flores, B. *Reading in the Bilingual Classroom: Literacy and Biliteracy.* Rosslyn, Virginia: National Clearinghouse for Bilingual Education, 1979.

Gould, S. J. *The Mismeasure of Man.* New York: W. W. Norton, 1981.

Graves, D. How do writers develop? *Language Arts,* February 1982, *59*(2), 173-179.

Gumperz, J. *Language in Social Groups.* Palo Alto, California: Stanford University Press, 1971.

Gusfield, J. *The Culture of Public Problems.* Chicago: The University of Chicago Press, 1981.

Hall, W. S., Cole, M., Reder, S., and Dowley, G. Variations in young children's use of language: Some effects of setting and dialect. In R. Freedle (Ed.), *Discourse Production and Comprehension.* Norwood, New Jersey: Ablex, 1977.

Heath, S. B. Toward and ethno-history of writing on American education. In M. Whiteman (Ed.), *Variation in Writing: Functional Linguistics and Cultural Differences.* Norwood, New Jersey: Erlbaum, 1981.

_____. Questioning at home and at school: A comparative study. In G. Spindler (Ed.), *Doing the Ethnography of Schooling: Educational Anthropology in Action.* New York: Holt, Rinehart & Winston, 1982.

————. *Ways with Words: Ethnography of Communication in Communities and Classrooms.* New York: Cambridge University Press, 1983.

Herrnstein, R. J. *I.Q. in the Meritocracy.* Boston: Little Brown & Co., 1974.

Hess, R. D., and Shipman, V. C. Early experience and the socialization of cognitive modes in children. *Child Development,* December 1965, *36*(4), 869-885.

Hymes, D. What is ethnography? In P. Gilmore and A. A. Glatthorn (Eds.), *Ethnography and Education: Children In and Out of School.* Washington, D.C.: Center for Applied Linguistics, 1982.

Jencks, C., Smith, M., Acland, H., Bane, M. J., Cohen, D., Gintis, H., Heynes, B., and Michelson, F. *Inequality: A Reassessment of the Effect of Family and Schooling in America.* New York: Basic Books, 1972.

Jensen, A. R. How much can we boost IQ and scholastic achievement? *Harvard Educational Review,* 1969, *39*, 1-123.

John, V. P. Styles of learning-styles of teaching: Reflections on the education of Navajo children. In C. Cazden, V. John, and D. Hymes (Eds.), *Functions of Language in the Classroom.* New York: Teachers College Press, 1972.

Jules-Rosette, B. The veil of objectivity: Prophecy divination, and social inquiry. *American Anthropologist,* September 1978, *80*(3), 549-570.

Kagan, Spencer. Cooperative learning and sociocultural factors in schooling. In *Beyond Language: Social and Cultural Factors in Schooling Language Minority Students.* Los Angeles, California: Evaluation, Dissemination and Assessment Center, California State University, Los Angeles, 1986.

Labov. W. The logic of nonstandard English. In P. P. Giglioli (Ed.), *Language and Social Context.* London, England: Penguin Books, 1972.

Laboratory of Comparative Human Cognition. A model system for the study of learning difficulties. *The Quarterly Newsletter of the Laboratory of Comparative Human Cognition,* July 1982, *4*(3), 39-66.

————. Culture and cognitive development. In W. Kessen (Ed.), *Mussen's Handbook of Child Psychology: Vol. I. History, Theory, and Method.* (4th ed.). New York: John Wiley & Sons, 1983.

Lennenberg, A. N. *Biological Foundations of Language.* Cambridge, Massachusetts: MIT Press, 1966.

Leont'ev, A. Some problems in learning Russian as a foreign language (Essays on Psycholinguistics). *Soviet Psychology,* Summer 1973, *11*, 4.

McDermott, R. P. *Kids Make Sense: An Ethnographic Account of the Interactional Management of Success and Failure in One First Grade Classroom.* Unpublished doctoral dissertation, Department of Anthropology, Stanford University, 1976.

————. Social relations as contexts for learning in school. *Harvard Educational Review,* 1977, *47*, 298-313.

————, and Roth, D. R. The social organization of behavior: Interactional approaches. *Annual Review of Anthropology,* 1979, *7*, 321-345.

Mehan, H., Moll, L. C., Riel, M. M., Tum Suden, M., Maroules, N., Drale, C., Boruta, M., Whooley, K., and Newcomb, A. *Computers in Classrooms: A Quasi Experiment in Guided Change.* (Final Report No. NIE-G-83-0027). San Diego, California: University of California, Interactive Technology Laboratory, Center for Human Information Processing, 1985.

————. Structuring school structure. *Harvard Educational Review,* 1978, *45*(1), 311-338.

————. *Learning Lessons.* Cambridge, Massachusetts: Harvard University Press, 1979.

Moll, L., and Díaz, E. Bilingual communication and reading: The importance of Spanish in learning to read in English. *Elementary School Journal,* in press.

_____, and Díaz, R. Teaching writing as communication: The use of ethnographic findings in classroom practice. In D. Bloom (Ed.), *Language, Literacy and Schooling.* Norwood, New Jersey: Ablex, 1986.

Morris, R. W., and Louis, C. N. *Improving the Functional Writing of Urban Secondary School Students.* (Final Report. No. NIE-400-81-0019). Washington, D.C.: National Institute of Education, 1982.

Ogbu, J. Racial stratification and education: The case of Stockton, California. *IRCD Bulletin,* 1977, *12*(3), 1-26.

Philips, S. V. Participant structures and communicative competence: Warm Springs Indian children in community and classrooms. In C. Cazden, V. John, and D. Hymes (Eds.), *Functions of Language in the Classroom.* New York: Teachers College Press, 1972.

_____. *The Invisible Culture: Communication in Classroom and Community on the Warm Springs Indian Reservation.* New York: Longmans, 1982.

Piattelli-Palmarini, M. (Ed.) *Language and Learning: The Debate Between Jean Piaget and Noam Chomsky.* Cambridge, Massachusetts: Harvard University Press, 1980.

Ramírez, M. *Nuevas Fronteras de Aprendizaje: Teachers Manual and Curriculum Guide.* Mimeo, June, 1979.

Ramírez, M. A., and Castañeda, A. *Cultural Democracy, Bicognitive Development, and Education.* New York: Academic Press, 1974.

Schultz, J., Florio, S., and Erickson, F. Where's the floor?: Aspects of the cultural organization of social relationships in communication at home and at school. In P. Gilmore and A. Glatthorn (Eds.), *Ethnography and Education: Children In and Out of School.* Georgetown, Virginia: Center for Applied Linguistics, 1982.

Shuy, R., and Griffin, P. The Study of Children's Functional Language and Education in the Early Years. (Final Report to the Carnegie Corporation of New York.) Arlington, Virginia: Center for Applied Linguistics, 1978.

Sinclair, J. McH., and Coulthard, R. M. *Towards an Analysis of Discourse.* New York: Oxford University Press, 1975.

Slobin, D. Cognitive prerequisities for the development of grammar. In C. A. Ferguson and D. I. Slobin (Eds.), *Studies of Child Language Development.* New York: Holt, Rinehart & Winston, 1973.

Smith, F. *Writing and the Writer.* New York: Holt, Rinehart & Winston, 1982.

Spindler, George D. (Ed.). *Education and Culture--Anthropological Approaches.* New York: Holt, Rinehart & Winston, 1963.

Sue, Stanley, and Padilla, Amado. Ethnic minority issues in the United States: Challenges for the educational system. In *Beyond Language: Social and Cultural Factors in Schooling Language Minority Students.* Los Angeles, California: Evaluation, Dissemination and Assessment Center, California State University, Los Angeles, 1986.

Talyzina, N. F. One of the paths of development of Soviet learning theory. *Soviet Education,* 1978, *20*(11), 28-48.

Tharp, R. G. The effective instruction of comprehension: Results and descriptions of the Kamehameha Early Education Program. *Reading Research Quarterly,* 1982, *17*(4), 503-527.

Trueba, H., Moll, L. C. and Díaz, S. *Improving the Functional Writing of Bilingual Secondary School Students.* (Context No. 400-81-0023.) Washington, D.C.: National Institute of Education, 1982.

Vygotsky, L. S. Interaction Between Learning and Development. In M. Cole, V. John-Steiner, S. Scribner, and E. Souberman (Eds.). *Mind in Society: The Development of Higher Psychological Process.* Cambridge, Massachusetts: Harvard University Press, 1978.

Willis, P. *Learning to Labor.* London: Routledge & Kegan Paul, 1977.

Witkin, H. A., and Berry, J. W. Psychological differentiation in cross-cultural perspective. *Journal of Cross-Cultural Psychology,* 1975, *6*(1), 4-87.

————, Dyk, R. B., Faterson, H. F., Goodenough, D. R., and Karp, S. A. *Psychological Differentiation.* New York: Wiley, 1962.

COOPERATIVE LEARNING AND SOCIOCULTURAL FACTORS IN SCHOOLING

Spencer Kagan
University of California, Riverside

I. INTRODUCTION

Cooperative learning, the structuring of classrooms so that students work together in small cooperative teams, holds the potential to provide educational outcomes far more positive than presently provided--especially for minority students. There are three pressing problems facing the educational system in the United States: (1) failure to hold and educate minority students; (2) failure to successfully create positive race relations among students; and (3) failure to socialize students toward prosocial values and behaviors such as respect and care for others, and knowledge of when and how to cooperate and help. Cooperative learning methods directly address these problems.

After describing these three educational problems in some detail (see Section II) and describing the nature of cooperative learning methods (see Section III), the present chapter will overview the research results of cooperative learning with emphasis on how cooperative learning addresses the three major deficiencies of our present educational system (see Section IV). Given the positive results of cooperative learning, it is appropriate to examine in some detail the probable mechanisms by which cooperative learning produces positive educational outcomes. Thus, the main body of the present chapter (see Section V) is devoted to reviewing the theoretical and empirical evidence for various explanations of how cooperative learning works, with special attention to how cooperative learning produces gains for minority students. In the last substantive section of the chapter (see Section VI), there is an overview of the training models and resources available for teachers and schools wishing to institute cooperative learning, including a discussion of how training in cooperative learning addresses some inadequacies in present approaches to teacher training and development.

This chapter is not written in the spirit of proclaiming cooperative learning to be a panacea capable of curing the academic and social problems associated with educating a population that is increasingly diverse socioculturally. In the past decades, schools have been the victims of fad-like programmatic swings--each of which claims to be the cure. For the most part, these programs can be seen as end points of a pendulum swing that oscillates between two poles: open-education/humanistic vs. back-to-basics. One refreshing aspect of the cooperative learning approach is that it incorporates both poles of the pendulum: Some of the cooperative learning methods have as their focus the acquisition of basic skills; others aim more at humanistic concern for allowing students to follow and develop their curiosity and their identities as independent learners and loving individuals. Cooperative learning incorporates the goals and methods of both the behaviorist and humanistic traditions and appears to be qualitatively different from educational fads, which represent just one more swing of the school-reform pendulum. The new philosophical synthesis and positive results of cooperative learning merit close examination by educators concerned with the problems created by increased sociocultural diversity.

II. THREE PRESSING PROBLEMS FOR EDUCATION: EDUCATIONAL DEMOCRACY, RACE-RELATIONS, AND PROSOCIAL DEVELOPMENT

Educational Democracy

The United States public school system proclaims as one of its highest values the democratic principle of equal educational opportunity for all pupils regardless of race and economic class. This principle of educational democracy is not being realized. In this chapter, evidence will be provided indicating that part of the reason we do not have educational democracy is that the competitive structure of most classrooms biases educational outcomes against minority and low-income students who are more cooperatively oriented than majority and higher income students. Although the reasons that minority students are not receiving educational benefits comparable to majority students are varied and complex, there can be no doubt that our public school system is failing to hold and educate minority students at levels comparable to majority students. This fact has been documented in detail (Carter and Segura, 1979; Coleman *et al.* 1966; Cortes, this volume; McGroarty, this volume).

The case is well illustrated by two types of data: school holding power and academic achievement for minorities.

School holding power. Taking the percentage of those enrolled in southwestern schools in 1970 by age, we find that minority and majority students approach full enrollment through elementary school, but differential dropout among minority groups begins during middle and high school. For example, only 60 percent of the Mexican-Americans who begin United States public schools finish high school; the figure for Anglos is approximately 86 percent (United States Commission of Civil Rights, 1973).

Academic Achievement. Turning to the question of academic performance of children in school, the data is even more alarming. Academic performance of minority pupils is considerably below majority norms across the United States (Coleman *et al.,* 1966; National Commission on Secondary Education for Hispanics, 1984), and it falls increasingly behind with each school year (Kagan and Zahn, 1975; Okada, 1968).

Reading is central to the achievement of children in all subjects, and it is in reading that the achievement gap is greatest. If we examine the proportion of children who are two or more years behind grade level in reading, we find that in the fourth grade 16.9 percent of the Mexican-American, but only 6.0 percent of Anglos, children fall in that category. Rather than decreasing this gap, successive years of schooling increase it. By the eighth grade, 39.9 percent of Mexican-American children are two or more years behind in reading, compared to 12.8 percent of Anglos (Carter and Segura, 1979). These figures do not reveal the problem in its depth because a higher percentage of Mexican-American than Anglo children have dropped out of school by the eighth grade; if there were no dropout, the achievement gap of remaining students would be even worse. Overall, the United States public school system is failing with regard to the achievement of minority children.

Although the academic outcomes crisis is particularly intense for students from minority groups, their low achievement needs to be viewed against the backdrop of a general decline of achievement in United States public schools. About 20 percent of all American 17-year-olds are functionally illiterate, unable to comprehend simple written instructions (Lerner, 1981); nearly half of our graduating high school students do not know the basics of how our government works (Johnson *et al.,* 1984). Compared to the former Soviet Union students (Wirszup, 1981), one tenth the number of United States students take some calculus in high school or college (Johnson *et al.*, 1984). There has been a steady decline in the average and top scores on the College Entrance Examination Board's Scholastic Aptitude Test for the past 20 years. (Johnson and Johnson, 1983b).

Race Relations

The second major way in which United States public schools are failing minority students is with regard to the nature of race relations, which are fostered within classrooms. Children enter school relatively color-blind, willing to play with and be friends with other children regardless of ethnic, cultural, or racial background. Each year, however, pupils increasingly choose their own race peers as friends. Informal and formal observations converage on the same picture: Children in the lower elementary school grades play in a relatively integrated fashion; by the time they reach fifth and sixth grade, however, they self-segregate along race lines. This trend can be observed informally by watching playground behavior; it is readily described by most teachers in integrated schools and has been documented by sophisticated research methods (this will be discussed in Section IV of this chapter). This progressive racism is evident also to those of us who are bringing cooperative learning to desegregated classrooms. Children in elementary school show little or no resistance to being grouped in mixed-ethnic learning teams; middle school children show some initial resistance. By high schol, however, the resistance is often strong, necessitating extensive use of team-building techniques for the successful introduction of integrated cooperative teams.

The generally poor job our schools are doing with regard to race relations among students is understandable. Whereas the courts mandated desegregation of schools, they did not provide models or resources for integration of classrooms. Desegregating students into competitively structured classrooms has a negative rather than a positive impact on race relations among students.

The failure of schools to foster positive race relations among students has negative effects on the achievement and self-esteem of minority students (Kagan *et al.*, 1985). Unless school practices are changed to promote positive race relations among students, there can be no hope of realizing the democratic promise of an integrated, democratic society in which ability rather than color determines the limits of a person. The ongoing failure of schools to effectively address the problem of race relations among students represents perhaps the greatest missed opportunity in our public education system. As will be shown, the results of cooperative learning studies indicate that with relatively little time and expense, by reorganizing the social structure of the classroom, radical improvements in race relations can be obtained consistently. It is important to note that the need for an effective approach to improving race relations among students will become increasingly great: Demographic trends indicate our schools will be faced with increased sociocultural diversity among students (Cortés, this volume).

Prosocial Development

The third major problem facing our public schools is an increasing prosocial socialization void and the consequent lack of prosocial attitudes and behaviors among our nation's youth.

Nature and causes of the prosocial socialization void. Economic and social forces are reshaping our patterns of family and community life so children in urban settings increasingly are cut away from the socialization experiences that once directed their behavior toward positive behaviors such as cooperation, helping, sharing, and caring. The prosocial socialization void results from urban family structure, television, and school practices.

1. Family Structure. Within the last generation, the American urban family has undergone a radical restructuring. Parent-child, grandparent-child, and teenage-child interactions within the family have been reduced dramatically as a function of the increased percentage of small, non-extended, and single-parent families. Economic forces and social values have shifted so that most women have abandoned the full-time homemaker role to join the workforce. Among two-parent families who have school-aged children, more than half have both parents employed; and more than 30 percent of mothers with preschoolers are employed (United States Department of Commerce, 1979). Mother, traditionally the most important force for prosocial socialization, often is not home; the trend for maternal employment will increase.

Since the late 1960s, the divorce rate has doubled; one out of five United States families are supported by the mother (Bronfenbrenner, 1976). Children today are subject to less contact and supervision with those most invested in the prosocial development. Negative academic and social consequences have been documented for extended periods following divorce (Hetherington, 1979). United States Census Bureau statistics for 1985 indicated that slightly over one out of every four families in the United States is headed by one parent; it was estimated that by 1990 somewhere between one-third and one-half of all families in the United States were in single family units (Gelman *et al.*, 1985). In the ten-year period from 1970 to 1980, the percentage of once married persons who were divorced or separated at the time of the census doubled (United States Department of Commerce, Bureau of the Census, 1984). Further, the children of divorced parents display a variety of behaviors indicating divorce has a negative impact on socialization. These children are not different from children of two-parent families in intellectual ability or academic aptitude, but their grades are lower, their teachers rate them as less motivated, they are absent more often, more disruptive in class, and have poorer study habits (Hetherington *et al.*, 1978).

At the same time, fertility trends have left children with far fewer siblings. Since 1957, when the post-war fertility rate boom peaked, there has been a 50 percent decline in the fertility rates among women aged 15-44 (National Center for Health Statistics, 1951, 1979). There is no evidence that the downward trend in family size begun in the late 1950s will reverse. The absence of siblings, especially older siblings, may have a negative effect on moral development. As children of high stage moral development interact with those of a lower stage, the moral development of the lower-stage children increases (Kohlberg, 1973). Further, it is assumed that the ability to take the role of the other, rule making, and rule enforcing behaviors facilitated by peer interaction are needed to develop a morality based on mutual consent and cooperation among equals (Piaget, 1932).

Families are now mobile units. Less than half of the United States families interviewed for the 1980 census were living in the same house as in 1975. More than half of those who had moved relocated to a different county (United States Department of Commerce, Bureau of the Census, 1984). As a result, children lose the stabilizing influences of long-term neighborhood and community support systems. Neighbors do not know or care for other children as much as they once did. Regular attendance at churches and temples has dropped off dramatically; when interviewed in 1958, half of those 30 years or under indicated they had attended within the last seven days; by 1981, the figure was down to less than one-third (United States Department of Commerce, Bureau of the Census, 1984). Parents often work in settings that do not permit children to visit, so an additional important prosocial modeling experience is lost. In sum, children now less often enjoy the enduring, caring contact with those who could best provide prosocial socialization experiences.

2. Television. As children are increasingly cut free from the positive socializing experiences previously provided by parents, grandparents, older peers, and neighbors, they have turned to television. America's children too often view rather than participate in social interaction. Ninety-eight percent of all American households have a television; more than half have at least two (Nielsen Television Index, 1982). Children 2-11 years spend more than 25 hours a week watching television (Comstock *et al.*, 1978)--approximately the same number of hours they spend in school. This very extensive television viewing has three negative effects on the prosocial development of youth: First, it restructures family activity away from positive social interaction; second, it fosters, through advertisements, a materialistic and manipulative social orientation; and third, it provides aggressive and antisocial models.

Although a family may be sitting in close physical proximity, if the television is on, the probability of meaningful interaction among family members is decreased. Children are increasingly oriented toward the advertisements and program content, not toward older family members who could provide valuable prosocial socialization experiences.

Advertisements differ in their specific content, but the underlying message is consistent: The passport to fulfillment is product acquisition, not positive interpersonal relationships. Enormous resources are spent to convey the message that friendship, status, and pleasure are obtained by what one buys, not how much one cares. It is alarming in this regard to note that often young children, unlike adults, do not discount advertisements as commercially motivated and may interpret them as positive socialization messages.

The third negative aspect of television, of course, is the program content. As often noted, there is far too much violence and antisocial content and far too little prosocial modeling. More than 70 percent of prime-time dramatic fiction programs sampled from 1967 to 1979 contained violence; children's cartoon and weekend morning programs have the highest levels of violence of all types of programming (Gerbner *et al.*, 1980; Gerbner *et al.*, 1979). There is little parental control over television viewing, and children perceive far fewer controls that parents report (Bower, 1973; Lyle and Hoffman, 1972; Rossiter and Robertson, 1975; Stein and Friedrich, 1972).

In spite of considerable research, the extent of the negative impact of aggressive and antisocial television content has not been established unequivocably. A host of experimental studies support the conclusion that viewing aggressive and antisocial television content increases the probability of aggressive and antisocial behavior in children, adolescents, and adults (Berkowitz, 1971; Liebert and Baron, 1972; Parke *et al.*, 1977). The results hold for naturalistic and controlled lab viewing (Bandura, 1965; Steuer, 1971) and following individual and group viewing (Berkowitz, 1971; Parke *et al.*, 1977). Nevertheless, the relationship between experimental studies and real-world television is unclear. Determining that a child will hit a bobo doll after watching a television model do so, especially when there are few other alternatives available to the children tested, allows us to conclude little or nothing about the real-world effects of television content. Studies that manipulate television diet introduce the confounding factor of frustrating children who normally watch aggressive television. Studies that correlate naturally occurring viewing habits with aggressive behavior leave unanswered the cause-effect relation: Aggressive children may choose aggressive program content. The one cross-legged design demonstrating that childhood preference for violent programs relates to aggressive behavior in adolescence (Eron *et al.*, 1972) may have serious flaws (Kaplan, 1972). Nevertheless, we can assert unqualifiedly that the program content of present-day television is not providing the prosocial socialization models necessary to fill the increasing prosocial socialization void.

   3. Competitive and Individualistic School Practices. United States public schools can be characterized as generally competitive, individualistic, and autocratic. Comparing the descriptions of classroom life offered by Julius Maller with that offered by John Goodlad, we can note a shift from competitive to individualistic emphasis, but in both cases the lack of cooperative activities are noted. Maller (1929) concluded his classical experimental study of cooperation and competition with the following statement:

> *The frequent staging of contests, the constant emphasis upon making and breaking of records, and the glorification of the heroic individual achievement and championship in our present educational system lead toward the acquisition of the habit of competitiveness. The child is trained to look at the members of his group as constant competitors and urged to put forth a maximum effort to excel them. The lack of practice in group activities and community projects in which the child works with his fellows for a common goal precludes the formation of habits of cooperativeness and group loyalty. (p. 163)*

Goodlad's survey (1984) of American classrooms involving observations from more than 1,000 classrooms echoes Maller's lament regarding the lack of cooperative structures.

> *No matter how we approach the classroom in an effort to describe and understand what goes on, the teacher comes through as coach, quarterback, referee, and even rule-maker. But there the analogy must stop because there is no team. There is, instead, a loosely knit group. Each student/player plays the same position, with varying degrees of skill. There is no inherent opportunity or reason to admire performances in other positions and how each contributes to effective team accomplishment. There is little or nothing about classroom life as it is conducted, so far as I am able to determine, that suggests the existence of or need for norms of group cohesion and cooperation for achievement of a shared purpose.(p. 108)*

Researchers agree that in typical classrooms, students are expected to sit quietly and work independently most of the day (Dunkin and Biddle, 1974). Teachers are emitters and directors; rarely are they targets of student communication (Adams and Biddle, 1970; Perkins, 1964). Remarkably, our society, which prides itself on democratic principles, has settled on autocratic models of teaching.

> *For the most part, the teachers in our sample of schools controlled rather firmly the central role of deciding what, where, when, and how the students were to learn....When students played a role, it was somewhat peripheral, such as deciding where they sat. (Goodlad, 1984, p. 109)*

Schools have become increasingly isolated from parents and communities. In general, schools are larger, more impersonal, and further away from homes. Both children and staff often commute. These trends work against the possibility of cooperative models for children. Parents and teachers are not likely to know or work with each other; teachers are not likely to draw on community resources.

> *As schools are moved to the outskirts of a town, they become compounds, physically and socially insulated from the life of the community, neighborhood, and families as well as from the life for which they are supposedly preparing the children. The insularity is repeated within the school itself, where*

*children are segregated in classes that often change yearly in
composition, have little or no social identity of their own, and
have little connection with each other or with the school as a
common community for which the members share active
responsibility.... (Bronfenbrenner, 1979)*

Consequences of the prosocial socialization void. The lack of prosocial socialization experiences for children has resulted in alarming increases in antisocial behavior and decreases in prosocial attitudes and
behavior. Each year more than $200 million is spent repairing damage to
school property in the United States. Each month more than 100,000
teachers and 2 million students report a theft of their property in school;
more than 5,000 teachers and 250,000 students report being physically
attacked (Bybee and Gee, 1982). The problem of violence and vandalism
in schools is national; schools across the nation have security budgets,
often security forces (Committee on the Judiciary of the United States
Senate, 1975). The rate of violence to teenagers is greater in school than
any other single place (Johnson *et al.,* 1984). In almost all Gallup Polls
on education, respondents name discipline as the most important
problem in the schools (Perry and Duke, 1978).

The depth of alienation and lack of prosocial ties felt among our
students is perhaps most clearly reflected in the percentage of students
committing, attempting, or contemplating suicide. More than one-sixth
of high school students contemplate suicide. Of every 640 high school
students, each year on the average ten make a serious attempt to end
their lives, and one succeeds. The suicide rate among teenagers has risen
250 percent since the 1960s (Bronfenbrenner, 1976).

A consequence of the socialization void is the inability of students at
all levels to behave cooperatively in some situations in which it is adaptive to do so. Urban students in grades ranging from two to college level
consistently adopt nonadaptive competitive strategies in experimental
situations in which the way to maximize rewards is to behave
cooperatively (Edney, 1980; Edney and Harper, 1978; Kagan and
Madsen, 1971; 1972; Madsen and Shapira, 1970).

Future of the prosocial socialization void. The lack of prosocial
abilities among our students will be felt more intensely as our economy
shifts increasingly toward high technology and interdependence in the
workplace (Reich, 1983; Naisbitt, 1984). Even now, social skills are
more in demand in the workplace than are academic skills (Crain, 1984)
and because novel problem solving associated with technological ad-

vances in the workplace are best solved by cooperating teams, social skills in the future will be at an increasing premium. Rapid urbanization also brings with it a demand for increased social skills needed to cope with increased interdependence and sociocultural diversity; a competitive and individualistic social orientation will be out of step with our future economic and social realities. Ironically, as economic forces are bringing a greater need for a prosocial orientation, they at the same time are eroding what historically were the primary prosocial socialization opportunities for our youth. It appears that the burden on prosocial socialization will increasingly shift from families and communities to the schools.

III. COOPERATIVE LEARNING METHODS

There now exists a number of cooperative learning methods. The methods differ along various dimensions, including philosophy of education, types of learning and cooperation promoted, student and teacher roles, and modes of reward and evaluation (Kagan, 1985c). For example, Johnson *et al.* (1984) of the Cooperative Learning Center, University of Minnesota, included the teaching of social skills as a defining characteristic of cooperative learning groups. In contrast, teaching social skills is not an element in the four cooperative learning methods: (1) Student Teams-Achievement Divisions (STAD), (2) Teams-Games-Tournaments (TGT), (3) JIGSAW, and (4) Team Assisted Individualization (TAI) sponsored by the Center for Social Organization of Schools, Johns Hopkins University (see Appendix 1). One feature that distinguishes all cooperative learning methods from traditional or whole-class instructional formats is the division of the class into small teams whose members are positively interdependent. Positive interdependence among teammates is created by task and/or reward structures, which make the achievement of any team member contribute to the rewards of all. In such situations, students hope and work for the achievement of their teammates.

Five distinct types of cooperative learning methods can be distinguished: Peer Tutoring, Jigsaw, Cooperative Projects, Cooperative/Individualized, and Cooperative Interaction (see Appendix 1). Although not all existing methods fit neatly into just one of the five categories, the five categories are useful because they indicate the diversity of organizational principles underlying cooperative learning methods.

Peer Tutoring

Peer tutoring methods are designed to maximize the probability that teammates will help each other master predetermined content. Teamwork in the peer tutoring methods often consists of teammates drilling each other (using flash cards or worksheets) with the aim of bringing each member up to his or her highest possible level of proficiency. Peer tutoring methods are most often used with high consensus and relatively low difficulty academic tasks such as acquisition of math or spelling facts.

Jigsaw

Jigsaw methods are based on the principles of interdependence and division of labor. Each team member is given primary responsibility for a unique portion of the learning unit. Teammates leave their teams to work with the members of other teams who have been assigned the same portion of the learning unit. In these "expert groups" students work together to master their common topic. When the students return to their teams, each team member is dependent on his or her teammates to provide the information on the other portions of the learning unit. Each individual is responsible for mastering the whole learning unit. Thus, teamwork in the Jigsaw methods consists of team members taking turns teaching their teammates the part of the learning unit they have mastered. Although drill may be involved in the Jigsaw methods, especially if team members are instructed to quiz each other on the material, peer tutoring in Jigsaw takes the form of sharing information. The basic organizational principle in Jigsaw classrooms is the division of the learning unit into unique individual portions. Jigsaw methods are most often used with medium-consensus, medium-difficulty academic tasks such as mastering text material in social studies or social sciences.

Cooperative Projects

In this approach, students work together to produce a product such as a written paper, mural, or group presentation. Each team member receives a grade based on the success of the group product. Teamwork in the Cooperative Projects methods consists of cooperative planning, coordinated research, analysis and synthesis of ideas, and/or debate among team members as to the meaning of materials and how to report or present them. The Cooperative Projects approaches are most often used with low-consensus, complex academic content. Students in this approach assume the greatest responsibility for what and how to study.

Cooperative/Individualized

Students progress at their own rate through individualized learning materials in the Cooperative/Individualized approach, but their progress contributes to a team grade so that each pupil is rewarded by the achievements of his or her teammates. There may be little or no teamwork in this approach as the learning units are designed to be self-explanatory; for the most part, students work alone. Team members sit together, check each other's work, may tutor each other, and receive a common group grade based on the individual progress of all members of the team.

Cooperative Interaction

Students in the Cooperative Interaction method work together as a team to master a learning unit. There is no graded group project; each student completes the assignment for him or herself and is graded individually. Nevertheless, completion of the unit demands cooperative interaction. For example, students must coordinate their efforts to complete a lab experiment. The Cooperative Interaction approach is distinguished from the Jigsaw approach because all students have equal access to and responsibility for all learning materials, although distinct student roles (such as clean-up monitor and safety inspector) may be created for management purposes. The Cooperative Interaction approach is distinguished also from the Cooperative/Individualized approach because the materials are group-paced and all students complete the same assignments.

Within the five major categories of cooperative learning methods, there are from one to several cooperative learning methods. (A thumbnail sketch of the various cooperative learning methods is presented in Appendix 1, by category, with a reference to the major source of that method.)

IV. RESULTS OF COOPERATIVE LEARNING

The effects of cooperative learning have been researched extensively, and positive outcomes have been documented in a number of domains including academic achievement; ethnic relations; prosocial development; and liking for class, school, learning, and self. The empirical evidence in support of these claims has been reviewed and summarized in a number of major publications (Aronson et al., 1978; Johnson et al., 1984; Johnson et al., 1983; Johnson et al., 1981; Sharan, 1980; Sharan et *al.*, 1984; Slavin, 1980, 1983a, 1983b). Of most concern for the present review is the impact of cooperative learning on academic achievement, especially minority group achievement, ethnic relations, and prosocial development.

Academic Achievement

In their meta-analysis of 122 achievement-related studies conducted between 1924 and 1981, Johnson *et al.* (1981) concluded that cooperative learning almost always promotes higher achievement than do competitive and individualistic learning structures, across all age levels, subject areas, and almost all tasks. The Johnson *et al.* (1981) conclusions have been criticized, however, as a generalization that glosses over significant interactions with factors such as task type (Cotton and Cook, 1982; McGlynn, 1982). It has been claimed also that the Johnson *et al.* (1981) meta-analysis includes studies that are little related to academic achievement in classroom settings (Slavin, 1983a) and that it ignores important differences among cooperative learning methods (Slavin, 1983b).

In an attempt to provide a more analytic analysis, Slavin (1983b) reviewed only those controlled research studies conducted for an extended time in regular elementary and secondary school classrooms. The review supported the conclusion that there is a general superiority of cooperative learning: Of the 46 studies reviewed, 63 percent showed superior outcomes for cooperative learning; 33 percent showed no significant differences; and only 4 percent showed higher achievement for the control groups. Most important, however, a dramatic difference emerged among the studies as a function of cooperative learning method. Almost all studies (89 percent), which used group rewards based on individual achievement, produced achievement gains. In contrast, among the studies that used only individual grades or a group grade based on a group product with no individual accountability for amount or quality of input into the group product, achievement was about equal to that obtained in control classes.

Slavin (1983b) concluded that the critical element producing achievement gains in cooperative learning methods is individual accountability for individual achievement, which contributes to a group reward, not peer tutoring or group study. Support for that conclusion comes from individual studies, which have found that group rewards based on individual achievement produce achievement gains even if there is no opportunity for group study (Slavin, 1983a), and group study in the absence of group rewards does not produce achievement superior to individual study (Slavin, 1983a).

Achievement of minority groups. One of the most important findings to emerge from the cooperative learning research is the strong achievement gains among minority pupils in cooperative classrooms. Three studies, using two different cooperative learning methods and samples of minority students from different geographic areas have produced a similar result: Anglos show equal or somewhat greater academic gains in cooperative classrooms compared to traditional classrooms, but minority students show far greater gains in the cooperative compared to traditional methods (Aronson *et al.*, 1978; Slavin, 1977; Slavin and Oickle, 1981). In the Aronson *et al.* (1978) study, Black and Mexican-American students learned more in Jigsaw than in traditional classes; in the Slavin (1977) and Slavin and Oickle (1981) studies, Black students learned more in the STAD treatments than in traditional classrooms. The results of the latest of these studies, plotted in Figure 1, are particularly dramatic.

Figure 1

LANGUAGE ACHIEVEMENT
(Classroom Structure x Ethnicity)

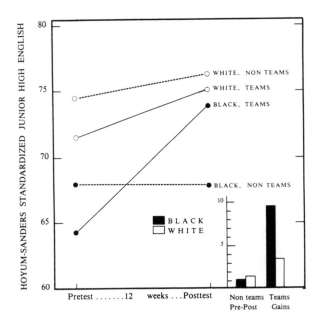

Source: Kagan *et al.*, 1985, p. 290.

As pictured in Figure 1, Black students in traditional classrooms showed almost no gains, whereas Black students in cooperative classes gained more than twice as much as any other group. It was as if the Black students were not motivated to learn in the traditional competitive/individualistic classroom structures, whereas they were highly motivated to learn when their learning contributed to the team score and was associated with peer approval. It is important to note that the very dramatic gains of minority students were not bought at the expense of achievement gains for majority students; both majority and minority students gained more using student teams.

It appears that the special benefits for minority and lower-status students in cooperative learning classrooms may have considerable generality. In Israel, children from a Middle Eastern background share the same lower-status position in their society as do minority students in the United States; they are subject to the same negative ethnic stereotypes and manifest a similar academic achievement gap. It has been found, however, that when the classroom is restructured to include cooperative small-group activities, it is the Middle Eastern children who display the greatest achievement gains (Klein and Eshel, 1980).

A number of studies in the United States have examined separately the gains of high-, medium-, and low-achieving students in cooperative learning classrooms (Armstrong et al., 1981; Martino and Johnson, 1979; Nevin et al., 1982; Smith et al., 1981, 1982, 1984; Skon et al., 1981). The results of these studies indicate that it is the medium and low achievers who benefit most from the cooperative methods. It is important to note, however, that the benefit obtained for the lower achievers is not bought at the expense of the higher achievers; the high achieving students generally perform about as well in traditional and cooperative classrooms.

The very dramatic "catch-up" effect for minority students that occurs in cooperative learning has profound implications for educational practice and theory. Traditionally, the achievement gap between minority and majority students has been attributed to deficits among minority students in intelligence or motivation. These attributions now appear to be context-bound. That is, minority students may lack motivation to learn, but only when they are placed in traditional, competitive/individualistic classroom structures. As demonstrated so clearly by the results plotted in Figure 1, in a relatively short time what appears to be a long-term minority student deficiency in basic language skills can be overcome by transforming the social organization of the classroom.

Thus, the gap in achievement between majority and minority students is best not attributed to personal deficiencies of minority students, but rather to the relatively exclusive reliance in public schools on competitive and individualistic classroom sturctures. (For more on the effects of the education context on the achievement of minority students, see Díaz *et al.,* this volume.)

Ethnic Relations

It was well established at the time of the initial court-mandated desegregation that the nature of the contact between members of different racial groups would determine how desegregation would proceed (Cook, 1979; Slavin, 1981). In the famous social science statement (Minnesota Law Review, 1953), leading social scientists of the time warned that successful desegregation would depend on "the absence of competition for a limited number of facilities or benefits...and the possibility of equivalence of positions and functions among all of the participants within the desegregated situation" (p. 438). By failing to heed this warning, teachers and school administrators have recreated in the classroom the out-group status for minority students accorded them in the larger society. Researchers have noted that desegregation into classrooms that employ traditional, whole-class structures has not led to improved ethnic relations. For example, in their analysis of ethnic relations in the desegregated Riverside (California) Public Schools, Gerard *et al.* (1975) concluded:

> *The unprecedented amount of data we have examined points unmistakably to the conclusion that, with the exception of playground interaction, little or no real integration occurred during the relatively long-term contact situation represented by Riverside's desegregation program. If anything, we found some evidence that ethnic cleavage became somewhat more pronounced over time. (p. 237)*

Broad reviews of school desegregation have been negative with regard to impact on race relations (St. John, 1975; Stephen, 1978).

In contrast, a consistent finding in the cooperative learning research has been improved ethnic relations among students participating in cooperative learning groups. In summarizing that literature, Slavin (1983a) examined 14 experiments involving students from grades 3 through 12. Overall cross-ethnic friendships improved in the cooperative learning classrooms over control classes. In the studies using the original

Jigsaw method, only one of the five ethnic relations measures showed improvement of the Jigsaw method over the control classrooms. In the remainder of the studies, however, 63 percent of the 19 tests of ethnic relations showed better ethnic relations in cooperative than control classrooms. The remaining comparisons showed no difference; never were ethnic relations significantly better in control classrooms.

Caution is needed in interpreting the positive outcomes of cooperative learning on interethnic relations. Much of the evidence is based on weak measures of cross-race friendship patterns, which might reflect transitory or superficial friendship changes occurring as a result of participation in cooperative teams. For example, most studies simply have students list the names of their friends in the classroom and then count percentage of cross-race friendship choices. Students might well be less likely to write down the names of others if they cannot spell them. Thus, if racially mixed student teams lead only to the learning of how to spell one's teammates' names, this might appear as an increase in cross-racial friendships.

There are, however, indications that the interethnic relations gains in cooperative learning classrooms, are more than a temporary function of working together with others from other racial groups. In a follow-up study, one academic year after a cooperative learning project had been conducted, students from the cooperative and control conditions were asked to list their friends. Students in the control group listed 9.8 percent of their friends as from a race other than their own; the STAD students listed 37.9 percent of the friendship choices outside their own race (Slavin, 1979). Johnson and Johnson (1981) observed patterns of cross-ethnic interaction during free-time periods immediately following either cooperative or individualistic interventions. There was greater Black-white interaction following the cooperative rather than individualistic classes.

Typically, in desegregated classrooms, racial groups self-segregate along racial lines increasingly with increased grade level. Casual observations of play patterns on most desegregated elementary school playgrounds will confirm that children from kindergarten through grade 4 play in a relatively integrated pattern, but by fifth grade there is a strong tendency for children to group along race lines. This trend continues increasingly through middle and high school. When forming mixed-ethnic cooperative groups, there are almost never objections among the elementary school age children, but some middle and high school children manifest a strong initial dislike for working in mixed-ethnic groups.

To determine the impact of cooperative teamwork on racial integration among students of grades 2-4 and 5-6, student-teachers at the School
of Education, University of California, Riverside were randomly
assigned to teach using cooperative (TGT or STAD) or traditional
methods (Kagan *et al.,* 1985). The *Interpersonal Relations Assessment
Technique (IRAT)* (Schwarzwald and Cohen, 1982) was administered to
the pupils of the study following six weeks of cooperative or traditional
learning. The IRAT allows each student to respond to each of his or her
classmates on each of several items that indicate degree of friendship,
such as willingness to loan a classmate a pencil, sit next to him or her, or
invite him or her home. The ethnic composition of the 900 pupils involved in the study was 66 percent white, 20 percent Mexican-American,
and 13 percent Black. The results are presented in Figure 2.

Figure 2

FRIENDLINESS (IRAT) AND RACE RELATIONS
(Class Structure x Grade x Ethnicity x Ethnicity of Other)

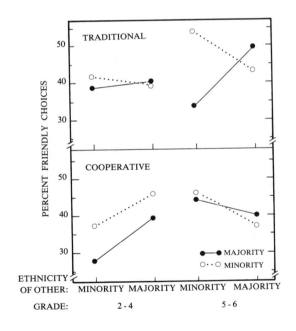

Source: Kagan *et al.,* 1985, p. 306.

As can be seen in Figure 2, in traditional classrooms with increased grade level there was the usual increased segregation among students along race lines. At grades two to four there is only a very slight preference of minority and majority students for their own race. In contrast, by grades five and six, being of the same race becomes almost a prerequisite for friendship among minority students. The picture is quite different in the cooperative classrooms: The very strong ethnic cleavage observed in the traditional classrooms was reduced to insignificance. This very dramatic interaction of Technique with Age x Ethnicity x Ethnicity of the Other was very reliable statistically, $F(1,495) = 18.62$, $p < .00001$. Clearly, cooperative learning methods can radically improve ethnic relations among students.

Prosocial Development

There are important theoretical reasons for predicting that students in cooperative learning classrooms should become more prosocial. To make those reasons clearer, let's first consider peer relations in a traditional classroom. In the traditional classroom the teacher is in front of the class; he or she asks the students questions. Following each question a number of hands go up. Some students are anxiously stretching their hands in the hopes of being called. Others, of course, do not have their hands up and try not to have their eyes meet those of the teacher in hopes they will not be called. The teacher calls on Juan. Peter, who sits next to Juan, knows the right answer. As Juan begins to hesitate, Peter becomes glad and stretches his hand higher. Peters knows that if Juan misses, the teacher may call on him. In fact, the only way Peter can obtain a reward in this situation is if Juan fails. It is only natural in this competitive class structure for students to begin to take pleasure in the failures of others: Their own rewards are contingent on the failures of others. Traditional classrooms provide a negative interdependence among students in which each failure of one student is associated with a success for another. In many cases, this negative interdependence is further institutionalized by grading on the curve, announcing or posting only the top grades or papers, and/or displaying a chart indicating the performance of students relative to one another.

In contrast to the peer relations in a traditional classroom is the positive interdependence among team members in cooperative classrooms. The success of any team member leads to increased rewards (grades, recognition, pride) for the others. Students in this structure naturally begin hoping for their teammates to do well. They begin to adopt a prosocial orientation toward their teammates, which probably generalizes to others as well.

The empirical research analyzing the prosocial development of students in cooperative and control classrooms is generally quite supportive of the conclusion that cooperative learning increases prosocial development. Slavin (1983a) lists eight cooperative learning studies which examined cooperativeness as an outcome variable. In six of the eight studies, cooperativeness was greater among the students in the cooperative learning conditions; in the remaining two comparisons, no differences were found.

Although the box score looks quite favorable for cooperative learning, there are serious methodological problems in a number of the prosocial development studies. For example, in one study teachers were allowed to pick other teachers with whom to be compared; another study used invalid cooperation-competition choice-cards which confounded individualism with the cooperative alternative making the results uninterpretable. Sometimes prosocial development measures that appear to have face validity do not. For example, investigators have reported more helping behavior among students in the cooperative than traditional classrooms, but the experimental conditions demand that students in the cooperative classrooms work together and those in the individualistic conditions work alone; listing more helpers in the cooperative classrooms, thus, may be a function of the situational press, not a generalized increase in prosocial development. Similarly, when students in the cooperative classrooms less often positively answer the question, "I would rather beat a classmate at schoolwork than help him," not too much should be inferred. It is possible that the students in the cooperative classrooms are thinking of their teammates and that they are individualistic rather than cooperative, knowing that helping a teammate will improve their own grade. That is, the social orientation of students in cooperative classes may not have changed but rather only their social situation.

In response to the weaknesses of previous studies of cooperative learning and prosocial development, social orientation choice-cards were included as a dependent variable in the Riverside Cooperative Learning Project described previously (Kagan et al., 1985). There is an extensive, valid literature surrounding the choice-card methodology: Cooperative behaviors on the choice-cards reflects a generalized tendency toward prosocial behavior. For example, cooperativeness as assessed by valid cooperation-competition choice-cards is associated with affiliative motivation, cooperative behavior in a variety of social interaction situations, and peer ratings of cooperativeness (Kagan, 1984). The choice-card cooperativeness of minority and majority students in the cooperative and traditional classrooms at grades 2-4 and 5-6 is pictured in Figure 3.

Figure 3

COOPERATIVE (SSBS) AND RACE RELATIONS
(Class Structure x Grade x Ethnicity x Ethnicity of Other)

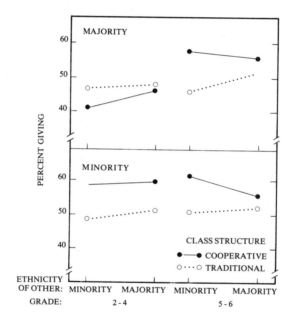

Source: Kagan *et al.*, 1985, p. 302.

The cooperative treatments produced more cooperativeness among students than the traditional treatment at grades 5-6, for both minority and majority students. At grades 2-4 the cooperative treatments produced more cooperativeness than the traditional class structure for the minority students, but unexplicably not the majority students. The class structure grade, by ethnic group, and by ethnicity of other interaction was significant, $F(1,512) = 12.91$, $p < .001$. Thus, in six of the eight comparisons, cooperative classroom structures produced substantially more cooperativeness among students than did the traditional structures.

An important interaction with regard to race relations emerged in the upper grades: Under the traditional class structure, both minority and majority students were more cooperative to majority than minority students, giving them more. In contrast, when cooperative student teams were employed, both minority and majority students were more cooperative toward the minority students. It may be that older minority students are given higher social status in cooperative than traditional class structures. Most important, students become generally more cooperative after participating in cooperatively structured classrooms.

V. THEORETICAL EXPLANATIONS: HOW DOES COOPERATIVE LEARNING WORK?

There remains the task of explaining how cooperative learning methods produce the academic and social gains observed. The methods are complex and work in a variety of ways. There are a number of plausible theoretical explanations that merit examination. The academic achievement gains, ethnic relations gains, and prosocial development gains observed in cooperative classrooms are to some extent undoubtedly interrelated. That is, positive cross-race relations and prosocial disposition among students almost certainly are part of a classroom climate conducive to academic progress. Conversely, solid academic progress among majority and minority students would probably predispose them toward positive peer relations. There are many factors in cooperative learning environments that contribute to the observed academic and social gains. These factors will be described and discussed in five topics: Academic Task Structure, Academic and Social Reward Structure, Teacher Roles and Behaviors, Student Roles and Behaviors, and Cultural Compatibility of Classroom Structure.

Academic Task Structure

The learning task in cooperative classrooms is different from that in traditional classrooms in a number of ways that are likely to foster academic achievement. Those ways include the amount of comprehensible input, complexity of input, amount of comprehensible output, frequency and type of practice, clarity of task structure, subdivision of learning unit, and time-on-task.

Comprehensible Input.   It is possible that students discussing an academic task provide one another more comprehensible input than do teachers lecturing.   Certainly, the interactive nature of the cooperative learning groups allows students to ask for clarification and for communication to be adjusted so that it is comprehensible.   It is in the interest of each student to make his or her communication comprehensible because the more that is learned by his or her teammates, the greater will be the rewards for each team member.   It is clear that cooperative learning groups contain greater amounts of low-level (repetition of information), intermediate-level (stating of new information), and high-level (explanations, rationales, and integration) verbal input to students than do individualistic learning structures (Johnson and Johnson, 1983a; Johnson *et al.,* 1983).   Comprehensible input and the concomitant negotiation of meaning between communicating individuals are critical elements in language acquisition (Krashen, 1982; Long, 1983).   Thus, we would expect particular benefits of cooperative learning for students of Limited English Proficiency (LEP).

Complexity of Input.   Anyone who has overheard a cooperative learning group interact will recognize the rich, complex input provided to students by their teammates, expecially in the Jigsaw, Cooperative Projects, and Cooperative Interaction methods.   Complexity and variety of input leads to higher level cognitive development (Bloom, 1964; Bruner, 1961, 1966).   Students exposed to Group-Investigation (See Appendix 1) made more high-level cognitive gains than those exposed to peer tutoring and whole-class methods (Sharan *et al.,* 1984).   It may be that some of the gains associated with controversy in groups are due to the increased complexity of input associated with controversy.   Controversy, when handled constructively, demands that students confront apparently opposing points of views or facts and search for a higher level of synthesis. Constructive controversy has been associated with higher achievement and retention of materials (Johnson, 1980; Johnson and Johnson, 1979; Lowry and Johnson, 1981; Johnson *et al.,* 1984; Smith *et al.,* 1981, 1982, 1984).

Comprehensible output.   It may be that the opportunity to express oneself is a critical feature distinguishing cooperative and whole-class methods.   In traditional classrooms, students have remarkably little opportunity to express themselves to teachers or peers (Adams and Biddle, 1970; Dunkin and Biddle, 1974; Perkins, 1964).   This is due, in part, to the fact that teachers take almost exclusive responsibility for teaching and expect students to be relatively passive recipients of knowledge.   It is due also to the structure of the traditional classroom: Only one person at a time speaks. In contrast, during drill for STAD and TGT, it is expected that about half the class is speaking at any one given moment; in Jigsaw, Co-op Co-op, and Group-Investigation (see Appendix 1), one member of each team is presenting at any given moment. Thus, in traditional formats, at any given moment usually the teacher is presenting material; during the same time, in cooperative learning classrooms, from one half to one-sixth of the class is presenting material.

The cognitive activity involved in preparing materials for oral presentation is almost certainly an important determinant of understanding and long-term comprehension. Further, the press to produce comprehensible output is a critical determinant of the extent to which LEP students will acquire native-speaker productive competence (Swain, 1983).

Frequency and type of practice. In the well-structured STAD, TGT, and TAI methods, students spend a great deal of practice on the items they most need to learn. The students use flash cards and worksheets for spelling or math facts, receiving repeated contact with missed items. There is an opportunity for drill and practice also in the Jigsaw methods following the expert presentations. This structured, frequent, and often interactive practice in cooperative learning methods is probably superior for most students to group-paced work on worksheets or in workbooks. There is evidence that cooperative learning groups involve more frequent helping, tutoring, and practice than do competitive or individualistic class structures (Armstrong *et al.,* 1981; Cooper *et al.,* 1980; Johnson & Johnson, 1981, 1982a, 1982b, 1983a).

Clarity of task structure. Although the learning tasks differ across cooperative learning methods, a common aspect of the task structure in cooperative learning methods is the extreme clarity with which the tasks are structured. Students know what their goals are and the steps they must follow to reach those goals. Research has indicated that direct instruction is superior to a variety of other methods for acquisition of basic skills, especially for lower socio-economic level children (Stebbins *et al.,* 1977). It may be that lower socio-economic class students profit more from highly structured learning environments, and the highly structured nature of cooperative learning methods is particularly beneficial for that group.

Subdivision of learning unit. Because the learning unit is subdivided in some of the cooperative learning methods, students may experience the learning task as less overwhelming. For example, a student who could be intimidated by a whole learning unit, when faced with mastering one Jigsaw topic or one Co-op Co-op mini topic, may attack the task with confidence and enthusiasm.

Time-on-task. A consistent finding in the cooperative learning research has been that students spend more time-on-task. Slavin (1983a) reviewed ten studies examining time-on-task in cooperative and control classrooms. In seven of the ten studies, time-on-task was greater in cooperative classrooms. As with academic achievement, those cooperative learning methods that provided group rewards based on individual achievement most consistently related to increased time-on-task. Increased time-on-task has been associated with increased achievement across a variety of learning methods (Stallings, 1980). Increased time-on-task in the cooperative learning methods probably results from the game-like nature of the learning tasks, the clarity of task structures, the subdivision of the task into easily mastered parts, and most important, the interactive nature of the task. Students like to talk. The desire to express themselves to their peers, a constant problem in the traditional classroom, is channeled in the cooperative classroom toward academic achievement. So, rather than taking time away from task in the cooperative formats, peer interaction directs students toward the academic task. This is especially true because of the incentive reward structure; peers are motivated to keep their teammates on task because that behavior will result in higher rewards for their team.

Academic and Social Reward Structure

The reward structure in cooperative learning classrooms is radically different from that found in traditional classrooms. Rewards in cooperative learning classrooms are frequent and peer supported. In most of the methods the rewards are group based. In some of the methods, the rewards are also individually normed and equally accessible. Although in most cooperative learning methods, there are no explicit rewards for cooperative behavior (because cooperative behavior is instrumental in achieving group success), peers become supportive and rewarding of cooperativeness among their teammates, therefore, a social reward system evolves that is parallel to the academic reward system.

Frequent immediate rewards. Rewards for achievement in the cooperative learning methods are more frequent and immediate than individual or competitive classes. As a student learns material in the peer tutoring, Jigsaw, and cooperative/individualized methods, or as he or she makes progress toward the goal in the group project or group interaction methods, there is immediate reinforcement from peers. In addition, there are weekly quizzes, newsletters, and/or classroom bulletin boards that give recognition to team and individual achievements. The frequency and immediacy of rewards in cooperative learning classrooms are in contrast to those received in traditional classrooms. It is much more efficient to have each student rewarded immediately by several peers when he or she makes progress than to have rewards primarily following quizzes and tests. If rewards are grades and/or written praise by the teacher following a good test performance, the rewards probably follow the learning by days. Such rewards are pitifully weak in contrast to peer praise immediately following learning successes.

Peer rewards. In contrast to systems that have students compete individually for teacher praise or recognition, cooperative learning places students on the same side with fellow students. Teammates support rather than put down or dismiss the achievements of others. Rewards from peers mean far more to most students than rewards from teachers, so the peer support for achievement in cooperative learning is probably one of the most important explanations for achievement gains observed. Peer acceptance and support is particularly important for some minority groups (Hare, 1977); therefore, peer support for achievement may explain the particularly strong gains made by some minority students in cooperative learning. In their review of the literature, Johnson and Johnson (1985) cite 14 studies demonstrating that cooperative learning groups involve more facilitative and encouraging interaction among students than do competitive or individualistic learning situations.

Group-based rewards. Not all cooperative learning methods have explicit group-based rewards. In both the original Jigsaw and Descubrimiento methods (see Appendix 1), students take individual quizzes. In the remaining cooperative learning methods, however, there are group rewards. As indicated, Slavin (1983a, 1983b) has made the case that group rewards for individual achievement are consistently associated with achievement gains. Achievement gains are not found as consistently in those techniques like original Jigsaw, which do not provide group rewards. Relatively little research has been completed on Descubrimiento, but the lack of group rewards in the method may possibly prove a weakness.

In the group project methods there is group reward, but individuals may or may not be individually accountable for their contribution to the project. Individuals in the group project approaches may be more or less individually accountable for their contributions to the group, and they may be more or less individually evaluated for those individual contributions, depending on how the group project methods are operationalized. In Co-op Co-op, for example, individual team members are evaluated by their teammates with regard to their contribution to the team effort, and they may be evaluated by the teacher as well on their mini-topic contribution. In some Learning Together methods, in contrast, the group may complete a project without individual accountability.

In a revealing set of experiments, Hamblin *et al.* (1971) demonstrated that group rewards have a direct effect on peer tutoring and student achievement. The experimenters manipulated which students' scores would be used to determine the group grade and also how many students in a group would receive the group grade. As more students' grades were dependent on the scores of the lowest three members in the group, peer tutoring and student achievement rose. When the group grade was contingent on the scores of the highest achievers, it was the highest achievers who learned most; when the group grade was contingent on the scores of the lowest achievers, it was the lowest achievers who learned most. The group grade motivates achievement among those students who are responsible for it. The extent to which this is a push or pull effect is not clear. That is, it remains to be determined the extent to which others pull achievement out of those upon whom their grade is dependent, and the extent to which individuals experience an internal push to perform well when others are depending on them. In either case, the group reward is a powerful motivator for achievement. Group rewards also promote pro-social behaviors (Kagan, 1977; Kagan and Madsen, 1971; Madsen and Shapira, 1970); group rewards create interdependence among students which increases cooperative behaviors.

Rewards for improvement. A unique and important aspect of STAD and Jigsaw II scoring methods is that students earn points depending on how their performance each week compares to the weighted running average of their past scores, with more weight given to recent past performances. Thus, every student in a class could receive a top score if he or she improves. This is in contrast to grading on the curve in which the basis for comparison is not individual past performance but rather the performance of other students. The use of improvement scores probably goes a long way in decreasing competition among students; students compete with themselves, not others.

The use of improvement scores also probably increases the sense of internal control felt by students. A student knows how to control how hard he or she tries, and so can control improvement, whereas he or she does not know how to control how hard others will try. When others are the basis for comparison, academic outcomes are externally determined. In five of the six cooperative learning studies examining locus of control, students in cooperative classroom become more internal (Slavin, 1983a).

Equal reward opportunity. In the STAD, Jigsaw II, TGT, and TAI methods (see Appendix 1), all students have an equal opportunity to receive rewards each week, but for different reasons. As indicated, in STAD and Jigsaw II, each student's performance is compared with his or her past performance; therefore, weak and strong students have an equal chance to earn top grades. In TGT, it is the bumping system that ensures that students compete against those of equal ability. In TAI, progress through the individual workbooks can occur at an equal rate for those working on beginning or advanced workbooks. Students bring their new knowledge to each workbook; therefore, difficulty remains relatively constant as students progress through the individual learning materials.

That rewards are equally accessible to all students is an important distinguishing characteristic of all the Johns Hopkins methods (STAD, TGT, Jigsaw II, and TAI). In a traditional classroom, students know before a quiz who will bring back top grades; week after week the same students are winners and the same students are losers. It is no wonder that grading system produces alienation and drop outs. In contrast, in the cooperative learning methods, each student can make a valuable contribution and therefore has access to rewards from peers.

Teacher Roles and Behaviors

Teacher roles in cooperative learning classrooms are quite different from those of traditional classrooms; along with the changed social structure comes a changed pattern of teacher attention, expectations, and discipline. The need for discipline, especially individual discipline is reduced, and the ability of teachers to consult with individual students is increased.

Attention and expectation. In traditional classrooms, negative effects sometime result from teacher attention and expectation patterns. The traditional assignment of students to groups based on ability carries with it expectation patterns that have a profoundly negative impact on the attitudes and performance of low-achieving children:

> *From the day that the class was assigned permanent seats, the activities in the classroom were perceivably different....The fundamental division of the class into those expected to learn and those expected not to, permeate the teacher's orientation to the class. (Rist, 1970, p. 423)*

Teachers adopt four qualitatively different relationships with children: attachment, concern, indifference, and rejection. They tend to be attached to high achievers and conformists; concerned for students who make demands appropriate to the classroom activity; indifferent to silent children; and rejecting of children whose demands are seen as illegitimate (Silberman, 1969; 1971). There is a general preference among teachers for rigid, orderly, and conforming students over active, independent, and assertive students (Feshbach, 1969; Brophy and Good, 1974; Levitin and Chananie, 1972). These preferences, however, might well be a function of the traditional classroom structures in which order and conformity are at a premium. In the cooperative learning classroom, teachers can afford to value independence and assertiveness more as those qualities can be channeled into productive work in the cooperative setting.

Most important, in the cooperative setting, teachers may have a more equitable distribution of their expectations and attention, especially toward minority students. Generally, high achievers are given more opportunities to participate in traditional classrooms and are given more praise and less criticism than lower achievers (Cooper, 1979). Minority and low-income students more often are rejected and less often liked (Leacock, 1969).

Of particular concern is that teachers may be agents of social stratification, socializing minority students toward lower status social positions. Communication patterns toward lower-middle-class and upper-middle-class students differ along a number of dimensions consistent with the conclusion that teachers are socialization agents preparing students for social roles similar to those of their parents (Cicourel and Mehan, 1985; Wilcox, 1982). Communication toward lower socioeconomic class students tends to be characterized by less teaching, more control, and by patterns that do not emphasize learning how to learn (Mehan, 1984). Beyond the complex analyses of the meta-communication differences that occur between teachers and students as a function of socio-economic class, stands the simple fact that teachers treat majority students better than they do minority students. The United States Commission on Civil Rights (1973) sampled student-teacher interaction in 429 classrooms in California, New Mexico, and Texas. Even after correcting for class size and ratio of Anglo and Mexican-American students, the Commission found the following significant differences: Compared to Mexican-American students, Anglo students were praised 36 percent more often; had their ideas built upon 40 percent more often; were responded to positively 40 percent more often; had questions directed to them 21 percent more often; and received more attention overall.

Cooperative learning may, therefore, have beneficial effects, especially for minority students, by distributing teachers' attention more equally and by taking the emphasis away from teacher-student communication. In cooperative classrooms, groups are heterogeneous with regard to achievement level and teachers attend more to groups than individuals. Further, cooperative classrooms are not structured around an elevated importance of teacher praise and attention; the teacher generally becomes more of a consultant than an emitter, director, and evaluator.

Discipline. Probably because cooperative learning activities are very highly structured and because there are strong peer norms for cooperation and achievement, there is generally less need among teachers to resort to individual student discipline in cooperative classrooms. Another reason that discipline is less of an issue in cooperative classes is that students are being allowed to do what they enjoy most: interact with their peers. Research supports the conclusion that there is more emphasis on control of social behavior in traditional programs (Miller and Dyer, 1975; Minuchin and Shapiro, 1983). Relieving the teacher of some of the burden of discipline frees him or her for attention to academic content issues.

Individual consultation. In cooperative classrooms, the role of the teacher shifts from director to consultant. Well-managed cooperative classrooms run themselves to a remarkable extent, freeing the teacher to give attention to individuals or small groups most in need. In TAI, small group pull-out of students with similar needs is an integral part of the structure; in the other methods, pull-out is included less formally, at the teachers' discretion. Individual achievement, especially among minority and low-achieving students who most need individual attention, may be increased because of the redefinition of teacher role. Teachers in cooperative classrooms are freed to do more of what they do best, teach, because many of the management and discipline issues are taken care of by the classroom structure.

Student Roles and Behaviors

The roles of students in cooperative classrooms are quite different than in traditional classrooms. In the cooperative structures students are active, self-directing, and communicative. Student behaviors, norms, and relationships change: Students engage in peer tutoring, evolve norms and sanctions supporting achievement, and have relationships that are more often characterized by equal status.

Activity.   Perhaps more than anything else, cooperative learning classrooms are active classrooms.   The nature of the activity differs depending on the technique, but no matter whether the students are involved in peer tutoring, consulting in expert groups, or designing a cooperative project, they are involved and active.   This activity level in cooperative classes may account in part for achievement gains.

Cooperative classrooms are active classrooms, involving movement, interaction, and a variety of alternating roles for students.   In contrast, traditional classrooms usually involve fixed roles and a great deal of seat work with little interaction.   Traditional classroom structures are boring for students who, as a consequence, do not remain on task and find with time learning is less and less attractive.

Students in cooperative classrooms report that they are less often bored (Aronson *et al.,* 1978) and like class more (Kagan *et al.,* 1985; Slavin, 1983a).   There is strong evidence that the active oral involvement of students in cooperative learning classrooms is critical for achievement gains.   Active engagement, providing task-related information, and explanations have been found to relate to achievement gains (Johnson *et al.,* 1983; Webb, 1980a, 1980b).

Self-Direction.   The behavior of students in cooperative classrooms is (to use the terms favored by deCharms, 1968), more origin-like than pawn-like.   As noted, five out of six studies that have included locus of control as dependent measures find students in cooperative learning classrooms to be more internal in contrast to students in traditional classrooms who feel more externally controlled (Slavin, 1983a).   Researchers have also reported greater intrinsic motivation among students in cooperative classrooms (Johnson *et al.,* 1976).

It is logical that students in cooperative classrooms would feel that academic outcomes are more under their control than do students in traditional classrooms because, in an important sense, they are.   That is, if there is equal opportunity for high and low achievers to bring back points for their team or to make an important contribution to a group project, success is properly attributed to individual effort, not to the characteristics of the teacher, task, or reward structure.   When students attribute success or failure to their own behavior rather than external factors, their achievement efforts increase.   An internal locus of control is related to academic achievement (Brookover *et al.,* 1979; Coleman *et al.,* 1966) and may be a cause as well as a consequence of academic success in cooperative learning classrooms.

Communication.   There is a great deal of academic content-related communication in cooperative classrooms.   This communication among students provides verbal input absent in individual work in traditional classrooms and allows a chance for students to formulate and express their ideas. Content-related communication in the cooperative classroom is the vehicle for students to do one of the things they most want: talk with their peers. Thus, academic talk is reinforced.

Because cooperative learning groups are interactive, the pace of communication becomes more student-centered than in traditional classrooms. In the traditional format, a teacher is bound to proceed too slowly for some students and too fast for others; in contrast, students adjust the pace of their communications in cooperative learning groups to the understanding level of their peers. They know that if they go too fast the team will suffer because of lost information.

There develops over time considerable attention among team members to the understanding level of others. This may be a partial explanation of the increased cognitive and affective role-taking abilities observed among students following cooperative learning activities (Johnson and Johnson, 1983a). Theoretically, role-taking and cooperative interaction opportunities have been related to the development of a higher level of morality (Kohlberg, 1973; Piaget, 1932). Experiences in situations in which bilateral and multilateral communication are necessary probably increases the general sense of interdependence among students which, in turn, increases their prosocial orientation.

In traditionally structured bilingual classrooms, LEP students, compared with other students, are the recipients of less teacher and peer communication and communication at a lower cognitive and linguistic level (Arthur *et al.,* 1980; Long, 1980; Schinke-Llano, 1983). This "foreigner talk" does not allow important educational opportunities for LEP students. In cooperatively structured classrooms, students need to communicate; it is likely that communication with LEP students is at a higher level. In the Jigsaw method, for example, students must learn what each other student knows, and so they patiently draw out the LEP students (Aronson *et al.,* 1978). In Descubrimiento and Jigsaw III (see Appendix 1), bilingual students serve as translators for LEP students. It is likely that the increased need for communication is responsible for important gains among both the bilingual and LEP students in the cooperative formats. It has been noted that in the Descubrimiento science program, LEP students make substantial gains in English proficiency (Cohen *et al.,* 1981).

Peer tutoring. As indicated in the overview of the outcomes of cooperative learning, a surprising result emerged: Peer tutoring without group reward was not associated with achievement gains beyond those found in traditional classroom formats. This finding runs counter to a large literature indicating positive effects of peer tutoring for both tutees and tutors (Devin-Sheehan *et al.,* 1976; Ellson, 1975; Fitz-Gibbon, 1977; Rosenshine and Furst, 1969). A meta-analysis of the effects of peer tutoring on mathematics concluded that peer tutoring was more effective than individualized teaching methods such as computer-based instruction, programmed instruction, and instruction with individual learning packages (Hartley, 1977). A larger meta-analysis of 65 objective studies of peer tutoring concluded that peer tutoring was effective in producing positive academic and social outcomes for both tutors and tutees (Cohen and Kulik, 1981). In 87 percent of studies, students from classes that included tutoring programs outperformed students from control classes. The average effect size across studies was .40, equivalent to raising the performance of students from the 50th to the 66th percentile. Importantly, in all of the eight studies that included tutee attitudes toward subject matter, student attitudes were more positive in peer tutoring classes for a significant effect size of .29. The effects on tutors were equally impressive: Tutors moved in achievement an equivalent of from the 50th to the 63rd percentile (ES = .33 for 38 studies) and had more positive attitudes toward the subject matter (ES = .42 for five studies).

In the face of its generally positive outcomes, peer tutoring cannot be dismissed as an unimportant aspect of cooperative learning. This is especially so since highly structured peer tutoring programs produce more positive effects than do less structured programs (Cohen and Kulik, 1981; Ellson, 1975; Rosenshine and Furst, 1969), and the peer tutoring programs in cooperative learning methods are highly structured.

There is one plausible reconciliation of the apparent contradiction of positive results for peer tutoring in general and lack of positive results for cooperative learning methods that use peer tutoring but do not include a group reward and individual accountability. Peer tutoring is probably almost always effective, but in team situations in which there is no group reward or individual accountability for contribution to the team reward, there is little motivation for peer tutoring and, in fact, little peer tutoring probably occurs. Support for that conclusion comes from a series of studies that found less peer tutoring occurs when opportunity for group study is not accompanied by a group reward based on individual achievement (Hamblin *et al.,* 1971; Slavin, 1980). Thus, it appears that peer tutoring, when properly motivated, may be a very important element of cooperative learning, producing both positive academic and attitudinal outcomes.

Peer norms for achievement. In cooperative learning classrooms, individual achievement helps one's teammates obtain the best possible grade. Teammate approval of individual achievement is a natural consequence. Three studies indicate that, following cooperative learning, peer norms shift in favor of achievement (Slavin, 1983a; Madden and Slavin, 1983; Slavin, 1978a). This finding may be particularly important in explaining the greater achievement of minority students in cooperative learning classrooms, because, as indicated, there is evidence that peer norms are particularly important for some minority students (Hare, 1977). In cooperative classrooms, there may be less of a need for minority students to assume an "oppositional identity" (see Ogbu and Matute-Bianchi, this volume), particularly an anti-achievement orientation, because achievement is associated with supporting peer, rather than exclusively teacher-defined goals. In their review of the literature, Johnson and Johnson (1985) cite 21 studies indicating that students in classrooms using cooperative student teams believe that other students care for how much one learns and wants to help one learn.

Although it is clear that cooperative learning methods create a shift in peer norms to favor achievement, it is not clear how much that shift leads to increased achievement. Studies of the "transmission-of-values" hypothesis have been mixed; early studies were supportive of the notion that peer achievement norms led to achievement; later studies have cast doubt on that hypothesis. The early studies of the effects of school desegregation reported results consistent with the hypothesis that having majority friends and having achievement-oriented values is important for the achievement of minority students (Coleman *et al.,* 1966; Crain and Weisman, 1972; United States Commission on Civil Rights, 1967). A more direct test of the "transmission-of-values" hypothesis, using a longitudinal design and causal modeling, found support for the hypothesis that peer acceptance and achievement norms positively affected grades among minority students (Lewis and St. John, 1974). The transmission-of-values hypothesis, however, has not received support in other work. A review of the work is provided by Maruyama (1985). In a re-analysis of both the Gerard and Miller (1975) and the Lewis and St. John (1974) data using sophisticated structural equation techniques, Maruyama and associates found achievement to exert a causal influence on popularity, but popularity not to influence achievement.

Equal status. Cooperative classroom structures operate to equalize the status among high and low achievers, majority and minority students. The equalization of status is perhaps best exemplified by the

Jigsaw techniques in which each student is an expert who is responsible for teaching the team an important segment of the learning unit. Significant equalization of status occurs also in Co-op Co-op, in which each team member has a unique and valuable mini-topic, and in STAD, TGT, and TAI (see Appendix 1) because each team member has an equal opportunity to earn points for the team. Rotating roles in the Descubrimiento method also acts to equalize status. There is evidence that interracial contact in the presence of equal status tends to overcome racial stereotypes and discrimination (Allport, 1954; Cohen, 1980; Cohen and Roper, 1972). Thus, the equalization of status among students is probably an important contributor to the cross-racial friendship gains observed among students in cooperative learning classrooms.

Cultural Compatibility of Classroom Structure

The theory that goes most directly toward explaining the exceptionally positive effects of cooperative learning methods for minority groups involves the concepts of cultural compatibility and classroom structure. Each cooperative learning classroom structure is a complex, multifaceted environmental setting. The classroom structure provides a context within which behavior occurs. The many aspects of that context may be more or less compatible with the cognitive, emotional, and behavioral modes of individuals of a given culture. If there is incompatibility between the classroom structure and the behavior patterns or values or individuals from a cultural group, that group may be said to suffer structural bias (Kagan, 1980; 1983; Kagan et al., 1985). That is, the choice of a particular classroom structure may result in more positive academic and social outcomes for some groups.

Focus on the interaction of cultural patterns with classroom structures is in the spirit of interactional psychology or systems approaches. To emphasize that individual characteristics will lead to quite different behaviors, depending on the context within which the behavior occurs, represents a shift from traditional scientific paradigms that tend to seek linear and invariable relationships rather than global and context-bound relationships. Some of those who have emphasized in their studies the importance of context and the interaction of individuals with settings are Díaz et al., this volume; Cronbach, 1957; Cronbach and Snow, 1977; Hunt, 1975; Endler and Magnusson, 1976; Messick, 1970; and Minuchin and Shapiro, 1983). In spite of the attractiveness of the approach, reviews have not supported the general utility of matching individual differences with teaching methods (Bracht, 1970; Cronbach and Snow,

1977). A number of explanations for the generally poor results found in the attribute-treatment interaction (ATI) literature have been offered, including: (1) speculative pairing of person and treatment variables, (2) testing of short, ill-defined treatments with inappropriate statistical methods (Cronbach and Snow, 1977), and (3) the lack of appropriate categories and labels with which to identify individual differences likely to interact with educational treatments (Gordon and Shipman, 1979).

Nevertheless, we know that cultural characteristics do interact with classroom structures. Anthropologists have provided several critical examples of cultural groups responding with failure to school settings that are culturally inappropriate. In one experiment, Hawaiian children performing at the 27th percentile, when a phonics-based methods of reading instruction was used, responded positively to a more culturally appropriate comprehension-based reading program; their scores jumped to the 67th percentile (Au, 1980). According to Au and Jordan (1980), the comprehension-based method was culturally appropriate because it incorporated small group discussions of the reading stories that matched the "talk story" speech experiences of the Hawaiian children. (For more on this experiment, see Díaz *et al., this volume.*) Classroom sturctures that emphasize individual performance, a single directive or controlling authority, and lack of student control over degree of participation are "culturally incongruent" with the background of many Native American groups (Philips, 1970; Erickson and Mohatt, 1982). Native American children who are not language deficient in certain contexts appear language deficient in the traditional classroom context because the speech settings provided by the context are incompatible with the interactional etiquette of Native Americans (Philips, 1982).

Several researchers have documented an "incompatibility of cultures" or a "school-home discontinuity" with regard to Mexican-Americans in school. Luis Laosa (1982) provided support for his "general continuity-discontinuity hypothesis" with evidence that the discrepancy between parent and teacher communication styles may be partially responsible for the lower achievement and higher drop-out rate among Mexican-American compared to Anglo students. Laosa claimed that inquiry-based teaching methods common in schools are compatible with the parental teaching styles in Anglo but not Mexican-American families; Mexican-Americans are said to prefer a modeling approach. In some ways, Laosa's work echoed the work of Ramirez and Castañeda (1974), who indicated that the cognitive styles of Mexican-Americans include learning, incentive, relational, and communication styles, all of which are in conflict with traditional Anglo educational practices. Ramírez and Castañeda (1974) noted that "the mutual dependence and cooperative achievement characteristic of interpersonal relationships in traditional Mexican-American culture contrasts with the achievement through individual competition encouraged by the culture of the schools" (p. 45).

In their detailed analysis of the cooperativeness of a South Pacific Island population, Graves and Graves (1983) found that children from more traditional homes were more cooperative on both social motive and social interaction games. Importantly, increased identification with school values was associated with increased competitiveness. The school system on the island, though staffed with natives, reflects Western values: Children are to suppress their help-giving, rewards are administered individually, and authority is vested in a single adult. Children from traditional homes adjust slowly to these values and those who were least identified with the school values were the most cooperative. Near the onset of schooling, more than 50 percent of the students could be classified as generous on cooperation-competition choice-cards; following six years of school, only 15 percent were generous. There is evidence that cooperativeness is a characteristic of minority students in general. Extensive research documents the cooperativeness of Mexican-American students (Kagan, 1977; 1984). There is evidence also that Black, Asian, and Native American students are relatively more cooperative than Anglo students (Caudill and DeVos, 1956; DeVoe, 1977; Philips, 1970, 1982; Richmond and Weiner, 1973; Kagan et al., 1985; Sampson and Kardush, 1965). Independent of the minority status of a cultural group, low income is also associated with cooperative among Anglo and minority groups (Kagan, 1984; Knight et al., 1981; Pepitone, 1985). Cooperativeness is generally characteristic also of cultural groups from rural and traditional settings; in urban settings, the more recently immigrated and less acculturated the cultural group, the more cooperative their social style is likely to be (Kagan, 1981; Knight and Kagan, 1977).

The cooperative social orientation of low income and minority students may interact with the competitive and individualistic classroom structures commonly found in American public schools, producing negative academic and social schooling outcomes. Public school classrooms, thus, may be generally biased against minority students due to their relatively exclusive reliance on competitive and individualistic classroom structures. This structural bias hypothesis has been detailed and supported (Kagan, 1980; 1983; Kagan *et al.,* 1985). The kinds of negative effects that are likely to result from structural bias include achievement bias, ethnic-relations bias, and cultural value bias.

Achievement bias. There are different rewards for achievement associated with different types of classroom structures. Some of these rewards are extrinsic, including teacher praise, peer approval, and points or rewards that are given for superior performance. In each classroom structure, there are also various kinds of cooperative and competitive outcomes associated with achievement that can be rewarding. For example, in a competitive class structure, achievement may be associated with advancing to the highest achievement group in the class or with having one's name at the top of a performance list. In a cooperative classroom structure, achievement may be associated with helping one's teammates learn, receiving good grades, or class recognition. Because various individuals and ethnic groups place a different value on these cooperative and competitive outcomes, different classroom structures are differentially rewarding of achievement for various individuals and groups. Thus, a given classroom structure can be biased for or against the academic achievement of certain individuals and groups.

Obviously, it would be unfair to give pink bracelets to all students--boys and girls--who do well on their spelling tests each week. With that type of reward, girls probably would be more motivated to learn spelling than would boys, even though the rewards (and standards for achieving it) are ostensibly equal. Given that some individuals and groups come to school with a high value on competitive rewards and others with a high value on cooperative rewards, it is unfair to set up a class structure that provides exclusively or even primarily competitive rewards. When achievement is equivalent to "winning" in a competitive social comparison situation, individuals and groups who place a high value on winning will be more motivated to achieve than those who do not value, or who negatively value, obtaining more than others.

Structural bias against the achievement of cooperatively-oriented students is not always as easy to recognize as would be the use of only pink bracelets as rewards. Competitive rewards are embedded within the context of classroom structures that have been accepted unquestioningly for years. Often these competitive rewards are not overt and tangible; they are part of an implicit social comparison process that occurs among students as a function of classroom reward and task structures. A relatively common reward structure in traditional classrooms is to indicate the names of students who have reached criterion on some academic task. Colorful rocket ships with students' names on them may show how "high" students have advanced in the math or spelling tasks; a bar graph or posted exam testifies as to the number of perfect tests students have obtained. Given such rewards, competitive students will find it rewarding to learn because they value "besting" others. When such rewards are used, however, students who come to school with a value on equality rather than superiority will find the rewards for achievement of little or even negative value. Similarly, even if the competitive rewards in a classroom are covert, involving a competitive social comparison process that results from the classroom structure, competitively-oriented students will find the rewards for achievement more worth working for than will cooperatively-oriented individuals and groups. Research indicates that cooperatively-oriented students perform better in cooperatively-structured classrooms; and competitively-oriented students perform better in competitively-structured classes (Kagan *et al.,* 1985; Wheeler, 1977).

In a classroom that emphasizes student team learning, minority students and other cooperatively-oriented students will find achievement particularly rewarding; in cooperative classrooms, achievement is associated with increasing the positive outcomes of others. In a particularly revealing set of experiments, it was established that compared to majority students, Mexican-American and other minority students have lower achievement motivation if achievement is for themselves, but have higher achievement motivation if achievement is for their family (Gray, 1983).

Since many minority and low-income students have a more cooperative social orientation, it appears that traditional classroom structures are biased against those groups. The majority-minority school achievement gap may be attributed in part to the pervasive tendency of schools to rely almost exclusively on competitive classroom structures that provide more valued rewards for majority than minority students.

Ethnic-relations bias. A classroom structure can create a social climate or pattern of social relations in which members of a group are either accepted and valued by their peers or in which they are disparaged and alienated. Thus, classroom structures can be said to have either a positive or negative ethnic-relations bias. It is likely that minority students will suffer most from classroom structures that have a negative ethnic-relations bias.

The United States courts have indicated that separate schools are by their essence not equal and have demanded desegregation in our public school systems. By mandating desegregation, the courts cast on the schools the racial problem of the larger society. Unfortunately, schools were ill-prepared to deal with this problem; they maintained traditional, competitive, and individualistic classroom structures that recreated society's segregation within the classroom. We now know that if desegregated students had been sent to classrooms in which cooperative, racially integrated, classroom structures had been used, students would be less likely to suffer the negative consequences of within-class segregation (Slavin, 1980; 1983a). Traditional, competitive classroom structures, in contrast, lead students to segregate along racial lines, causing the creation of a minority outgroup. This negative ethnic-relations bias is probably associated with alienation, lower self-esteem, and lower academic achievement among minority students.

Cultural value bias. A classroom structure may be more or less in synchrony with the cultural values of a group. When a desegregated classroom relies exclusively on certain classroom structures, it will create value conflicts for groups that do not share those values. For example, if minority students come to school with cooperative values, but the classroom structure provides a strong press for competitive and individualistic behaviors, then a value conflict is created for minority students. Serious value conflicts create identity confusion and can interfere with the learning of academic material. Students can resolve home-culture/school-society value conflicts only by suffering negative consequences: They become alienated from the school and society, alienated from their home and culture, or alienated from both. Thus, the exclusive reliance within public schools on certain kinds of classroom structures can have the effect of systematically undermining core cultural values and the psychological stability of certain minority students. Internal conflict, alienation, and drop-out are some of the probable consequences of cultural value bias.

VI. COOPERATIVE LEARNING TEACHER TRAINING MODELS AND RESOURCES

Teacher training in cooperative learning has been approached in different ways, each of which has some advantages and disadvantages. The approaches differ along several dimensions. General principles approaches emphasize the general principles of cooperative learning; cookbook approaches teach the specific steps a teacher must take to operationalize particular methods. The author's own approach attempts to synthesize the general principles and cookbook approaches and has been detailed elsewhere (Kagan, 1985b). Some trainers have involved teachers as long as a full school year in training; others certify teachers as trained after as few as four hours. Teacher training differs also in the extent to which it relies on modeling, guided practice, feedback, and the development of teacher support groups. There are a number of resources including films, synchronized cassette/filmstrips, books, games, newsletters, and organizations for teachers involved in cooperative learning.

Teacher Training

The general principles approach. For years, through their writing and workshops, David and Roger Johnson and their associates at the Cooperative Learning Center, University of Minnesota, have stressed teaching teachers the basic concepts of cooperative learning. Johnson *et al.* (1984) spelled out their approach to teacher training in detail. The approach included training in basic principles, training in differentiating effective from ineffective implementation, using a cooperative supervision model, and structuring professional support groups.

The Johnson *et al.* (1984) study provided the example of Diane Browne, an outstanding trainer, who trained teachers one-on-one. Ms. Browne gave an awareness in-service session to an entire school, but then worked with each teacher individually. She modeled cooperative learning in the teacher's class; cooperatively planned a lesson plan with the teacher to be taught in the class; co-taught the lesson; and made repeated visits to the classroom and teacher, offering new techniques and materials tailored to the teacher's content and problems. After a number of teachers were trained, a support group was formed and trained. Ms. Browne maintained contact with the teachers and sent out monthly newsletters. She also met with curriculum directors, parent groups, principals' cabinets, and coordinated collaboration between teachers.

When the general principles approach is combined with intensive individual training like that offered by Diane Browne, it actually includes much of the cookbook approach as well. When the general principles approach is given in a workshop only, as often is the case, teachers may not have sufficient grasp of how to apply the techniques to their own classes. Or worse, they may believe they know how when actually they do not.

The cookbook approach. At Johns Hopkins University, the Center for Social Organization of Schools distributes a teachers' manual on cooperative learning (Slavin, 1978b) and provides workshops. After a few hours of training, teachers can be certified in their knowledge of a cooperative learning method. The teachers' manual and workbooks describe in detail the step-by-step procedures of assigning students to teams, preparing lesson plans and worksheets, scoring students, and providing recognition for team achievement.

The cookbook approach has the advantage of creating a great deal of conformity among teachers with regard to the methods they are using, with teachers converging on the predetermined, most effective methods. The disadvantage of this approach is that teachers are less prepared to institute creative adaptations of the cooperative learning methods to special problems and content areas. When teachers are trained in cooperative learning methods in a workshop format without individual feedback following real class experiences, some teachers will encounter problems for which they are not prepared and will abandon the techniques. Others will deviate from the techniques in ways that are not positive for academic and social outcomes.

A student-teacher training model. At the University of California, Riverside, the School of Education has included training in cooperative learning methods for its student teachers. The training program is intensive; competence in the theory and practice of cooperative learning is a requirement for the credential for many student-teachers.

The University of California, Riverside training model includes full-day workshops on the principles and techniques of the methods; a course on the theories, methods, and research in cooperative learning; classroom supervision that includes cooperative learning experiences for student teachers using the techniques; and intensive feedback for student teachers using the techniques in their classes. Effort has been made also to train the master teachers in whose classrooms student teachers practice the techniques of cooperative learning.

Many teachers who have graduated from the University of California, Riverside training program now use the cooperative learning methods regularly; some have trained their fellow faculty in their school settings.

Elements of successful teacher training. Although formal research on the training of teachers in cooperative learning has not been conducted, personal experience in working with student teachers and in-service teachers leads this author to conclude that a combination of the basic principles and cookbook methods is best. Most important, however, training must go beyond the workshop model; no amount of workshop and class time alone is sufficient to ensure competence. Important elements of successful teacher training include: repeated opportunities to view and interact with successful instructor/models; guided practice and coaching; intensive immediate feedback in a supportive environment; opportunities to successively approximate successful practices; peer support groups and the opportunity to experience cooperative activities within a meaningful context (for example, cooperatively plan lesson plans or school activities with fellow teachers).

A full discussion of the formidable problems faced by those responsible for teacher training and development is far beyond the scope of this chapter. Joyce and Clift (1984) have outlined the problems with our approaches to teacher education. Teachers in training too often face a fragmented curriculum that fails to integrate theory and practice. Training seldom includes models for anything but the didactic approach. Once teachers are placed in schools, the cellular, individualistic approach to school organization provides a powerful structural constraint that funnels practice away from innovation and toward recitation; there is seldom enduring administrative, structural, or peer support for innovation or variety in approaches to curriculum and the social organization of the classroom. There is little wonder that teachers often move rapidly from idealism toward resignation, from innovation toward stagnation.

Successful training of teachers for cooperative learning has the potential of addressing a number of critical problems in teacher training and support. Most important, training in cooperative learning provides an antidote to the isolation of the individual teacher due to the cellular organization of the school (Joyce and Clift, 1984). During training in cooperative learning, teachers enjoy peer coaching and support. Just as individual students in traditional classrooms are denied peer support for achievement because of the classroom structure, so too are individual teachers in traditional school denied peer support. Teachers seldom have the opportunity to learn from or support one another. Training in cooperative learning, by including cooperative activities among teachers and the establishment of on-going supportive networks, can reorganize the social structure of the school faculty away from isolation and insecurity toward cooperation and mutual support.

Teacher Resources

There are a variety of manuals, books, training tapes and films, and games available to teachers wishing to incorporate cooperative learning in their classrooms. These resources are cataloged in Appendix 2.

VII. CONCLUSIONS

Cooperative learning holds promise for the schooling of minority pupils and for pupils in general. It is somewhat unique as an innovation for teaching as it is not content-specific nor limited to one pole of the humanistic-basic skills continuum. Results of numerous controlled studies of cooperative learning indicate it has positive effects on academic achievement and a number of achievement-related schooling outcomes. It also has positive effects on cooperativeness and ethnic-relations among students. Thus, cooperative learning addresses some of our most pressing national educational problems.

Schools cannot choose not to affect race relations and prosocial development; the only question is what kind of impact they will provide. The choice of any classroom structure brings with it certain kinds of socialization experiences. Our nation's schools have settled *de facto* on a massive competitive and individualistic socialization program, with adverse consequences for our pupils, especially those from minority populations. If we continue to rely almost exclusively on competitive and individualistic class structures, we will continue to bias educational outcomes against minority and other cooperatively oriented students and produce students who are blind to the many positive cooperative possibilities in the academic, economic, and social spheres. If we are to have a population that is rational and adaptive, we must provide all types of learning experiences--cooperative, competitive, and individualistic--so that our students will develop the ability to adapt rationally to the full range of human situations. At the present moment, the need for cooperative learning is especially intense as rapid urbanization and social restructuring combine to create a prosocial socialization void. The burden is on schools to respond to that void. By including meaningful cooperative experiences that are an integral part of the school experience, we can better meet the challenges provided by rapid urbanization, social restructuring of our work and home settings, and the increased numbers of ethnic and cultural minority group members in our schools and society.

REFERENCES

Adams, R. S., and Biddle, B. J. *Realities of Teaching: Explorations with Video Tape.* New York: Holt, 1970.

Allport, G. *The Nature of Prejudice.* Cambridge, Massachusetts: Addison-Wesley, 1954.

Armstrong, B., Johnson, D. W., and Balow, B. Effects of cooperative versus in-dividualistic learning experiences on interpersonal attraction between learning-disabled and normal-progress elementary school students. *Contemporary Educational Psychology,* 1981, *6,* 102-109.

Aronson, E., Blaney, N., Stephan, C., Sikes, J., and Snapp, M. *The Jigsaw Classroom.* Beverly Hills, California: Sage, 1978.

―――――, and Goode, W. Training teachers to implement jigsaw learning: A manual for teachers. In S. Sharan, P. Hare, C. D. Webb, and R. Hertz-Lazarowitz (Eds.), *Cooperation in Education.* Provo, Utah: Brigham Young University Press, 1980.

Arthur, B., Weiner, R., Culver, M., Lee, Y. J., and Thomas, D. The register of imper-sonal discourse to foreigners: Verbal adjustments to foreign accent. In D. Larsen-Freeman (Ed.), *Discourse Analysis in Second Language Acquisition.* Rowley, Massachusetts: Newbury House, 1980.

Au, K. H. Participation structures in a reading lesson with Hawaiian children: Analysis of a culturally appropriate instructional event. *Anthropology and Education Quarterly,* 1980, *11*(2), 91-115.

―――――, and Jordan, C. Teaching reading to Hawaiian children: Finding a culturally ap-propriate solution. In H. Trueba, G. P. Guthrie, K. H. Au (Eds.), *Culture in the Bi-lingual Classroom.* Rowley, Massachusetts: Newbury House, 1980.

Bandura, A. Influence of model's reinforcement contingencies on the acquisition of im-itative responses. *Journal of Personality and Social Psychology,* 1965, *1,* 589-595.

Berkowitz, L. The contagion of violence: An S-R mediational analysis of some effects of observed aggression. In W. J. Arnold and M. M. Page (Eds.), *Nebraska Symposium of Motivation (Vol. 19).* Lincoln, Nebraska: University of Nebraska Press, 1971.

Bloom, B. S. *Stability and Change in Human Characteristics.* New York: Wiley, 1964.

Bower, R. T. *Television and the Public.* New York: Holt, 1973.

Bracht, G. H. The relationship of treatment tasks, personological variables, and depen-dent variables to aptitude-treatment interactions. *Review of Educational Research,* 1970, *40,* 627-645.

Bronfenbrenner, U. Contexts of child rearing: Problems and prospects. *American Psychologist,* 1979, *34*(10), 844-850.

―――――. Who cares for America's children? In V. Vaughn and T. Brazelton (Eds.), *The Family--Can It Be Saved?* New York: Year Book Medical Publishers, 1976.

Brophy, J. E., and Good, T. L. *Teacher-Student Relationships: Causes and Conse-quences.* New York: Holt, Rinehart and Winston, 1974.

Brookover, W., Beady, C., Flood, P., Schweitzer, J., and Wisenbaker, J. *School Social Systems and Student Achievement.* New York: Praeger, 1979.

Bruner, J. S. *The Process of Education.* Cambridge, Massachusetts: Harvard University Press, 1961.

―――――. *Toward a Theory of Instruction.* Cambridge, Massachusetts: Harvard Univer-sity Press, 1966.

Bybee, R., and Gee, E. *Violence, Values and Justice in the Schools.* Boston, Massachusetts: Allyn and Bacon, 1982.

Carter, T. P., and Segura, R. D. *Mexican Americans in School.* New York: College Entrance Examination Board, 1979.

Caudill, W., and DeVos, G. Achievement, culture and personality: The case of the Japanese Americans. *The American Anthropologist,* 1956, *58,* 1102-1126.

Cicourel, A. V., and Mehan, H. Universal development, stratifying practices, and status attainment. *Research in Social Stratification and Mobility,* 1985, *4,* 3-27.

Cohen, E. G. Design and redesign of the desegregated school: Problems of status, power, and conflict. In W. G. Stephan and J. R. Feagin (Eds.), *Desegregation: Past, Present, and Future.* New York: Plenum Press, 1980.

_____, DeAvila, E., and Intiti, J. A. *Multi-Cultural Improvement of Cognitive Ability.* Unpublished manuscript. Palo Alto, California: Stanford University, 1981.

_____, and Roper, S. Modification of interracial interaction disability: An application of status characteristic theory. *American Sociological Review, 1972, 37*(6), 643-657.

Cohen, P. A., and Kulik, J. A. Synthesis of research on the effects of tutoring. *Research Information Service, 1981, 39,* 227-229.

Coleman, J. S., Campbell, E. Q., Hobson, C. J., McPortland, J., Mood, A. M., Weinfeld, F. D., and York, R. L. *Equality of Educational Opportunity.* Washington, D.C.: United States Department of Health, Education and Welfare, Office of Education, U.S. Government Printing Office, 1966.

Committee on the Judiciary of the United States Senate. *Our Nation's Schools--A Report Card: "A" in School Violence and Vandalism.* (Preliminary report of the Subcommittee to Investigate Juvenile Delinquency.) Washington, D.C.: U.S. Government Printing Office, 1975.

Comstock, G., Chaffee, S., Katzman, N., McCombs, M., and Roberts, D. *Television and Human Behavior.* New York: Columbia University Press, 1978.

Cook, S. W. Social science and school desegregation: Did we mislead the Supreme Court. *Personality and Social Psychology Bulletin, 1979, 5,* 420-437.

Cooper, H. M. Pygmalion grows up: A model for teacher expectation, communication and performance influence. *Review of Educational Research, 1979, 49,* 389-410.

Cooper, L., Johnson, D. W., Johnson, R., and Wilderson, F. The effects of cooperation, competition, and individualization on cross-ethnic, cross-sex and cross-ability friendships. *Journal of Social Psychology, 1980, 111,* 243-252.

Cotton, J., and Cook, M. Meta-analyses and the effects of various systems: Some different conclusions from Johnson *et al. Psychological Bulletin, 1982, 92,* 176-183.

Cortés, Carlos E. The education of language-minority students: A contextual interaction model. In *Beyond Language: Social and Cultural Factors in Schooling Language Minority Students.* Los Angeles, California: Evaluation, Dissemination and Assessment Center, California State University, Los Angeles, 1986.

Crain, R. L. *The Quality of American High School Graduates: What Personnel Officers Say and Do About It.* Report No. 354. Baltimore, Maryland: Center for Social Organization of Schools, Johns Hopkins University, 1984.

_____, and Weisman, C. S. *Discrimination, Personality, and Achievement: A Survey of Northern Blacks.* New York: Seminar Press, 1972.

Cronbach, L. J. The two disciplines of scientific psychology. *American Psychologist,* 1957, *12,* 671-684.

_____, and Snow, R. E. *Aptitudes and Instructional Methods.* New York: Wiley, 1977.

de Charms, R. *Personal Causation.* New York: Academic Press, 1968.

Devin-Sheehan, L., Feldman, R. S., and Allen, V. L. Research on children tutoring children: A critical review. *Review of Educational Research, 1976, 46*(3), 355-385.

DeVoe, M. W. Cooperation as a function of self-concept, sex, and race. *Educational Research Quarterly, 1977, 2,* 3-8.

Díaz, Stephen, Moll, Luis C., and Mehan, Hugh. Sociocultural resources in instruction: A context-specific approach. In *Beyond Language: Social and Cultural Factors in Schooling Language Minority Students.* Los Angeles, California: Evaluation, Dissemination and Assessment Center, California State University, Los Angeles, 1986.

Dunkin, J. M., and Biddle, B. J. *The Study of Teaching.* New York: Holt, 1974.

Edney, J. J. The commons problem: Alternative perspectives. *American Psychologist,* 1980, *35,* 131-151.

_____, and Harper, C. S. Heroism in a resource crisis: A simulation study. *Environmental Management,* 1978, *2*(6), 523-527.

Ellson, D. G. Tutoring. In N. Gage (Ed.), *The Psychology of Teaching Methods.* Chicago, Illinois: University of Chicago Press, 1975.

Endler, N. S., and Magnusson, D. (Eds.), *Interactional Psychology and Personality.* New York: Wiley, 1976.

Erickson, F., and Mohatt, G. Cultural organization of participation structures in two classrooms of Indian students. In G. Spindler (Ed.), *Doing the Ethnography of Schooling.* New York: Holt, Rinehart and Winston, 1982.

Eron, L. D., Huesmann, L. R., Lefkowitz, M. M., and Walder, L. O. Does television violence cause aggression? *American Psychologist,* 1972, *27,* 253-263.

Feshbach, N. D. Student teacher preferences for elementary school pupils varying in personality characteristics. *Journal of Educational Psychology,* 1969, *60,* 126-143.

Fitz-Gibbon, C. T. *An Analysis of the Literature of Cross-Age Tutoring.* Washington, D.C.: National Institute of Education, 1977.

Gelman, D., Greenberg, N. F., Cappola, V., Burgower, B., Doherthy, S., Anderson, M., and Williams, E. The world of single parents. *Newsweek,* July 15, 1985, *106*(3), 42-50.

Gerard, H. B., Jackson, T. D., and Conally, E. S. Social contact in the desegregated classroom. In H. B. Gerard and N. Miller (Eds.), *School Desegregation: A Long-Term Study.* New York: Plenum Press, 1975.

_____, and Miller, N. *School Desegregation.* New York: Plenum Press, 1975.

Gerbner, G., Gross, L., Morgan, J., and Signorielli, N. The mainstreaming of America. *Journal of Communication,* 1980, *30,* 12-29.

_____, Gross, L., Signorielli, N., Morgan, M., and Jackson-Beeck, M. The demonstration of power: Violence profile No. 10. *Journal of Communication,* 1979, *29,* 177-196.

Gonzalez, A., and Guerrero, M. *A Cooperative/Interdependent Approach to Bilingual Education: Jigsaw Teacher's Handbook.* Hollister, California: Hollister School District, 1983.

Goodlad, J. I. *A Place Called School: Prospects for the Future.* New York: McGraw Hill, 1984.

Gordon, E. W., and Shipman, S. Human diversity, pedagogy, and educational equity. *American Psychologist,* 1979, *34,* 1030-1036.

Graves, N. B., and Graves, T. D. The cultural context of prosocial development: An ecological model. In D. Bridgeman (Ed.), *The Nature of Prosocial Development.* New York: Academic Press, 1983.

Gray, T. C. The cognitive correlates of bicultural achievement motivation. In E. Garcia (Ed.), *The Mexican American Child: Language, Cognition, and Social Development.* Tempe, Arizona: Center for Bilingual Education, University of Arizona, 1983.

Hamblin, R. L., Hathaway, C., and Wodarski, J. S. Group contingencies, peer tutoring and accelerating academic achievement. In E. Ramp and W. Hopkins (Eds.), *A New Direction for Education: Behavior Analysis.* Lawrence, Kansas: The University of Kansas, Department of Human Development, 1971.

Hare, B. R. Racial and sociometric variations in preadolescent area-specific and general self-esteem. *International Journal of Intercultural Relations,* 1977, *1,* 31-51.

Hartley, S. S. *Meta-Analysis of the Effects of Individually Paced Instruction in Mathematics.* Unpublished doctoral dissertation, University of Colorado, 1977.

Hetherington, E. M. Divorce: A child's perspective. *American Psychologist,* 1979, *34*(10), 851-858.

————, Cox, M., and Cox, R. The aftermath of divorce. In J. H. Stevens, Jr., and M. Mathews (Eds.), *Mother-Child, Father-Child Relations.* Washington, D.C.: National Association for the Education of Young Children, 1978.

Hunt, D. E. Person-environment interaction: A challenge found wanting before it was tried. *Review of Educational Research,* 1975, *45*, 209-230.

Johnson, D. W. Group processes: Influences of student-student interactions on school outcomes. In J. McMillan (Ed.), *Social Psychology of School Learning.* New York: Academic Press, 1980.

————, and Johnson, R. Conflict in the classroom: Controversy and learning. *Review of Educational Research,* 1979, *49*, 51-70.

————, and ————. Effects of cooperative, competition, and individualistic learning experiences on cross-ethnic interaction and friendships. *Journal of Social Psychology,* 1982a, *118*, 47-58.

————, and ————. Effects of cooperative and individualistic instruction on the relationships and performance of handicapped and non-handicapped students. *Journal of Social Psychology,* 1982b, *118*, 257-268.

————, and ————. Effects of cooperative and individualistic learning experiences on interethnic interaction. *Journal of Educational Psychology,* 1981, *73*, 444-449.

————, and ————. Social interdependence and perceived academic and personal support in the classroom. *Journal of Social Psychology,* 1983a, *120*, 77-82.

————, and ————. The socialization and achievement crisis: Are cooperative learning experiences the solution? In L. Bickman (Ed.), *Applied Social Psychology, Annual 4.* Beverly Hills, California: Sage Publications, 1983b.

————, and ————. The internal dynamics of cooperative learning groups. In R. Slavin, S. Sharan, S. Kagan, R. Hertz-Lazarowitz, C. Webb, and R. Schmuck (Eds.), *Learning to Cooperate, Cooperating to Learn.* New York: Plenum, 1985.

————, ————, Holubec, E. J., and Roy, P. *Circles of Learning: Cooperation in the Classroom.* Alexandria, Virginia: Association for Supervision and Curriculum Development, 1984.

————, ————, Johnson, J., and Anderson, D. The effects of cooperative vs. individualized instruction on student prosocial behavior, attitudes toward learning, and achievement. *Journal of Educational Psychology,* 1976, *68*, 446-452.

————, ————, and Maruyama, G. Interdependence and interpersonal attraction among heterogeneous and homogeneous individuals: A theoretical formulation and a meta-analysis of the research. *Review of Educational Research,* 1983, *53*, 5-54.

————, ————, and Tiffany, M. Structuring academic conflicts between majority and minority students: Hindrance or help to integration. *Contemporary Educational Psychology,* 1984, *9*, 61-73.

————, ————, ————, and Zaidman, B. Are low achievers disliked in a cooperative situation? A test of rival theories in a mixed-ethnic situation. *Contemporary Educational Psychology,* 1983, *8*, 189-200.

————, Maruyama, G., Johnson, R., Nelson, D., and Skon, L. Effects of cooperative, competitive and individualistic goal structures on achievement: A meta-analysis. *Psychological Bulletin,* 1981, *89*, 47-62.

Johnson, R., Johnson, D. W., DeWeerdt, N., Lyons, V., and Zaidman, B. Integrating severely adaptively handicapped seventh-grade students into constructive relationships with nonhandicapped peers in science class. *American Journal of Mental Deficiency,* 1983, *83,* 611-618.

Joyce, B., and Clift, R. The phoenix agenda: Essential reform in teacher education. *Educational Researcher,* 1984, *13*(4), 5-18.

Kagan, S. Co-op Co-op: A flexible cooperative learning technique. In R. Slavin, S. Sharan, S. Kagan, R. Hertz-Lazarowitz, C.Webb, and R. Schmuck (Eds.), *Learning to Cooperate, Cooperating to Learn.* New York: Plenum, 1985a.

————. Cooperation-competition, culture, and structural bias in classrooms. In S. Sharan, A. P. Hare, C. Webb, and R. Lazarowitz (Eds.), *Cooperation in Education.* Provo, Utah: Brigham Young University Press, 1980.

————. Ecology and the acculturation of cognitive and social styles among Mexican American children. *Hispanic Journal of Behavioral Sciences, 1981, 3*(2), 111-144.

————. Interpreting Chicano cooperativeness: Methodological and theoretical considerations. In J. L. Martinez and R. H. Mendoza (Eds.), *Chicano Psychology.* 2nd ed. New York: Academic Press, 1984.

————. Social motives and behaviors of Mexican-American and Anglo-American children. In J. L. Martinez (Ed.), *Chicano Psychology.* New York: Academic Press, 1977.

————. *Cooperative Learning Resources for Teachers.* Riverside, California: University of California, Riverside, Printing and Reprographics, 1985b.

————. Social orientation among Mexican-American children: A challenge to traditional classroom structures. In E. Garcia (Ed.), *The Mexican American Child: Language, Cognition, and Social Development.* Tempe, Arizona: Center for Bilingual Education, University of Arizona, 1983.

————. The dimensions of cooperative classroom structures. In R. Slavin, S. Sharan, S. Kagan, R. Hertz-Lazarowitz, C. Webb, and R. Schmuck (Eds.), *Learning to Cooperate, Cooperating to Learn.* New York: Plenum Press, 1985c.

————, and Madsen, M. C. Cooperation and competition of Mexican, Mexican-American, and Anglo-American children of two ages under four instructional sets. *Developmental Psychology,* 1971, *5,* 32-39.

————, and ————. Experimental analyses of cooperation and competition of Anglo-American and Mexican children. *Developmental Psychology,* 1972, *6,* 49-59.

————, and Zahn, G. L. Field dependence and the school achievement gap between Anglo-American children. *Journal of Educational Psychology,* 1975, *67,* 643-650.

————, ————, Widaman, K. F., Schwarzwald, J., and Tyrrell, G. Classroom structural bias: Impact of cooperative and competitive classroom structures on cooperative and competitive individuals and groups. In R. E. Slavin, S. Sharan, S. Kagan, R. Hertz-Lazarowitz, C. Webb, and R. Schmuck (Eds.), *Learning to Cooperate, Cooperating to Learn.* New York: Plenum Press, 1985.

Kaplan, R. M. On television as a cause of aggression. *American Psychologist,* 1972, *27,* 968-969.

Klein, Z., and Eshel, Y. *Integrating Jerusalem Schools.* New York: Academic Press, 1980.

Knight, G. P., and Kagan, S. Acculturation of prosocial and competitive behaviors among second- and third-generation Mexican American children. *Journal of Cross-Cultural Psychology,* 1977, *8,* 273-284.

————, ————, and Buriel, R. Confounding effects of individualism in children's cooperation--competition social motive measures. *Motivation and Emotion*, 1981, *5*, 167-178.

Kohlberg, L. The contribution of developmental psychology to education--Examples from moral education. *Educational Psychologist*, 1973, *10*(1), 2-14.

Krashen, S. D. *Principles and Practice in Second Language Acquisition*. Oxford: Pergamon, 1982.

Laosa, L. M. School, occupation, culture, and family: The impact of parental schooling on the parent-child relationship. *Journal of Education Psychology*, 1982, *74*(6), 791-827.

Leacock, E. B. *Teaching and Learning in City Schools*. New York: Basic Books, 1969.

Lerner, B. The minimum competence testing movement: Social, scientific, and legal implications. *American Psychologist*, 1981, *27*, 1057-1066.

Levitin, T., and Chananie, J. Responses of female primary school teachers to sex-typed behaviors in male and female children. *Child Development*, 1972, *43*, 1309-1316.

Lewis, R., and St. John, N. Contribution of cross-racial friendship to minority group achievement in desegregated classrooms. *Sociometry*, 1974, *37*, 79-91.

Liebert, R. M., and Baron, R. A. Short-term effects of televised aggression on children's aggressive behavior. In J. P. Murray, E. A. Rubinstein, and G. A. Comstock (Eds.), *Television and Social Behavior: II. Television and Social Learning*. Washington, D.C.: U. S. Government Printing Office, 1972.

Long, M. H. *Input, Interaction, and Second Language Acquisition*. Unpublished doctoral dissertation, University of California, Los Angeles, 1980.

————. Native speaker/non-native speaker conversation and the negotiation of comprehensible input. *Applied Linguistics*, 1983, *4*(2), 126-141.

Lowry, N., and Johnson, D. W. The effects of controversy on students' motivation and learning. *Journal of Social Psychology*, 1981, *115*, 31-43.

Lyle, J., and Hoffman, H. Children's use of television and other media. In E. A. Rubinstein, G. A. Comstock, and J. P. Murray (Eds.), *Television and Social Behavior: IV. Television in Day-to Day Life: Patterns of Use*. Washington, D.C.: U.S. Government Printing Office, 1972.

Madden, N. A., and Slavin, R. E. Effects of cooperative learning on social acceptance of mainstreamed academically handicapped students. *Journal of Special Education*, 1983, *17*, 171-182.

Madsen, M. C., and Shapira, A. Cooperative and competitive behavior or urban Afro-American, Anglo-American, Mexican-American, and Mexican village children. *Developmental Psychology*, 1970, *3*, 16-20.

Maller, J. B. *Cooperation and Competition: An Experimental Study in Motivation*. New York: Teachers College, Columbia University, 1929.

Martino, L., and Johnson, D. W. Cooperative and individualistic experiences among disabled and normal children. *Journal of Social Psychology*, 1979, *107*, 177-183.

Maruyama, G. Relating goal structures to other classroom processes. In R. Slavin, S. Sharan, S. Kagan, R. Hertz-Lazarowitz, C. Webb, and R. Schmuck (Eds.), *Learning to Cooperate, Cooperating to Learn*. New York: Plenum Press, 1985.

McGlynn, R. A comment on the meta-analysis of goal structures. *Psychological Bulletin*, 1982, *92*, 184-185.

McGroarty, Mary. Educators' responses to sociocultural diversity: Implications for practice. In *Beyond Language: Social and Cultural Factors in Schooling Language Minority Students.* Los Angeles, California: Evaluation, Dissemination and Assessment Center, California State University, Los Angeles, 1986.

Mehan, H. Language and schooling. *Sociology of Education,* 1984, *57,* 174-183.

Messick, S. The criterion problems in the evaluation of instruction: Assessing possible not just intended outcomes. In M. C. Wittrock and D. C. Wiley (Eds.), *The Evaluation of Instruction: Issues and Problems.* New York: Holt, Rinehart and Winston, 1970.

Miller, L. B., and Dyer, J. L. Four preschool programs: Their dimensions and effects, with commentary by H. Stevenson and S. H. White. *Monographs of the Society for Research in Child Development,* 1975, *40*(162).

Minnesota Law Review. The effects of segregation and the consequences of desegregation: A social science statement. Appendix to appellant's briefs of *Brown* vs. *Board of Education of Topeka, Kansas,* 1953, *37,* 427-439.

Minuchin, P. P., and Shapiro, E. K. The school as a context for social development. In P. H. Mussen (Ed), *Handbook for Child Psychology, Vol. IV, 4th Ed.* New York: Wiley, 1983.

Naisbitt, J. *Megatrends: Ten New Directions Transforming our Lives.* New York: Warner Books, 1984.

National Center for Health Statistics. Final natality statistics, 1977. *Monthly Vital Statistics Report, 1979, 27*(12). (Supplement).

————. *Vital statistics for the United States (Vol. 1).* Washington, D.C.: United States Department of Health, Education, and Welfare, 1951.

National Commission on Secondary Education for Hispanics. *Make Something Happen: Hispanics and Urban High School Reform.* Volume 2. Washington, D.C.: National Commission on Secondary Education for Hispanics, Hispanic Policy Development Project, 1984.

Nevin, A., Johnson, D. W., and Johnson, R. Effects of groups and individual contingencies on academic performance and social relations of special needs students. *Journal of Social Psychology,* 1982, *116,* 41-59.

Nielson Television Index. *National Audience Demographics Report, 1982.* Northbrook, Illinois: A./C. Nielsen Company, 1982.

Ogbu, John U., and Matute-Bianchi, Maria. Understanding sociocultural factors: Knowledge, identity and school adjustment. In *Beyond Language: Social and Cultural Factors in Schooling Language Minority Students.* Los Angeles: Evaluation, Dissemination and Assessment Center, California State University, Los Angeles, 1986.

Okada, T. Dynamics of achievement: *A Study of Differential Growth of Achievement Over Time.* Technical Note No. 53, National Center for Educational Statistics, Office of Education, United States Department of Health, Education and Welfare. Washington, D.C.: U.S. Government Printing Office, 1968.

Parke, R. D., Berkowitz, L., Leyens, J. P., West, S. G., and Sebastian, R. J. Some effects of violent and nonviolent movies on the behavior of juvenile delinquents. In L. Berkowitz (Ed.), *Advances in Experimental Social Psychology (Vol. 10).* New York: Academic Press, 1977.

Pepitone, E. A. Children in cooperation and competition: Antecedents and consequences of self-orientation. In R. Slavin, S. Sharan, S. Kagan, R. Hertz-Lazarowitz, C. Webb, and R. Schmuck (Eds.), *Learning to Cooperate, Cooperating to Learn.* New York: Plenum Press, 1985.

Perkins, H. V. A procedure for assessing the classroom behavior of students and teachers. *American Educational Research Journal*, 1964, *1*(4), 249-260.

Perry, C., and Duke, D. Lessons to be learned about discipline from alternative high schools. *Journal of Research and Development in Education*, 1978, *11*, 77-91.

Philips, S. Acquisition of roles for appropriate speech usage. In *Monograph Series on Languages and Linguistics, 21st Annual Round Table, No. 23.* Georgetown University, School of Languages and Linguistics, Georgetown University Press, 1970.

_____. *The Invisible Culture: Communication in Classroom and Community on the Warm Springs Indian Reservation.* New York: Longmans, 1982.

Piaget, J. *The Moral Judgment of the Child.* New York: Harcourt, 1932.

Ramírez, M., and Castañeda, A. *Cultural Democracy, Bicognitive Development and Education.* New York: Academic Press, 1974.

Reich, R. B. The next American frontier. *The Atlantic Monthly,* April, 1983, 97-108.

Richmond, B. O., and Weiner, G. P. Cooperation and competition among young children as a function of ethnic grouping, grade, sex, and reward condition. *Journal of Educational Psychology,* 1973, *64*, 329-334.

Rist, R. Student social class and teacher expectations: The self-fulfilling prophecy in ghetto schools. *Harvard Educational Review,* 1970, *40*(3), 411-450.

Rosenshine, B., and Furst, N. *The Effects of Tutoring upon Pupil Achievement. A Research Review.* Washington, D.C.: Office of Education, 1969.

Rossiter, J. R., and Robertson, T. S. Children's television viewing: An examination of parent-child consequences. *Sociometry,* 1975, *38*, 308-326.

Sampson, E., and Kardush, M. Age, sex, class, and race differences in response to a two-person non-zero-sum game. *Conflict Resolution,* 1965, *9*, 212-220.

Schinke-Llano, L. A. Foreigner talk in content classrooms. In H. W. Seliger and M. H. Long (Eds.), *Classroom Oriented Research in Second Language Acquisition.* Rowley, Massachusetts: Newbury House Publishers, 1983.

Schwarzwald, J. and Cohen, S. Relationship between academic tracking and the degree of interethnic acceptance. *Journal of Educational Psychology,* 1982, *74*, 588-597.

Sharan, S. Cooperative learning in small groups: Recent methods and effects on achievement, attitudes, and ethnic relations. *Review of Educational Research,* 1980, *50*, 241-271.

_____, and Hertz-Lazarowitz, R. A group-investigation method of cooperative learning in the classroom. In S. Sharan, P. Hare, C. D. Webb, and R. Hertz-Lazarowitz (Eds.), *Cooperation in Education.* Provo, Utah: Brigham Young University Press, 1979.

_____, Kussell, P., Hertz-Lazarowitz, R., Bejarano, Y., Raviv, S., and Sharan, Y. *Cooperative Learning in the Classroom: Research in Desegregated Schools.* Hillsdale, New Jersey: Erlbaum, 1984.

Silberman, M. Behavioral expression of teachers' attitudes toward elementary school students. *Journal of Education Psychology,* 1969, *60*, 402-407.

_____. Teachers' attitudes and actions toward their students. In M. Silberman (Ed.), *The Experience of Schooling.* New York: Holt, Rinehart and Winston, 1971.

Skon, L., Johnson, D. W., and Johnson, R. Cooperative peer interaction versus individual competition and individualistic efforts: Effects on the acquisition of cognitive reasoning strategies. *Journal of Educational Psychology,* 1981, *73*, 83-92.

Slavin, R. E. *Cooperative Learning.* New York: Longman, 1983a.

————. Cooperative learning. *Review of Educational Research,* 1980, *50,* 315-342.

————. Cooperative learning and desegregation. *Journal of Educational Equity and Leadership,* 1981, *1,* 145-161.

————. Effects of biracial learning teams on cross-racial friendships. *Journal of Educational Psychology,* 1979, *71,* 381-387.

————. How student learning teams can integrate the desegregated classroom. *Integrated Education,* 1977, *15,* 56-58.

————. Student teams and comparison among equals: Effects on academic performance and student attitudes. *Journal of Educational Psychology,* 1978a, *70,* 532-538.

————. Team-assisted individualization: Combining cooperative learning and individualized instruction in mathematics. In R. Slavin, S. Sharan, S. Kagan, R. Hertz-Lazarowitz, C. Webb, and R. Schmuck (Eds.), *Learning to Cooperate, Cooperating to Learn.* New York: Plenum Press, 1985.

————. *Using Student Team Learning.* Baltimore, Maryland: Johns Hopkins University, Center for Social Organization of Schools, 1978b.

————. When does cooperative learning increase student achievement? *Psychological Bulletin,* 1983b, *94*(3), 429-445.

————, and Oickle, E. Effects of learning teams on student achievement and race relations: Treatment by race interactions. *Sociology of Education,* 1981, *54,* 174-180.

Smith, K., Johnson, D. W., and Johnson, R. Can conflict be constructive? Controversy versus concurrence seeking in learning groups. *Journal of Educational Psychology,* 1981, *73,* 651-663.

————, ————, and ————. Effects of controversy on learning in cooperative groups. *Journal of Social Psychology,* 1984, *122,* 199-209.

————, ————, and ————. Effects of cooperative and individualistic instruction on the achievement of handicapped, regular, and gifted students. *The Journal of Science Psychology,* 1982, *116,* 277-282.

Stallings, J. Allocated academic learning time revisited, or beyond time on task. *Educational Researcher,* December 1980, 11-16.

Stebbins, L. B., St. Pierre, R. G., Proper, E. C., Anderson, R. B., and Cerva, T. R. *Education as Experimentation: A Planned Variation Model, IV-A, An Evaluation of Follow Through.* Cambridge, Massachusetts: Abt Associates, 1977.

Stein, A. H., and Friedrich, L. K. Television content and young children's behavior. In J. P. Murray, E. A. Rubinstein, and G. A. Comstock (Eds.), *Television and Social Behavior: II. Television and Social Learning.* Washington, D.C.: U.S. Government Printing Office, 1972.

Stephen, W. G. School desegregation: An evaluation of predications made in *Brown vs. Board of Education. Psychological Bulletin,* 1978, *85,* 217-238.

Steuer, F. B., Applefield, J. M., and Smith, R. Televised aggression and the interpersonal aggression of preschool children. *Journal of Experimental Child Psychology,* 1971, *11,* 442-447.

St. John, N. H. *School Desegregation: Outcomes for Children.* New York: Wiley, 1975.

Swain, M. *Communicative Competence: Some Roles of Comprehensible Input and Comprehensible Output in Its Development.* Paper presented at the Xth University of Michigan Conference on Applied Linguistics, University of Michigan, Ann Arbor, October 28-30, 1983.

United States Commission on Civil Rights. *Racial Isolation in the Public Schools: A Report.* Washington, D.C.: U.S. Government Printing Office, 1967.

_____. *The Unfinished Education* (Report II: Mexican American Education Study). Washington, D.C.: U.S. Government Printing Office, 1973.

United States Department of Commerce, Bureau of the Census. *National Data Book and Guide to Sources: Statistical Abstract of the United States 1985.* 105th edition. Washington, D.C.: U.S. Government Printing Office, 1984.

_____. *Population Profile of the United States: 1978, Population Characteristics* (Current Population Reports, Series P-20, No. 336). Washington, D.C.: U.S. Government Printing Office, April 1979.

Webb, N. M. A process-outcome analysis of learning in group and individual settings. *Educational Psychologist,* 1980b, *15,* 69-83.

_____. Group process: The key to learning in groups. *New Directions for Methodology of Social and Behavioral Science,* 1980a, *6,* 77-87.

Wheeler, R. *Predisposition toward Cooperation and Competition: Cooperative and Competitive Classroom Effects.* Paper presented at the meeting of the American Psychological Association, San Francisco, August 1977.

Wilcox, L. Differential socialization in the classroom: Implications for equal opportunity. In G. Spindler (Ed.), *Doing the Ethnography of Schooling: Educational Anthropology in Action.* New York: Holt, Rinehart and Winston, 1982.

Wirszup, I. The Soviet challenge. *Education Leadership,* 1981, *38,* 358-366.

Appendix 1

MAJOR COOPERATIVE LEARNING METHODS
PEER TUTORING

STAD

Student Teams-Achievement Divisions (STAD) has been described in detail by Slavin (1978b). There are five components of STAD, as follows:

Class presentations. Material to be learned is initially presented to the whole class by the teacher or in an audiovisual presentation.

Teams. Teams are composed of four or five students who are carefully selected to represent a cross-section of the class; the teams are as heterogeneous as possible with regard to the sex, ethnic background, and ability-level of students. The team members work together in a peer-tutoring format to master the material of the learning unit. Most often the team members quiz each other, working from worksheets that consist of problems and/or information to be mastered.

Quizzes. Students are evaluated via individual quizzes. The quizzes assess individual achievement on the material presented in the class and practiced in teams.

Individual improvement scores. A detailed scoring system allows students to earn points for their teams based on improvement over a running average of their past scores. The scoring system is based on a periodically readjusted "base score" for each student; each student earns points for his or her team based on improvement over past performance.

Team recognition. Teachers use newsletters, bulletin boards, or other forms of social recognition and rewards to teams for high individual weekly performance and/or high cumulative standings. Recognition is provided for individuals who perform exceptionally well or who are most improved.

TGT

Teams-Games-Tournaments (TGT) is identical to STAD except quizzes are replaced with academic game tournaments and individual improvement scores are replaced with a bumping system (Slavin, 1978b), as follows:

Game tournaments. Students play games in which they win points by demonstrating knowledge of the academic material that has been practiced in teams. The games have simple rules that allow students to take turns answering content-relevant questions. Students can earn extra points by correctly challenging the answer of another student. Students play the academic games at tournament tables consisting of three students of similar ability level. The highest scorer from each tournament table earns six points for his or her team; the middle scorer earns four points; and the lowest scorer earns two.

Bumping system. To ensure that students have an equal opportunity to earn points for their team, tournament tables are homogeneous with regard to ability level. Initially, the teacher assigns students to tournament tables; later, a bumping system reassigns students to tournament tables: Following each tournament, the highest scorer at each table advances to higher ability-level table and the lowest scorer moves to a lower ability-level table.

JIGSAW

Jigsaw I

The original Jigsaw method was developed to place students in situations of extreme interdependence. To do so, each student is provided with only part of the materials of an academic unit but is evaluated on how well he or she masters the whole unit. In a sense, each student of a learning team has but one piece of a jigsaw puzzle; the learning task for each student is to obtain the information from every piece of the puzzle. To do well, students have to learn the unique information possessed by each other member (See Aronson *et al.*, 1978; Aronson and Goode, 1980).   The elements of the original Jigsaw method include:

Specially designed curriculum materials. Curriculum materials are designed or rewritten so that each member of a learning team has a unique source that is comprehensible without reference to the other sources.

Team-building and communication training. Because communication among team members is an essential part of Jigsaw, special team-building and communication training activities are included to prepare students to cooperate and communicate in groups. Team building is extensive; it involves role-playing, brainstorming, and specially designed group activities.

Student group leader. During the extensive team building, the importance of a group leader is stressed. Group leaders are selected by the teacher; and they receive special training, including discussions and role-playing. The group leader is expected to help organize the group, keep the group on task, serve as group/teacher liaison, model productive social and academic behaviors, and help resolve conflicts.

Teams. Teams range in size from three to seven members, but five- or six-member teams are recommended. Students are assigned to teams so that the teams will be heterogeneous with regard to ability level, racial and sex characteristics, and personality factors such as assertiveness. Teachers are to use their knowledge and intuition in forming groups.

Expert groups. Each team member is assigned to an expert group composed of members of other teams who have been assigned the same expert topic. Students meet in expert groups to exchange information and master the material each student is to present to his or her team.

Individual assessment and reward. Students take individual tests or quizzes covering all the material of the learning unit; there is no group reward.

Jigsaw II

Jigsaw II was adapted from the original Jigsaw method to use existing curriculum materials and to take advantage of some of the features of STAD, which are not part of the original Jigsaw (Slavin, 1978b). The typical sequence of events in Jigsaw II is as follows: students are assigned to teams as in STAD; they are assigned to expert topics within teams; they read the whole learning unit, with emphasis on their expert topic; they meet in expert groups to discuss and master their topics; they report to their teams; they take an individual quiz that contributes to a team score; and they receive individual and team recognition. Jigsaw II differs from Jigsaw I in a number of important respects, including the following:

Use of existing curriculum materials and universal access. Because all students have access to all learning materials, interdependence among students is lessened. The use of existing curriculum materials, however, makes Jigsaw II practical and economical.

Use of STAD scoring and team recognition techniques. Jigsaw II uses base scores, improvement scores, team scores, and individual and team recognition techniques used in STAD, which are not part of the original Jigsaw. Also, Jigsaw II uses four-person teams, in contrast to the original Jigsaw, which usually uses five- or six-member teams. Teams in Jigsaw II are formed as in STAD and TGT; personality factors and teacher intuition are not part of the formula used to form teams.

Absence of team building and differentiated student roles. Unlike the original Jigsaw, Jigsaw II does not include team building and communication training, and no attempt is made to have students become differentiated with regard to their roles within teams; no team leader is appointed.

Jigsaw III

Jigsaw III, a cooperative/interdependent approach to bilingual education, was developed for the Hollister School District, California, as a Title VII demonstration program by Gonzalez and Guerrero (1983). The technique, in many respects, is similar to the original Jigsaw, but it contains some unique elements.

Similarities to original Jigsaw. Like the original Jigsaw approach, Jigsaw III includes variable team size (from three to six members), some teacher discretion in team formation, inclusion of differentiated student roles in teams, team building, and individual testing rather than group rewards.

Unique elements. Unique to Jigsaw III are elements adopted for use in bilingual classrooms. They include: bilingual group composition, bilingual learning materials, and extreme emphasis on team building. Groups are composed so that each group contains one English speaking, one non-English speaking, and one bilingual student. This structure was selected to force students to interact in mixed-language groups. Materials are specially designed for bilingual classes; the content lesson as well as all of the expert sheets, worksheets, and quizzes are bilingual.

Jigsaw III places a great emphasis on team building and activities designed to teach students the structure of Jigsaw. For example, there are not only team building activities but also transition team building activities that prepare students to participate in Jigsaw. Students also engage in "wrap up" following participation in Jigsaw and expert groups. During wrap up, students examine group processes and determine how they could behave to make the group work more effectively. For example, they evaluate whether they have allowed others to speak, listened well, had equal participation, and treated each other with kindness and respect. Through the wrap-up activities, students take responsibility for group process and learn prosocial interpersonal styles.

COOPERATIVE PROJECTS

Group Investigation

Group Investigation was designed to provide students with very broad and diverse learning experiences, quite in contrast to the STAD, TGT, and the Jigsaw techniques, which are oriented toward student acquisition of predetermined facts and skills. A detailed presentation of the philosophy and technique of Group Investigation has been presented by Sharan and Hertz-Lazarowitz (1979). The method requires coordination of four dimensions of classroom life: (1) the organization of the classroom into a "group of groups," (2) use of multifaceted learning tasks for cooperative group investigation, (3) inclusion of multilateral communication among pupils and active learning skills, and (4) teacher communication with and guidance of groups.

In Group Investigation, pupils progress through six consecutive stages, as follows:

Stage I: Identifying the topic and organizing pupils into research groups. Various techniques are used to have students identify and classify topics to form inquiry groups. Students join the group of their choice within the limits of forming three- to six-member groups. Ideally, groups are composed of pupils of both sexes with different abilities and from varying ethnic backgrounds. Although student choice of inquiry groups and ethnic and ability-level heterogenity within groups are sometimes initially inconsistent with goals, they are reconciled over time with discussion and active assistance of the teacher.

Stage II: Planning the learning task. Group members or pairs of group members determine subtopics for investigation. Tasks appropriate for group investigation pose problems that can be dealt with in a variety of ways; they are complex tasks, unlike the information and skill acquisition tasks toward which STAD and TGT are oriented. Groups decide what is to be studied, how it is to be studied, and determine the goal of their study.

Stage III: Carrying out the investigation. Students gather information, analyze and evaluate the data, and reach conclusions. Multilateral learning is stressed, which includes communication with collaborators, teacher, and other sources of information, including feedback loops among participants.

Stage IV: Preparing a final report. The group must engage in activities that culminate in a report, event, or summary. Organizing, abstracting, and synthesizing information are stressed. There is an opportunity for members of different groups to coordinate activities.

The steering committee, consisting of representatives of each group, meet and are active in coordinating time schedules, reviewing requests for resources, and ensuring that the ideas of the groups are realistic and interesting. The steering committee also makes sure that all pupils are involved and contributing to the group's work. Groups decide the content and method of their presentation.

Stage V: Presenting the final report. The final report may take various forms including exhibition, skit, debate, or report. Members of the class may participate in various reports. The presentation involves multilateral communication and interaction, and often a moving emotional experience.

Stage VI: Evaluation. Assessment of higher-level learning is emphasized, including applications, synthesis, and inferences. Affective experiences should be evaluated also, including level of motivation and involvement. Various forms of evaluation are possible. Teachers and pupils can collaborate on evaluation, including the formulation of exams. The steering committee may work with the teacher in selecting exam questions that are submitted by the groups.

Co-op Co-op

The essence of Co-op Co-op is structuring the classroom so that students work in cooperative teams toward a goal that will help the other students in the class. A detailed presentation of the philosophy and technique of Co-op Co-op is presented by Kagan (1985a). Like Group Investigation, Co-op Co-op is oriented toward complex, multifaceted learning tasks and student control of what and how to learn. There are important differences in the techniques, however, as Co-op Co-op involves a simpler classroom organization--there is no steering committee and little interrelation among groups.

There are ten steps to Co-op Co-op, as follows:
1. *Student-centered class discussion.* Initial experiences, including class discussion are designed to uncover and stimulate student curiosity.
2. *Selection of student learning teams.* As in STAD, this step usually is designed to maximize heterogenity within teams along the dimensions of ability level, sex, and ethnic background.
3. *Team-building.* As in the original Jigsaw, team building is incorporated to increase within-team cooperation and communication skills.
4. *Team-topic selection.* Students divide the learning unit into topics so that each team is responsible for one aspect of the learning unit and the work of teams will complement each other in moving the whole class toward mastery of the learning unit.
5. *Mini-topic selection.* As in Jigsaw, each student becomes an expert in one aspect of the team learning goal; unlike Jigsaw, students determine how to divide the topic, and mini-topics are selected by students rather than assigned by the teacher.
6. *Mini-topic preparation.* Students individually gather and organize materials on their mini-topics.
7. *Mini-topic presentations.* As in Jigsaw, each student presents to the group what they have learned on their individual topic. A second round of mini-topic presentations follows an opportunity to respond to the group's discussion of each individual mini-topic and its relation to the whole topic.
8. *Preparation of team presentations.* Teams prepare a presentation to the whole class of what they have learned on their team topic.
9. *Team presentations.* Presentations are made to the whole class. Non-lecture presentations such as demonstrations, role-plays, and use of audiovisual media are preferred.
10. *Evaluation.* Evaluation is made of individual mini-topic presentations to the team (usually by teammates), team presentations to the whole class (usually by classmates), and an individual paper or project by each student on his or her mini-topic (usually by teacher).

COOPERATIVE/INDIVIDUALIZED

TAI

Team Assisted Individualization (TAI) was designed to create a happy marriage between cooperative and individualized learning methods. TAI relies on group support to encourage progress through carefully designed individualized learning modules. Because the team score is based on how many individual learning modules are completed by the team members, they provide support for individual achievement. There are some elements of peer tutoring that are incorporated in TAI: Team members are instructed to turn to their teammates for help. However, because the individual learning modules are designed to be as self-explanatory as possible, and because teammates are usually working at quite different levels, cooperative interaction is held to a minimum. At present, TAI is available for math for grades one through six, but math materials are being extended for middle-level schools. A TAI reading program was developed by Robert Slavin and his associates at Johns Hopkins University. A full description of TAI, including a review of the research on the method has been provided by Slavin (1985).

COOPERATIVE INTERACTION

Finding Out/Descubrimiento

The Descubrimiento method developed by DeAvila (Cohen *et al.*, 1981) consists of 170 different math/science activities used over 14 weeks. Twelve activities are scheduled per week; the activities are designed to teach thinking skills such as hypothesizing, describing, constructing, measuring, examining, inquiring, comparing, experimenting, and drawing conclusions. The activities each week are on a theme such as measurement, optics, electricity, or water; they provide numerous redundant opportunities to experience the same underlying concept. For example, if the unit is on probability, students may graph the height of a bouncing ball, the frequency of outcomes on a flipped coin, and the frequency of outcomes of spinning a polysided object.

The classroom in the Finding Out/Descubrimiento method is organized around multiple-learning centers that operate simultaneously. There is an initial bilingual activity panel that presents the instruction of a task. For about 90 percent of the tasks, students must complete a worksheet before the activity to demonstrate comprehension. Students are expected to ask for and give help to their group mates. The groups are heterogeneous with regard to language background. Following the activity, students fill out individual worksheets to demonstrate competency. The method also relies on content-referenced, individual mini-tests and teacher observation forms to assess implementation of the program.

Although students individually write up each learning activity and receive individual grades, the activities are group-paced and involve cooperative interaction. For example, a group cannot work with the materials at a learning center until all the group members understand what is to be done. Peer norms for giving and receiving help are an integral part of the approach. Further, a number of the activities demand cooperative interaction for completion. For example, while one student drops a ball, another charts the height of its bounce.

Rotating individual roles within teams are an additional feature of the Descubrimiento method. At a given learning center one team member may be the safety officer, one the facilitator, another the checker, and yet another in charge of clean up.

The Descubrimiento method, like Jigsaw III, was designed to be used in bilingual/bicultural classrooms. All materials are in English and Spanish, and bilingual students serve as translators for monolingual students within groups.

Appendix 2

COOPERATIVE LEARNING RESOURCES

1. Theory and Introduction

Dewey, J. *Experience and Education.* New York: Macmillian, 1957.

Johnson, D. and Johnson, R. *Learning Together and Alone: Cooperation, Competition, and Individualization.* Englewood Cliffs, New Jersey: Prentice Hall, 1975.

Kagan, S. The dimensions of cooperative classroom structures. In R. Slavin, S. Sharan, S. Kagan, R. Hertz-Lazarowitz, C. Webb, and R. Schmuck (Eds.), *Learning to Cooperate, Cooperating to Learn.* New York: Plenum, 1985.

Schmuck, R. A. and Schmuck, P. A. *Group Processes in the Classroom.* Dubuque, Iowa: William C. Brown, 1983.

Sharan, S., Hare, P., Webb, C. D., and Hertz-Lazarowitz, R. (Eds.), *Cooperation in Education.* Provo, Utah: Brigham Young University Press, 1980.

_____, and Sharan, Y. *Small-group Teaching.* Englewood Cliffs, New Jersey: Educational Technology Publications, 1976.

2. Classroom Teaching Methods

Aronson, E., Blaney, N., Stephan, C., Sikes, J., and Snapp, M. *The Jigsaw Classroom.* Beverly Hills, California: Sage, 1978.

————, and Goode, E. Training teachers to implement jigsaw learning: A manual for teachers. In S. Sharan, P. Hare, C. D. Webb, and R. Hertz-Lazarowitz (Eds.), *Cooperation in Education*. Provo, Utah: Brigham Young University Press, 1980.

Caplan, R. and Keech, C. *Showing Writing: A Training Program to Help Students to Be Specific*. Berkeley, California: Bay Area Writing Project, University of California, Berkeley, 1980.

Dishon, D. and O'Leary, P. W. *A Guidebook for Cooperative Learning: A Technique for Creating More Effective Schools*. Holmes Beach, Florida: Learning Publications, Inc., 1985.

Gartner, A., Kohnler, M. C., and Riessman, F. *Children Teach Children: Learning by Teaching*. New York: Harper & Row; 1971.

Healey, M. K. *Using Student Response Groups in the Classroom*. Berkeley, California: Bay Area Writing Project, University of California, Berkeley, 1980

Johnson, D. W. and Johnson, R. T., Holubec, E. J., and Roy, P. *Circles of Learning*. Alexandria, Virginia: Association for Supervision and Curriculum Development, 1984.

Johnson, R. T. and Johnson, D. W. (Eds.). *Structuring Cooperative Learning: Lesson Plans for Teachers*. Minneapolis, Minnesota: Interaction Book Company, 1984.

Kagan, S. Co-op Co-op: A flexible cooperative learning technique. In R. Slavin, S. Sharan, S. Kagan, R. Hertz-Lazarowitz, C. Webb, and R. Schmuck (Eds.), *Learning to Cooperate, Cooperating to Learn*. New York: Plenum, 1985.

Poirier, Gerrard A. *Students as Partners in Team Learning*. Berkeley, California: Center of Team Learning, 1970.

Sharan, S. and Hertz-Lazarowitz, R. A group-investigation method of cooperative learning in the classroom. In S. Sharan, P. Hare, C. D. Webb, and R. Hertz-Lazarowitz (Eds.), *Cooperation in Education*. Provo, Utah: Brigham Young University Press, 1980.

Slavin, R. E. Student team learning: A manual for teachers. In S. Sharan, P. Hare, C. D. Webb, and R. Hertz-Lazarowitz (Eds.), *Cooperation in Education*. Provo, Utah: Brigham Young University Press, 1980.

————. Team-assisted individualization: Combining cooperative learning and individualized instruction in mathematics. In R. Slavin, S. Sharan, S. Kagan, R. Hertz-Lazarowitz, C. Webb, and R. Schmuck (Eds.). *Learning to Cooperate, Cooperating to Learn*. New York: Plenum, 1985.

Stein, S. K. and Crabill, C. D. *Elementary Algebra. A Guided Inquiry.* Boston, Massachusetts: Houghton Mifflin, 1972.

Weissglass, J. *Exploring Elementary Mathematics: A Small-group Approach for Teaching.* San Francisco, California: W. H. Freeman, 1979.

3. Team Building, Class Environment, and Group Processes

Co-operative College of Canada. *Co-operative Outlooks.* Saskatoon, Saskatchewan: Co-operative College of Canada, 1980.

Gibbs, J. and Allen, A. *Tribes: A Process for Peer Involvement.* Oakland, California: Center-Source Publications, 1978.

Glassman, M., Kisiow, E., Good, L., O'Connor, M., Alderson, I., and Kutz, S. *Cooperation and Community Life.* Saskatoon, Saskatchewan: Co-operative College of Canada, 1980.

Graves, N. B. and Graves, T. D. Creating a cooperative learning environment: A ecological approach. In R. Slavin, S. Sharan, S. Kagan, R. Hertz-Lazarowitz, C. Webb, and R. Schmuck (Eds.), *Learning to Cooperate, Cooperating to Learn.* New York: Plenum, 1985.

Hill, W. F. *Learning Through Discussion: Guide for Leaders and Members of Discussion Groups.* Beverly Hills, California: Sage Publications, 1977.

Johnson, D. W. and Johnson, F. P. *Joining Together: Group Theory and Group Skills.* Englewood Cliffs, New Jersey: Prentice Hall, 1975.

Moorman, C. and Dishon, D. *Our Classroom: We Can Learn Together.* Englewood Cliffs, New Jersey: Prentice Hall, 1983.

Prutzman, P. *The Friendly Classroom for a Small Planet.* Wayne, New Jersey: Avery Publishing Group, Inc. 1978.

Raths, L. E., Harmin, M., and Simon, S. B. *Values and Teaching: Working with Values.* Columbus, Ohio: Charles E. Merrill, 1966.

Schmuck, R. A. and Schmuck, P. A. *Group Processes in the Classroom.* Dubuque, Iowa: William C. Brown Co., 1983.

Saskatchewan Department of Co-operation and Co-operative Development. *Working Together, Learning Together.* Saskatoon, Saskatchewan: The Stewart Resource Center, 1983.

Simon, S. B., Howe, L. W., and Kirschenbaum, H. *Values Clarification: A Handbook of Practical Strategies for Teachers and Students.* New York: Hart Publishing Co., Inc., 1972.

Stanford, G. *Developing Effective Classroom Groups.* New York: Hart Publishing, 1977.

_____. *Learning Discussion Skills Through Games.* New York: Citation Press, 1969.

Vacha, E. F. *Improving Classroom Social Climate.* Orcutt, California: Orcutt Union School District, 1977.

4. Cooperative Sports, Games, and Activity

Animal Town Game Company. *The Animal Town Game Company Catalog of Board Games.* Santa Barbara, California: Animal Town Game Company, 1984.

Deacove, J. *Cooperative Games Manual.* Perth, Ontario, Canada: Family Pastimes, 1974.

_____. *Sports Manual of Co-operative Recreation.* Perth, Ontario, Canada: Family Pastimes, 1974.

Family Pastimes. *Family Pastimes Catalog of Cooperative Games.* Perth, Ontario, Canada: Family Pastimes, 1985.

Fluegelman, A. (Ed.). *The New Games Book.* New York: Dolphin/Doubleday, 1976.

Harrison, M. *For the Fun of It! Selected Cooperative Games for Children and Adults.* Philadelphia, Pennsylvania: Philadelphia Yearly Meeting of the Religious Society of Friends, 1975.

Lentz, T. F. and Cornelius, R. *All Together. A Manual of Cooperative Games.* St. Louis, Missouri: Character Research Association/Peace Research Laboratory, 1950.

Michaelis, B. and Michaelis, D. *Learning Through Noncompetitive Activities and Play.* Palo Alto, California: Learning Handbooks, Pitman Learning, 1977.

Orlick, T. *Every Kid Can Win.* Chicago, Illinois: Nelson Hall Publishers, 1975.

_____. *The Cooperative Sports & Games Book: Challenge Without Competition.* New York: Pantheon, 1978.

_____. *The Second Cooperative Sports and Games Book.* New York: Pantheon, 1982.

_____. *Winning Through Cooperation: Competitive Insanity; Cooperative Alternatives.* Washington, D.C.: Hawkins & Associates Publishers, 1977.

Sobel, J. *Everybody Wins: 393 Non-competitive Games for Young Children.* New York: Walker, 1983.

Weinstein, M. and Goodman, J. *Playfair: Everybody's Guide to Noncompetitive Play.* San Luis Obispo, California: Impact, 1980.

5. Cooperative School-Wide Organization

Neale, D. C., Bailey, W. J., and Ross, B. E. *Strategies for School Improvement: Cooperative Planning and Organization Development.* Boston, Massachusetts: Allyn & Bacon, Inc., 1981.

Schmuck, R. A. Students as organizational coparticipants. In S. Sharan, P. Hare, C. D. Webb, & R. Hertz-Lazarowitz (Eds.), *Cooperation in Education.* Provo, Utah: Brigham Young University Press, 1980.

_____, Chesler, M., and Lippit, R. *Problem Solving to Improve Classroom Learning.* Chicago, Illinois: Science Research Associates, 1966.

_____, and Schmuck, P. A. *A Humanistic Psychology on Education. Making School Everybody's House.* Palo Alto, California: Mayfield Publishing, 1974.

Schwartz, M. N., Steefel, Q., and Schmuck, R. A. *The Development of Educational Teams.* Eugene, Oregon: Center for Educational Policy and Management, 1976.

Wynn, R. and Guditus, C. W. *Team Management: Leadership by Consensus.* Columbus, Ohio: Charles E. Merril Publishing, 1984.

6. Research Reviews and Overviews

Graves, N. B. and Graves, T. D. The cultural context of prosocial development: An ecological model. In D. Bridgeman (Ed.), *The Nature of Prosocial Development: Interdiciplinary Theories and Strategies.* New York: Academic Press, 1983.

Johnson, D. W., Johnson, R., and Maruyama, G. Interdependence and interpersonal attraction among heterogeneous and homogeneous individuals: A theoretical formulation and a meta-analysis of the research. *Review of Educational Research,* 1983, *53,* 5-54.

_____, Maruyama, G., Johnson, R., Nelson, D., and Skon, L. Effects of cooperative, competitive and individualistic goal sructures on achievement: A meta-analysis. *Psychological Bulletin,* 1981, *89,* 47-62.

Kagan, S., Zahn, G. L., Widaman, K. F., Schwarzwald, J., and Tyrrell, G. Classroom structural bias: Impact of cooperative and competitive classroom structures on cooperative and competitive individuals and groups. In R. E. Slavin, S. Sharan, S. Kagan, R. Hertz-Lazarowitz, C. Webb, and R. Schmuck (Eds.), *Learning to Cooperate, Cooperating to Learn.* New York: Plenum, 1985.

Sharan, S. Cooperative learning in small groups: Recent methods and effects on achievement, attitudes, and ethnic relations. *Review of Educational Research,* 1980, *50,* 241-271.

_____, Kussell, P., Hertz-Lazarowitz, R., Bejarano, Y., Raviv, S., and Sharan, Y. *Cooperative Learning in the Classroom: Research in Desegregated Schools.* New York: Erlbaum, 1984.

Slavin, R. E. Cooperative learning. *Review of Educational Research,* 1980, *50,* 315-342.

_____. *Cooperative Learning.* New York: Longman, 1983.

_____. When does cooperative learning increase student achievement? *Psychological Bulletin,* 1983, *94,* 429-445.

_____, Sharan, S. Kagan, S., Hertz-Lazarowitz, R. Webb, C., and Schmuck, R. (Eds.). *Learning to Cooperate, Cooperating to Learn.* New York: Plenum, 1985.

EDUCATORS' RESPONSES TO SOCIOCULTURAL DIVERSITY: IMPLICATIONS FOR PRACTICE

Mary McGroarty

University of California, Los Angeles

ANOTHER EDUCATIONAL CRITIQUE?

Before reading this book, educators and members of the public interested in education may well ask why there is a need for yet another volume on the problem areas in American education. Already more than enough reports and recommendations have been published to direct those who wish to improve the nation's schools; can this volume add any new information or insights to the debates on education? Two major reports on education are *A Nation At Risk* (National Commission on Excellence in Education, 1983) and *High School: A Report on Secondary Education in America* (Boyer, 1983). (For a full list of the numerous monographs and books on education produced, see "Symposium on the Year of the Reports," 1984 and Gross and Gross, 1985.) California, too, has sounded the call for reform in *Raising Expectations* (California State Department of Education, 1983). From the many recommendations made, educators are still trying to select those that suit their circumstances. Should we not simply allow the educational system some time to absorb the deluge of information and formulate solutions to the problems identified in the reports?

Of course, educators must address the issues identified in the national reports. However, merely selecting recommendations for improvement from the many lists available will not provide California with optimal opportunities to make education more effective for all students and teachers. There is nothing wrong with the laudable aims of all the reports mentioned; nevertheless, all of them are, in important ways, incomplete. They are incomplete because they neglect the sociocultural influences that, along with traditional matters of curricular offerings and time available for instruction, affect educational outcomes for students.

The suggestions of the editorial team of the Bilingual Education Office under the coordination of Daniel D. Holt and the field reviewers have been extremely helpful, and I am grateful for the constructive criticism of the many individuals who offered comments on this chapter.

Strengthening curricular offerings and increasing the amount of time available for instruction are indeed reasonable means of improving education. Their potential impact, though, is mediated by the local circumstances in which they are applied; these circumstances are shaped in fundamental ways by the sociocultural influences that permeate the educational process. These influences are the central topic of this volume. Described from several different disciplinary perspectives-- historical, sociological, linguistic, anthropological, and psychological-- sociocultural influences interact with the usual content and structure of school learning to create differential outcomes for different groups of students (Cicourel and Mehan, 1984). If educators are both aware of these influences and willing to modify current practices, they will be better able to serve the ever more diverse students enrolled in California classrooms more effectively.

Dealing effectively with diversity is the key to California's educational future. In the introductory chapter to this volume, Carlos Cortés documents the changing composition of the students in California schools. Using demographic data, he shows that the proportion of students who are members of linguistic or cultural minority group members will grow rapidly in the next decades. At the same time, his work and that of the other contributors to this book, notably Stanley Sue and Amado Padilla, John Ogbu and Maria Matute-Bianchi, and Spencer Kagan, provide convincing documentation of the relative lack of success that students from minority groups have experienced in school (see also Carter and Segura, 1977). Clearly, then, school personnel must consider the provision of some new approaches to learning if they are to reach students who have not been well served in schools. Moreover, the diversity characterizing California schools affects all participants, all students and teachers, not just those who are members of linguistic and cultural minority groups. Growing diversity means that all parties involved in education will often interact with people unlike themselves, both during instruction and in other school-related activities. New methods that enhance learning by taking diversity into account are, thus, in order.

The information in this volume will help educators interested in devising some new approaches to learning. These new approaches should be viewed as complementary to the recommendations for reform offered in the other reports. The current prescriptions for reform make traditional recommendations for improving the school experience of students. Among them are: requiring students to take a more rigorous--

that is, more structured--program of study with fewer electives and more required courses in English, mathematics, science, social studies, and foreign language; demanding more, and more frequent, assessment of formal skills possessed by students (and sometimes by teachers); emphasizing writing skills by calling attention to the need for more frequent composition practice; and asserting that all students, even those not bound for additional formal education after high school, need such skills. (See United States Department of Education, 1984 for a state-by-state list.) These valuable and often very detailed recommendations address issues that are narrowly related to the usual domain of schooling: the subjects required of students and the time that should be allocated to them. Furthermore, many reports are limited to the secondary level of education. Consideration of the subjects to be studied, the time devoted to them, and the methods to be used in assessing them plays a part in educational reform, but only a part: Equally critical is the ability of educators to provide these useful areas of learning to the many different types of students enrolled in school (Levin, 1985; Resnick and Resnick, 1985; Alexander and Pallas, 1984). This volume shows that, by understanding cultural influences on education and the context of instruction and shaping educational experiences accordingly, educators have a much greater chance of developing the knowledge and skills specified in the critiques of education in all the students in their charge.

WHAT CULTURE MEANS TO SCHOOLING

We will discuss the implications of the chapters included here for all those involved in the educational system: parents and students, teachers, resource teachers and trainers, and administrators. The main audience is teachers, resource teachers, and administrators since it is their professional reponsibility to provide formal instruction for students. Yet, as those concerned with contextual influences on education hold, and as anthropologists and psychologists have observed for some time, a great deal of learning and teaching is done in informal, out-of-school situations (Rogoff and Lave, 1984). Thus, we cannot ignore such situations in discussing the educational implications of the chapters in this book. The notion that culture and context, both of them dynamic and subject to change over time, affect educational outcomes is a powerful one; it motivates all the work contained here. This notion means different things for different parties to the educational contract. Some of these implications follow directly from the scholarship included here. Indeed, some of these chapters such as those by Shirley Brice Heath; by Stephen Díaz, Luis Moll, and Hugh Mehan; and by Spencer Kagan, are directly concerned with the interpersonal processes that mediate instruction in and outside of classrooms; these chapters speak directly to possible changes in educational practice. The other chapters, those by Stanley Sue and Amado Padilla and by John Ogbu and Maria Matute-Bianchi, offer more global insights into the educational experiences of minority groups. They also imply certain changes in our understanding of education, though not always as directly as the other chapters. Whether focused at the micro-level of classroom interaction or the macro-level of societal power relationships, all the chapters suggest some changes in the role definitions and actual behaviors of educators that must occur if all students, including language minority students, are to be well served in school (Cummins, 1985).

A common thread linking all the chapters in this book is the notion that cultural and social factors play a critical role in education. These are not the only influences that could be mentioned; economic and political considerations also figure in education, and they are, in fact, described in the Cortés chapter and in the analysis presented by Ogbu and Matute-Bianchi. However, the main thrust of the book is the description of the sociocultural influences that have shaped the experiences of diverse cultural groups in California's classrooms and the presentation of some guidelines for improving the academic and social outcomes of education for students and teachers alike.

Education as an Expression of Cultural Values

Let us briefly review the case for careful attention to cultural and social-interactional influences on educational processes and outcomes. The indissoluble relationship between education and culture has been axiomatic in many academic disciplines as well as in the experiences of educators themselves. Philosophers and social scientists have emphasized the central role of values, the ideals of a culture, in education. In the words of educational philosophers, education "is more especially a value-realizing institution than is any other institution with the exception of religion" (Butler, 1970, p. 58). "The school, ideally, is a setting in which values, beliefs, and opinions can be examined both critically and appreciatively" (Noddings, 1984, p. 184). This position, echoed in the analyses of schooling presented by Cortés, Ogbu and Matute-Bianchi, and Kagan, holds that schools reflect, impart, and contribute to the values of the society at large. One of the ways they do this is through the variety of social structures used to provide education, structures that usually reflect a society's dominant values, according to many critics (see, for example, Anyon, 1981; Apple, 1979; and Bowles and Gintis, 1976), and often do not accommodate the experiences of students from cultural, class, or ethnic minority groups. These educational structures allow students to learn the norms that embody prevailing social and cultural values. Sociologist Robert Dreeben noted "the social experiences available to pupils in schools, by virtue of the nature and sequence of their structural arrangements, provide opportunities for children to learn norms characteristic of several aspects of adult life" (1968, p. 65). Education is aimed at teaching students the skills and behaviors valued in their society; it is, thus, a form of cultural transmission, which has been the dominant model in educational anthropology for decades (Spindler, 1982). Anthropologist George Spindler pointed out that "we must study cultural transmission if we are to study education" (1982, p. 312). Those who wish to understand education need to understand the cultural and interactional patterns shaping the process.

The chapters included here reveal the necessity of knowing the students' cultures, particularly as these cultures affect interaction in school. Such knowledge is seen as a key to understanding. This point of view echoes Ruth Benedict's classic statement of the importance of culture in individual development:

> *The life-history of the individual is first and foremost an accommodation to the patterns and standards traditionally handed down in his community. By the time he can talk, he is the little creature of his culture, and by the time he is grown and able to take part in its activities, its habits are his habits, its beliefs his beliefs, its impossibilities his impossibilities. (1934, pp. 2-3)*

The cultural background of an individual is an essential aspect of personal identity that directs all interactions, including those with the formal educational system. If the culture of student is significantly different from that reflected in the educational system, one of the explanations for school failure discussed by Sue and Padilla, we may expect conflict to ensue. The consequences of conflicts between the cultural norms of a group and the expectations embodied in the American educational system have been varied. By themselves, such conflicts do not always condemn students to decreased earnings or other adverse consequences;

local economic conditions and other historical patterns make a difference, as Steinberg's work (1981) showed. Nevertheless, as successful completion of the formal educational system becomes a more common prerequisite for later advancement, it becomes more important to know how cultural discontinuities between groups of students and mainstream educational institutions can be bridged successfully.

Organizational Constraints of School Culture

Even when the culture of the child matches that of most adults in the school system, another aspect of culture figures in the discussions here: that is, the organizational culture of the school, the possibilities and constraints peculiar to educational settings. This aspect of culture is not directly addressed in the chapters here, although those by Ogbu and Matute-Bianchi, Heath, and Kagan allude to its importance. As remarked by many careful observers of schooling (see, Cuban, 1984a, 1984b; Sarason, 1971; and Jackson, 1968), educational institutions have their own internal logic and preferred modes of action that shape events. This theme was reiterated in Goodlad's study of 1,000 classrooms in 38 American schools (Goodlad, 1984). The highly variable development of each individual within a cultural group and the institutional constraints on educational activity may mean that conflicts between children, even children from a majority group background, and school demands will occur as students progress through the grades. Individual differences cannot always be accommodated by the entrenched regularities of school life (Wang and Lindvall, 1984); cultural differences, too (systematic differences that, to one degree or another, characterize many members of a cultural group), pose a further challenge to educational arrangements.

Hence, both the culture of the students and the culture of the school are important in understanding the educational experience of an individual or a group. Nevertheless, a focus on cultural identity may lead to inaccurate interpretations; stereotyped interpretations, and stereotyped educational recommendatons, may then develop. The study of cultural differences demands both courage and caution of those who seek to use this knowledge for the improvement of education. As remarked by linguist Lily Wong Fillmore:

> ...while I regard the question of cultural influences on learning--especially on language--as an important one for us to consider, it is one that I approach with a good deal of caution and trepidation. Such considerations all too easily become the basis for creating stereotypes, and for misjudging the complexity of learning problems. (1981, p. 24)

The study of cultural influence on educational outcomes proposed in this volume rests on a paradox: By learning more about groups of students and mastering methods suitable for many different groups, majority and minority group students, we become more capable of teaching individual students well. Knowing more about systematic differences related to student background and modes of behavior and adopting a variety of instructional strategies are effective pedagogical responses to cultural diversity. Teachers need to be able to use knowledge of culture judiciously in order not to stereotype students but to serve them better; this means using cultural knowledge in conjunction with other types of information related to the content and skills to be taught and individual student preferences and personalities to promote learning.

THE INTERACTIONAL DIMENSION: CONTEXTS FOR BEHAVIOR

Knowledge of culture alone will not provide educators with sufficient knowledge to understand and modify school-related behavior. Equally important, the authors of these chapters imply, and equally applicable to all students (those who are members of linguistic or cultural minority groups and those who are not) is a thorough grasp of the contextual influences on behavior, both linguistic behavior and other kinds of actions. In most current social science models, contextual influences are conceptualized as reciprocal, involving dynamic accommodation between persons and circumstances or elements within a system, rather than unidirectional (James *et al.,* 1982). The scholarship from various disciplines included in this book fits this pattern in its emphasis on interaction.

Contexts for skill acquisition change according to physical, temporal, and social conditions, as the Cortés chapter notes. For example, scholars concerned with definitions of linguistic competence have noted that, until recently, "little attention has been given to the role of specific acquisition contexts in determining the interrelationships and development of different aspects of communicative competence" (Cummins, 1981, p. 8); however, theories of first- (Nelson *et al.,* 1985; John-Steiner and Tatter, 1983; Bates and MacWhinney, 1982; Snow, 1977) and second-language acquisition (Hatch, 1983b; Long and Sato, 1984) both emphasize the interactive nature of the operative processes: Interaction creates the opportunity for language and shapes its use. Research like that of Heath (this volume; 1982a; 1982b, 1983b), Wells (1981, 1985), Maynard (1985) Mehan (1979, 1984), and Díaz *et al.* (this volume) helps educators see how children learn and demonstrate different kinds of linguistic behavior according to the interactions, socialization patterns, and educational contexts they experience. Contexts affect pedagogy, an issue Richards (1985) discussed with reference to second language teaching and one that merits exploration in other curricular areas as well. In this volume, Díaz *et al.* use an interactionist approach, an approach emphasizing the reciprocal demands of setting and participants on each other, to explore culturally appropriate provision of reading and writing instruction. In all these situations, it is clear that student behavior both within and across ethnic groups varies according to the setting. Furthermore, contexts themselves change over time: American classrooms of the 1980s were both similar to (Cuban, 1984a) and different from their counterparts of the 1930s (Tyack *et al.,* 1984). The importance of local and historical context is part of the intellectual base of ethnography, the continuous, repeated observational technique that has yielded many of the insights included in these two chapters.

The definition of context relevant here includes the physical, temporal, and social-psychological aspects of any human situation; it encompasses the roles played by the participants, the expectations they have of each other (as in the Ogbu and Matute-Bianchi chapter), the purposes for which they interact and the language used to accomplish the interaction (see the Díaz *et al.* chapter), and the personal histories and cultural resources they bring to individual and group interaction, described at different levels of analysis by Sue and Padilla and Heath. Like much work in all the social sciences, the concept of context employed in these papers reflects attention to participants' interpretations of events as well as descriptions of their actions and raises the additional questions of the accuracy and adequacy of any observer's interpretation of social interaction (Geertz, 1983). The different definitions of context that inform the work of all the authors in this volume (see also Erickson and Shultz, 1981) attest to the multiplicity of factors bearing on all behavior, including the educational behavior that is the focus of this book.

Contextual influences affect all participants. Spindler explained, "The ethnographic world view also holds that all behaviors occur in contexts, and that not only do contexts continuously change, but people change with contexts" (1982, p. 491). It is, thus, not enough to know about the general tendencies labeled cultural differences in behavior; we also need to know how these tendencies change according to different situations, how individuals respond to different circumstances according to cultural predispositions; in other words, we need to know how cultures create and construe contexts. This dynamic aspect of behavior is also an integral part of culture; another definition of culture emphasizes that "culture is process...it involves a series of actions and operations that are cyclical and repetitive" (Arvizu *et al.*, 1980, p. 6). The work of Heath and Díaz *et al.* in this volume illustrates some of the contextual influences on language acquisition and development in and out of school settings. Kagan's work illuminates the social structures that create competition of cooperative learning environments. Examining the larger social context of historical and contemporary relationships between minority and majority group members, Ogbu and Matute-Bianchi analyze interactions between different cultural groups that have shaped the nature of the educational experience available to students who are members of those groups.

The aim of this volume is to shed light on the sociocultural factors that shape educational experiences, to get at "the knowledge participants (students teachers, principals, mothers, fathers, friends...) use to guide their behavior in the various social settings they participate in" (Spindler, 1982, p. 5). The book as a whole draws attention to the dynamic contextual influences on educational behavior as they are constructed and sustained by the cultural and linguistic characteristics of those involved. The authors describe many types of sociocultural influences--a group's past history, own in-group interpretation of that history, typical patterns of linguistic socialization, and preferred modes of learning--that affect educational outcomes. While there are differences in the approach used for each chapter and the level of specific attention to educational issues, all the chapters illustrate sociocultural influences on the educational process. As Cortés and Ogbu and Matute-Bianchi point out, the problem of differential outcomes in schooling for members of some language minority groups is not limited to California or to the United States; it has been observed in many countries. (See Cziko and Troike, 1984; Skutnabb-Kangas, 1984; and Paulston, 1980 for considerations of bilingual issues in several settings around the world.) In the first chapter of the book, Cortés shows how each chapter offers a different perspective on the sociocultural factors which influence education and consequently suggests a different response or set of responses for educators. In this chapter, we will direct our attention to that latter issue to see what these chapters mean for different groups concerned with education. Each of these chapters implies different courses of action for the parents, teachers, and administrators wishing to make schools more effective for diverse groups of students; it is to these courses of action that we now turn.

IMPLICATIONS FOR PARENTS: THE PRIMARY EDUCATORS

The chapters included here imply several kinds of activity for parents who are concerned about the progress of their own children and other children who share their cultural identity.   While teachers and administrators cannot presume to tell parents how to raise their children, as Heath (this volume) observes, they can still offer some suggestions to parents who want to make schools more responsive to cultural diversity. Also, parents can take steps toward building the skills needed by their children and those needed by school personnel to build the foundations for positive educational experiences. The authors show some ways of accomplishing these goals; we will now set out their recommendations.

Becoming Aware of Their Own Beliefs

Ogbu and Matute-Bianchi suggest that parents need to be aware of their own ideas about status mobility, or "folk beliefs about making it" to see what these beliefs mean in terms of the behavior promoted in children. Of particular importance is the orientation toward school success that parents support.   These authors see differences between the minority groups they call "caste-like" and "non-caste-like"; while these labels are grounded in historical experiences, they also include different kinds of parental support for both the ends and the means required for success in school.   As Sue and Padilla point out, minority parents, like majority parents, universally desire their children to be successful in school, although they may not be aware of the means required to promote educational progress in mainstream terms. In contrast, Ogbu and Matute-Bianchi imply that different minority groups may have different conceptions and expectations about educational success; these differing conceptions of success may transmit different kinds of messages to children. In either case, the matter of parental beliefs about education and the kinds of behavior that come about because of these beliefs is an issue. Parents need to understand what they mean by success, the kind of student and parent behavior required for it, and the ways to help children attain it.

Building Children's Language Skills

Among the activities parents can undertake are building the children's verbal skills and exposing them to a variety of situations that demand that the children learn to make their meanings explicit. The Heath chapter (this volume) suggests some activities for accomplishing these goals. As Heath notes, it is important that children master the ability to provide labels, tell stories, give accounts of events, and provide clear in-structions; they can learn these in any language if they are given the chance to do so and encouraged to practice. Parents can provide much of this learning if they are willing to spend the time needed to supply the "redundant, reiterative, and interdependent occasions for practice." This will help children learn to "negotiate meaning" through language (Wells, 1981), an ability needed in school settings.

It is important to note that verbal skills can be developed in the parents' first language as well as in English; the choice of which language to speak is less important than the uses to which that language is put. If parents speak a language other than English, they should know that maintenance and development of the first language can provide children with benefits such as the cognitive flexibility associated with well-developed bilingualism (Cummins, 1981; Kessler and Quinn, 1980; Ben-Zeev, 1977; for a more comprehensive review, see Hakuta, 1985 and Díaz, 1983). Dolson (1985) found that, in the Los Angeles area, children from Spanish-speaking homes where the use of Spanish was maintained showed consistently better academic achievement than similar children whose families made no attempt to retain Spanish. Moreover, as Cummins remarked (1984), parents who are fluent in their native language but not comfortable in English and nevertheless decide to use only English with their children may unwittingly lessen "quantity and quality of adult-child interaction" (p. 272). The frequency and variety of parent-child interaction, not the language chosen for the interaction, is central to the children's academic development, as Heath's work (this volume; 1982a; 1983b) implies. Language skills of potential academic value can be built in any language.

Besides building oral language skills, parents can show children how other language-related activities fit into their lives. Perhaps parents write letters to friends and family members; almost certainly, they use various types of functional writing skills to make lists, pay bills, take messages, or help students with their homework, like the parents in the junior high schools studied by Díaz et al. (this volume). Through the example of parents and other caregivers, children can come to see writing as a natural part of many transactions at home and in the community. Parents can encourage students to assist them in functional writing tasks and to write their own lists, letters, or stories as soon as they can. Reading, too, is interwoven in home and community activities even more than writing. Parents can read to children, support children's reading competence by asking them to read signs, labels, maps, and more extended texts when appropriate, and, as children grow older, include them in public activities such as operating a business or participating in religious exercises that require reading and writing (Heath, this volume; 1983b; Trueba, 1984).

In reading, as in oral language development, lack of fluency in English is no barrier to parent participation; a research team in England found that having children read to their parents, even if the parents did not speak or read English, improved the children's reading skills significantly (Tizard *et al.,* 1982). All these activities do not always translate directly into school applications, but they serve to make reading and writing familiar skills (Leichter, 1984). To the extent that they require children to make meaning clear to non-intimates, the literacy activities conducted at home also prepare students to approach academic tasks more successfully.

Practicing Cooperation as well as Competition

In addition to helping children master the kinds of language needed as a prerequisite to school experiences, parents can give children practice in different kinds of task structures. Kagan (this volume) shows that members of different cultural groups may have different preferences for cooperative or competitive tasks. The work included there suggests that, while parents may not wish to change their preferred mode of accomplishing activity, they would do well to give children practice in both kinds of situations.

In the area of verbal skills, there is evidence that cooperative, interactive activity is beneficial: Research shows that children who participate in social symbolic play requiring them to resolve a conflict or incongruity acquired better narrative competence than children who engaged in similar play by themselves (Pellegrini, 1985). In other areas, children can cooperate as well as compete with siblings or friends in games, running errands, or helping parents. This is important not only for success in school but also for abilities that may be needed in later life. As Kagan (this volume) mentions and other studies imply (California Postsecondary Education Commission, 1984), there is some evidence that California, like the rest of the country, is moving toward a service economy where ability to work cooperatively will be more important than it has been in the past.

Also, cooperative activities at home or in school model a variety of problem-solving strategies, and variability in finding successful solutions to problems is characteristic of skilled performance in a variety of occupations (Scribner, 1984). Hence, practice in cooperative as well as competitive activities would eventually be adaptive in contexts besides school.

Educating Schools About the Community

School personnel must understand the communities from which their students come; and parents, along with other community members, can assist them by providing information on local conditions. As the authors in this volume, particularly Sue and Padilla and Heath emphasize, there is great variation within language minority communities everywhere, and members of any community may not conform to generalized descriptions. Also, there is regional variation: The circumstances of Hispanic, Chinese, or Vietnamese groups in one part of California can be very different from those in another. Educators need specific knowledge about those they serve; this means understanding broad cultural patterns and individual and local variations. To help them better understand the out-of-school context of their students, parents can cooperate with research efforts as they did in the ethnographic work described in this volume. Furthermore, they can actively seek to make community consultants available to educators seeking expertise on local languages, customs, or economic or political issues.

The pressure of parents as members of cultural groups can be a successful tool in educational intervention. Cortés (this volume) summarizes some of the political pressures, many brought by parents and other community group members, that effected change in school curricula and policies in the 1960s. Ogbu and Matute-Bianchi (this volume) provide other examples of the impact groups of Black and Hispanic parents have had in some northern California schools. Acuña (1984) and Warren (1982) gave similar case histories showing that Spanish-speaking parents in areas of southern California also have been successful (sometimes after protracted effort) in moving schools toward acceptance of bilingual education and other educational programs designed to recognize and promote their heritage and to make school practices more responsive to their needs. Thus, there is precedent for seeing parents as effective in making schools take cultural differences into account.

Parents also can affect educational outcomes by demonstrating that they are interested in what happens in school and making it clear that they wish to see programs they perceive as successful continued and others changed. We have already noted that political pressure can shape school practices. Here, too, lack of ability to speak English need not preclude participation in school activities. In a study of Chicano parents in northern California, Torres (1982) found that higher levels of participation were, in fact, associated with higher levels of Spanish dominance. While this association cannot be generalized to all language minority communities, the research shows that parents who do not speak English can still become involved in school decision making.

Summary

The chapters in this book offer several suggestions for parents: They can work with their children on language development, building the verbal skills needed to succeed in school; they can provide practice in both cooperative and competitive activities in play or work settings; they can organize with other parents to promote activities they see as positive or press schools to change. From the historical evidence provided here (see the Cortés, Sue and Padilla, and Ogbu and Matute-Bianchi chapters), it is clear that schools have not always been receptive to the concerns of parents. It is also true that today's changing social circumstances, summarized in Kagan's chapter, mean that many children live in one-parent families and that all parents are less likely to have the time to volunteer in schools or attend school meetings. Yet, even given the constraints of current conditions, parents can help their children succeed in school. They can demonstrate their own approach to the issue of bicultural identity, as Sue and Padilla imply; they can become more aware of their own beliefs about success and the impact these beliefs have on the school-related expectations and experiences of their children, themes that Ogbu and Matute-Bianchi develop; they can help children master verbal skills in ways that Heath specifies; they can provide topics of interest to their children for instruction, a point mentioned by Díaz et al; they can show support and provide practice for cooperative forms of activity, as described by Kagan. Also, they can serve as active agents in changing the cultural dynamics that affect their children as Ogbu and Matute-Bianchi describe. In all of these ways, parents can affect the sociocultural contexts that, in turn, affect the educational progress of children.

DIRECTIONS FOR TEACHERS AND AIDES:
KNOWING CULTURES AND CONTEXTS

These chapters suggest many courses of action for classroom teachers who wish to learn more about sociocultural diversity and become better able to teach diverse students. In many schools, teacher aides also play important instructional roles in the classroom; hence, they should be included in the training and activities suggested here. Teachers may also

need to develop additional strategies for effective use of aides in the provision of instruction. Some of these directions involve study projects or
activities that teachers can undertake individually; others demand active
cooperation among teachers, aides, parents, resource teachers and
trainers, administrators, and others who have a stake in realizing the
goals of education. In this section, we will concentrate on actions that
individual teachers and aides can undertake to make good education
possible in settings of sociocultural diversity. Teachers can have a
positive impact on the instruction they provide (Good *et al.,* 1975).

Knowing Their Own Cultures

Teachers can begin by improving their understanding of cultures, both
their own and the cultures to which their students belong. To achieve a
clearer concept of the powerful influence of cultural values on education-
related beliefs and behaviors, they can start with themselves. Like their
students, teachers are cultural beings (Spindler, 1974; Cleghorn and
Genesee, 1984) and need to know what that means. Teachers can learn
to see themselves as agents and expressions of culture, a role they fulfill
with respect to conceptual and linguistic learning and interactional style,
as many of the chapters here imply. One way to begin to see how personal identity is shaped by culture is to explore family history; Cortés
(1984) provided several relevant resources. Anthropologist Ruth Landes
(1976) described a group of southern California educators who became
much better able to articulate their culturally-based expectations and
values through the study of their families' backgrounds, including immigration experiences and beliefs about education. In the course of
defining the values and ways of behavior they had learned while growing
up, they began to see how many of these still influenced their professional behavior.

Some guidelines for providing improved general understanding of
culture and its many influences on education are provided by Arvizu *et
al.* (1980) and Spindler (1982). Wilcox (1982) and Erickson (1984) provided comprehensive discussions of the importance of ethnographic
techniques and their applicability to education; Romaine (1984) and
Saville-Troike (1982) applied some of these techniques to the understanding of language use in ways that helped teachers appreciate what it means
for them and their students to be effective communicators in educational
settings. Research described by Au and Mason (1981) and Barnhardt
(1982) showed how information drawn from students' home cultures
guided educators in improving academic skills. Even when teachers

work in heterogeneous, rather than ethnically uniform settings, they can use such knowledge to diversify instructional approaches. These resources offer points of departure for teachers who wish to deepen their knowledge of cultural influences on education and use it to provide more effective instruction. If teachers and aides are themselves members of linguistic or ethnic-minority groups, they can draw on their own experiences in moving through the educational system to assist them in understanding the challenges facing their students. Although sharing minority identity does not automatically ensure similarity of experience, it can provide important insights into the educational situation of students from non-mainstream backgrounds.

There is one kind of cultural learning that we have not yet discussed, but has considerable potential for improving instruction: language learning. Research conducted in California (Merino *et al.,* 1979; Ramírez and Stromquist, 1979) suggested that teacher fluency in the students' first language, in this case Spanish, is linked to better student achievement in English and Spanish. The case study on reading presented by Díaz *et al.* in this volume also implies that teacher skills in Spanish can benefit English reading instruction. Teachers who want to develop or refine the ability to use the students' first language in instructional settings should know that this skill can, if used appropriately, assist them in educating their students.

The dimension of a teacher's professional culture should also be mentioned, for personal and professional cultures interact in actual behavior. Studies by Lortie (1978) and Cuban (1984a) can give teachers insights into the way teaching as an occupation shapes an individual's ideals, expectations, and experiences. The chapters by Díaz *et al.* and Kagan attest to the multiple demands made on teachers in school settings, as do other commentators (Sykes and Devaney, 1985; Koehler, 1984; Shulman and Carey, 1984; Goodlad, 1984). Teachers routinely operate in an environment of multiple claims on their attention; their own cultural and occupational habits may sometimes determine the choices thay make regarding which method of reading instruction to use, which student or students to select as leaders, which forms of feedback and evaluation to use with students and parents. In such environments, teachers often make pedagogical decisions based on their "common sense" as adult members of a culture and on occupation, yet even notions of common sense can be culture-specific (Geertz, 1983). Understanding that these pedagogical choices are just that--choices--may help them see that their established cultural and professional patterns often do not preclude trying alternative methods.

Knowing Student Contexts and Interaction Preferences

Besides knowing more about their own cultures, teachers need to learn about the cultures of their students. This means knowing about past experience of various cultural groups in a community in order to see if any of the conditions discussed by Ogbu and Matute-Bianchi (this volume) occur locally. In addition to gathering information regarding the past, teachers need to know about the current conditions in the communities from which their students come. Some of the questions to be answered are: What is the situation in the community regarding immigration? Mobility? Literacy practices in the first language and in English? Educational activities carried out in out-of-school settings such as homes, churches, stores, neighborhood clubs? What are typical patterns of employment? Child raising? Skills expected of adults and children? In all these areas, information regarding culturally-based patterns of activity will offer teachers more comprehensive pictures of their students' social worlds. In addition, such work can begin to reveal more subtle cultural variations even in apparently universal constructs such as intelligence (Greenfield and Bruner, 1969). The authors of the chapters in this volume are careful to point out that generalized descriptions of minority or majority students are less valuable than specific information regarding Mexican-Americans, Blacks, Asian, or Anglo communities served by a certain school. To better understand their own classroom experiences, teachers need local cultural knowledge about a group's history, economic circumstances, religions and social organizations, socialization practices, conceptualization of social competence, and language uses.

These kinds of cultural knowledge are not only ends in themselves; they will help teachers and aides gain a broader perspective on one of the main themes in this book: the influence of cultural background on interaction in the school context. The matter of teacher and student cultural background is critical because it influences their interactions with each other and with the materials they encounter in school. Hence, teachers need to know about the interactional styles preferred by them and their students. Interactional style here includes two areas of behavior: verbal discourse patterns and the task structures used to effect classroom learning. Knowing one's personal interactional style in each of these areas has different implications for teachers. The three chapters that deal directly with classroom processes--those by Heath, Díaz et al., and Kagan--all suggest that patterns of interaction make a difference in students' access to knowledge and ability to take advantage of school opportunities (see also Marshall and Weinstein, 1984). Thus, teachers need to know about the kinds of interaction they permit and encourage, perhaps without even knowing it, in their classrooms.

Seeing Interaction Patterns: Language

Linguistic interaction patterns bear close examination here. As work in classroom language (Cazden, 1982; 1986) and Heath's analyses (this volume; 1983a, 1983b) also show, teachers may often use question forms and conventions for giving commands and providing information different from those their students have learned at home. In some communities, including both communities where English is the usual language and groups that use languages other than English, adults and children speak to each other in ways very different from those encountered in school where differences are marked. Where the school-related forms of language are never used at home and where home-and community-based language forms are not found in school, the discontinuities in language use may pose unnecessary difficulties for children. These discontinuities may relate to the kinds of language activities encouraged for children, the rights to adult-like speech enjoyed by children, or the way written information is regarded within the community. The knowledge of genres of language use governing verbal interaction is especially crucial, Heath (this volume) implies, for those teachers providing initial school experience and literacy instruction for young children. These teachers need to help children acquire and build the text-related forms of knowledge that will serve as a means of mastering the rest of the curriculum as they move through school. To see what kinds of verbal interaction occur in their classrooms and determine whether these are optimal, teachers need to know about their own verbal behavior and that their students experience outside of school. Knowledge of one's own typical patterns of asking and answering questions (Heath, this volume; 1982a; 1983a; 1983b), waiting for response (Greenbaum, 1985; Philips, 1972), providing praise, correction, or clarification (Heath, 1982a, 1983b; Philips, 1972), nominating individual students or groups to answer, and maintaining discipline would allow teachers to see how their usual methods of providing instruction may unintentionally reach fewer students than they expected.

Teachers cannot, of course, stop with learning about their own usual patterns of verbal behavior; they also must see how these correspond to the ways of talking their students have learned outside of school. Some of these ways of talking may extend to ways of using languages other than English, and teachers can then draw on these if they are able. Indeed, the case studies on reading and writing in the Díaz *et al.* chapter suggest that teachers' use of the students' first language may be beneficial in checking reading comprehension or motivating students to write in English. Both this chapter and Heath's chapter imply that the choice of language used for instruction--whether it is English, Spanish, or Cantonese--may be less important than the variety of uses realized in that language. Where there are significant differences between teacher and student patterns of verbal interaction, learning is impeded.

What can teachers do to discover their own interactional style? Certainly it is nearly impossible to teach and observe oneself at the same time. However, teachers can use the assistance of technological aids, peers, or supervisors to help them see how they use language in a classroom. An audio cassette or videotape recorder allows teachers to make records of their own classes; they can then play the tapes back to see what kinds of questions they have used, whether they have waited a reasonable length of time for student answers, what kinds of positive, corrective, or disciplinary comments they have made, and to which students. Another means of discovering typical patterns of verbal interaction is through a peer observation system. Teachers can work with other teachers who will visit classrooms, make a record and perhaps use an observation system developed to identify patterns of verbal interaction, and share results to help their peers get a sense of their classroom style. Extensive work with interested peer coaching teams is one of the trademarks of many successful staff development efforts (Showers, 1985). Supervisors may also be called upon to perform observations if they are available and the teacher is willing.

These suggestions for peer observation demand administrative support and cooperation between teachers who volunteer to assist each other; thus, they require planning beyond that needed for classroom instruction. Nevertheless, they have the potential to provide teachers with relevant comments from trusted observers regarding classroom patterns. A similar system has been used to good effect among ESL (English as a second language) teachers in San Francisco (Doherty, 1984), and by elementary teachers in Santa Clara County who wished to improve skills in classroom management and instruction (Servatius and Young, 1985). All those involved understand that the process is aimed simply at helping teachers, and the observation records are not part of any formal evaluation record and do not go to administrators; they are viewed as the teacher's personal information profile, to be used according to each teacher's aims.   Other observation systems suitable for individual teachers or for peer or supervisory feedback are described in Acheson and Gall (1980).

For an observation to be pedagogically and culturally useful, any observation instrument or analytical system should draw on research in classroom interaction, instructional effectiveness, and cultural appropriateness.   Research on the instructional effectiveness of various language use patterns is exemplified in the work of Legarreta (1977, 1979), Ramírez and Stromquist (1979), and Stallings *et al.* (1979).   In these studies, observation instruments related to bilingual language use, elementary level ESL techniques, and methods used to teach reading in high school helped teachers see which uses of language were more or less effective in their classrooms.   To add the dimension of cultural appropriateness, we must specify ways for teachers to get information about the uses of language that are typical for their students outside of school.   Some of these include conducting observations outside the school (Heath, 1983a, 1983b; Philips, 1972), asking community members to act as informants about language, and enlisting the help of students to become ethnographers of their own communication (Heath and Branscombe, 1985). The case study on writing (Díaz, *et al.,* this volume) demonstrates some of these approaches to gathering community data. Systematic observation of one's own classroom interaction patterns, then, is one way teachers and aides can begin to address some of the issues raised in this book.

While observation will not provide comprehensive information about all aspects of a teacher's pedagogy (Stodolsky, 1984), it can help teachers gain a more accurate sense of their own interaction patterns. With additional data from community sources, teachers can then make some determinations about possible changes that might benefit their students. If they are concerned about the way they typically use language as compared with the uses of language most familiar to their students, they can follow some of the suggestions made by Heath (this volume; 1983a, 1983b).   If teachers work with a large number of students learning English as a second language, they can make some decisions regarding the instruction by consulting the work of Hatch (1983a, 1983b) and Fillmore (1985, 1982a) who show how classroom language can serve as input for learners. Also, knowing how the students will use the second language can help teachers plan appropriate learning activities (McGroarty, 1984; Fillmore, 1982b). In either case, observations allow teachers to see what kinds of verbal contexts for learning they create during interaction with their students.

Seeing Interaction Patterns: Task Structure

Verbal contexts are only part of the learning environment; equally important, as Kagan's work (this volme) shows, are the task structures used in classroom activities. Developing skill in using cooperative learning arrangements with students is another way teachers can work for success in culturally diverse classrooms; many cooperative strategies make steps in task completion clearer to students and thus provide better "scaffolding" for learning, an attribute typical of teaching outside the classroom (Greenfield, 1984b). There are several different types of cooperative learning strategies, all described in Kagan's chapter. Teachers interested in using them should make an effort to see how they are alike and how they are different. The cooperative learning strategies outlined in the Kagan chapter show different configurations of group and individual responsibility for learning, activities to ensure mastery, correction and clarification, and reward for the final effort. Each of these arrangements is slightly different, and their appropriateness depends on the nature of the content to be taught and the range of academic skills in the class as well as on students' cultural backgrounds and levels of language proficiency.

Indeed, teachers and aides who implement cooperative learning plans should know that they need to ensure relatively equal involvement by all the students if they are to exploit the academic and social potential of cooperative plans; cooperative learning using only traditional reading and writing activities as vehicles for learning may not provide maximal opportunities for students with weak skills in these areas, as some research showed (Cooper *et al.,* 1982; Cohen, 1984). Nevertheless, cooperative learning offers potential for improving student learning and students' attitudes toward each other (Johnson, 1980; Weigel *et al.,* 1975) and making classroom activity more varied for teachers. As the results of research in northern California showed (Cohen and DeAvila, 1984), cooperative learning plans using a variety of activities and repeated practice of central concepts through different media have been remarkably successful in effecting both better academic performance and better social skills such as self-discipline and ability to work with others. Encouraging children "to learn from each other as well as from teachers and books" (Noddings, 1984, p. 190) helps them become more responsible community members in addition to being better students. The time, energy, and imagination that teachers must devote to producing equal involvement can result in social as well as academic benefits.

The studies conducted by Kagan and other investigators show that cooperative learning is a powerful tool for all teachers, particularly those who work in settings of cultural diversity. Teachers can educate themselves about this approach to learning and see how it might fit their circumstances. Those who wish to pursue comprehensive implementation need training, peer support groups, continued contact with a knowledgeable person, and administrative endorsement to do so. Individual teachers interested in cooperative learning need not wait until all these conditions are met, however, they can begin by experimenting with cooperative learning activities in one subject or trying a single cooperative learning strategy to see how these arrangements might help them.

A similar process of experimentation and gradual adoption was described by Raquel Muir (1980), an experienced teacher who wished to use findings from the "Beginning Teacher Evaluation Study" in her southern California classroom. Over the course of two years, she tried out several methods of improving the academic learning time available to her students and began to integrate new practices into her usual pattern of teaching. While, as she noted, the experimentation was never finished--there was no point at which an unvarying method useful in all classes had been achieved--by the end of this period she was confident in her ability to employ a variety of classroom practices, many based on the research she had read. Teachers interested in cooperative learning could begin work on their own and then, if possible, set up some limited cooperative plans to see how the new strategies work. At the same time, because working alone to implement changes is both more difficult and less enjoyable than working with colleagues, teachers can let fellow teachers, resource teachers, and administrators know of their interest in this approach and request that appropriate training be established.

Improving Professional Knowledge

There are some additional steps that teachers, who wish to be effective in diverse cultural settings, can take. Many of the studies included here illustrate instruction in basic areas such as reading and writing instruction, both central skills in any student's school experience. Teachers of other subjects, though, can use many of these techniques; the cooperative learning approaches described by Kagan (this volume) span a range of subjects and student levels. To be able to use these approaches effectively, teachers should have a good grasp of the subject matter they wish to convey; this may mean, for some teachers, improving their own knowledge in the areas they teach. As Goodlad (1984) observed, many teachers are now asked to teach subjects for which they have little preparation. Indeed, the junior high teachers surveyed by Díaz et al. (this volume) had had little or no preparation in the teaching of writing. The study of classroom interaction patterns and different task structures, while very beneficial as the chapters here show, will not substitute for knowledge of the subject to be taught (Buchmann, 1982). Hence, teachers who wish to improve their pedagogical skills may find it wise to improve their knowledge of both the subject they teach and the related processes of student skill development. Improved expertise, achieved through an in-service program, an extra course, or participation in a special summer experience such as an intensive program affiliated with the National Writing Project, will give teachers a stronger background on which to base new approaches to learning. This is an area that teachers might wish to explore as one avenue for building the knowledge base they will use in all contexts.

Summary

Teachers and aides interested in becoming more effective in socioculturally diverse classrooms can, thus, make many kinds of efforts as individuals. They can improve their understanding of their own culture and students' cultures, particularly as these shape interactional preferences; they can learn to identify the linguistic patterns and the task structures they typically use and learn to vary them according to student response; they also can work to improve their knowledge of the subjects they teach. Some of these efforts require support from personnel outside the classroom--resource teachers, teacher trainers, and administrators--if they are to be effective. It is to these key people we now turn.

RESOURCE TEACHERS AND TEACHER TRAINERS: PROVIDING THE MEANS

To bring about effective instructional change, teachers need support from several sources. The variety of support needed ranges from explicit training and continued supervised practice of new skills to provision of new instructional materials to allocation of the time and money required for planning good projects. In this section we will see how resource teachers and teacher trainers, those whose responsibility it is to assist teachers in their instructional roles, can help teachers provide good classroom instruction for socioculturally diverse students.

Knowing Past History and Current Possibilities

First of all, resource teachers and teacher trainers working with individual schools, school districts, training consortia, or universities need to be well informed about the reciprocal influences of culture, the social context, and the educational system. They can begin by reading this book and pursuing other sources of information suggested, the chapters by Cortés, Sue and Padilla, and Ogbu and Matute-Bianchi set out much information about the way American education has dealt with issues of cultural diversity. The chapters by Heath, Kagan, and Díaz et al. demonstrate some ways that teachers have learned to provide good instruction in settings of sociocultural diversity. Resource personnel and trainers need current and clear information about these instructional innovations, and these chapters provide it.

Resource teachers and trainers interested in providing better instruction for students of varied cultural backgrounds can take the steps recommended for classroom teachers in the previous section. In addition, they can make it possible for groups of teachers with whom they work to be trained in some of the methods suggested. Resource people have a central role as conduits of information and services; they will be the ones to make it possible for teachers to take advantage of the better understanding of culture and context as influences on education. Hence, they need to know the rationale for the suggestions made, some of the research evidence that supports their use; the most approapriate way to train those with whom they work; and the best ways to draw parents, administrators, and others concerned about education into the process as needed.

Resource teachers interested in the ideas in this book can influence the staff development plans for the teachers with whom they work. The work here, particularly that included in the Heath, Kagan, and Díaz et al. chapters shows that teachers welcome assistance from those who understand their classroom realities and are willing to work within the many constraints imposed thereby. Teachers are justifiably tired of criticism from outsiders who have not experienced the multiple daily demands of a classroom; Kagan's research, grounded in classroom life, gives teachers many effective ways to improve learning in their classrooms. Resource teachers and trainers, people who have themselves been teachers in circumstances similar to those of their colleagues who remain in the classroom full time, can be catalysts in bringing some of the methods outlined here to the attention of fellow teachers and helping them develop skill in their use.

Resource teachers and trainers need to provide resources; they serve as the links between the scholarship embodied in this volume and the teachers who have great potential use for the innovations described. What are the kinds of resources needed to ensure that teachers take culture and context into account in providing instruction? Of the many that might be mentioned, we will concentrate on three: pedagogical, personal, and material. Resource teachers and trainers can assist teachers in locating and taking advantages of better means of instruction in these three areas.

Helping Teachers See What They Do and Change If They Wish

By pedagogical resources, we mean the behavioral skills related to providing effective instruction. These are the skills related to creating optimal contexts for education. They include a teacher's verbal patterns and the structural arrangements a teacher uses to help students master the material to be taught. As noted in the previous section, the work done by Heath (this volume) shows that teachers will profit from examining their own patterns of verbal interaction and comparing them with those that the students encounter outside school. Resource teachers and trainers can help teachers become aware of this issue, gather data on their own behavior, and learn how to collect information from members of the students' communities to help them see how verbal interaction in the classroom might be modified. Some of the observation techniques described in Acheson and Gall (1980), coupled with the types of observations discussed by Heath (1982b, 1983a, 1983b) can supply needed information. Community-based information can yield stimulating topics for instruction as well; in the writing study reported in this volume by Díaz et al., we see how community language use patterns were used as a vehicle for improving writing skills.

Besides helping teachers identify the verbal patterns they used in the classroom and those most often employed in the students' communities, resource teachers and trainers who aim to develop strong pedagogical skills must identify and demonstrate for teachers a variety of general learning formats. Only if teachers can first see for themselves how a variety of new learning strategies, including the cooperative learning plans discussed by Kagan (this volume), look in the classroom can they begin to determine which arrangements might best suit their circumstances. Hence, teacher training aiming to build pedagogical skills in new strategies must begin with observations of expert models, an approach grounded in social psychological learning theory (Bandura,

1977), and include guided practice under the guidance of both experts and peers (Showers, 1985; Joyce and Clift, 1984). Thus, teacher trainers need to show teachers how to employ innovative materials and practices; provision of new materials or exposure to a single expert demonstration is not enough to ensure transfer of the training to the classroom. If teachers have neither been trained in optimal ways to use new materials nor shown how to monitor their own success in doing so, they are likely to depend on their already established methods of teaching that may or may not complement new approaches. This result, observed in numerous assessments of educational innovation, among them a national study of bilingual education materials (Horst *et al.*, 1980) and an investigation of English language teaching for adults in the Los Angeles area (Megowan, 1985), attests to the need for thorough and continuous teacher training to support innovations. A promising model that incorporates observation of behavior, expert guidance, and peer coaching was developed by California educators working on services for language-minority students (Calderón and Spiegel-Coleman, 1984). In this approach, potential trainers see demonstrations, learn how to present them to teachers, and show teachers how to work with each other over a two- to three-year training cycle. While long-term results of this model are being evaluated (Calderón, 1985), it has proven more successful in the view of administrators and more popular in terms of teacher acceptance than traditional approaches to staff development.

Another aspect of personal resources needed for effective instruction is that of preparation in the subjects to be taught and the possibilities for student skill development each entails. In this area, too, resource teachers and trainers can help teachers locate opportunities to improve their own academic backgrounds in order to be more capable of presenting a variety of curricular options to students. In this volume (see the Kagan and Díaz *et al.* chapters), the continued participation and support of academic experts and teachers trainers is essential to the interventions described: cooperative learning methods and community-based writing instruction. Long (1985a, 1985b) proposed a similar approach to educating teachers about second-language acquisition that drew on theoretical insights to develop techniques and materials that promote active use of language. An experimental study of in-service training using this approach showed it was generally effective (Long *et al.*, 1984). Gaies (1986) and Palmer and Rodgers (1985) provided additional guidelines to show how teachers can set up peer work in second-language classrooms where a variety of school language skills is typical. All these effort show that in-service programs must address both substantive and methodological concerns to be effective.

Creating Attitudes to Help Teachers Grow

Related to the personal resources needed to offer good instruction in socioculturally diverse contexts is that of attitudes--teacher attitudes toward themselves, their students, the potential for success their students can attain, and their work. The issue of teacher attitudes is a complex one; we will not go into detail here because the nature and strength of causal links between teacher attitudes and classroom behaviors is not clear and because it is not apparently the case that change in teacher attitudes necessarily brings about change in teacher behaviors. Nevertheless, the matter of teacher attitudes is important (Good, 1980) because it seems clear that attitudes affect expectations that affect behavior on the part of both teacher and students. It is important that teachers have positive attitudes about themselves, their students, and the ability of their students to learn; they must have high expectations that their students can profit from learning and be able to communicate these expectations to students. Indeed, the very title of California's proposal for improving high school education, *Raising Expectations* (California State Department of Education, 1983) reflects this philosophy. If this position is to be more than a slogan, teachers need help from resource people and teacher trainers in creating and sustaining positive expectations for themselves and their students. This means giving teachers and students the opportunity to demonstrate their competence to each other during classroom encounters. Many of the techniques suggested here can help teachers and students communicate more effectively and learn better through a variety of task arrangements; these experiences can do much to create positive attitudes in teachers and students. The best way to improve attitudes may be to improve performance, and the pedagogical suggestions included here make this possible. Hence, while the importance of a positive personal attitude must be emphasized, the means for achieving this may best be defined in terms of pedagogical skill. In fact, research done with California teachers (Ramírez *et al.,* 1982; Ford 1984) showed that simply exposing teachers to information about ethnically marked varieties of English language use did not make them more favorably inclined toward the learning potential of students who spoke these varieties of English; this kind of training apparently may reinforce stereotypes rather than build confidence in students' potential to learn. Teachers' academic backgrounds form part of the resources they need to teach well; their attitudes make an equally critical contribution. After conducting extensive research on the skills and abilities of teachers in bilingual education programs in northern California, linguist Robert Politzer remarked, "Teachers whose knowledge of linguistics, psycholinguistics, sociolinguistics is not matched by a knowledge of the culture of the pupil's dominant language and cultural background, and by empathy with the community in which the pupil lives, are not likely to make a very significant contribution to the goals of bilingual/cross-cultural education" (1978, p. 15). Teachers need more than academic knowledge to provide good instruction in culturally diverse settings; their attitudes are also a determinant of effectiveness, and trainers thus need to help teachers develop and maintain positive attitudes toward themselves and their students.

Besides teachers' attitudes toward their own performance and that of their students comes consideration of their flexibility and ability to work with others on instructional improvement. Resource teachers can be the key to creation of an environment that supports mutual efforts by their provision of expertise and by their demonstration of willingness to attend to teachers' concerns. Classroom teachers typically work in isolation from one another (Little, 1982; Lortie, 1978) and, hence, themselves need to acquire skills in cooperative endeavor to make improvement possible. Too many recommendations for the reform of teacher education ignore this basic workplace condition (McLaughlin, 1984) and may, hence, fail to produce changes in teaching practices. Through their own demonstration of new practices along with an ability to help teachers work together, resource personnel help build the kind of atmosphere that makes continuous staff development possible. To create such an atmosphere, resource teachers can work to establish norms of collegiality, experimentation, and mutual assistance (Showers, 1985; Little, 1982). Some ways of doing this are engaging teachers in cooperative planning, assisting them in implementing new methods, becoming more precise and perceptive judges of teaching, and rewarding their cooperative efforts through public interest and recognition. These efforts signify the "equality of effort by the parties involved [and] equal humility in the face of the complexity of the task" (Little, 1982, p. 335) that characterize schools where continuous staff development is encouraged. Through their ability to shape organizational arrangements for training and their skill in inspiring collegial efforts, resource teachers help create a school climate that promotes student success.

Finding Materials, Media, and Time

The third area that resource teachers and trainers must consider in assisting teachers is the area of material resources needed for instruction. This is a vital one. Good classroom teaching depends not only on the effective pedagogy and personal background of the teacher but also on the materials used to challenge, stimulate, organize, and reinforce student learning. This is particularly true in the cooperative learning plans suggested here (Kagan, this volume). To make cooperative learning effective, teachers need to employ a variety of media so that all students can participate fully in the learning tasks. The work in science and math teaching done by Cohen and DeAvila and their colleagues in their *Descubrimiento/Finding Out* program (see Cohen, 1984; Cohen and DeAvila, 1984) demonstrated the necessity of using a variety of materials to make cooperative learning work. The cooperative learning research demonstrates that a variety of interesting materials--books, workbooks, realia, audio cassettes, filmstrips, records, art materials, measuring instruments, objects with scientifically provocative properties (magnets, live animals)--are essential to make the learning tasks appealing and rewarding for all the students (Dickson, 1982). While cooperative learning as described here also strengthens basic skills such as reading, writing, and computation, it is clear from most of the studies that materials cannot be restricted to traditional text-based presentations if they are to involve all the students in the activity (see Cohen, 1984; Cohen and DeAvila, 1984). Varied materials are essential, and resource personnel must assist teachers in locating or developing good materials in addition to undertaking training in their use.

The materials needed to provide better instruction in settings of sociocultural diversity are not limited to those typically found in classrooms. Implied in some of these chapters is the need for educators to come to terms with technological media that can amplify and extend the learning opportunities available to students inside and outside of school. Heath (this volume) offers some suggestions for incorporating television viewing into active language development efforts. Mehan and his colleagues (Mehan and Souviney, 1984; Mehan *et al.,* 1984) have shown that, if used interactively, the computer has potential for improving language skills. Educators in any setting would do well to learn how to use technological means to enhance learning; we may speculate that educators working in settings of sociocultural diversity will find it particularly beneficial to do so, for in so doing, they may be able to interest students who otherwise find in school an atmosphere entirely divorced from the more interesting phenomena of daily life. In her assessment of the impact of media on the development of intellectual, emotional, and social skills, psychologist Patricia Greenfield (1984a) provided educators--parents and teachers--with useful information regarding optimal use of these technologies. Resource teachers and teacher trainers can help teachers come to terms with new instructional media by providing both the machines and the instructional packages needed (hardware and software) and the training that will help teachers see how instructional goals can be met via effective use of television, video games, and computers.

Many of the suggestions regarding the resources needed to help teachers provide effective instruction in diverse settings require an investment of time and money. Resource personnel and teacher trainers need to know that instructional improvement demands these precious resources; they must be prepared to provide realistic estimates and make a good case for the potential value of the work required. Cohen and DeAvila (1984) offered some information about the costs and time involved in their program for elementary math and science instruction. Stallings *et al.* (1979) gave a detailed time frame for a large-scale project in the improvement of secondary reading skills. In both of these instructional improvement efforts, the initial investment in time and the relatively modest cost for materials was judged worthwhile because the teachers who were first trained were then able to train their peers. Hence, the initial training provided school districts with a core of trained teachers able to work with other teachers to achieve the goals identified for their projects. Resource personnel and teacher trainers should determine whether this is possible in their circumstances, and, if they can, set up training programs that will continue after the initial training efforts end. Many of the cooperative learning arrangements described by Kagan (this volume) fit this pattern. Resource providers should be prepared to make sufficient time and financial support available to teachers who want to master contextually appropriate learning methods. Knowing that once well trained, these teachers can work with peers and, if appropriate, outside training agencies or consultants to refine and monitor new approaches to learning will allow resource personnel to make a good case with administrators and others whose potential support is needed.

Summary

Those who train teachers, thus, must work to provide the many resources needed for interesting and effective instruction in classrooms characterized by sociocultural diversity and heterogeneity in student language backgrounds and skill levels. They can do this by making it possible for teachers to develop the pedagogical and personal skills needed to deal effectively with a variety of cultures and learning contexts. Resource teachers and trainers can also assist teachers in locating and developing the training models and materials that they and the teachers feel promise some benefits for them and their students. Providing these resources also requires the active support of administrators. We will now consider their potential contributions to improving education in schools where sociocultural diversity compels renewed attention to the goals and means of education.

IMPLICATIONS FOR ADMINISTRATORS: MAKING CONNECTIONS

If schools are to be effective in meeting the challenge of sociocultural diversity, school and school district administrators must take an active part in supporting the effort. Some of the ways they can do this are making connections between the parties who can provide assistance and their teachers; informing themselves of the potential benefits of the learning approaches suggested here; making this information available to other educators, to parents and community members and to policymakers; supporting the efforts of resource teachers and trainers to provide appropriate experiences for teachers; and following the progress of innovative efforts. Administrators have many duties, as Bridges (1975) showed; it is usually rare for them to be able to devote more than 30 minutes to an item that comes across their desks, and most of their activities are completed in less than 10 minutes. However, administrative support is essential if these suggestions, like the innovations of the 1960s and 1970s, studied by Berman and McLaughlin (1975), are to have any impact on the educational experiences of teachers and students.

Knowing Themselves and Their School Settings

Many of the steps in awareness and knowledge of cultures and contexts recommended here for teachers also apply to administrators. They can begin to address sociocultural diversity by better understanding their own cultural and interactional styles and those of their students. Even now, there are few teachers and even fewer administrators who belong to linguistic and cultural minority groups (Richards, 1983); hence, administrators will need to make active efforts to find out about communities they serve. Where administrators share membership in one of the cultural groups their students represent, as in the bilingual/bicultural program described by Warren (1982), they can use common cultural background to create and maintain communication with community members. (However, work like that by Ogbu and Matute-Bianchi presented here implies that teachers and administrators who have succeeded in the educational system may not be typical members of minority communities; thus, they cannot take common cultural background as a guarantee of open communication.) Whether or not administrators share the cultural background of some of their students, they can take steps to improve their understanding of cultures and contexts as these issues bear on educational behavior. Administrators can support efforts to gather community information that would help them and their teachers work more effectively with students. This book, especially the chapters by Díaz et al. and Heath, suggest that educators will derive valuable insights and guidelines for practice from ethnographic information collected from the communities represented by their students. Because such information demands time, attention, and training to collect, it may fall to the administrator to make a case for its importance before district administrators or boards of education. Working with local training centers or institutions of higher education may also be necessary. If administrators cannot undertake the job of making these connections--if the responsibility in their circumstances belongs to resource teachers or trainers--they can still make it clear that they wish to learn more about innovative efforts made, support these efforts, and stand ready to assist those who will carry them through. Long-term workshops, such as the training institute for principals in the Los Angeles area (Spiegel-Coleman, 1984) can help administrators stay informed of theoretical and pedagogical developments so that they can enhance school-level programs.

Lending Material and Moral Support

Administrators often make critical decisions about resource allocation. In this capacity, too, they can respond to sociocultural diversity by making the resources needed for personnel, training, or technological assistance available to teachers who can use them. None of the innovations described in this book--the cooperation between teachers and researchers, the use of cooperative approaches to learning, the use of technological aids like tape recorders in gathering information for language instruction--can take place unless the administrators involved support the expenditure of time and money required. High school principal Robert McCarthy (1985) presented additional recommendations on ways to enhance the quality of instruction by improving the level of technological support, ranging from staplers to computers, available to teachers. Although the amount of teacher time and the money needed for all these improvements varies greatly, the authors recommend that administrative support be given to undertake these efforts.

Beyond the matter of fiscal and material support comes another kind of support: The support in the school's climate of opinion that comes about in part because of administrators' encouragement of teachers' efforts to improve instruction. Educational history shows that, in a varied sample of American school districts, successful administrators have helped to bring about good instruction by building a "community of commitment" (Tyack and Hansot, 1982) composed of teachers, students, and parents striving for common goals. Administrators can build such communities by working with teachers, parents, and resource personnel to define instructional goals and then recognizing the student and teacher efforts to meet these goals. Like resource teachers, they must work to promote norms of cooperation among teachers and, thus, create an organizational climate that fosters professional growth (Little, 1982). Important for any educational program, these efforts are doubly so in circumstances of sociocultural diversity where administrators must work with many groups to build consensus on educational goals and then help teachers meet the goals set. In making this possible, an administrator's positive regard for the efforts being made and the people making them is vital.

Such positive public regard must extend beyond the school walls. Administrators often have contact with other administrators, curriculum specialists, and policymakers such as members of boards of education and superintendents. All individuals in these latter positions need current and accurate information about the relative merits of different approaches to education. School administrators involved in improvement efforts need to speak up for their schools to let other decision makers see what is promising and feasible in different circumstances.

Leading the Way

In smaller schools or districts where administrators also serve as resource teachers, it may be up to them to adopt some of the suggestions offered here for resource personnel. Thus, administrators may be the instructional leaders who help fellow teachers build the pedagogical and personal skills they need and supply the material resources needed. Principals can be effective instructional leaders as they work along with teachers to gather the necessary information, make appropriate instructional plans, and modify efforts as the strengths and weaknesses of any new instructional approach becomes apparent. Working with teachers does not mean abandoning the responsibility to exercise appropriate authority, as Carmichael attested (1985); on the contrary, it gives teachers a model of clear expectations that can guide their efforts at instructional innovation and professional growth. Innovative efforts may need to be gradual to allow the principal time to build up the trust and expertise of teachers, but there is still great potential benefit to be gained. An elementary school principal in northern California has shown that work with a group of teachers over a two-year period provided most of them with better instructional techniques, and these techniques were reflected in improved skill mastery by students (Noli, 1980). The process of improvement there was at times slow and uneven but ultimately worth the principal's efforts.

Summary

All administrators can play important roles in helping to establish and maintain good communication among parents, students, teachers, community members, and policymakers. In this volume, Ogbu and Matute-Bianchi point out the necessity for members of minority groups to make their voices heard in matters of school governance. Goodlad (1984) made the same observation regarding all parents and those students old enough to take an interest in their education. Administrators can help achieve better communication by publishing newsletters in appropriate languages; scheduling school events at staggered times so that working parents can attend when possible; providing child care, translators, and interesting programs to encourage attendance at parent meetings; and making it clear that they welcome community comments on educational matters.

Besides being receptive to the comments of teachers, students, and others, administrators must act to implement the provision of quality instruction in their schools. Through better knowledge of their own school settings, consistent efforts to support the pedagogical work of teachers, and ability to take the instructional initiative when prudent, administrators can shape effective schools in circumstances of sociocultural diversity.

FINAL COMMENTS:
WHAT DIVERSITY MEANS FOR EDUCATORS

Let us reconsider the original question. With the many useful recommendations for reform made in various reports, why should educators seek out additional directions for change? Why should they encourage fellow teachers, resource personnel, parents, and administrators to do the same? The rationale can be found in the early chapters of this book: those show that minority students have, for the most part, not been successful in school. As the demographic picture in California changes, it becomes even more crucial to see that students from these groups can progress in school. Too often, students who are members of linguistic or cultural minority groups have been taught as if they were no different from majority group students who come to school already fluent in English and familiar with the kinds of language use and interaction patterns they find in school. While the distinction between adapting instruction appropriately and diluting it unnecessarily (Carew and Lightfoot, 1979) is sometimes subtle, it can be drawn in sensible and defensible terms.

Beyond the issue of equality of access to the learning opportunities presented in school comes the matter of better performance for all students, those who are members of mainstream groups as well as minority group members. Many of the innovations suggested in this book have given convincing proof that they lead to improved performance on the part of all students, majority and minority group members alike. Learning to use community information in the classroom and developing skills in cooperative as well as competitive learning environments offer great promise for all students. Furthermore, these techniques offer teachers an opportunity to expand their repertoire of pedagogical skills.

No serious observer of American education can argue with the goals or recommendations for reform articulated in the many reports on education. Nevertheless, they are striking in their lack of concern for sociocultural diversity and individual as well as cultural variation in student background and behavior. The themes of diversity, of cultural and contextual influences on the interactions between students and teachers, motivate this book because of their importance on California's educational scene. In this large, varied, and rapidly growing state, those who implement the traditional educational reforms--lengthening the school day, adding more required subjects, establishing more and more frequent tests--will deprive themselves and their students of the maximal opportunities to improve academic and social outcomes of education unless they also deal with some of the issues raised by sociocultural diversity (Politzer, 1981).

We must be careful not to oversell any of the approaches included here. All of them offer great possibilities for improving student performance and teacher effectiveness in different curricular areas. Following the advice of Sue and Padilla (this volume), we should not rely on single solutions to educational problems but should employ varied and divergent approaches to change. By themselves, research result are insufficient guides for educational practice; they are limited by the conditions from which they emerge. Changing circumstances as well as the unpredictability of behavior mean that it is neither possible nor wise to suggest that what has happened because of an innovation in one classroom will of necessity happen in another (Buchmann, 1984). Nevertheless, the scholars whose work is included here have offered persuasive evidence that the approaches to learning they and their cooperating teachers employed brought about improved academic achievement and social orientation in the diverse classrooms they studied. Hence, educators who work in similar settings and share similar goals of improving both academic attainment and social environment in schools have reason to expect that these approaches might be useful.

Educators interested in meeting both of these worthy goals need to reflect carefully on the ideas presented here and test their applicability to local circumstances. Adoption of these guidelines could help to make the difference between "more of the same"--a school experience sharply bounded, as in the past, by linguistic and cultural barriers for certain students--and "more of the best"--a school experience that offers all students a variety of ways to improve the mastery of skills and concepts and learn to work with one another as they do so. We cannot raise our expectations without increasing our ability as educators to reach diverse groups of students effectively. This volume offers persuasive evidence that educators can learn to respond to sociocultural diversity to good effect and, in so doing, make California's schools better places for all students and teachers involved.

REFERENCES

Acheson, Keith, A., and Gall, Meredith Damien. *Techniques in the Clinical Supervision of Teachers.* New York: Longman, 1980.

Acuña, Rodolfo F. *A Community Under Seige: A Chronicle of Chicanos East of the Los Angeles River 1945-1975.* Monograph No. 11. Los Angeles California: UCLA Chicano Studies Research Center Publications, 1984.

Alexander, Karl L., and Pallas, Aaron M. Curriculum reform and school performance: An evaluation of the "new basics." *American Journal of Education,* 1984, *92*(4), 391-420.

Anyon, Jean. Social class and school knowledge. *Curriculum Inquiry,* 1981, *11*(1), 3-42.

Apple, Michael W. *Ideology and Curriculum.* London: Routledge and Kegan Paul, 1979.

Arvizu, Steven F., Synder, Warren A., and Espinosa, Paul T. Demystifying the concept of culture: Theoretical and conceptual tools. *Bilingual Education Paper Series,* June, 1980, *3*(11). Los Angeles: National Dissemination and Assessment Center, California State University, Los Angeles.

Au, Kathryn H., and Mason, J. Social organizational factors in learning to read: The balance of rights hypothesis. *Reading Research Quarterly,* 1981, *17*(1), 115-152.

Bandura, Albert. 1977. *Social Learning Theory.* Englewood Cliffs, New Jersey: Prentice-Hall, 1977.

Barnhardt, Carol. Tuning-in: Athabaskan teachers and Athabaskan students. In R. Barnhardt (Ed.) *Cross-cultural Issues in Alaskan Education,* Vol. 2. Fairbanks Alaska: Center for Cross-cultural Studies, University of Alaska, 1982. (ERIC Document ED 282 814.)

Bates, Elizabeth, and MacWhinney, Brian. Functionalist approaches to grammar. In Eric Wanner and Lila R. Gleitman (Eds.), *Language Acquisition: The State of the Art.* Cambridge, England: Cambridge University Press, 1982.

Benedict, Ruth. *Patterns of Culture.* Boston: Houghton Mifflin Co., 1934.

Ben-Zeev, Sondra. The influence of bilingualism on cognitive development and cognitive strategy. *Child Development,* 1977, *48*(4), 1009-1018.

Berman, Paul, and McLaughlin, Milbrey Wallin. *Federal Programs Supporting Educational Change, Vol. IV: The Findings in Review.* Santa Monica, California: Rand Corporation, 1975.

Bowles, Samuel, and Gintis, Herbert. *Schooling in Capitalist America: Educational Reform and the Contradictions of Economic Life.* New York: Basic Books, 1976.

Boyer, Ernest L. *High School: A Report on Secondary Education in America.* New York: Harper and Row, 1983.

Bridges, Edwin M. *The Nature of Leadership.* Paper presented at conference on "Educational Administration Twenty Years Later: 1954-1974," Ohio State University, Columbus, Ohio, April, 1975.

Buchmann, Margret. The flight away from content in teacher education and teaching. *Journal of Curriculum Studies,* 1982, *14*(1), 61-68.

_____. The use of research knowledge in teacher education and teaching. *American Journal of Education,* 1984, *92*(4), 421-439.

Butler, J. Donald. The role of value theory in education. In Philip G. Smith (Ed.), *Theories of Value and Problems of Education.* Urbana: University of Illinois Press, 1970.

Calderón, Margarita. *Organizational Structures for Ensuring Transfer in Bilingual Staff Development Programs.* Paper presented at American Educational Research Association Conference, Chicago, Illinois, April, 1985.

_____, and Spiegel-Coleman, Shelly. Effective instruction for language minority students. *Teacher Education Quarterly,* 1984, *2*(3), 73-79.

California Postsecondary Education Commission. *Social and Economic Trends: 1985-2000.* Sacramento, California, June, 1984.

California State Department Board of Education. *Raising Expectations: Model Graduation Requirements.* Sacramento, California: California State Department of Education, 1983.

Carew, Jean V., and Lightfoot, Sara Lawrence. *Beyond Bias: Perspectives on Classrooms.* Cambridge, Massachusetts: Harvard University Press, 1979.

Carmichael, Lucianne B. Working within the authority pyramid: The principal as learner. *Education and Urban Society,* 1985, *17*(3), 311-323.

Carter, Thomas P., and Segura, Roberto D. *Mexican Americans in School: A Decade of Change.* New York: College Entrance Examination Board, 1977.

Cazden, Courtney B. Classroom discourse. In M. C. Wittrock (Ed.) *Handbook of Research on Teaching.* 3rd ed. New York: Macmillan, 1986.

_____. Four comments. In Perry Gilmore and Allan A. Glatthorn (Eds.), *Children in and out of School.* Washington, D.C.: Center for Applied Linguistics, 1982.

Cicourel, Aaron V., and Mehan, Hugh. *Universal Development, Stratifying Practices, and Status Attainment.* Unpublished manuscript. San Diego: University of California at San Diego, 1984.

Cleghorn, Ailie, and Genesee, Fred. Languages in contact: An ethnographic study of interaction in an immersion school. *TESOL Quarterly,* 1984 *18*(4), 595-625.

Cohen, Elizabeth G. Talking and working together. In Penelope Peterson, Louise Cherry Wilkinson, and Maureen Hallinan (Eds.), *The Social Context of Instruction.* New York: Academic Press, 1984.

_____, and DeAvila, Edward. *Learning to Think in Math and Science: A Program for Linguistic and Academic Diversity.* Report to National Curriculum Dissemination Network. Palo Alto, California: Stanford University School of Education, 1984.

Cooper, Catherine R., Marquis, Angela, and Ayers-Lopez, Susan. Peer learning in the classroom: Tracing developmental patterns and consequences of children's spontaneous interactions. In Louise Cherry Wilkinson (Ed.), *Communicating in the Classroom.* New York: Academic Press, 1982.

Cortés, Carlos. *Introductory Bibliography on Family and Community History.* Riverside, California: Department of History, University of California, Riverside, 1984.

_____. The Education of Language Minority Students: A Contextual Interaction Model. In *Beyond Language: Social and Cultural Factors in Schooling Language Minority Students.* Los Angeles, California: Evaluation, Dissemination and Assessment Center, California State University, Los Angeles, 1986.

Cuban, Larry. *How Teachers Taught: Constancy and Change in American Classrooms 1890-1980.* New York: Longman, 1984a.

_____. Policy and research dilemmas in the teaching of reasoning: Unplanned designs. *Review of Educational Research,* 1984b, *54*(4), 655-681.

Cummins, James. *Bilingualism and Special Education: Issues in Assessment and Pedagogy.* Clevedon, England: Multilingual Matters, 1984.

_____. *Disabling Minority Students: Power, Programs, and Pedagogy.* Paper presented at Conference of the Society for Research on Child Development, 1985.

_____. The role of primary language development in promoting educational success for language minority students. *Schooling and language minority students: A Theoretical Framework.* Los Angeles: Evaluation, Dissemination and Assessment Center, California State University, Los Angeles, 1981.

Cziko, Gary A., and Troike, Rudolph C. Contexts of bilingual education. *AILA Review/Revue de l' AILA,* 1984, (1), 7-33.

Díaz, Rafael M. Thought and two languages: The impact of bilingualism on cognitive development. In Edmund W. Gordon (Ed.), *Review of Research in Education,* Vol. 10. Washington, D.C.: American Educational Research Association, 1983.

Díaz, Stephen, Moll, Luis C., and Mehan, Hugh. Sociocultural resources in instruction: A context-specific approach. In *Beyond Language: Social and Cultural Factors in Schooling Language Minority Students.* Los Angeles, California: Evaluation, Dissemination and Assessment Center, California State University, Los Angeles, 1986.

Dickson, W. Patrick. Creating communication-rich classrooms: Insights from the sociolinguistic and referential traditions. In Louise Cherry Wilkinson (Ed.), *Communicating in the Classroom.* New York: Academic Press, 1982.

Doherty, Cecelia. *Peer Observation for Staff Development Purposes.* Paper presented at 18th Annual Convention of Teachers of English to Speakers of Other Langauges, Houston, Texas, March, 1984.

Dolson, David P. The effects of Spanish home language use on the scholastic performance of Hispanic pupils. *Journal of Multilingual Multicultural Development,* 1985, *6*(2), 135-155.

Dreeben, Robert. *On What Is Learned in School.* Reading, Massachusetts: Addison-Wesley, 1968.

Erickson, Frederick. School literacy, reasoning and civility: An anthropologist's perspective. *Review of Educational Research,* 1984, *54*(4), 525-546.

_____, and Shultz, Jeffrey. When is a context? Some issues and methods in the analysis of social competence. In Judith L. Green and Cynthia Wallat (Eds.), *Ethnography and Language in Educational Settings.* Norwood, New Jersey: Ablex, 1981.

Fillmore, Lily Wong. Cultural perspectives on second language learning. *TESL Reporter,* 1981, *14*(2), 23-31.

_____. Instructional language as linguistic input: Second language learning in classrooms. In Louise Cherry Wilkinson (Ed.), *Communicating in Classrooms.* New York: Academic Press, 1982a.

_____. Language minority students and school participation. What kind of English is needed? *Journal of Education,* 1982b, *164*(2), 143-156.

_____. When does teacher talk work as input? In Susan Gass and Carolyn Madden (Eds.), *Input in Second Language Acquisition.* Rowley, Massachusetts: Newbury House, 1985.

Ford, Cecilia E. The influence of speech variety on teachers' evaluation of students with comparable academic ability. *TESOL Quarterly,* 1984, *18*(1), 25-40.

Gaies, Stephen J. *Peer Involvement in Language Learning.* Orlando, Florida: HBJ International, 1986.

Geertz, Clifford. *Local Knowledge.* New York: Basic Books, 1983.

Good, Thomas L. Classroom expectations: Teacher-pupil interactions. In James H. McMillan (Ed.), *The Social Psychology of School Learning*. New York: Academic Press, 1980.

_____, Biddle, Bruce J., and Brophy, Jere E. *Teachers Make a Difference*. New York: Holt, Rinehart, and Winston, 1975.

Goodlad, John. *A Place Called School*. New York: McGraw-Hill, 1984.

Greenbaum, Paul E. Nonverbal differences in communication style between American Indian and Anglo elementary classrooms. *American Educational Research Journal*, 1985, *22*(1), 101-115.

Greenfield, Patricia Marks. *Mind and Media: The Effects of Television, Video Games, and Computers*. Cambridge, Massachusetts: Harvard University Press, 1984a.

_____. A theory of the teacher in the learning activities of everyday life. In Barbara Rogoff and Jean Lave (Eds.), *Everyday Cognition*. Cambridge, Massachusetts: Harvard University Press, 1984b.

_____, and Bruner, Jerome S. Culture and cognitive growth. In David A. Goslin (Ed.), *Handbook of Socialization Theory and Research*. Chicago: Rand McNally and Company, 1969.

Gross, Beatrice, and Gross, Ronald. *The Great School Debate*. New York: Simon and Schuster, 1985.

Hakuta, Kenji. *Mirror of Language: The Debate on Bilingualism*. New York: Basic Books, 1985.

Hatch, Evelyn. Input/interaction and language development. In Evelyn Hatch (Ed.), *Psycho-linguistics: A Second Language Perspective*. Rowley, Massachusetts: Newbury House, 1983a.

_____. Simplified input and second language acquisition. In Roger Andersen (Ed.), *Pidginization and Creolization as Language Acquisition*. Rowley, Massachusetts: Newbury House, 1983b.

Heath, Shirley Brice. Sociocultural contexts of language development. In *Beyond Language: Social and Cultural Factors in Schooling Language Minority Students*. Los Angeles, California: Evaluation, Dissemination and Assessment Center, California State University, Los Angeles, 1986.

_____. What no bedtime story means: Narrative skills at home and at school. *Language in Society*, 1982b, *11*(1), 49-76.

_____. Questioning at home and at school: A comparative study. In George Spindler (Ed.), *Doing the Ethnography of Schooling*. New York: Holt, Rinehart, and Winston, 1982a.

_____. Research currents: A lot of talk about nothing. *Language Arts*, 1983a, *60*(8), 999-1007.

_____. *Ways with Words*. Cambridge: Cambridge University Press, 1983b.

_____, and Branscombe, Amanda. "Intelligent writing" in an audience community: Teacher, students, and researchers. In Sarah W. Freedman (Ed.), *The Acquisition of Written Language: Revision and Response*. Norwood, New Jersey: Ablex, 1985.

Horst, D. P., Douglas, D. E., Friendly, L. D., Johnson, D. M., Luber, L. M., McKay, M., Nava, H. G., Piestrup, A. M., Roberts, A. O., and Valdez, A. *An Evaluation of Project Information Packages (PIPs) as Used for the Diffusion of Bilingual Projects (Vols. 1 and 2)*. Mountain View, California: RMC Research Corporation, 1980.

Jackson, Phillip W. *Life in Classrooms.* New York: Holt, Rinehart, and Winston, 1968.

James, Lawrence R., Mulaik, Stanley A., and Brett, Jeanne M. *Causal Analysis: Assumptions, Models, and Data.* Beverly Hills, California: Sage Publications, 1982.

Johnson, David W. Group processes: Influences of student-student interaction on school outcomes. In James H. McMillan (Ed.), *The Social Psychology of School Learning.* New York: Academic Press, 1980.

John-Steiner, Vera, and Tatter, Paul. An interactionist model of language development. In Bruce Bain (Ed.), *The Sociogenesis of Language and Human Conduct.* New York: Plenum Publishing, 1983.

Joyce, Bruce, and Clift, Renee. The Phoenix agenda: Essential reform in teacher education. *Educational Researcher,* 1984, *13*(4), 5-18.

Kagan, Spencer. Cooperative learning and sociocultural factors in schooling. In *Beyond Language: Social and Cultural Factors in Schooling Language Minority Students.* Los Angeles, California: Evaluation, Dissemination and Assessment Center, California State University, Los Angeles, 1986.

Kessler, Carolyn, and Quinn, Mary Ellen. Positive effects of bilingualism on science problem-solving abilities. In James E. Alatis (Ed.). *Current Issues in Bilingual Education.* Washington, D.C.: Georgetown University Press, 1980.

Koehler, Virginia. *Inside the Classroom.* Paper prepared for American Educational Research Association Project on Research Contributions for Educational Improvement. Washington, D.C.: American Educational Research Association, 1984.

Landes, Ruth. Teachers and their family cultures. In Joan I. Roberts and Sherrie K. Akinsanya (Eds.), *Schooling in the Cultural Context.* New York: David McKay Co., 1976.

Legarreta, Dorothy. The effects of program models on language acquisition by Spanish-speaking children. *TESOL Quarterly,* 1979, *13*(4), 521-534.

_____. Language use in bilingual classrooms. *TESOL Quarterly,* 1977, *11*(1), 9-16.

Leichter, Hope Jensen. Families as environments for literacy. In Hillel Goelman, Antoinette A. Oberg, and Frank Smith (Eds.), *Awakening to Literacy.* Exeter, New Hampshire: Heinemann Educational Books, 1984.

Levin, Henry M. *Educational Reform for Disadvantaged Students: An Emerging Crisis.* Project report 85-B1. Philadelphia, Pennsylvania: Public/Private Ventures, 1985.

Little, Judith Warren. Norms of collegiality and experimentation: Workplace conditions of school success. *American Educational Research Journal,* 1982, *19*(3), 325-340.

Long, Michael H. A role for instruction in second language acquisition: Task-based language teaching. In Kenneth Hyltenstam and Manfred Pienemann (Eds.), *Modeling and Assessing Second Language Acquisition.* Clevedon, England: Multilingual Matters, 1985a.

_____. *Task-Based Language Teaching.* Manuscript. Honolulu, Hawaii: University of Hawaii at Manoa, 1985b.

_____, and Sato, Charlene. Methodological issues in interlanguage studies: An interactionist perspective. In Alan Davies, Clive Criper, and A.P.R. Howatt (Eds.), *Interlanguage.* Edinburgh, Scotland: Edinburgh University Press, 1984.

_____, Brock, Cindy, Crookes, Graham, Deicke, Carla, Potter, Lynn, and Zhang, Shuguiang. *The Effect of Teachers' Questioning Patterns and Wait-time on Pupil Participation in Public High School Classes in Hawai for Students of Limited English Proficiency.* Technical Report No. 1, Center for Second Language Classroom Research. Honolulu, Hawaii: University of Hawaii at Manoa, 1984.

Lortie, Dan C. *School Teacher.* Chicago: University of Chicago Press, 1978.

Marshall, Hermine H., and Weinstein, Rhona S. Classroom factors affecting students' self-evaluations: An interactional model. *Review of Educational Research,* 1984, *54*(3), 301-325.

Maynard, Douglas W. How children start arguments. *Language in Society,* 1985, *14*(1), 1-29.

McCarthy, Robert B. Technology time and participation: How a principal supports teachers. *Education and Urban Society,* 1985, *17*(3), 324-331.

McGroarty, Mary. Some meanings of communicative competence for second language students. *TESOL Quarterly,* 1984, *18*(2), 257-272.

McLaughlin, Milbrey Wallin. *The Limits of Policies to Promote Teaching Excellence.* Paper prepared for American Educational Research Association. Project on Research Contributions for Educational Improvement. Washington, D.C.: American Educational Research Association, 1984.

Megowan, Lorraine Barajas. *Intercultural Communication through American Holiday-Related Materials.* Unpublished masters thesis, University of California, Los Angeles, 1985.

Mehan, Hugh. Language and schooling. *Sociology of Education,* 1984, *57*(2), 174-183.

————. *Learning Lessons.* Cambridge, Massachusetts: Harvard University Press, 1979.

————, and Souviney, Randall (Eds.). *The Write Help: A Handbook for Computers in Classrooms. Report No. 6.* La Jolla, California: Center for Human Information Processing, University of California, San Diego, 1984.

————, Miller-Souviney, Barbara, and Riel, M. Margaret. Research currents: Knowledge of text editing and control of literacy skills. *Language Arts,* 1984, *65*(5), 510-515.

Merino, Barbara J., Politzer, Robert L., and Ramirez, Arnulfo G. The relationship of teachers' Spanish proficiency to pupils' achievement. *NABE Journal,* 1979, *3*(2), 21-37.

Muir, Raquel. A teacher implements instructional changes using the BTES framework. In Carolyln Denham and Ann Lieberman (Eds.), *Time to Learn.* Washington, D.C.: National Institute of Education, 1980.

National Commission on Excellence in Education. *A Nation at Risk.* Washington, D.C.: National Commission on Excellence in Education, 1983.

Nelson, Katherine, Engel, Susan, and Kyratzis, Amy. The evolution of meaning in context. *Journal of Pragmatics,* 1985, *9*(4), 453-474.

Noddings, Nel. *Caring.* Berkeley: University of California Press, 1984.

Noli, Pamela M. A principal implements BTES. In Carolyn Denham and Ann Lieberman (Eds.), *Time to Learn.* Washington, D.C.: National Institute of Education, 1980.

Ogbu, John U., and Matute-Bianchi, Maria. Understanding sociocultural factors: Knowledge, identity, and adjustment. In *Beyond Language: Social and Cultural Factors in Schooling Language Minority Students.* Los Angeles, California: Evaluation, Dissemination and Assessment Center, California State University, Los Angeles, 1986.

Palmer, Adrian S., and Rodgers, Theodore A., with Olsen, Judy Winn-Bell. *Back and Forth: Pair Activities for Language Development.* Hayward, California: Alemany Press, 1985.

Paulston, Christina Bratt. *Bilingual Education: Theories and Issues.* Rowley, Massachusetts: Newbury House, 1980.

Pellegrini, A. D. The relations between symbolic play and literate behavior: A review and critique of the empirical literature. *Review of Educational Research,* 1985, *55*(1), 107-121.

Philips, Susan U. Participant structures and communicative competence: Warm Springs children in community and classroom. In Courtney B. Cazden, Vera P. John, and Dell Hymes (Eds.), *Functions of Language in the Classroom.* New York: Teachers College Press, 1972.

Politzer, Robert L. Social class and bilingual education: Issues and contradictions. *Bilingual Education Paper Series,* 1981, *5*(2). Evaluation, Dissemination and Assessment Center, California State University, Los Angeles.

_____. *Some Reflections on the Role of Linguistics in the Preparation of Bilingual/Cross Cultural Teachers.* Unpublished manuscript. Palo Alto, California: Stanford University Program on Teaching and Linguistic Pluralism, 1978.

Ramírez, Arnulfo G., and Stromquist, Nelly P. ESL methodology and student language learning in bilingual elementary schools. *TESOL Quarterly,* 1979, *13*(2), 145-158.

_____, Edgardo, Arce-Torres, and Politzer, Robert L. Language attitudes and the achievement of bilingual pupils in English language arts. In Joshua A. Fishman and Gary D. Keller (Eds.), *Bilingual Education for Hispanic Students in the United States.* New York: Teachers College Press, 1982.

Resnick, Daniel P., and Resnick, Lauren B. Standards, curriculum, and performance: A historical and comparative perspective. *Educational Research,* 1985, *14*(4), 5-20.

Richards, Craig. *Bilingualism and Hispanic Employment: School Reform or Social Control?* Project report 83-A16. Palo Alto, California: Institute for Finance and Governance, Stanford University, 1983.

Richards, Jack C. The context of language teaching. In Jack C. Richards (Ed.), *The Context of Language Teaching.* Cambridge, Massachusetts: Cambridge University Press, 1985.

Rogoff, Barbara, and Lave, Jean. *Everyday cognition: Its Development in Social Context.* Cambridge, Massachusetts: Harvard University Press, 1984.

Romaine, Suzanne. *The Language of Children and Adolescents: The Acquisition of Communicative Competence.* Oxford, England: Basil Blackwell, 1984.

Sarason, Seymour B. *The Culture of the School and the Problem of Change.* Boston: Allyn and Bacon, 1971.

Saville-Troike, Muriel. *The Ethnography of Communication.* Oxford, England: Basil Blackwell, 1982.

Scribner, Sylvia. Studying working intelligence. In B. Rogoff and H. Lave (Eds.), *Everyday Cognition: Its Development in Social Context.* Cambridge, Massachusetts: Harvard University Press, 1984.

Servatius, Joanna Dee, and Young, Shareen E. Implementing the coaching of teaching. *Educational Leadership,* 1985, *42*(7), 50-53.

Showers, Beverly. Teachers coaching teachers. *Educational Leadership,* 1985, *42*(7), 43-48.

Shulman, Lee S., and Carey, Neil B. Psychology and the limitations of individual rationality: Implications for the study of reasoning and civility. *Review of Educational Research*, 1984, *54*(4), 501-524.

Skutnabb-Kangas, Tove. *Bilingualism or Not: The Education of Minorities*. Translated by Lars Malmberg and David Crane. Clevedon, England: Multilingual Matters, 1984.

Snow, Catherine E. Mothers' speech research: From input to interaction. In Catherine E. Snow and Charles A. Ferguson (Eds.), *Talking to Children: Language Input and Acquisition*. Cambridge, England: Cambridge University Press, 1977.

Spiegel-Coleman, Shelly. *Proposal for Multidistrict Principals' Training Institute (MPTI)*. Los Angeles, California: Office of Los Angeles County Superintendent of Schools, 1984.

Spindler, George D. Beth Anne--a case study of culturally defined adjustment and teacher perceptions. In George D. Spindler (Ed.), *Education and Cultural Process*. New York: Holt, Rinehart, and Winston, 1974.

————. (Ed.). *Doing the Ethnography of Schooling*. New York: Holt, Rinehart, and Winston, 1982.

Stallings, Jane, Needels, Margaret, and Stayrook, Nicholas. *How to Change the Process of Teaching Basic Reading Skills in Secondary Schools*. Phase II and Phase III. Final report of Grant No. NIE-G-77-0001. Washington, D.C.: National Institute of Education, 1979.

Steinberg, Stephen. *The Ethnic Myth*. Boston: Beacon Press, 1981.

Stodolsky, Susan S. Teacher evaluation: The limits of looking. *Educational Researcher*, 1984, *13*(9), 11-18.

Sue, Stanley, and Padilla, Amado M. Ethnic minority issues in the United States: Challenges for the educational system. In *Beyond Language: Social and Cultural Factors in Schooling and Language Minority Students*. Los Angeles, California: Evaluation, Dissemination and Assessment Center, California State University, Los Angeles, 1986.

Sykes, Gary, and Devaney, Kathleen. Editor's introduction: A blight on the apple for teacher. *Education and Urban Society*, 1985, *17*(3), 243-249.

Symposium on the year of the reports: Responses from the educational community. *Harvard Educational Review*, 1984, *54*(1), 1-31.

Tizard, Jack, Schofield, W. N., and Hewison, Jenny. Collaboration between teachers and parents in assisting children's reading. *British Journal of Educational Psychology*, 1982, *52*(1), 1-15.

Torres, Maria E. *Participatory Democracy and Bilingual Education: The Case of San Jose, California*. Unpublished doctoral dissertation, Stanford University, Stanford, California, 1982.

Tyack, David, and Hansot, Elisabeth. *Managers of Virtue: Public School Leadership in America, 1820-1980*. New York: Basic Books, 1982.

————, Lowe, Robert, and Hansot, Elisabeth. *Public Schools in Hard Times: The Great Depression and Recent Years*. Cambridge, Massachusetts: Harvard University Press, 1984.

Trueba, Henry T. The forms, functions, and values of literacy: Reading for survival in a barrio as a student. *NABE Journal,* 1984, *9*(1), 21-39.

United States Department of Education. *The Nation Responds: Recent Efforts to Improve Education.* Washington, D.C.: U.S. Government Printing Office, 1984.

Wang, Margaret C., and Lindvall, Mauritiz C. Individual differences and school learning environments. In Edmund W. Gordon (Ed.), *Review of Research in Education,* Vol. 11. Washington, D.C.: American Educational Research Association, 1984.

Warren, Richard L. Schooling, biculturalism and ethnic identity: A case study. In George Spindler (Ed.), *Doing the Ethnography of Schooling.* New York: Holt, Rinehart, and Winston, 1982.

Weigel, Russell H., Wiser, Patricia L., and Cook, Stuart W. The impact of cooperative learning experiences on cross-ethnic relations and attitudes. *Journal of Social Issues,* 1975, *31*(1), 219-244.

Wells, Gordon. Language and learning: An interactional perspective. In Gordon Wells and John Nicholls (Eds.), *Language and Learning: An Interactional Perspective.* Lewes, East Sussex, England: The Falmer Press, 1985.

_____. *Learning through Interaction.* Cambridge, Massachusetts: Cambridge University Press, 1981.

Wilcox, Kathleen. Ethnography as a methodology and its application to the study of schooling: A review. In George Spindler (Ed.), *Doing the Ethnography of Schooling.* New York: Holt, Rinehart, and Winston, 1982.

EPILOGUE

FAR BEYOND LANGUAGE

Charles F. Leyba
California State University, Los Angeles

As the title of this volume implies, there are political, cultural, and psychological forces lying beyond or outside of language that are seemingly related to academic deficiencies in certain minority groups. Title VII legislation, on the other hand, rests largely on a philosophical base that predicates language deficiency as the main cause.

This epilogue joins the other authors in arguing that extralinguistic characteristics have a primordial importance in the academic performance of students. Its focus will be on culture as the preeminent factor-- not in explaining deficiencies, for cultures internally viewed are not primarily deficient, but as the ground that must be carefully understood before any remediation to alleged deficiencies is to be applied.

The concept of culture or the word itself has immediate meaning for all who employ it so that both speaker/writer and listener/reader share or feel they share sufficient mutual understanding about its meaning to obviate questions concerning its content. People generally are quite comfortable with the manner in which they use the word or find others using it. Important words are like that. It is for this reason that special attention should be accorded their usage.

The purpose of this paper, then, is to explore the concept of culture from a reflective, analytical perspective. This is not to avoid empirical approaches that are, in fact, the final touchstones of the validity of any effort at theory construction or verification. However, the explanatory infrastructure or framework for phenomena, that which unifies data, reduces perplexity, and creates intelligibility, is theory. This paper will largely be concerned with theory.

The importance of this topic to Title VII is as follows. Little as we know about culture and little as we discuss the concept of culture, there is considerable support for bilingual education as an educational program that will provide equitable learning opportunities for its target population. It does this largely through its major funding title, Transitional Bilingual Education. This funding title is clearly assimilative in design and purpose. Yet its effect on cultures of the target populations is hardly assessed or even addressed.

Perhaps there is an assumption here that lies just beyond the pale of discussion, a powerful but questionable one that culture will abide or needs little tending.

This paper attempts--the literal meaning of the word *essay*--to provide analyses of the inner structure of culture as a basis for the reader's efforts or interest in assaying the real or possible effects of bilingual education as an acculturational tool. This paper places culture in the foreground of the discussion.

The topics to be treated are as follows:

a) cultural characteristics as "imprints" on the psychological dimensions of cultural participants.

b) the order/interrelationships of cultural characteristics.

c) the relationship of the characteristics as one of superordination-- subordination, not in a spatial sense but in the sense of being essential vs. nonessential.

d) cultural characteristics as providing a culture with relative temporal persistence or permanence, i.e., how deeply does a culture imprint itself on the participant's way of thinking?

e) views of cultural characteristics as positive and negative.

Cultural Characteristics as Imprints

The word *characteristics* is employed to designate behaviors, traits, attitudes, orientations, etc., in fact, any element that can be used to describe a culture's influence on human behavior. What is being referred to, therefore, are not cultural externals or products but something residing within the combined psyche of the participants of a culture. Since these characteristics govern behavior, they also can be referred to as values.

These characteristics are the result of human conventions or agreements as opposed to behavior-governing characteristics that are instinctually derived. It is true that cultural values fully incorporated into the behavioral repertoire of individuals lead to activities that function with the mechanical regularity of instincts and can be mistaken for instincts. Nevertheless, because they have been fashioned and adopted by the least of instinct-driven entities, namely man, these cultural characteristics share man's status of freedom and rationality, which are the very opposite of instinctual behavior.

Cultures, as has been said, have characteristics residing in the psyche and because of this can be referred to as values. Since value has a behavior-governing quality as we are using the word, these characteristics can just as easily be referred to as "meanings." Again, the focus is on features that give rise to or govern behavior or actions. These combined characteristics, values, and meanings are what constitute a culture in its inner dimension.

Schema I graphically attempts to portray these notions.

Schema I

Cultural Dimensions:
Imprints and Products

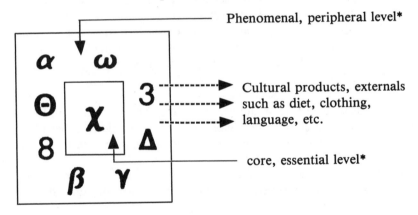

Phenomenal, peripheral level*

Cultural products, externals such as diet, clothing, language, etc.

core, essential level*

Culturally Imprinted Psyche

* inner dimension of culture including the inner and outer square.

Interpretation

The above schema portrays the following:

a.   the x represents the presumed essential or core level of the culture.

b.   the numbers and letters in the square surrounding the x represent dispositions to behave in culturally conditioned styles. These are proximate sources of culturally conditioned behaviors or styles.

c.   entirely outside the square are cultural products: artifacts and behaviors--all externally observable.

d.   items a and b (possibly) represent the culturally imprinted characteristics.

The use of the words "values" and "meanings" as alternates for cultural imprints has special significance. Cultural knowledge has a personalistic or emotive dimension which the above two words convey. In this respect, cultural knowledge is clearly different from mathematical knowledge, which is not infrequently described as "acultural." Consider the number 307 as a mathematical notation to be the sum of a given set of numbers. It is accurate or not accurate but otherwise lacks meaning, or, if you will, significance. But let this number be endowed *culturally* with the character of the ominous or the propitious and it takes on significance, i.e., meaning and value. Cultural meaning adds to spare cognition an emotional value that summons a behavioral response (emotional or otherwise) as well.

Cultural values have precisely this sort of quality. As Spindler states:

> It is clear that each culture selects certain conditions of living, certain objects of possession, certain characteristics of personality, as more desirable than others. And these desirables are seen as motivating people to behave in acceptable and worthwhile ways, as underlying complex and highly specific manners and customs. (1963, p. 20)

Cultural values, as Spindler states, are "desirables," that is, have motivating force that channel behaviors in certain directions rather than others and explain why in identical circumstances members of different cultures posit different behaviors.

Furthermore, Spindler correctly places or locates these desirables beneath "manners and customs," i.e., in the psyche of the cultural participant.

Clearly, knowledge that has the character of moving individuals to actions has the quality of a good to be attained or accomplished. Moreover, it takes on the character of stimulating regularized, patterned behavior, given the proper circumstances. So, one may expect, for example, that on certain holidays, specific foods will be served by individuals within a given culture. In a real sense, it may be said that individuals are driven in the direction of certain behaviors and ways of thinking by cultural values. Still another way of putting it would be to observe that since thinking precedes acting or doing, not necessarily in a temporal order of precedence, cultural conditioning frames, in the initial stage, the person's perceptions or ways of thinking and acting. These values, consensually arrived at in their origin, receive the stamp of authenticity and in some cases sacredness through their persistence over time and become the veritable flywheel of the culture. For this reason,

culture can be literally described as the skin coloring of the soul of man
so that identification with a culture transcends such pedestrian markers
as surname, pigmentation, and the like.

In essence, this is what Sapir is referring to when he noted:

> The so-called culture of a group of human beings, as it is ordinarily
> treated by the cultural anthropologist, is essentially a systematic list
> of all the socially inherited patterns of behavior which may be il-
> lustrated in the actual behavior of all or most of the individuals of
> the group. The true focus, however, of these processes which,
> when abstracted into a totality, constitute culture is not in a
> theoretical community of human beings known as society, for the
> term "society" is itself a cultural construct which is employed by
> individuals who stand in significant relations to each other in order
> to help them in the interpretation of certain aspects of their
> behavior. The true focus of culture is in the interactions of specific
> individuals and, on the subjective side, in the world of meanings
> which each one of these individuals may unconsciously abstract for
> himself from his participation in these interactions." (1949, p. 515)

Because cultural characteristics govern behaviors focusing them in one
direction rather than another, cultures take on distinctiveness and
separateness or identifiability. The most obvious characteristics are
found in the cultivation of distinct forms of dress, music (at times), and
certainly food preparation. This focus on forms or styles is logically
derived from shared meanings among the participants of each given
culture. Because they are shared meanings, individuals bound by them
are identifiable as belonging to or sharing a cultural community.

Cultural values or characteristics, therefore, have a strong influence
on human behavior, conative as well as cognitive. It is, however, the
influence of cultural characteristics on the cognitive aspects of human
behavior that is critical. Culture does, in fact, divert intellectual focus in
the direction of certain aspects of reality and just as important *away*
from others. Seen in this light, cultures are positive but may be labeled
deficient when a given culture is accepted as a standard against which
other cultures are measured.

Order and Interrelationship of Cultural Characteristics

A careful reading of the Sapir quote, while supporting the construct
presented in the previous section, namely, the inner dimension of
culture, initiates an additional consideration. If these values can be seen

as "essentially a systematic list of all the socially inherited patterns of behavior..." as Sapir observed, it may be asked whether these values exist simply as separate and distinct entities within the culturally imprinted psyche or is there an order and integration of these values with a mutually causal interplay among them.

Some serious considerations in the form of further questions call for attention. If these cultural characteristics as imprints exist within individuals, and there is an order among them, i.e., a scale of priority among these meanings, the next question that presents itself asks, which values and how some of these values are more important than others. Is there a Maslovian hierarchy among these values? If there is such a hierarchy, then what are these values that are more important than others, does the culture and its survival depend on these, can the culture be destroyed simply by obliterating these values?

The importance of these questions cannot be overstated. In the first instance, there is Title VII legislation which at bottom is based on equal opportunity philosophy. Stated in other words and more mechanistic ones, Title VII legislation has as its goal to take an individual "from here to there." This means from a condition of need or deficiency to one of empowerment, i.e., capacity to share in the goods of the mainstream society. The bulk of Title VII funding is focused this way and explicitly so in the title: Transitional Bilingual Education (TBE). Is empowerment merely this? Is it simply an invitation to participate in the life of the most powerful economy currently in existence, or is empowerment far less a matter of civic justice and more a vehicle of cultural transformation and assimilation? Is empowerment culturally neutral? The schools as conveyors of empowerment certainly are not.

Additionally, the authors in this volume very appropriately address factors correlated with minority academic failure and success (Ogbu and Matute-Bianchi, this volume) or varieties of methodologies that might improve minority performance in academic tasks required in this culture (see Kagan especially, this volume). The appropriateness of this approach is based on the fact that bilingual education is primarily an equity issue (see the *Lau v. Nichols* decision) intending that students advance, other factors taken into consideration, with proportional equality in the acquisition of academic subject matter and the development of academic skills. It is the equity issue that the authors directly address or assume as needing attention. No consideration is given to the effect this acculturational effort may or may not have on the culture the target population brings to the classroom.

To return to the topic under consideration, left unquestioned is whether the academic content and skills to be acquired are merely adjectival to the deeper thrust of a given culture and its imprinted characteristics, values, and meanings. In other words, are these academic contents and skills purely adventitious and accidental, or do they represent a gradual displacement of the culture of the target population?

If culturally imprinted characteristics indeed have an order among them, the immediate relevance to the above question is evident. If there is an order among them, the first relationship must be that of "greater or lesser" importance or perhaps "lasting" vs. "transient." The less important may be referred to as peripheral, phenomenal, or superficial, the more important as essential, sub-phenomenal, or core level. Does this order of greater or lesser importance mean that certain cultural characteristics (lesser ones) may be dislodged and replaced without affecting the core of the culture itself? In this sense, empowerment efforts may be only slightly accultural, i.e., culture-displacement efforts.

It will be readily conceded that something of the above relationship exists among cultural characteristics. Those characteristics related, for example, to dress or diet may undergo modification or extinction without a sea-change in culture itself. Cultural permanence (core?) would seem unaffected by modifications of peripheral characteristics. One might remove Mexican food permanently from the diet of a given Mexican American and ask this person whether he/she remains fully a Mexican American in cultural identity. The answer would most likely be affirmative. Of how many cultural characteristics is this true? We don't have the answer.

Pursuing this line of reasoning further, it may be said that if phenomenal level characteristics taken singly may be removed from a person's cultural psyche, would the sub-phenomenal or core level characteristics abide? Also, do these core characteristics exist independently of one another, resting, so to speak in the psyche, alongside one another like silverware on a table? Or are these characteristics more like piano keys, each one independent of the other, yet combining to form a chord as it were? Is there an interplay among them and if so, which combination of them forms the essence of the culture? If there is an interplay among them forming the essence of a culture, is this what we mean by core level or essential characteristics? At present, we do not know the answers to any of these questions.

Is language a peripheral, accidental characteristic? (Language is the overriding concern of Title VII legislation.) When the topic of language in relation to culture is introduced, one has the sensation of having entered the very penetralia of a given culture. Indeed, most individuals regardless of their having reflected at all on the matter will instinctively concur with the suggestion that the culture at its sub-phenomenal, essential or deepest levels is inextricably linked to the given culture's language. So much is this felt that the weakening of the language resonates with a threat to the culture itself.

Yet a plethora of difficulties, as ever, accompanies this seeming truism. The example comes to mind of a foreigner who has fully mastered the border version of Spanish. Has this person become Mexican American culturally or does this person remain a participant in the culture of his/her origin and upbringing? What of the person (Anglo) who has earned a Ph.D. in Spanish? Is such a person more Mexican American in culture than the Mexican American student in the class who speaks deficient Spanish? Certainly the students and community would not admit it. Apparently the culture is constituted of something deeper than mere language. Language is not necessarily or logically transposable with the culture.

If one considers the phenomenal level of the culture, perhaps it may be easily conceded that the individual described above is at very least bicultural, or, as Sue and Padilla and Ogbu and Matute-Bianchi (this volume) would express it, this person would be capable of contextual interaction. Furthermore, if there is little more to culture than amassing items such as authentic language-production skills, participating in culturally based activities in a spontaneous, i.e., nonawkward fashion, possessing a knowledge of items such as listed by Hirsch (1987), then one might go further and consider, perhaps, this individual to be acculturated or to be a full, i.e., authentic participant in the second culture.

On the basis of this model, there would be no real superordination-subordination of cultural characteristics, simply an array of culturally defined and relevant capabilities. Without an essential-nonessential relationship among cultural characteristics, cultural genocide would be hardly more than the suspension of activities that are culturally relevant, perhaps until they are in a state of remission. The associated feelings of loss and nostalgia would perhaps be the only tangible and reprehensible element. An example of this might be an urbanized Native American who has not participated in culturally determined activities over a lifetime.

This position is not without advantages. The human agent is a carrier of culture or, more accurately, of cultural characteristics. In the case/model above, these cultural characteristics are of coordinate importance though some may *seem* to occupy a central position. Removal or erasure of some characteristics constitute no profound loss to the individual or group, though feelings may make it seem so. Any mystique about culture and its importance to the group and individual dissolves in the face of an atomistic rationalism. It, therefore, frees the human agent from any other than an imagined responsibility for cultural preservation. Schema II portrays this condition.

Schema II

No core level characteristics
only peripheral ones*

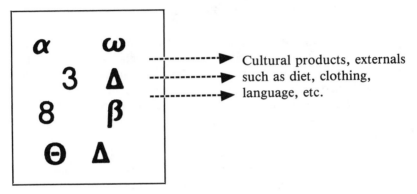

Cultural products, externals
such as diet, clothing,
language, etc.

Culturally Imprinted Psyche

*But a, ɵ, w, for example *taken together* might be the core level cultural characteristics.

Relationship: Superordination-Subordination

The previous analysis has explored the concept or hypothesis that there may be no cultural characteristics of lesser or greater importance to a culture. Untutored good sense, however, persuades one that there must be. Yet untutored good sense has it that one important characteristic (language) is of great importance to culture, but was found on analysis to lack the cultural hegemony popular perception endows it with.

Together with our current ability to distribute cultural externals or products into categories, the inner structure of culture also appears to have lesser and greater (in the valuational sense) categories of characteristics. Though it was considered a possibility that all culture was a mere capacitation of the human being through the acquisition of skills and information, like a veneer on the psyche (Schema II), this position would very likely enjoy small support, if any, especially among the nonspecialists.

Despite its few adherents, this point of view cannot be easily shunted aside, especially since it suggests that what might be considered a core level characteristic of the culture is simply one or other element coequal with the rest but which nevertheless enjoys a status, albeit specious, above them. The reason for this contradictory state of affairs must be sought out.

The explanation that comes most readily to mind is that the *affect* garnered from members of the culture serves to apotheosize the given characteristic. In this schema, no cultural characteristic is more important than the other, there is no essential/nonessential level but what willing or attachment to it makes it so. The importance of the given characteristic consists precisely in the reluctance, the stubborn resistance of the cultural participants to parting with it. In this instance, its importance is a *perceived* importance. The *intrinsic* importance any given characteristic may seem to have is factually nonexistent, and democratic equality pervades all cultural characteristics. The way then to test for significance or importance among cultural characteristics is not to ask which characteristic (or characteristics) is essential but to ask which one a group of participants in the culture would be most reluctant to give up, which one they are most attached to. Importance now takes on a psychological dimension. The key question becomes, why the given cultural characteristic must be retained, why it is difficult to part with.

The brief analysis used previously that demonstrated that language is not the core level characteristic that it appears to be could be iterated with every cultural characteristic once they have been fully taxonomized. It would not be surprising to find out that no single characteristic can carry the burden of being the soul and substance of the culture or of being the core level characteristic as we have been referring to it.

This leaves the analysis with two possibilities, one of which has been alluded to. We shall refer to or categorize these as "possibility a" and "possibility b."

1) *Possibility a.* This possibility was earlier analogized to a chord, the individual notes of which were representative of cultural characteristics. If cultural characteristics are like individual notes in a chord played singly, neither one of which is of core level value, the possibility was raised that a combination of cultural characteristics, like several musical notes played simultaneously, might assume the role of being the core level of the culture. The question becomes this: What combination of cultural characteristics, if it can be determined, constitute what we have defined as the core level of a culture? See Schema III.

Schema III

Certain cultural characteristics as representing
the essence of the culture (w, Θ, ▲).

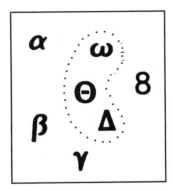

Culturally Imprinted Psyche

Interpretation

Three characteristics designated by Greek letters together constitute
the essential or core level of the culture.

2) *Possibility b.* This possibility raises the notion that, since
neither a single cultural characteristic nor a combination *may*
constitute what we consider the core level of a culture, the core
level has more of the nature of being a mood, feeling, or a sense
or a vague-but-real inclination or propensity toward certain
values or meanings which when occurring at the behavioral
(phenomenal level) of a culture constitute the observable items
of the culture under consideration. See Schema IV.

Schema IV

Core level of culture
as a "mood," "sense," "inclination,"
"propensity"

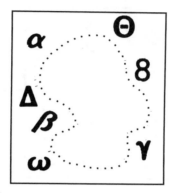

Culturally Imprinted Psyche

Interpretation

The letters are behavior traits, i.e., sources of behavior expressing
the mood, sense, etc. of the culture. Nothing lies within the dotted
lines since the essence or core level of the culture consists of a vague
or indefinable mood, a penchant or psychological gravitation, if
you will, toward certain behaviors or products.

"Possibility b" is not without its adherents and suggestive evidence.
One of the informants, when queried about what constitutes core level
values in Hispanic culture asserted that "what a Chicano feels within is
what defines the culture." Furthermore, the Dahaf Research Institute in
Tel Aviv conducted research interviews in 1988 (Montgomery, 1993) to
determine who the man in the street would grant immigrant status to
under the Law of Return. Seventy-eight percent would grant this status
to Jewish believers in Jesus as the Messiah as long as the person is "born
to a Jewish mother, pays his taxes to the state, serves in the army,

celebrates the Jewish holidays, keeps the commandments of Israel's tradition, [and] *feels he is a Jew"* (emphasis added).   These characteristics, in effect, define a Jewish cultural participant both on the basis of internal and external characteristics.   The only internal one designated is "feeling."

Research involving preverbal communication emphasizes tonality as a strong communicative element, possibly the primary vehicle for transmitting lexical/cognitive content.   This is certainly generative of a "feeling" sense of meaning associated to a vaguely elaborated cognitive content on the part of the recipient of communications (the infant).   It is tentatively suggested that this "feeling" abides and is augmented during the years of communication formulation and subsequently reinforced during the life of the culture participant.

Whether there is a core level that a culture identifies as such, or there exist characteristics singly or in combination that perform this function, it appears there is something of this sort in a culture that has so imprinted its members as to make them identifiable as members and persist in that identity over time.

The common perception of human beings that this is one of the functions of a culture is verified or supported by expressions of criticism such as "an Oreo cookie" (African American), "coconut" (Mexican American), and so on.   Here the distinction in the popular mind is very clear.   The cultural member under such criticism is able to be identified as a superficial participant in the culture in certain respects (usually physiognomic) but in other respects, essential in the mind of the critic, the member is seriously *manque.*

Through this analysis the suggestion remains that (1) a culture has a core, whatever it consists of; (2) the culture imprints its members in an identifiable way; and (3) the culture has a persistence over time.

The Concept of Culture

The analysis engaged in thus far has focused on attempting to define the inner structure of a culture.   No attention has been given to defining even in a general way what the word means at least as it is being and will be employed in this writing.

As noted earlier, the word is sufficiently vague as to garner intelligibility and comfort with its use on the part of everyone that employs it.   To a large extent this is attributable to the omnipresence, in fact, of culture among human beings.   Every person seems to have a mental referent for the word that suffices to provide it with meaning.   There is, for example, the culture of the city or even of neighborhoods, the culture of the bar, or football crowds. Examples could be endlessly multiplied. There is "culture" or "a culture" everywhere. In terms of the examples given, this is not primarily what culture will be held to mean here.

Perhaps one can begin to reach in the direction of a quasi definition in this fashion. Consider a Society of Hispanic engineers. Is the principal or basic cultural specification that of being Hispanic, or that of being an engineer? Clearly, the basic or principal cultural specification is the former. But why? The answer must reside in the fact that being Hispanic relates more deeply to the basic organization of human life--its activities, its curiosity about the mystery or meaning of living, living well, dying--than does being an engineer, who might be more interested in distributing different forms of energy. Since a person is human 24 hours a day, 168 hours a week, and an engineer only one-third, or less, of that time, then the element which touches, governs, or imprints a person's humanity more deeply will be that person's basic cultural specification. In other words, a person's basic cultural specifier imprints more deeply and organizes ones behavior and thinking more continuously than the less basic cultural characteristics do.

This is the basic sense in which culture is considered here. While it is not essential to the argument being constructed, other questions do arise. How many basic cultures are there? Is there a culture more basic than that of being, in this example, Hispanic? Do basic cultures differ as genera or as species? Is being a participant in Western culture a deeper cultural specification than being a participant in Hispanic culture? Something like this question will be considered later.

Culture as Deep Imprint

It has been noted that culture exists in its inner dimension as a cultural imprint on the psyche and also has the effect of governing behavior, that is, causing reality to be viewed in one way rather than another and causing certain purposes to be selected rather than others. Now the question is raised as to how deeply a culture imprints itself on the psyche. A corollary of this question is to ask the possibility of a basic culture's being extinguished and under what conditions this might occur. Or, is it really possible to be bicultural in terms of basic cultural imprints? Or does a person *behave* biculturally but remain monocultural? These latter questions, together with others raised earlier, despite the seeming interstices, are all interconnected.

It should be remembered that since Title VII is an inductive procedure, the culture of the participants will undergo change. How much depends on the answers given to the above questions.

Returning to the question "How deeply does a culture imprint itself on the participants' psyche?," the writer has conducted informal, oral inquiries on this topic over a period of fifteen years. The informants have been exclusively professors, members of ethnic minority groups.

In a conversation with an internationally known informant of Jewish extraction, the query was made this way: If at the moment of birth you were placed in a family (non-Jewish) and raised there to adulthood, and then, by happenstance you were to enter a Jewish temple, would you sense even vaguely a belonging, a calling to return as to some ancestral home? The informant asserted without hesitation that such a sense or tendency would indeed be felt, unmistakably so.

This is indeed a remarkable observation since the informant is professional in every respect and not given to hyperbole. The response confirms the depth to which a culture is considered imprinted and even suggests it being inscribed in genetic material.

The same topic was approached from a different vantage point with Hispanic informants. The topic was framed this way: The Nobel Prize is a world mark of high renown and of outstanding contributions made in the field in which it is awarded. In the first 75 years of its establishment (1901-1976) one Hispanic person, identified by country, has been a laureate in the hard sciences (physics, chemistry), while in the same period six have been laureates in literature. Additionally, world renown and distinction has accrued to Hispanics in large numbers in literature, arts, and philosophy. The discussion sought the causes of this imbalance. Alternative possible explanations were explored: cultural deficiency and backwardness, national poverty affecting investment in physical science plant, lack of emphasis on subject matter relating to the needs, interests, and focus of contemporary society, etc.

The informants readily rejected any notion of deficiency, cultural or financial. A lack of emphasis on subject matter relating to the needs, interests, and focus of contemporary society also was given short shrift.

The discussion trended inevitably and inexorably toward basic culture as a *verbum,* the word or expression, of a given group. As such, culture was seen to exist by convention as language does. It was consequently also seen to have a core that over time focuses the perceptions of its participants and vectors their aspirations and interests in one direction rather than another. Because culture was seen as analogous to language, no single culture would be considered superior to the other. All cultures were then seen to be, in distinct and concerted ways, partial-to-fuller expressions of how humans can have a satisfying set of meanings for life. Each culture then is a value-filled statement, no better and no worse than any other with the consequence that questions regarding failure to receive recognition in one field or several is not a deficiency but simply an alternative group statement, expression, or verbum. As an alternative group statement, a given culture may be far off the mark of contemporaneity.

Why, then, are there what I would call "omnibus" cultures, that is, cultures within which are found individuals of world distinction in practically every field of human endeavor? Jewish culture certainly is an example of this. What is it that empowers individuals in this particular culture to have this capability? Also, if it has this capability as it surely does, does this very capability raise questions such as are implied in the comparability of cultures in terms of the culture's greater or less effectiveness in developing excellence in its participants?

In a context where comparisons among strongly held values inevitably have pejorative or meliorative connotations, it verges on the odious to raise such issues. Yet the comparisons, voiced or not, are there.

If a culture has the resiliency or adaptability to engage surrounding cultures with success while retaining its identifiability, its inner core intact, are other cultures to be considered more fragile or vulnerable in this regard?

How many cultures have been weakened to the point of losing their identity through contact with other cultures? What cultural values have had to be "sacrificed" to gain the "opportunities" provided by contact with other cultures? When other cultures have been more or less preserved, at what social and psychological expense to its participants has this been accomplished?

There is a generally accepted perception that the populations in Western countries are living in a scientific-technological culture, a culture that has displaced the theocentric-philosophic culture of the Middle Ages. This scientific-technological culture has centered on man as knower--reconstructor of the environment, whether it be from the infinitesimal depths of the organization of the material universe to as far out as the universe of matter extends. In turn, this has required that man *(homo intelligens et faber)* understand how matter behaves so that matter may be shaped to behave in modes subservient to man's interests. The epistemological mechanics in this activity are rudimentary: Human intelligence penetrates the material universe and disassembles it (i.e., atomizes) to fabricate new material structures. An example of this is biogenetics.

Yet what of cultures whose knowing styles are more noninvasive and passive than penetrative, where the object-to-be-known presents itself to human consciousness and gaze and is understood in its being-structure not in a becoming-structure? The epistemological mechanics here are equally simple: Human intelligence reflects or mirrors (speculate from the Latin *speculor,* vb., to watch or *speculum,* n., a mirror) the world reality, i.e., leaves reality unchanged. In this case, the material universe etches itself within human consciousness. Human consciousness comes to know what something is in the fundamental sense of letting the object gazed upon continue to exist, thereby validating knowledge of it over long periods of time.

Are there cultures like this? It appears that there are. Native American cultures seem to be this way. Elements of Hispanic culture seem to share this trait also. If you ask an inheritor of scientific-technological culture what an earthworm is, it will be shortly sacrificed, i.e., altered fundamentally. It will be fixed in a desirable medium, microtomed, laid out on microscopic slides, etc. The observer will then know what the earthworm *was.* Ask the Hispanic or Native American what an earthworm is and you will be presented with some artistic portrayal: a chant, a myth, a philosophy, a pictograph, etc. This results in nothing but good fortune for the earthworm since it remains what it is, namely, alive. There are further dividends. If the world-as-object is not primarily seen as something to be transformed or manipulated into structures for human service, the world becomes a place that is largely left alone and respected in its pristine condition. This is certainly a characteristic of southwestern Native American culture. It would never be said that this culture is bent on altering the world as is the essential thrust of a scientific-technological culture.

As Kluckhohn and Leighton observed:

For the most part The People (Navahos) try to influence her (Nature) with various songs and rituals, but they feel that the forces of nature, rather than anything that man does, determine success or failure of crops, plagues of grasshoppers, increase of arroyos, and decrease of grass. If a flood comes and washes out a formerly fertile valley, one does not try to dam the stream and replace the soil; instead one moves to a floodless spot. One may try to utilize what nature furnishes, such as by leading water from a spring or stream to his fields, but no man can master the wind and the weather. This is similar to the attitude toward sex, which is viewed as part of nature, something to reckon with, but not a thing to be denied.

Many white people have the opposite view: namely, that nature is a malignant force with useful aspects that must be harnessed, and useless, harmful ones that must be shorn of their power. They spend their energies adapting nature to their purposes, instead of themselves to her demands. They destroy pests of crops and men, they build dykes and great dams to avert floods, and they level hills in one spot and pile them up in another. Their premise is that nature will destroy them unless they prevent it; the Navahos' is that nature will take care of them if they behave as they should and do as she directs.

In addition to all the other forces which make the acceptance of the current program of soil erosion control and limitation of livestock slow and painful, this premise plays an important and fundamental part. To most Navahos it seems silly or presumptuous to interfere with the workings of nature to the extent that they are being told to do. Besides, they believe it won't bring the benefits the white people promise. If anything is wrong these days, it is that The People are forgetting their ways and their stories, so of course anyone would know that there would be hard times. It has nothing to do with too many sheep. (1946)

Relative to the underlying topic of this chapter, what would "opportunity" mean for a Navajo or Hispanic cultural participant when opportunity is couched in such terms as to require a transformation of one's basic cultural outlook in favor of another?

Biculturalism

Authors in this book (Sue and Padilla) present a Contextual Interaction model for dealing with conflicting values (functioning within two cultures with opposed and mismatched values as is apparent in the case described above).

As the authors note:

....the contextual interaction approach does not view groups as culturally deficient or inferior. Although persons may have to acquire new skills, these skills need not mean a loss of one's ethnic culture. This perspective is much more tolerant of ethnics who espouse a bicultural philosophy as a means of accommodating to the demands of the mainstream as well as their own ethnic community.

The above citation passingly suggest biculturalism (bicultural philosophy) as a possible solution to underachievement arising from intercultural contact. It assures, moreover, that the acquisition of new skills need not mean the loss of one's ethnic culture. Later in the same paragraph, language is used as an example of a skill with the statement that attaining high levels of English proficiency does not necessarily imply the elimination of proficiency in one's native language.

A study of Sue and Padilla's entire chapter reveals that culture is dealt with at the level of skills or operations. Employing language as an example is an indication of this point of view. It should be remembered that language per se was earlier shown to be a non-essential indicator or marker of being a participant of a basic culture though language may be taken that way from the standpoint of mere appearances or as a rule-of-thumb identifier or marker of cultural membership.

The Contextual Interaction Model raises the issue of biculturality. The analysis of the concept of culture we are working with questions the meaning of biculturality just as we are examining the concept of culture itself.

A person may be considered bicultural when he/she posits culturally appropriate behavior as may be testified to by a community of observers in two cultures. Now, employing the schemata discussed earlier, there are several ways to explain biculturalism.

a) The culturally appropriate behaviors are the product of acquired culture-specific traits, which are phenomenal or adventitious cultural elements. These cultural elements can exist within human consciousness in two groups, so to speak. An individual demonstrating biculturality would elicit cultural behaviors or actions appropriate to the cultural environment in which the individual is found, now in one cultural environment, later in another.

If being bicultural means only this--a developed habituation to positing appropriate behaviors in two cultural ambiences--then, to an *external* observer, which culture the bicultural individual *really* belongs cannot be discerned. In this instance, the person is considered effectively or operationally bicultural with no necessary pretentions as to core level or basic cultural characteristics. See Schema II.

b) The culturally appropriate behaviors arise from phenomenal, adventitous cultural elements as the proximate sources of behavior, but these cultural elements are essentially or vitally linked to core level characteristics. This essential or vital link means that the culturally appropriate and distinct behaviors can be posited by one cultural member or "persona." The behaviors are no longer mere psychic veneer but expressions of an authentic cultural personality.

Now, functioning biculturally involves summoning, as it were, the culturally appropriate (imprinted) persona to the fore to function in the given cultural ambience and later summoning another culturally appropriate persona as the cultural ambience changes.

To an observer, a person functioning in this way clearly gives the appearance of *full* (i.e., core level) biculturalism, but is this condition possible? Can a single human being be invested with two cultural personae? The very unity of the human person militates against this line of explanation and, what on the face of it appears a deviant condition (psychologically, a dual personality), should not be used to explain that which the word "biculturalism" seems to connote, namely a desirable and meritorious condition.

c) The culturally appropriate behaviors arise from causes as mentioned (a & b) but in one case these behaviors are representative of a culturally authentic persona (behaviors, e.g., appropriate to Mexican American culture produced by a person imprinted at the core level with Mexican American cultural values); in another case, in the same person, the behaviors spring from characteristics that are genuinely adventitious and overlie the core values of the genuine cultural persona. In this schema, a person would, or might, be referred to as bicultural at the phenomenal level but not authentically so since the individual's cultural persona is singly that found at the core level.

This explanation is one that persons would be most comfortable with and seems to accord easily with human experience. It protects the normal attachment humans have to a single basic culture (the culture of origin) and it redefines biculturalism in defensible terms, assuming the validity of all the analyses engaged in thus far.

Cultural Deficiency

Cultures probably share the characteristic of being considered "the best" or "as good as any" by its participants. Certain major cultures definitely have this characteristic. We refer here to the Chinese and Greek cultures as examples; the former with its notion of Middle Kingdom as the center of, and superior to, other civilizations; the latter with its reference to surrounding non-Greek speakers as *barbaroi,* i.e., barbarians. These are obvious examples.

However, what of cultures where no such superiority is explicitly displayed? Here, there is a given group of persons with a hegemonic possession of knowledge and skills associated to a reward structure (occupations with better incomes) that is mediated by the acquisition of the necessary knowledge and skills that in turn have been curricularized by the schools.

The reward structure is staffed by individuals whose membership is in the nonminority culture, for the most part. This culture can be described or named as Anglo, majority, scientific-technological, etc. The important factor is that its investigative epistemology represents an invasive (to the world of nature) matter-manipulative thrust into the structure of the world which is not congenial (as shown earlier) to the culture of the Navajo nor arguably to Hispanic culture in general.

The members of minority cultures come to be seen both by the majority culture (and members of the minority culture) as experiencing deficiencies (lack of proportionate representation in the reward structure). The schools, the only governmentally controlled organization to touch all citizens in their formative years, are given support to "intervene," i.e., upgrade minority academic skills. This is accomplished quite properly and honestly under a variety of "equal opportunity" based policies.

It is inevitable that in the popular as well as informed mind cultures whose members have high dropout rates, lower grade level of achievement, poor matriculation rates, and the like, will begin to be seen as deficient. It may be impolitic to speak publicly of these cultures as deficient, but not everything that is impolitic goes unspoken, or even less, unthought of.

Nevertheless, the offer of an opportunity to succeed is made on the majority culture's terms, which is simply to say that there is a distinct potential for assimilation in the effort. As long as there is no *societally* generated reward structure for the skills and products of minority cultures (outside of entertainment and folk art), the pathway to success must require adopting the skills and knowledge of the broader or majority culture.

Conclusion

The chapter's argumentation has been to question the exaggerated facility with which the concept culture is normally utilized. To initiate a discussion of culture, various meanings or values internal to the concept were elucidated. In addition, a variety of schemata or structures were provided that, together with the meanings and values, were used as a glossary of conceptual paradigms for interpreting certain cultural phenomena or data that were adduced.

The clear intent has been to introduce a minimal caution in dealing with "culture" and to suggest that legislative policy honestly intending to create and facilitate pathways to success as contemporarily defined may (or will) have the effect of creating a subtle, incremental erosion of core values or elements of the culture being served. Depending on the model chosen to portray the structure of culture, the effects may be interpreted as nugatory or lethal, regardless of reality.

Because of the seeming plasticity of human consciousness, hardly a question is raised as to the net effect, pro or con, resulting from intercultural contact and conflict, i.e., resulting from empowerment efforts. The responsibility has been that of the community when it is a question of language maintenance, not that of the federal government. The whole question of cultural maintenance seems to await proper attention.

REFERENCES

Hirsch, Jr., E. D. *Cultural Literacy.* Boston: Houghton Mifflin, 1987.

Kluckhohn, Clyde C., and Leighton, Dorothea. *The Navaho.* Cambridge, Mass.: Harvard University Press, 1946.

Montgomery, John Warwick. "When is a Jew not a Jew?" *New Oxford Review,* June 1993, p. 26.

Sapir, E. "Cultural Anthropology and Psychiatry." In David G. Mandelbaum (Ed.), *Selected Writing of Edward Spir.* Berkeley: University of California Press, 1949.

Spindler, G. *Education and Culture: Anthropological Approaches.* New York: Holt, Rinehart and Winston, 1963.

DATE DUE

OC 26 '05			